Pharmacy Administration

Pharmacy Administration

Prof. Dr. G. Vidya Sagar
Dean and Director
Veerayatan Institute of Pharmacy
Kutch 370 460
Gujarat

PharmaMed Press
An imprint of Pharma Book Syndicate
An unit of BSP Books Pvt., Ltd.
4-4-316, Giriraj Lane,
Sultan Bazar, Hyderabad - 500 095.

Third Reprint 2020

Published by

PharmaMed Press
An imprint of Pharma Book Syndicate
A unit of BSP Books Pvt., Ltd.
4-4-309/316, Giriraj Lane, Sultan Bazar, Hyderabad - 500 095.
Phone: 040-23445600, 23445688; Fax: 91+40-23445611
E-mail: info@pharmamedpress.com
www.pharmamedpress.com/pharmamedpress.net

Printed at

Aditya Offset Process (I) Pvt. Ltd.
Hyderabad.

Price: Rs. 450.00
ISBN: 978-81-78002-55-2 (Paperback)

Foreword

In the last two decades Indian Pharma industry has undergone a metamorphosis due to liberalization and globalization. The General Agreement on Tariffs and Trade (GATT) of 1948 has led to an unprecedented increase in international trade after the second world war. But GATT could not prevent a country from raising barriers to trade. When at Bretton Wood in July 1944, the allied countries agreed to establish the Internal Monctary Fund (IMF) and the International Bank for Reconstruction and Development (IBRD), which today is part of the World Bank Group, it was expected that an organization to regulate international trade would also be established. But it was only in 1995 that World Trade Organization with strong Dispute Settlement Mechanism could be set up. This has led to a healthy competition. Today to succeed in the world's marketplace, a pharmaceutical company requires continuous introduction of progressively superior products and services.

Besides developing more efficacious drugs, effective administration of clinical research trails, hospitals and retail pharmacy chains will be required to meet the challenge of providing user-friendly health care systems. Pharmacy administration focuses on managing the financial, physical and human resources efficiently. It is my pleasure to write a few words at the request of Professor G. Vidya Sagar, Principal and Director of Veerayatan Institute of Pharmacy, Kutch, Gujarat and the author of the book on Pharmacy Administration.

Dr. Sagar has informed me that this book explains the concepts in an easy to understand format and it includes nearly every facet of the Pharmacy administration. The book should, therefore, prove to be of use to both the students as well as managers in the pharmaceutical business.

I wish Dr. Vidya Sagar a great success in his career as a professor and as an author.

Ahmedabad
Date: 11/9/2010

Dr. Akshai Aggarwal
Vice-Chancellor

Preface

Indian pharmaceutical and health care industry is progressing by leaps and bounds. This has given impetus for opening more retail pharmacy outlets, chain pharmacy groups. There is a lot of activity in clinical research and new drug discovery sphere also.

During the last 15 years due to new GATT policy and open govt. licensing procedure, there is a sea change in the Indian Pharma segment. Due to new economic policy of the govt. and due to liberalization and globalization phenomena, Pharma industry in India has experienced a great metamorphosis. These developments have led to introduction of new drugs and technologies and new biotechnological innovations in drug discovery. Today there is a better understanding of diseases and disorders due to the availability of better diagnostic tools.

The common method of practice of pharmacy in our country is through pharmacy and medical store. In order to run a drug store, the pharmacist should be familiar with various management principles and techniques. Pharmacy Administration is a subject of academic B.Pharm curriculum in almost all universities in India.

Pharmacy administration will give a pharmacist abilities and skills to complete his responsibilities relateds to providing improved pharmaceutical care to the patient, developing better medication distribution system, providing better drug information to the patients and compiling better database of drug inventory, etc.

I hope my textbook will be a handy reference to fellow pharmacists and to be pharmacists of the country in learning the basic tenets of management. A Pharmacist is a vital link in the health care services of a nation. To run the drug store effectively and efficiently, management principles and techniques are very useful. This Textbook elucidates and gives a lucid exposition of essential management principles and practices for the pharmacy students.

All care has been taken to table the contents of the textbook in a simple and effective way for easy understanding of the students. The textbook covers the entire syllabus prescribed by JNTU for this subject in final B.Pharm 1st Semester. The present textbook provides updated and pertinent details on various issues of the subject in a simple and unambigous way.

I do not claim any originality of thought but I am profoundly indebted to all those persons from whom I have gained knowledge for authoring this book.

I have made every effort to avoid errors yet possibility of any printing error or otherwise due to oversight cannot be overruled. I shall be obliged if readers bring such mistakes to my notice for rectification.

I am confident that students and teachers will find this textbook worth reading. Comments and suggestions from the readers regarding the relevant improvements on the book are always welcome.

I express my sincere gratitude to Sri Anil Shah of Pharma Book Syndicate for encouraging me to take up this work and for bringing out the book in such a beautiful way.

Sep. 2010 ***Prof. Dr. G. Vidya Sagar***

Contents

Chapter - 1

Introduction to Business

When we look around us, we observe that most of the people are engaged in one activity or the other. Teachers teach in the schools, farmers work in the fields, workers work in the factories, drivers drive vehicles, shopkeepers sell goods, doctors attend to patients and so on. In this way, people are busy during the day and sometimes during the night throughout the year. Now the question arises as to WHY we all keep ourselves busy. The answer is to satisfy our wants. By doing so, we either fulfill various obligations or earn money through which we can buy goods and commodities.

Human Activities

Activities which human beings undertake are known as human activities. These may be cultivating land, growing plants, rearing animals, teaching in a school or college, working in a factory or office, watching television, listening to radio, reading newspaper, business studies, playing football, etc. We can divide these activities into two broad categories as (i) economic activities; and (ii) non-economic activities.

(i) ***Economic activities:*** Activities, which are performed with an objective to earn money, are known as economic activities. For example, a farmer grow crops to sell them, a factory or office employee works and gets wage or salary, a businessman earns profit through buying and selling of goods.

(ii) ***Non-economic activities:*** Activities, which are not performed to earn money but to get some satisfaction, are called non-economic activities. These activities are performed to discharge social obligation or for physical fitness or for recreation. People visiting places of worship, providing relief to the victims of flood and earthquake, engaging in sports activities, gardening, listening to radio or watching television are all examples of non-economic activities.

Types of Economic Activities

We know that economic activities are undertaken to earn money. Generally, people engage themselves in such activities on a regular basis and are said to be engaged in their occupation. Thus, occupation means keeping oneself engaged or occupied in some gainful economic activity on a regular basis to earn one's livelihood. For example, doctors treat patients, lawyers provide legal services, workers work in offices and factories, teachers teach in schools and colleges and shopkeepers buy and sell goods to earn their livelihood.

In this way, they are all engaged in occupations.

Occupations may be classified into three broad categories.

(a) Profession

(b) Employment

(c) Business

Let us now understand each of them:

(a) Profession: A person may not be an expert in every field. So, we require services of others who specialize in one field or other. For example, we need the services of doctors for our treatment, lawyers to get legal support etc. They are all engaged in when an individual is regularly engaged in a particular economic activity, it is known as his/her occupation. Individuals engaged in profession are called professionals.

Thus, profession refers to an occupation, which requires specialized knowledge and training to pursue it.

The characteristics of a profession:

(i) ***Specialized knowledge:*** We already know that every profession requires specialized knowledge to be acquired through training. This knowledge cannot be inherited. A doctor's son cannot become a doctor without pursuing the necessary course of studies for medical degree. A lawyer must have knowledge and training in law to be able to provide legal service to the people. To be a chartered accountant one has to pass the examinations conducted by the Institute of Chartered Accountants of India.

(ii) ***Service motive:*** The primary objective of every profession is to provide service. The professionals get some remuneration for providing such services. Thus, doctors, lawyers and other professionals work with service motive and in the process earn money for their livelihood.

(iii) ***Regulated by Professional body:*** A professional body regulates every profession. For example, Institute of Chartered Accountants of India, Bar Council of India, and Medical Council of India are the professional bodies established to regulate the functions of chartered accountants, lawyers and doctors in India respectively.

(iv) ***Code of conduct:*** These professionals have a code of conduct developed by the concerned professional body. This is to be followed strictly by each professional. This ensures uniformity in working of all the professionals.

(b) Employment: Employment refers to an occupation in which a person works regularly for others and gets wage/salary in return. Government servants, company executives, bank officials, factory workers are all said to be in employment. Let us learn about the characteristics of employment:

(i) *Work for others:* People engaged in employment always work for someone else. They are not free to decide the work to be done. They have to follow the instructions of their boss or employer.

(ii) *Terms and conditions:* In employment there are certain terms and conditions regarding work to be performed, hours of work, amount of remuneration and other facilities, if any. The employer who offers employment normally decides these conditions. The person seeking a job must join the work only after being satisfied with the terms

(iii) *Fixed income:* The remuneration payable to an employee is fixed and is paid in the form of wage or salary. An employee gets his wage or salary at regular intervals. This may be on daily or monthly basis. The increments in pay, dearness allowance and other allowances are also payable on the basis of the terms and conditions of employment.

(c) Business: Business refers to an occupation in which goods and services are produced, sold and exchanged in return of money. It is carried out on a regular basis with the prime objective of making profit. Mining, manufacturing, trading, transporting, storing, banking, and insurance are examples of business activities.

Vocation: Sometimes people earn their livelihood through vocation. Vocation basically means possession of a specific skill and its application towards earning a livelihood. For example people like carpenter, tailor, plumber, beautician, musician, electrician, computer operator etc. are said to be in a vocation as they all possess some special skills to keep themselves occupied either in business or in employment.

Meaning of Business

You find a variety of goods available in the market. You buy those goods as and when you require them. Do you know how these goods come to the market? Who makes these goods and who brings them to the market? Actually, all these goods are produced at some specific places, and then somebody brings these goods from the place of production to the market. Only then we are able to buy these goods and use them as per our requirement.

Again you must have observed some people are engaged in activities like transportation of goods and passengers, banking, insurance, advertising, supply of electricity, telephone etc. These are all service activities and are performed by the people to earn their livelihood.

In all the above activities, be it production, distribution, purchase or sale of goods and services, monetary gain is expected in each case and also, they are performed on a continuous basis. Thus, business refers to any human activity undertaken on a regular basis with the object to earn profit through production, distribution, sale or purchase of goods and services.

Business may be defined as "an activity involving regular production or purchase of goods and services for sale, transfer and exchange with an object of earning profit".

Importance of Business

Business is an integral part of modern society. It is an organised and systematic activity for earning profit. It is concerned with activities of people working towards a common goal.

The modern society cannot exist without business. The importance of business can be described as follows:

(i) Business improves the standard of living of the people by providing better quality and large variety of goods and services at the right time and at the right place.

(ii) It provides opportunities to work and earn a livelihood. Thus, it generates employment in the country, which in turn reduces poverty.

(iii) It utilizes the scarce resources of the nation and facilitates mass production of goods and services.

(iv) It improves national image by producing and exporting quality goods and services to foreign countries. By participating in international trade fairs and exhibitions it also demonstrates our progress and achievements outside the country.

(v) It enables the people of a country to use quality goods of international standard. This is possible by way of importing goods from foreign countries or by producing quality goods in the country by applying modern methods of production.

(vi) It gives better return to the investors on their capital investment and also provides opportunities to grow and expand the business.

(vii) It promotes social interest by providing tourist services, sponsoring cultural programmes, trade shows etc. in the country which enable people of different parts of the country to exchange their culture, traditions and practices. Thus, it promotes national integration. Introduction to Business

(viii) It also facilitates exchange of culture among the people of different nations and thus, maintains international harmony and peace.

(ix) It helps in the development of science and technology. It spends large amount of money on research and development in search of new products and services. Hence a number of innovative products and services are developed through industrial research.

Types of Business Activities

Broadly, business activities are classified into two categories:

(i) Industrial activities; and

(ii) Commercial activities.

Industrial activities refer to activities related to production or extraction of goods through utilisation of various resources. Growing crops and plants, extracting oil, natural gas and minerals from the surface of the earth, processing raw materials into finished and semifinished goods, construction of buildings, dams and bridges are examples of Industrial activities. A commercial activity includes all those business activities which are undertaken for sale or exchange of goods and services and facilitates their availability for consumption and use.

Thus, it includes trading activities and other service activities like transport, banking, insurance, warehousing etc. These service activities are known as auxiliaries to trade or aids to trade. They facilitate the business by carrying goods from the place of production to the place of consumption, providing finance, undertaking risk, systematic storing of goods etc.

1.1 Features of Business Organisation

Characteristics of Business

The essential characteristics of business are as follow:

(a) Deals in goods and services

(b) Sale or exchange of goods and services

(c) Regular exchange of goods and services

(d) Requires investment

(e) Aims at earning profit

(f) Involves risk and uncertainty of income.

(a) ***Deals in goods and services:*** People in business are engaged in production and distribution of goods and services. The goods may be consumer goods like bread, butter, milk, tea, etc. or capital goods like plant, machinery, equipments, etc. The services may be in the form of transportation, banking, insurance, warehousing, advertising and so on.

(b) ***Sale or exchange of goods and services:*** If a person produces or buys a product for self-consumption or for gifting it to another, he is not engaged in business. But when he produces or buys goods to sell it to somebody, he is engaged in business. Thus, in business the goods and services produced or purchased must be exchanged for money or for goods (under barter system) between the buyers and sellers. Without sale or exchange of goods the activities cannot be treated as business.

(c) ***Regular exchange of goods and services:*** The production or buying and selling activities must be carried out on a regular basis. Normally, an isolated transaction is not treated as business. For example, if Raju sold his old Maruti car to Hari, it is not considered as business, unless he continues to carry buying and selling of cars on a regular basis.

(d) ***Requires investment:*** Every business activity requires some amount of investment in terms of land, labour or capital. These resources are utilised to produce a variety of goods and services for distribution and consumption.

(e) ***Aims at earning profit:*** Business activities are performed with the primary objective of earning income by way of profit. Without profit it is not possible to survive for a long period. Earning of profit is also required to grow and expand the business.

(f) ***Involves risk and uncertainty of income:*** We know that every business aims at earning profit. The businessman who invests the various resources expects a fair amount of return. But, in spite of his/her best effort, the reward he/she gets is always uncertain. Sometimes he/she enjoys profits and also times may come when he suffers heavy losses. This happens because the future is unpredictable and businessman has practically no control over certain factors that affects his earnings.

Characteristics/Features of Organisation

The main characteristics or Features of organisation are as follows:

Outlining the Objectives: Born with the enterprise are its long-life objectives of profitable manufacturing and selling its products. Other objectives must be established by the administration from time to time to aid and support this main objective.

Identifying and Enumerating the Activities: After the objective is selected, the management has to identify total task involved and its break-up closely related component activities that are to be performed by and individual or division or a department.

Assigning the Duties: When activities have been grouped according to similarities and common purposes, they should be organized by a particular department. Within the department, the functional duties should be allotted to particular individuals.

Defining and Granting the Authority: The authority and responsibility should be well defined and should correspond to each other. A close relationship between authority and responsibility should be established.

Creating Authority Relationship: After assigning the duties and delegations of authority, the establishment of relationship is done. It involves deciding who will act under whom, who will be his subordinates, what will be his span of control and what will be his status in the organisation. Besides these formal relationships, some informal organizations should also be developed.

Importance / Need / Advantages / Significance of Organisation

The well-known industrialist of U.S.A. late Andrew Canrnegi, when sold his famous 'United State Steel Corporation', showed his confidence in organisation by uttering the following words, "Take away our factories, take away our trade, our avenues of transportation, our money, leave nothing but our organisation, and in four years, we shall re-established ourselves." Since ages and in every walk of life, organisation has been playing a vital role. The significance or main advantages of organisation are as follows:

It Facilitates Administration and management: Organisation is an important and the only tool to achieve enterprise goals set b administration and explained by management. A sound organisation increases efficiency, avoids delay and duplication of work, increases managerial efficiency, increases promptness, motivates employees to perform their responsibility.

It Helps in the Growth of Enterprise: Good organisation is helpful to the growth, expansion and diversifications of the enterprise.

It Ensures Optimum Use of Human Resources: Good organisation establishes persons with different interests, skills, knowledge and viewpoints.

It Stimulates Creativity: A sound and well-conceived organisation structure is the source of creative thinking and initiation of new ideas.

A Tool of Achieving Objectives: Organisation is a vital tool in the hands of the management for achieving set objectives of the business enterprise.

Prevents Corruption: Usually corruption exists in those enterprises which lack sound organisation. Sound organization prevents corruption by raising the morale of employees. They are motivated to work with greater efficiency, honesty and devotion.

Co-ordination in the Enterprise: Different jobs and positions are welded together by structural relationship of the organisation. The organizational process exerts its due and balanced emphasis on the co-ordination of various activities.

Eliminates Overlapping and Duplication of work: Over lapping and duplication of work exists when the work distribution is not clearly identified and the work is performed in a haphazard and disorganized way. Since a good organisation demands that the duties be clearly assigned amongst workers, such overlapping and duplication is totally eliminated.

Sound or Good Organisation

Organisation is not an end it itself but a means to achieve an end. Whether an organisation is good or bad depends on the fact as to how much efficiently and promptly it is in a position to achieve the objectives. An ideal organisation is one which is expected by all. Some people think that an ideal organisation stands in a dream only and actually it does not exist. However, it is a wrong concept. An ideal organisation is a reality which can be achieved through the active cooperation of all the members of an organisation and also by following the principles of organisation is not an exact science as physics and chemistry. Though a sound organisation is mainly based on the active cooperation of all the members of the organisation and on certain principles but also it is based on the capabilities of the individuals available to work along with its simplicity and flexibility. An organisation conceived and developed on the above lines will reward its leaders and well as its members (Personnel). Not only will the objectives be achieved more easily, and conveniently, but the physical operation of the organisation will also be greatly enhanced. Thus, a sound or good or ideal and result-oriented organisation must posses the following characteristics.

Realization of Objectives: Organisation is tool of achieving objectives of an enterprise. For this purpose, the organisation should be divided in several department, sub-departments, branches and units etc.

Harmonious Grouping of Functions etc: For achieving the organisation objectives there must be harmonious grouping of functions, jobs and sub-jobs in such a way so that there is action, consultation and co-ordination without any delay and difficulty.

Reasonable Span of Control: Another characteristic of organisation is that it should have reasonable span of control. Ordinarily, a person (personnel) cannot control more than five or six subordinates.

Clear-cut allocation of Duties and Responsibilities: There must be clear-cut allocation of duties and responsibilities in any scheme of sound organisation. Every executive must know his scope of activities, the ideal number is three

Promotion of Satisfaction: The most important element of any human organisation is the promotion of satisfaction of workers. Man works in a group or in an organisation and hence the success or failure of any organisation depends on as to how much the organisation is in a position to provide satisfaction to individuals or group working under him.

Fullest Utilization of Manpower: Another important characteristic of an ideal organisation is as to how far it is successful in making fullest and economical utilization of the available manpower.

Provision and Development and Expansion: Another important of an ideal organisation is that there exists the necessary provision for development and expansion so that it is possible to expand and develop any organisation according to needs and requirements and necessary changes alternatives may be made.

Coordination and cooperation: In order to achieve the objectives of the enterprise, there must be close coordination and cooperation in the activities of everybody working in the organisation. Further, there should also be active coordination and cooperation amongst the various departments and sub-departments. It will also assist in elimination of the evil of red tape.

Unity of Command: There must be unity of command. No one in any organisation should report to more than one line supervisor, and everybody must know to whom he reports and who reports to him. No subordinate should get orders from more than one supervisor, otherwise it will lead to confusion, chaos any conflict.

Effective System of Communication: An ideal organisation must possess effective system of communication. The inter-communication system should be clear and easier and there should be no ambiguity at any level.

High Morale: An ideal organisation is that in which the workers possess high morale. They work with full capacity, energy, enthusiasm, devotion and sincerity.

Flexibility: The last but not the least important characteristic of an ideal organisation is that it should be flexible so that necessary changes or modifications in the size of the organisation as well as technology could be easily and conveniently effected.

1.2 Organisation

An **organization** (or **organisation**) is a social arrangement which pursues collective goals, controls its own performance, and has a boundary separating it from its environment. The word itself is derived from the Greek word organon, itself derived from the better-known word ergon.

In the social sciences, organizations are the object of analysis for a number of disciplines, such as sociology, economics, political science, psychology, management, and organizational communication. In more specific contexts, particularly for sociologists, the term "institution" may be preferred. The broader analysis of organizations is commonly referred to as organizational studies, organizational behavior or organization analysis

Organization in Sociology

Sociology can be defined as the science of the institutions of modernity; specific institutions serve a function, akin to the individual organs of a coherent body. In the social and political sciences in general, an "organization" may be more loosely understood as the planned, coordinated and purposeful action of human beings working through collective action to reach a common goal or construct a tangible product. This action is usually framed by formal membership and form (institutional rules). Sociology distinguishes the term organization into planned formal and unplanned informal (i.e., spontaneously formed) organizations. Sociology analyzes organizations in the first line from an institutional perspective. In this sense, organization is a permanent arrangement of elements. These elements and their actions are determined by rules so that a certain task can be fulfilled through a system of coordinated *division of labor*.

An organization is defined by the elements that are part of it (who belongs to the organization and who does not?), its *communication* (which elements communicate and how do they communicate?), its autonomy (*Max Weber* termed autonomy in this context: *Autocephaly* (which changes are executed autonomously by the organization or its elements?), and its rules of action compared to outside events (what causes an organization to act as a collective actor?).

By coordinated and planned cooperation of the elements, the organization is able to solve tasks that lie beyond the abilities of the single elements. The price paid by the elements is the limitation of the *degrees of freedom* of the elements.

Advantages of organizations are enhancement (more of the same), addition (combination of different features) and extension. Disadvantages can be inertness (through co-ordination) and loss of *interaction*.

Organization in management and organizational stud *Management* is interested in organization mainly from an instrumental point of view. For a *company*, organization is a means to an end to achieve its goals - which are to create value for its stakeholders (stockholders, employees, customers, suppliers, communities

Organization Theories

Among the theories that are or have been most influential are:

Weberian organization theory (refer to *Max Weber*'s chapter on *Bureaucracy* in his book '*Economy and Society*')

Marxist organization analysis

Scientific management (mainly following *Frederick W. Taylor*)

Human Relations Studies (going back to the *Hawthorne studies*, *Maslow* and Hertzberg)

Contingency theory

New institutionalism and *new institutional economics*

Network analysis

Economic sociology

Organization ecology (or demography of organizations)

Agency theory (sometimes called principal - agent theory)

Studies of organization culture

Labour Process Theory

Critical Management Studies

Complexity Theory and Organizations

Transaction cost theory/Transaction cost Economics (TCE)

Garbage can model

Actor-Network Theory

Social entrepreneurship

Organizational Structures

The study of organizations includes a focus on optimizing *organizational structure*. According to *management science*, most *human* organizations fall roughly into four types:

Pyramids or hierarchies

Committees or *juries*

Matrix organizations

Ecologies

Pyramids or hierarchies

A *hierarchy* exemplifies an arrangement with a *leader* who leads leaders. This arrangement is often associated with *bureaucracy*. Hierarchies were *satirized* in *The Peter Principle* (1969), a book that introduced *hierarchiology* and the saying that "in a hierarchy every employee tends to rise to his level of incompetence".

These structures are formed on the basis that there are enough people under the leader to give him support. Just as one would imagine a real pyramid, if there are not enough stone blocks to hold up the higher ones, gravity would irrevocably bring down the monumental structure. So one can imagine that if the leader does not have the support of his lesser leaders, the entire structure will collapse.

An extremely rigid, in terms of responsibilities, type of organization is exemplified by *Führerprinzip*.

Committees or Juries

These consist of a group of peers who decide as a group, perhaps by voting. The difference between a *jury* and a *committee* is that the members of the committee are usually assigned to perform or lead further actions after the group comes to a decision, whereas members of a jury come to a decision. In *common law* countries legal juries render decisions of guilt, liability and quantify damages; juries are also used in athletic contests, book awards and similar activities. Sometimes a selection committee functions like a jury. In the Middle Ages juries in continental Europe were used to determine the law according to consensus amongst local notables.

Committees are often the most reliable way to make decisions. *Condorcet's jury theorem* proved that if the average member votes better than a roll of dice, then adding more members increases the number of majorities that can come to a correct vote (however correctness is defined). The problem is that if the average member is *worse* than a roll of dice, the committee's decisions grow worse, not better: Staffing is crucial.

Parliamentary procedure, such as *Robert's Rules of Order*, helps prevent committees from engaging in lengthy discussions without reaching decisions.

Staff Organization or Cross-functional Team

A *staff* helps an *expert* get all his work done. To this end, a "chief of staff" decides whether an assignment is routine or not. If it's routine, he assigns it to a staff member, who is a sort of junior expert. The chief of staff schedules the routine problems, and checks that they are completed.

If a problem is not routine, the chief of staff notices. He passes it to the expert, who solves the problem, and educates the staff – converting the problem into a routine problem.

In a "cross functional team", like an executive committee, the boss *has* to be a non-expert, because so many kinds of expertise are required.

Organization: Cyclical structure

A theory put forth by renowned scholar Stephen John has asserted that throughout the cyclical nature of one's life organizational patterns are key to success. Through various social and political constraints within society one must realize that organizational skills are paramount to success. Stephen John suggests that emphasis needs to be put on areas such as individual/ group processes, functionality, and overall structures of institutions in order to maintain a proper organization. Furthermore, the individual's overall organizational skills are pre-determined by the processes undertaken.

Matrix organization

This organizational type assigns each worker two bosses in two different hierarchies. One hierarchy is "functional" and assures that each type of expert in the organization is well-trained, and measured by a boss who is super-expert in the same field. The other direction is "executive" and tries to get projects completed using the experts. Projects might be *organized by regions, customer types, or some other source.*

Ecologies

This organization has intense *competition*. Bad parts of the organization starve. Good ones get more work. Everybody is paid for what they actually do, and runs a tiny business that has to show a *profit*, or they are fired.

Companies who utilize this organization type reflect a rather one-sided view of what goes on in *ecology*. It is also the case that a natural *ecosystem* has a natural border - *ecoregions* do not in general compete with one another in any way, but are very autonomous.

"Chaordic" organizations

The chaordic model of organizing human endeavors emerged in the 1990s. The idea is based on a blending of *chaos* and order (hence "chaordic"), and originated in the work of *Dee Hock* and the creation of the *VISA* financial network. Blending *democracy, complex systems, consensus decision making, co-operation* and *competition*, the chaordic approach attempts to encourage organizations to evolve from the increasingly nonviable hierarchical, command-and-control model.

Organizations that are legal entities: *government, international organization, non-governmental organization, armed forces, corporation, partnership, charity, not-for-profit corporation, cooperative, university.*

The organization of the artist

The organization of the artist is a term first used by architect *Frank Gehry* to denote the organizational set-up he enforces in order to ensure that the architect/artist is in control of design through construction. The organization of the artist deliberately eliminates the influence of politicians and business people on design. The purpose of the organization of the artist is to ensure that it is the design of the architect/artist that is actually implemented and not some compromise decided by political and business interests.

Gehry initially developed the concept of the organization of the artist as a reaction against what he calls the "marginalization of the architect/artist." Gehry explains:

"There's a tendency to marginalize and treat the creative people like women are treated, 'sweetie, us big business guys know how to do this, just give us the design and we'll take it from there.' That is the worst thing that can happen. It requires the organization of the artist to prevail so that the end product is as close as possible to the object of desire [the design] that both the client and architect have come to agree on."

Gehry argues that the organization of the artist, in addition to making possible artistic integrity, also helps keep his buildings on time and budget, which is rare for the type of innovative and complex designs that Gehry is known for. The organization of the artist thus serves the dual purpose of *artistic freedom* and economic prude.

Leadership in Organizations

An organization that is established as an *instrument* or means for achieving defined *objectives* has been referred to as a ***formal organization***. Its design specifies how goals are subdivided and reflected in subdivisions of the organization. Divisions, departments, sections, positions, *jobs*, and tasks make up this work *structure*. Thus, the formal organization is expected to behave impersonally in regard to relationships with clients or with its members. According to Weber's definition, entry and subsequent advancement is by merit or seniority. Each employee receives a salary and enjoys a degree of tenure that safeguards him from the arbitrary influence of superiors or of powerful clients. The higher his position in the hierarchy, the greater his presumed expertise in adjudicating problems that may arise in the course of the work carried out at lower levels of the organization. It is this bureaucratic structure that forms the basis for the appointment of heads or chiefs of administrative subdivisions in the organization and endows them with the authority attached to their position.

"An effective leader must be able to develop people."-R.Hewett

Leadership in Informal Organizations

In contrast to the appointed head or chief of an administrative unit, a leader emerges within the context of the ***informal organization*** that underlies the formal structure. The informal organization expresses the personal *objectives* and *goals* of the individual *membership*. Their objectives and goals may or may not coincide with those of the formal organization. The informal organization represents an extension of the social structures that generally characterize human life — the spontaneous emergence of groups and organizations as ends in themselves.

In prehistoric times, man was preoccupied with his personal security, maintenance, protection, and survival. Now man spends a major portion of his waking hours working for organizations. His need to identify with a community that provides security, protection, maintenance, and a feeling of belonging continues unchanged from prehistoric times. This need is met by the informal organization and its emergent, or unofficial, leaders.

Leaders emerge from within the structure of the informal organization. Their personal qualities, the demands of the situation, or a combination of these and other factors attract followers who accept their leadership within one or several overlay structures. Instead of the authority of position held by an appointed head or chief, the emergent leader wields influence or power. Influence is the ability of a person to gain cooperation from others by means of persuasion or control over rewards. Power is a stronger form of influence because it reflects a person's ability to enforce action through the control of a means of punishment.

Leader in Organizations

An individual who is appointed to a managerial position has the right to command and enforce obedience by virtue of the authority of his position. However, he must possess adequate personal attributes to match his authority, because authority is only potentially available to him. In the absence of sufficient personal competence, a manager may be confronted by an emergent leader who can challenge his role in the organization and reduce it to that of a figurehead. However, only authority of position has the backing of formal sanctions. It follows that whoever wields personal influence and power can legitimize this only by gaining a formal position in the hierarchy, with commensurate authority.

Hybrid Organizations

A *hybrid organization* is a body that operates in both the *public sector* and the *private sector*, simultaneously fulfilling public duties and developing commercial market activities. As a result the hybrid organization becomes a mixture of both a part of *government* and a private *corporation*.

1.3 Sole Proprietorship

We go to the market to buy items of our daily needs. In the market we find a variety of shops- some of them small and some of them big. We may find some persons selling vegetables, peanuts, newspapers etc. on the roadside. We may also find cobbler repairing shoes on the footpath. Everyday you come across such types of shops in your locality. The owner invests capital to start the business, takes all decisions relating to business, looks after the day to day functioning of the business and finally, is responsible for the profit or loss. The owner does exactly all these things. in some businesses a single individual and in some businesses a group of individuals perform all these activities.

Meaning of Sole Proprietorship

'Sole' means single and 'proprietorship' means ownership. It means only one person or an individual becomes the owner of the business. Thus, the business organization in which a single person owns, manages and controls all the activities of the business is known as sole proprietorship form of business organization. The individual who owns Business Studies and runs the sole proprietorship business is called a 'sole proprietor' or 'sole trader'.

A sole proprietor pools and organizes the resources in a systematic way and controls the activities with the sole objective of earning profit. Small shops like vegetable shops, grocery shops, telephone booths, chemist shops, etc. are some of the commonly found sole proprietorship form of business organization. Apart from trading business, small manufacturing units, fabrication units, garages, beauty parlors, etc., can also be run by a sole proprietor. This form of business is the oldest and most common form of business organization.

Definition of Sole Proprietorship

A business enterprise exclusively owned, managed and controlled by a single person with all authority, responsibility and risk

Characteristics of Sole Proprietorship

Sole proprietorship form of business organisations has the following characteristics.

(i) Single Ownership
(ii) No sharing of Profit and Loss
(iii) One-man's Capital
(iv) One-man Control
(v) Unlimited Liability
(vi) Less legal formalities

(i) ***Single Ownership:*** A single individual always owns sole proprietorship form of business organization. That individual owns all assets and properties of the business. Consequently, he alone bears all the risk of the business. Thus, the business of the sole proprietor comes to an end at the will of the owner or upon his death.

(ii) ***No sharing of Profit and Loss:*** The entire profit arising out of sole proprietor Sole Proprietorship ship business goes to the sole proprietor. If there is any loss it is also to be borne by the sole proprietor alone. Nobody else shares the profit and loss of the business with the sole proprietor.

(iii) ***One man's Capital:*** The capital required by a sole proprietorship form of business organization is totally arranged by the sole proprietor. He provides it either from his personal resources or by borrowing from friends, relatives, banks or other financial institutions.

(iv) ***One-man Control:*** The controlling power in a sole proprietorship business always remains with the owner. The owner or proprietor alone takes all the decisions to run the business. Of course, he is free to consult any body as per his liking.

(v) ***Unlimited Liability:*** The liability of the sole proprietor is unlimited. This implies that, in case of loss the business assets along with the personal properties of the proprietor shall be used to pay the business liabilities.

(vi) ***Less legal Formalities:*** The formation and operation of a sole proprietorship form of business organization requires almost no legal formalities. It also does not require to be registered. However, for the purpose of the business and depending on the nature of the business, the sole proprietorship has to have a seal. He may be required to obtain a license from the local administration or from the health department of the government, whenever necessary.

Advantages of Sole Proprietorship

The sole proprietorship form of business is the most simple and common in our country. It has the following advantages:

(i) ***Easy to Form and Wind up:*** A sole proprictorship form of business is very easy to form. With a very small amount of capital you can start the business. There is no need to comply with any legal formalities except for those businesses which required license from local authorities or health department of government. Just like formation it is also very easy to wind up the business. It is your sole discretion to form or wind up the business at any time.

(ii) ***Direct Motivation:*** The profits earned belong to the sole proprietor alone and he bears the risk of losses as well. Thus, there is a direct link between effort and Business Studies reward. If he works hard, then there is a possibility of getting more profit and of course, he will be the sole beneficiary of this profit. Nobody will share this reward with him. This provides strong motivation for the sole proprietor to work hard.

(iii) ***Quick Decision and Prompt Action:*** In a sole proprietorship business the sole proprietor alone is responsible for all decisions. Of course, he can consult others. But he is free to take any decision on his own. Since no one else is involved in decision making it becomes quick and prompt action can be taken on the basis of this decision.

(iv) ***Better Control:*** In sole proprietorship business the proprietor has full control over each and every activity of the business. He is the planner as well as the organizer, who co-ordinates every activity in an efficient manner. Since the proprietor has all authority with him, it is possible to exercise better control over business.

(v) ***Maintenance of Business Secrets:*** Business secrecy is an important factor for every business. It refers to keeping the future plans, technical competencies, business strategies, etc., secret from outsiders or competitors. In the case of sole proprietorship business, the proprietor is in a very good position to keep his plans to himself since management and control are in his hands. There is no need to disclose any information to others.

(vi) ***Close Personal Relation:*** The sole proprietor is always in a position to maintain good personal contact with the customers and employees. Direct contact enables the sole proprietor to know the individual likes, dislikes and tastes of the customers. Also, it helps in maintaining close and friendly relations with the employees and thus, business runs smoothly.

(vii) ***Flexibility in Operation:*** The sole proprietor is free to change the nature and scope of business operations as and when required as per his decision. A sole proprietor can expand or curtail his business according to the requirement. Suppose, as the owner of a bookshop, you have been selling books for school students. If you want to expand your business you can decide to sell stationery items like pen, pencil, register, etc. If you are running an STD booth, you can expand your business by installing a fax machine in your booth.

(viii) ***Encourages Self-employment:*** Sole proprietorship form of business organization leads to creation of employment opportunities for people. Not only is the owner self-employed, sometimes he also creates job opportunities for others. You must have observed in different shops that there are a number of employees assisting the owner in selling goods to the customers. Thus, it helps in reducing poverty and unemployment in the country.

Limitations of Sole Proprietorship

One-man business is the best form of business organization because of the above-discussed advantages. Still there are certain disadvantages too.

(i) ***Limited Capital:*** In sole proprietorship business, it is the owner who arranges the required capital of the business. It is often difficult for a single individual to raise a huge amount of capital. The owner's own funds as well as borrowed funds sometimes become insufficient to meet the requirement of the business for its growth and expansion.

(ii) ***Unlimited Liability:*** In case the sole proprietor fails to pay the business obligations and debts arising out of business activities, his personal properties may have to be used to meet those liabilities. This restricts the sole proprietor from taking risks and he thinks cautiously while deciding to start or expand the business activities.

(iii) ***Lack of Continuity:*** The existence of sole proprietorship business is linked to the life of the proprietor. Illness, death or insolvency of the owner brings an end to the business. The continuity of business operation is therefore uncertain.

(iv) ***Limited Size:*** In sole proprietorship form of business organisation there is a limit beyond which it becomes difficult to expand its activities. It is not always possible for a single person to supervise and manage the affairs of the business if it grows beyond a certain limit.

(v) ***Lack of Managerial Expertise:*** A sole proprietor may not be an expert in every aspect of management. He/she may be an expert in administration, planning, etc., but may be poor in marketing. Again, because of limited financial resources it is also not possible to employ a professional manager. Thus, the business lacks benefits of professional management.

Advantages

- Easy to form and wind up
- Direct Motivation
- Quick Decision and Prompt

Action

- Better Control
- Maintenance of Business Secrets
- Close Personal Relation
- Flexibility in Operations

Limitations

- Limited Capital
- Unlimited Liability
- Lack of Continuity
- Limited Size
- Lack of Managerial

Expertise

Suitability of Sole Proprietorship Form of Business

Sole proprietorship form of business organization is suitable:

- Where the market for the product is small and local. For example, selling grocery items, books, stationery, vegetables, etc.

- Where customers are given personal attention, according to their personal tastes and preferences. For example, making special type of furniture, designing garments, etc.
- Where the nature of business is simple. For example, grocery, garments business, telephone booth, etc.
- Where capital requirement is small and risk involvement is not heavy. For example, vegetables and fruits business, tea stall, etc.
- Where manual skill is required. For example, making jewellery, haircutting or tailoring, cycle or motorcycle repair shop, etc

1.4 Joint Stock Company

A joint stock company (JSC) is a type of business entity: It is a type of corporation or partnership involving two or more legal persons. Certificates of ownership (or stocks) are issued by the company in return for each financial contribution, and the shareholders are free to transfer their ownership interest at any time by selling their stockholding to others. In most countries, a joint stock company offers the protection of limited liability; a shareholder is not liable for any of the company's debt beyond the face value of their shareholding.

There are two kinds of joint stock company: Private and public companies. The shares of the former are usually only held by the *directors* and Company Secretary. The shares of the latter are bought and sold on the open market. The important features of a joint stock company are as follows

1. *Separate legal existence*: A company is an artificial person and has a legal entity quiet distinct from its members or owners. A shareholder can use a company and his investment as creditor has nothing to do with his investment in its share capital. As an artificial person, it enjoys all the rights enjoyed by such a natural person. Therefore, a company cannot marry, cannot take oath, cannot be sent to *jail*, cannot enter into partnership and cannot practice as a professional (lawyer, doctor).
2. *Division of capital into shares*: The capital of a company is divided into shares of small denominations which are readily transferable from one owner to another without much formality.
3. *Limited Liability*: The *liabilities* of the members is generally limited to the extent of the face value of the shares that a person has agreed to take up. For example, if a person has paid Rs. 5/- on a share of Rs. 10/-, his liability extends up to a further sum of Rs. 5/- only. Whatever may happen to the company and whatever may be the state of solvency of the company, his total liability does not exceed the face value of the share(Rs. 10/- in our case).

4. *Perpetual existence*: A company has the distinct characteristic of having perpetual existence. In other words, its existence is not affected by the death, *insolvency* or retirement of its shareholders or directors. The shares may constantly change hand and yet the company goes on. This characteristic gives life and *stability* to the company form of organization.
5. *Common seal*: A company has a common seal which is substitute for this signature as a company. Being an artificial person, it can not sign documents by itself. The name of the company is engraved on the common seal. The common seal is kept in safe custody by the secretary of the company, it is used accordingly to the directions of the Board of Directors. When this seal is affixed for the company on any document, it has to be witnessed by at least two directors.
6. Separation *of ownership from management*. As we know that the entity of a company is quite distinct from that of the members or shareholders who compose it, a shareholder cannot bind the company for his acts. All the shareholders do not manage the company themselves but they leave the management into the hands of their representative and trustees, i.e., The Board of Directors

Partnership

A **partnership** is an arrangement where entities and/or individuals agree to cooperate to advance their interests. In the most frequent instance, a partnership is formed between one or more *businesses* in which **partners** (owners) co-labor to achieve and share profits or losses.

Partnerships are also frequent regardless of and among sectors. Non-profit organizations, for example, may partner together to increase the likelihood of each achieving their mission. Governments may partner with other governments to achieve their mutual goals, as may religious and political organizations. In *education*, accrediting agencies increasingly evaluate schools by the level and quality of their partnerships with other schools and across sectors. Partnerships also occur at personal levels, such as when two or more individuals agree to domicile together. Partnerships between governments, interest-based organizations, schools, businesses, and individuals, or some combination thereof, have always been and remain commonplace.

Partnerships have widely varying results and can present partners with special challenges. Levels of give-and-take, areas of responsibility, lines of authority, and overarching goals of the partnership must all be negotiated. While partnerships stand to amplify mutual interests and success, some are considered ethically problematic, or at least debatable. When a politician, for example, partners with a corporation to advance the corporation's interest in exchange for some benefit, a *conflict of interest* may make the partnership problematic from the standpoint of the public good. Developed countries often strongly regulate certain partnerships via *anti-trust* laws, so as to to inhibit monopolistic practices and foster free market competition.

Among developed countries, business partnerships are often favored over *corporations* in taxation policy, since *dividend taxes* only occur on profits before they are distributed to the partners. However, depending on the partnership structure and the *jurisdiction* in which it operates, owners of a partnership may be exposed to greater personal liability than they would as *shareholders* of a corporation.

Types of Partnerships

Under *common law* legal systems, the basic form of partnership is a *general partnership*, in which all partners manage the business and are personally liable for its debts. Two other forms which have developed in most countries are the *limited partnership* (LP), in which certain limited partners relinquish their ability to manage the business in exchange for *limited liability* for the partnership's debts, and the *limited liability partnership* (LLP), in which all partners have some degree of limited liability.

There are two types of partners. General partners have an obligation of *strict liability* to third parties injured by the Partnership. General partners may have *joint liability* or *joint and several liability* depending upon circumstances. The liability of limited partners is limited to their investment in the partnership.

A ***silent partner*** is one who still shares in the profits and losses of the business, but who is uninvolved in its management, and/or whose association with the business is not publicly known; these partners usually provide capital

Different Types of Partnerships-Merits and Demerits.

General Partnership: The most simple and basic form of partnership, general partners are fully responsible for all business dealings done by any of the partner. For example, if A and B are partners and A deals and eventually defaults with a third party, it's not only A who is responsible for repairing the damages, B is equally liable, even to the extent of selling his own assets to settle the aggrieved party. This clause of the agreement makes it a risky undertaking. There's some respite in form of tax savings which is applicable on each partner's income and not on dividends. General partner actively participate in routine management and decision making of the business.

Limited Partnership: Not all partners enter into the partnership agreement in the same capacity. Limited partners are the inactive ones who do not take part in the management or decision making (that doesn't mean they have no say at all). Mostly they are investors who just put in their capital and take home profits. Quite obviously, a partnership business must have one or more general partners. In case of a default or lawsuit, limited partner's personal asset are not on stake, that is why limited partners are bound to make their position known before conducting business on company's behalf.

Limited Liability Company **(LLC):** As stated above, in a general partnership not all partners can join as limited partners. However, Limited Liability Company is a form of partnership that allows all partners to enter as limited liability partners. Limited Liability Company is pretty similar to the corporations. Best thing about LLC is that one partner is not responsible for another partner's actions. LLC is in fact a more flexible form of business and ideal for small businesses that do not require excessive capital. Usually businesses start as general partnership or LLC and move on to become corporations when they expand.

1.5 Public Enterprises

Public enterprises have become important instruments in nation-building to carry out entrepreneurial functions associated with economic and social development. To some extent, public enterprises have assumed a part role of the State in accelerating economic development and maintaining political stability where sole dependence upon ministerial departments to implement government programmes have proved to be ineffective.

The growth in number of these bodies has increased materially and this is reflected in their contribution to the Gross Domestic Product (GDP). Profits and taxes from these enterprises constitute about 80% of the national revenues. These examples are by no means isolated as similar trends are discernible in many countries in the Asian region and elsewhere. Public enterprises are financed in a variety of ways. Generally, the initial investment capital is provided from the government as a launching grant. Thereafter, the enterprise may receive annual grants for operating and development expenditure depending on the nature of the enterprise and its activities. Statutory corporations and government owned companies are generally expected to generate their own income and operate profitably, are allowed to raise loans on the domestic and foreign markets and in a number of cases offer equity participation to government and private sector agencies. Characteristically more companies are created to undertake commercial or semi-commercial activities of the State as it is generally assumed that these provide greater operational flexibility than is normally possible through the traditional departmental form.

Concepts of Public Enterprise

The following public enterprises are recognized:

Departmental undertakings, statutory corporations or autonomous bodies established by or under legislation, autonomous bodies set up by government resolution or order, and companies, nationalized or established under company law, where government has a controlling interest.

Departmental Undertakings

These are entities which organizationally are part of ministerial departments but operate in a commercial manner. They come within ministerial jurisdiction, receive direct appropriations for capital and operational purposes from the legislature, keep their accounts on an accrual basis and are staffed and managed by civil servants. General examples are railways, postal services, government printers, water boards, mints and such like bodies which are service rather than profit motivated. In some countries these bodies may even be established instead as statutory corporations depending on the amount of flexibility that is desired in carrying out their tasks. In general this form of public enterprise is not a legal entity in its own right.

1.6 Statutory Corporations, Bodies or Authorities

Statutory bodies are organizations which are established by or under legislation with their structure, powers and functions specifically prescribed. They are separate legal entities and can sue and be sued. They have far more autonomy than departmental undertakings and can in many cases invest, raise capital, borrow and lend within the terms of their statutes. Harbor boards, airlines, telecommunications, energy and banks are general examples. In this study, some countries have made a distinction between bodies established by separate laws which are labeled statutory corporations or statutory authorities and those established under omnibus legislation which are referred to as autonomous bodies. Whilst there may be some differences in autonomy and the powers they wield, these autonomous bodies should not be confused with the autonomous bodies established by government resolutions or orders.

Autonomous bodies established by Government Resolution or Order

These types of bodies are rare. They may be established by government order or Royal Decree for a public purpose. Examples of such entities are found in Thailand such as the National Housing Authority and the Bangkok Mass Transit Authority. In India they take the form of registered societies (under the Societies Registration Act) which receive government financial backing. Their powers and functions are as specified in the resolution or order establishing them.

Government Companies

These are bodies established under company law. They differ from other companies in as much as the State and/or public corporations hold the majority or all of their shares. Where equity in these companies is held jointly by public and private interests, they are generally referred to as 'mixed enterprises' or 'joint venture' companies.

Rationale of Public Enterprises

There are two qualitative dimensions to a public enterprise viz the 'public' and the 'enterprise' aspects. The 'public' aspect of the two dimensional concept envisages that an entity must serve a public purpose such as promoting industrial expansion, ensuring balanced regional development, and/or generally raising living standards. The 'enterprise' aspect connotes that the entity must function as a commercial organization trying to achieve the normal commercial objectives expected of such a body. The weight age given to either dimension will determine whether the enterprise will operate in the nature of a nonprofit service organization or a profit-orientated company.

In the First International Seminar held in Seoul, Korea (1982) a paper presented on "State Audit Systems for Economic Development" outlined the phases of economic development which, theoretically at least, the various countries had reached or would experience. It referred to a first stage of 'maintenance' where production functions were limited and based on less advanced science and technology. In the second stage of 'mobilization' the government mobilizes society towards a 'take off' providing incentives for industrial expansion by providing access to raw materials, education and protective trade policies so that there is a commitment towards modernization and industrial development. The third stage is one of 'guidance' of the economy in which modern technology and long range planning is prevalent with rapid urbanization and changing class structures. The last stage is one of 'co-ordination' when the economy reaches the mature stage of a welfare oriented industrial society. At this stage the government tries to adopt a regulatory role co-coordinating the various aspects of the private sector in order to achieve the most equitable distribution of wealth and services. This is reflected in the types of enterprises that are established in each country; the diverse rationale postulated for establishing them, and the wide range of their activities. Arguably, when countries reach the 'mature' stage the governments concerned, depending on their political philosophies, begin to think in terms of privatizing their enterprises, partly because they have become a burden on public coffers and/or because such enterprises are capable of functioning as private sector entities and still serve the public interests.

Public enterprises in some countries grew out of necessity or were developed for political, economic, social and historical reasons. Governments had to fuel the engines of growth in the economy and had to provide the vehicles for achieving this purpose. There was a need to promote self-reliance in strategic sectors of the economy, provide infrastructural facilities for promoting a balanced and diversified economic structure in development, reduce racial and regional disparities, increase employment, bridge the gap in the investment participation as between the public and private sectors in the country and generate surpluses for reinvestment; also to enforce State control on trade and industry by ensuring an equitable distribution of goods and services. There was, in addition, a desire for creating prestigious or research-oriented institutions for discharging specialized functions. Further, it was also recognized that there was a need to bring outside expertise into management of the activity in ways which were not otherwise practicable in a departmental setting. It was also incumbent on governments to venture into and fill the void in those areas where the private sector was not prepared to invest. Governments also felt it necessary to intervene in those areas which they considered were being run inefficiently by the private sector. In some other cases entities which were poorly managed and required rehabilitation or the nature of the undertakings involved the public interest, 'nationalization' or government take-over was warranted so as to prevent exploitation by the private sector. There were also certain types of enterprises, such as defense-oriented industries, which could not be left to the private sector for reasons of national security. Tied in with all these reasons was the desire to create infrastructural facilities to encourage economic growth by attracting domestic and foreign capital. In some situations there was a tendency to establish, 'mixed enterprises' or joint ventures with the private sector. There were additional 'spin offs' in this type of arrangement in that it facilitated transfer of technology, expertise and skills from the private sector to the public sector.

Most public enterprises can be further classified according to sectored or functional types including: public utilities, transport and communications, food and agriculture, development finance institutions, industrial, trading, manufacturing, regional development, oil, coal and gas and heavy engineering. In the various countries they may be grouped differently depending on how ministerial functions which determine ministerial responsibility, are allocated for particular enterprises. The number of enterprises within each sector may indicate the importance and priority each country places on these bodies for carrying out its policies, development plans and objectives. In Korea for example, there are more development finance institutions ie banks, insurance companies and the stock exchange, than any other types of public enterprise. In India on the other hand, commercial, manufacturing and industrial types predominate. In Malaysia the regional development and agricultural sectors are prominent reflecting the importance given to agricultural based industries and a commitment to improve the welfare of the rural population.

The range of activities is marked, touching on all aspects of the economy from the provision of basic amenities such as water and electricity, to tourist promotion, the management of ports, railways and airlines, to atomic energy. Public enterprises such as the manufacturing and industrial types are actively involved in production whilst other agencies such as development finance institutions, like banks and insurance companies, perform supportive functions providing technical and financial assistance to promote the development of both public and private enterprises. Many statutory corporations and companies have also established subsidiary companies to support their activities. For example, a housing authority may set up a construction company, a credit corporation and a cement factory help achieve its objectives. This sort of development has led to the creation of numerous subsidiary companies, many of which may provide similar services and perform overlapping functions. This proliferation of subsidiaries has resulted in a dilution of available expertise in those developing countries where staff are drawn from the public service. Of greater importance and concern however, is the potential for the weakening of controls exercised by the legislature and the executive over these bodies to the detriment of public accountability.

Legislatorial and Governmental Controls

Public enterprises, other than the departmental form, generally enjoy considerable autonomy but they nevertheless are subject to legislatorial and governmental controls because in many cases their funds are derived from the State. They are, then, publicly accountable. The nature and extent of controls vary between countries depending on the form and type of the enterprises and in some cases the extent of the investment. These controls are exercised directly by supervision and inspection, through committees of the legislature and institutions such as the Comptroller and Auditor General (CAG), or indirectly through government surveillance of performance. Generally, government controls over their policies, management and operations can be represented diagrammatically as follows:

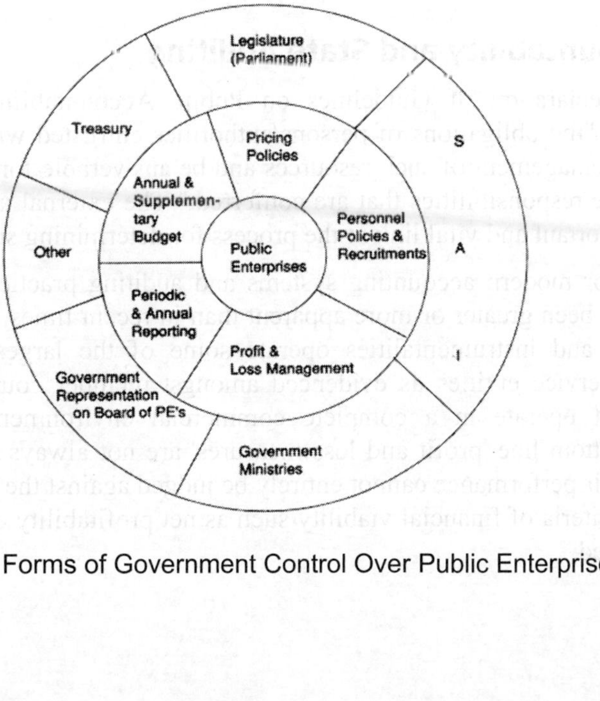

Fig. 1.1 Forms of Government Control Over Public Enterprises.

The main instruments of legislatorial controls in many of the countries are the budget debates, questions in the legislature, the annual accounts and reports of the enterprises tabled in the legislature, reports by the CAG and examination by legislatorial committees. The power of the government to exercise control stems primarily from the enabling statutes. Governments also supervise and control these bodies by ensuring that they comply with laws, rules and regulations issued by them and enforced by the central agencies such as the Treasury and public service personnel authorities. Controls are also exercised through pricing, lending and borrowing policies of the government. It is normal for most governments to appoint the boards of directors and also the chief executives. Apart from these organizational controls, procedural controls also exist. Systems for reporting on a regular basis and periodical review meetings between the Minister concerned and the managements of public enterprises are common. The CAG discharge a different responsibility by sustaining public accountability through their annual and special reports.

Governments are conscious of maintaining a proper balance between autonomy and control. Excessive controls could be counter productive to the very purpose of establishing an enterprise whilst on the other hand, too much autonomy could put public funds at risk in the event of poor management. Although comprehensive legislatorial and governmental controls exist, in practice some CAG have found them to be ineffective. There is often a lack of performance criteria and properly developed monitoring and evaluation systems, compounded by a shortage of adequately trained staff in the enterprise to ensure compliance with prescribed procedures. This perceived weakness could put at risk public accountability and thus increase the burden of public enterprises on government budgets.

Public Accountability and State Auditing

The Tokyo Declaration of Guidelines on Public Accountability defines public accountability as "the obligations of persons/authorities entrusted with public resources to report on the management of such resources and be answerable for the fiscal, managerial and Programme responsibilities that are conferred." The external audit through the CAG is the most important and vital link in the process for determining such accountability.

The need for modern accounting systems and auditing practices in government has probably never been greater or more apparent than in recent times. Governments through their agencies and instrumentalities operate some of the largest and most complex business and service entities as evidenced amongst member countries. Many of these entities do not operate in a complete commercial environment and the traditional commercial bottom line 'profit and loss measures' are not always relevant as a guide to efficiency. Their performance cannot entirely be judged against the back-drop of financial results using criteria of financial viability such as net profitability or the rate of return on capital employed.

The role of the State audit system has to be continuously adjusted to the ever expanding tasks required of it as the country's economy moves along to higher stages of development. In response to these changes a number of the member countries has shifted to comprehensive audits covering considerations of economy, and efficiency.

Nonetheless, in a number of countries, the main thrust of audit is still on financial and compliance audit. In so far as economy and efficiency audits are concerned these vary over a wide spectrum, in terms of scope, extent, methods and areas of audit concern. Thus at one end of the scale extensive performance audits are carried out by countries such as the Republic of Korea, Japan, Israel, Australia and India and at the other extreme there are some member countries where the CAG have not yet embarked on performance audits to any great extent.

Systems evaluation is commonly conducted and wherever possible transactions testing on a sampling basis is carried out. The extent of testing varies depending upon a detailed assessment of the system of internal controls.

As regards performance auditing, the approach and methods employed vary amongst the different CAG depending on the expertise, availability of qualified staff and the state of financial and other records of the public enterprises audited and their activities.

An important function of CAG is not only to attest the financial statements of public enterprises but also to assist the government and the enterprise management to improve financial and administrative efficiency and performance. In this context, the emphasis throughout the audit process is to serve as instruments of both accountability and improved public administration. Audit findings and reports thus not only express opinions on the financial statements but also include comments on the propriety of transactions, management decisions, waste and extravagance. Thus, not only are the results and operations of public enterprises evaluated but suggestions are also given for corrective actions and improvements.

However, CAG experience difficulty in evaluating the performance of public enterprises where the objectives of the enterprises are not clearly specified, or where multiple objectives are involved and there is no priority ranking to determine which objective takes precedence. It has been the experience of CAG that, more often than not, the social and economic objectives are not expressed in such detail as to serve as performance indicators, nor are the standards of performance specified by the authorities approving the socio-economic development programmes.

To carry out the performance audit effectively, the CAG has to remain abreast of developments in different fields of human knowledge and develop the vision and the intuitive flair for a creative evaluation of performance against the overall framework of national objectives and policy. This requires constant thought and conscious efforts to improve the technical skills of the audit personnel at all levels. Many member countries have expressed that lack of experienced and multidiscipline staff is a major constraint in development of this important area of audit.

Table 1.1 Form of Public Enterprises.

Countries	Departmental Undertaking	Public Corporation	Companies (Government/ corporation Owned)	Auto-nomous	TOTAL
1. Australia	20	**59**	77	Nil	156#
2. China	-	**-**	-		800,000
3. Cyprus	Nil	25	6	Nil	31
4. Hong Kong	6	**10**	-	-	16
5. India	298	**84**	1079	240	1701
6. Indonesia	2	27	157	Nil	186 34*
7. Israel	n/a	n/a	n/a	Nil	300
8. Japan	**17**	**81**	13	96	207
9. Jordan	n/a	**41**	6	-	n/a
10. Korea	**5**	25	70	Nil	100
11. Kuwait	n/a	**23**	36	-	n.a
12. Malaysia	18	480	847+	Nil	1345
13. Nepal	-	25	32	-	57
14. New Zealand	**14**	7	18	26	65
15. Pakistan	**41**	124	120	12	297
16. Papua New Guinea	Nil	44	37	-	81
17. Saudi arabia	Nil	30	65	Nil	**95**
18. Singapura	-	41	505	-	546
19. Sri Lanka	77	207	43	Nil	327
20. Thailand	10	35	**20**	Nil	**65**
21. United Arab	n/a	26	n/a		n/a

#At Federal level ie enterprises of the State governments are excluded.

*Unclassified. + There are 1,133 companies but only 847 are considered active:

Table 1.2 summarizes the mandate for audit of public enterprises by the CAG. Audit arrangements in a number of member countries include provision for three levels of audit viz: internal audit, external audit carried out by commercial accountants appointed by the government on the advice of the CAG or by the CAG direct, and finally by the CAG itself. In discharging its responsibility to the legislature, the CAG reviews and comments on the performance of both internal auditors and the commercial auditor.

Table 1.2 Mandate for Audit of Pubic Enterprises.

Type of PE	Public Corporations	Companies
Countries	**(Statutory Bodies)**	**(Government/Corporation Controlled)**
Australia	Appointment under the legislation relating to each statutory authority	Appointment under the Companies Act and the Audit Act
China	Authorisation under Article 91 of the Constitution of the People's Republic of China and Article 2 of the Provisional Regulations on Audit Work issued by the State Council in 1985	Authorisation under Article 91 of the Constitution of the People's Republic of China and Article 2 of the Provisional Regulations on Audit Work issued by the State Council in 1985
Cyprus	Authorisation under the "Public Corporate Bodies (Audit of Accounts) Law	Audited by private firms of auditors
Hong Kong	Audited by private firms of auditors. However, SAI has access to books and records of statutory bodies	
India	Authorisation under the provisions of the statute	Authorisation under the Companies Act 1956 as "superimposed" auditor over private auditor
Indonesia	Authorisation under Act No.5 of 1973	Audited by private firms of auditors
Israel	Authorisation under the State Comptroller's Law 1958	Appointment under the Companies Law, 1975
Japan	Authorisation under the Board of Audit Law, 1947	Authorisation under the Board of Audit Law 1947
Jordan	Authorised by legislation	Audited by private firms of auditors
Korea	Authorisation under - The Board of Audit and Inspection Law 1963	Authorisation under - The Board of Audit and Inspection Law 1963
	- The Budget and Accounting Law 1962	- The Budget and Accounting Law 1962
	- The respective laws establishing the corporation	
Kuwait	Authorisation under Law No. 30 of 1964 (Audit Bureau Legislation)	Authorisation under Law No. 30 of 1964

Table contd...

Type of PE	Public Corporations	Companies
Countries	(Statutory Bodies)	(Government/Corporation Controlled)
Malaysia	Appointment under the legislation relating to each authority or the Statutory Bodies (Accounts and Annual Reports) Act 1980	Only on order by the King under the provisions of the Constitution and Audit Act 1957. So far none given
	Authorisation under provisions of the Constitution and the Audit Act 1957	
Nepal	Authorisation under the provisions of the Constitution and the Audit Act	Authorisation under the Constitution, Audit Act and Companies Act
New Zealand	Authorisation under the State Owned Enterprises Act or specific enabling legislation	No specific authority necessary. C&A-G is appointed under normal provisions of company legislation
Pakistan	Enacting order 1973	Audited by firms of chartered accountants. SAI authorised by Government in 1977 to evaluate performance of companies
Papua New Guinea	Authorisation under - the Constitution - the Public Bodies (Financial Admin istration) Act 1969	Audit by private auditors but SAI may carry out such audits under provisions of the Constitution under special circumstances.
Saudi Arabia	Authorisation under the Act Establishing the General Auditing Bureau	Authorisation under the Act establishing the General Auditing Bureau
Singapore	Appointment under the legislation relating to each authority	Audited by private firms of auditors
Sri Lanka	Authorisation under - the Constitution - the Finance Act No.38 of 1971 - enabling statutes	Authorisation under the Companies Law
Thailand	Authorisation under - the State Audit Act, 1979 - the Accounts and Finance Regulations issued by the Ministry of Finance	Audited by private auditors but SAI has inspection rights
United Arab Emirates	Authorisation under the provisions of the Constitution and Federal Law No. 7 of 1976	Authorisation under the provisions of the Constitution and Federal Law No. 7 of 1976

CAG Reports to the Legislature

The general practice is for the CAG to present both annual and special reports to the legislature in the interests of public accountability. It has been noted, however, that in some countries this is not the procedure in respect of government-owned companies not subject to CAG audit either as appointed external auditor or in the exercise of powers to review the audit carried out by the commercial auditor. This is a perceived weakness in the accountability process.

The process adopted by most legislatures is for CAG reports to be reviewed by a committee such as a Public Accounts Committee. Depending on practices followed as between the government and the legislature which vary as between countries, action is taken to correct deficiencies and weaknesses raised by the CAG.

1.7 Changing Business Environment in Post Liberalization Era

Economic liberalization has changed the rules of the entrepreneurial game. The competencies required to thrive in the protected era may no longer be good enough.

The role of entrepreneurship in the economic development and growth of a country or region is often overlooked. In any case, it is not given the importance that it deserves, particularly in economic literature.

In fact, until recently, economists were reluctant to rely on entrepreneurship as a possible determinant of economic outcome. A standard economic explanation, if it is at all important, stems from testable hypotheses and quantifications.

Cultures and traditions are vague in determining economic outcomes although the same situations are tackled in economic literature with the help of multiple equilibrium conditions. Even then the explanations are incomplete. For example, within a geographical boundary, sufficient connections between socio-cultural values and economic outcomes are observed.

More specifically, at the household level often economic decisions are made in accordance with beliefs and traditions. For example, the choice of schools/colleges, professions to be taken up or to live in a particular area are not determined simply by economic decisions. In many of these situations ethnicity may play an important role.

In India, the government realized the importance of entrepreneurship and set up institutions at the national and State levels to develop entrepreneurship and also to provide assistance to first generation entrepreneurs. Though it is difficult to arrive at a firm conclusion on the creation of a new generation of entrepreneurs, the need to do it is clearly established.

What is Entrepreneurship?

Entrepreneurship is universal in any human activity — be it economic, political or social. Entrepreneurship has been defined as a creative human act involving the mobilization of resources from one level of productive use to a higher level.

Or, as "combining together factors of production" and the supply of entrepreneurship has been identified as critical in determining the wealth and growth of a nation's economy. In fact, entrepreneurship is a vital source of structural change and productivity improvement within economies.

First-generation entrepreneurs quite often start small firms with small investments and then, once established, some of them grow to larger firms. With shorter technology life cycles, the survival rate of these new small firms is expected to be low.

India's accelerated growth, post-liberalization, has not been accompanied by a commensurate expansion in employment. This suggests a restructuring in many sectors of the economy and also highlights the importance of entrepreneurship and new units in creating employment.

With development in knowledge and technology, the capital intensity of most production functions has increased. Simultaneously, this substitution of labor with capital has improved labor productivity. Productivity improvements have been significant in manufacturing. But, of late, the production of many services has also become capital intensive.

The infusion of technology and capital has enriched the content of many jobs; the capital required to set up even small firms has gone up. Entrepreneurship involves a willingness to take responsibility and the ability to put the mind to a task and see it through. An ingredient of entrepreneurship is sensing opportunities and serving as a change agent. An entrepreneur has to be a risk-taker; a calculated risk-taker and not a gambler.

An entrepreneur has to have a clear vision, be innovative and have a commitment to his goals with strong management and organizational skills.

Factors such as thrift, hard work, tenacity, honesty and tolerance are the key, though the main aspect is that of being a risk taker

Sociology of Entrepreneurship

Historically, Indian business has largely been mercantile. India and China were the world's largest manufacturing economies; manufacturing in India was entirely in the hands of small artisans.

The Parsees were the first Indian entrepreneurs to set up manufacturing units after the pioneering activities of the British. Around this time the Marwari trading community ventured into manufacturing. They acquired existing units and also set up new ones.

A new trend that has been observed the last 10-15 years is that the Generation Next of the traditional entrepreneurial communities are going for higher/professional education.

This has spawned a new breed of young entrepreneurs, particularly in the new sectors. The units are world class, able to survive and prosper in competitive market.

The key input provided by these new entrepreneurs in many cases is knowledge capital rather than only finance.

Although the economic environment and markets have changed, the traits required of an entrepreneur have remained the same. Economic liberalization has changed the rules of the entrepreneurial game.

The skills and competencies required to thrive in the earlier protected environment may not ensure survival in the open, liberalized milieu of today.

No longer do business culture and traditions matter for entrepreneurship. The new-age entrepreneurs and candidates can learn it by experience and training relating to risk-taking behavior. If such things are available, one can spring a surprise.

Questions

1. What are the merits and demerits of public sector organizations?
2. Discuss the different opportunities and challenges for a business organization
3. Compare and contrast between the public sector company and a joint stock company?
4. Explain the different types of business organizations?
5. Explain the post liberalization Indian economic developments and progress?
6. Define business and explain the significance of business?
7. Explain the basic characteristics of business organizations?
8. Explain the following (a) sole proprietorship (b) partnership company
9. Add a note on changing business environment in post liberalization scenario?
10. Explain briefly the functions of business?

Chapter - 2

Manufacturing Management

Manufacturing is the use of *machines*, *tools* and labor to make things for use or sale. The term may refer to a range of human activity, from *handicraft* to *high tech*, but is most commonly applied to *industrial* production, in which *raw materials* are transformed into *finished goods* on a large scale. Such finished goods may be used for manufacturing other, more complex products, such as *household appliances* or *automobiles*, or sold to *wholesalers*, who in turn sell them to *retailers*, who then sell them to end users - the "*consumers*".

Manufacturing takes turns under all types of *economic systems*. In a free market economy, manufacturing is usually directed toward the *mass production* of *products* for sale to *consumers* at a profit. In a *collectivist economy*, manufacturing is more frequently directed by the state to supply a centrally planned economy. In free market economies, manufacturing occurs under some degree of government *regulation*.

Modern manufacturing includes all intermediate processes required for the production and integration of a product's components. Some industries, such as *semiconductor* and *steel* manufacturers use the term *fabrication* instead.

History and Development

In its earliest form, manufacturing was usually carried out by a single skilled *artisan* with assistants. Training was by *apprenticeship*. In much of the pre-industrial world the *guild* system protected the privileges and trade secrets of urban artisans.

Before the *Industrial Revolution*, most manufacturing occurred in rural areas, where household-based manufacturing served as a supplemental subsistence strategy to *agriculture* (and continues to do so in places). Entrepreneurs organized a number of manufacturing households into a single enterprise through the *putting-out system*.

Toil manufacturing is an arrangement whereby a first firm with specialized equipment processes raw materials or semi-finished goods for a second firm.

2.1 Production Management

Production management, alternatively referred to as manufacturing management, is required for transforming raw materials and partly, fabricated materials into finished products. Production management does not imply management of productive process alone, but it covers all there activities which go into the making of production. To make production a concrete reality, one ,must pay heed to the factors of production like land, labor, capital and organization, or to speak in the language of business, materials, men, money, machines and methods. Production management thus calls for the work of planning and control pertaining to each of these factors of production.

Production management does not involve a mechanical assemblage of relevant factors. In contrast to mere transformation of raw materials into finished products, it aims at transmuting and permuting resources of higher productivity so that the greatest outputs are obtained from the least inputs. With its end in views, production management embraces the productive process too and involves planning, directing and controlling operations till their successful completion. Quality, quantity, cost and time of production have an important bearing on productivity of the manufacturing enterprise. Accordingly, it is the task of production management to see that effective utilization of resources is made, time is shortened, wastes and scrapings are avoided, and harmonious working is made to prevail in the plant.

For effective managerial performance, the work of production department is required to be organized on sound lines. All the principles and practices of organizing are to be applied in building a sound structure for improving the result of production management. Successful production management is not practicable without the existence of an appropriate organization structure. Consequently, managerial efforts are to be directed in designing an organization structure that conforms to the needs of the product, size of the enterprise and availability of production facilities. Organizing for production may be conceived in broader sense to include some aspects of works engineering or works organization like plant layout and factory building.

The problems of production management differ form case to case and are mainly related to the system of production. There are several systems of production which determine the magnitude of production work and the problems to be tackled in manufacturing operations. Hence, a familiarity with the different systems of production is required for understanding the intricacies of production management. Of course, the system of production is dictated in a particular case by the volume of sales and the nature of product. The quantity to be produced is nothing but an answer to the question of 'what can be sold". In the ultimate analysis, therefore, sales are the regulator of a system of production.

The management of transformation process of inputs into output is the essence of production management. In present competitive world the production process in every enterprise needs some effective and scientific planning as well as proper control. Thus production management can be defined as "Management which by scientific planning and regulation sets into motion the part of an enterprise to which it has been entrusted the task of actual transformation of inputs into output". In the words of Mr. E.L. Brech, "Production Management then becomes the process of effectively planning and regulating the operations of that part of an enterprise which is responsible for the actual transformation of materials into finished products".

This definition appears to be incomplete as it does not include the human factors involved in a production process. It lays stress only on the materialistic features.

In broader sense, production management actually deals with decision making related to production processes, so that the resulting goods and services are produced in accordance with the quantitative specifications and demand schedule with minimum cost. To attain these objectives the two main activities of Production Management are the Design and Control of production systems.

In production management effective planning and control are essential. In the absence of effective planning and regulation of any production activity the goals cannot be achieved, the customers may not be satisfied and ultimately certain activities may be closed which may lead to social evil

Measurement of Work

In an engineering sense efficiency can be simply stated as the ratio of useful energy obtained to energy applied. We can all understand that. Put succinctly, that is what is really meant by efficiency of production, but the difficulty is to see the relationship between input and output of production, or to measure performance. Which brings us right to the heart of the problem of efficiency of production: how to measure performances.

There is usually some difficulty about measuring the comparative performance of several departments in a Company or different companies. If two factories are turning out the same product which is measured in tons or feet, then overall cost per ton or per foot is a measure of performance which can be obtained readily and used for comparison. But how does one compare the costs or efficiency of two factories or department s making dissimilar products ? Cost per ton or unit is no good. As between two different firms, only the percentage net profit is any measure, and that is affected by the type of market and selling cost which are not production costs. And between different departments in the same firm there would seem to be, at first sight, no measure of efficiency on a common and therefore comparable basis.

If, however, the amount of "effort" (or cost-material, labor and overhead services) which should have been sued to make a given quantity of a product is known and also the amount actually used, then surely the correct amount as a proportion of the actual amount is a measure of performance of efficiency. It is in reality an efficiency formula again, output over input. The real value of output, in efforts or hours is the amount of cost which goes out of the factory or department in a useful form, i.e., it does not include all wastage and excess costs, avoidable, and of no benefit to customer or company. And input is the total of all effort and costs absorbed. Including excess costs.

Organization of Production Planning Department

The work of a Production Planning Department generally falls into three sections, dealing with three stages of the sequence of operations. They are:

(i) Compiling and recording facts.
(ii) Developing plans.
(iii) Putting plans into operation and controlling results.

In the first stage and section, information is gathered together, recorded and filed in a way which is suitable for use by planners, and so that reference to it is easy and rapid. The information is of three kinds, relating to:

(a) Customers' orders and requirements;
(b) Stocks of materials and components;
(c) Plant available, capacities, operations and times.

Unless the organization is of such a size that each kind of information is dealt with in a separate section, it is advisable for all of it to be handled by one section under the supervision of a person skill din the work. Its organization is mainly a problem of filing and entering-up figures or records form vouchers, i.e., transferring information and striking balances. It can usually be staffed with Juniors, female, or relatively unskilled labor, but must be carefully supervised and checked by very reliable people. The absolute accuracy and therefore double checking required in banks is not essential, but inaccuracies can be troublesome and costly.

The second stage and section comprises the vital part of planning. It is her that the effectiveness or indifference of results is ensured. And where the ability to scheme, think ahead and take all factors into account is so essential. It is a job mainly done on paper, juggling as it were with figures and charts. Sales budgets must be broken down into or integrated with long-term production plans, factory and departmental plans formulated, and weekly or daily or even hour-by-hour loads prepared. In small factories a few simple charts or schedules suffice, but in very large organizations a vast amount of detailed information, in the form of masses of figures, flows into the section, and must be rapidly and regularly collated and reissue for action. Extreme tidiness is essential, and if those concerned are not to be bogged down by a continuous stream of insistent inquiries demanding attention, much of the work must so be organized as to be dealt with in a routine manner by juniors.

The third stage consists of translating the plans into instructions and can be mainly of a clerical nature. In practice, however, it is at this stage that a certain amount of decentralization is advisable, and the hour-by-hour machine or operation loading and the actual issue of jobs to operators is done either in or adjacent to the Forman's office, or in a shop office. Progress work, that is, checking performance against plans and reporting results (with recommendations for corrective action and requests for urgent actions) to foremen or other supervisors, which is really an aspect of control, is frequently carried out form the same of and even by the same persons.

The complexity of an organization structure for production planning depe4nds on the type of industry or manufacture rather than its scale. In mass-production and continuous-process manufacture, production planning consist of balancing the flow of materials (or components) from outside or component manufacturing departments, with consumption by the factory or assembly departments. Particularly is this so in the automobile or similar industries, where a good deal of preliminary work on materials in subcontracted, no large stocks of materials are kept (or could be for the immense consumption rate) and a small interruption to production affects a large part of the factory and is very expensive. In those factories engaged on batch production of partly standardized products there is the added complexity of setting-up (time and cost), varying batch sizes, and the synchronization of finishing dates for parts and sub assemblies when batches vary so much. It is predominantly a question of continual adjustment in order to maintain balanced loads on departments and to correct for unforeseen delays. When the product is designed to customers' requirements, the total process time is increased by the time required for design or preparation for each order, and consequently the period over which planning must extend is greater, making the problem more complex. Production planning is most complex when the product is mainly to customers' requirements, but is designed to incorporate many standard parts kept in stock. When the number of orders exceeds something like 50 per week, the amount of information to be handled becomes large and the department correspondingly so.

Planning Methods

The purpose of production order is to provide information about various operations involved in a production process. Once a production order is formulated, there arises the necessity to determine that when and where each operation is to be done. The reasons in that the operations described in a production order may be executed in several ways to get the final product and one may like to use a production strategy which makes most effective use of an, machine and material in the system. The best strategy is planned through the methods of Routing and Scheduling. Thus scheduling and routing is the final stage in production planning and have the following objectives:

(i) to prescribe where and by whom each operation necessary to manufacture a product is to be executed. This is known as routing.

(ii) the establishment of times at which to begin and/or complete each even or operation. This is termed as scheduling.

Plant Layout

Layout problems are fundamental to every type of organization/enterprise and are experienced in all kinds of undertakings. Housewife must arrange her kitchen, retailer must arrange his counters and display the items in such a manner which facilitates movement and attract the attention of customers, office management positions the desks, tables and other equipment in such a way that it facilitates the flow of work. The manufacturing organizations must arrange their facilities, not only the department within the factory but also the plant, stores and services so as to achieve smooth flow of products.

The adequacy of layout affects the efficiency of subsequent operations. It is an important perquisite for efficient operations and also has a great deal in common with many of the problems.

The simplest of situations with comparatively fewer items to arrange have many alternatives available. Import the layout decisions were based merely on intuition, experience, judgment and some sort of improvisation but with increase in the complexities of organizations the layout problems are solved scientifically.

Once a decision about location of the plant has been taken, next important problem before the management is to plan suitable layout for the plant. Efficiency and performance of good machines and sturdy building depend to a great extent on the layout of a plant. Plat layout is the method of allocating machines and equipment, various production processes and other necessary services involved in transformation process of a product with the available space of the factory so as to perform various operations in the most efficient and convenient manner providing output of high quality and minimum cost.

In the words of James Lundy, "layout identically involves the location of space and the arrangement of equipment in such a manner that overall operating costs are minimized." Alternately, plant layout is an effort to arrange machines and equipment, and other services within a pre designed building ensuring steady, smooth and economical flow of material.

Planning the layout of a plant is a continuous process as there are always chances of making improvements over the existing arrangement specially with shifts in the policies of management of techniques of production.

The disposition of the various parts of a plant along with all the equipment used is known as plant layout. It should be so designed that the plant functions most effectively.

Layout problems are common to all kinds of organization. A retailer must arrange his counter, display of items etc., office management must position desks, tables etc. in such a way that it facilitates the flow of work. A manufacturing organization must position its machinery and other equipment so as to achieve smooth flow of products through their factories.

A good layout results in comforts convenience, safety, efficiency, Compactness and profits. A poor layout results in congestion, waste, frustration and inefficiency.

Thus after plant location the proper design of plant layout is most significant for smooth functioning and success of the organization.

These three aspects of works planning and organization, viz., the production system, plant layout and factory building, are interrelated and go to decide the shape of things to come into existence. Correct layout has an important contribution towards efficient running of production affairs, because it increases the speed of in-process work, reduces the manufacturing time, lowers the cost of handling materials, and secures an integrated working of all sequential operations. Besides planning for storage of materials and finished products, service facilities like repairs, maintenance, power generation and others, different sectional offices for managerial, supervisory or inspection work, areas for canteens, crèches and parking as well as for future expansion of the plant. In addition, a number of mechanical aids are used for handling materials and finished products. For the operation of mechanical equipments like chutes, conveyor belts, elevators, high-lift fork trucks, crane trucks, overhead cranes, trolleys, etc., sufficient spaces must be provided for the operation of equipment in making the layout of a plant.

There are two distinct types of layout that are to be found in different systems of production. Group layout or process layout is adopted in job production as well as in batch production to some extent, while line layout or product layout is the rule in the case of mass production and process production.

Under group layout, machines or operators of alike type are grouped into a unit for discharging a particular operation in the production run. For examples, all lathe machines, drilling machines, grinding machines, or milling machines are grouped into so many different units or sections of the plant. Similarly, operators are classified into specialized units like molding, assembling, painting, etc. on the other hand, line layout is based on the sequence of operations required for manufacturing a particular product or part. Under the layout, manufacturing operations are analyzed and sequenced in such an order that work in-process moves in one direction with no backtracking or retracting of the path. In line layout, materials are worked out into finished products through a series of integrated operations that is arranged in a straight line fashion. Line layout is the only choice available to mass production and process-production.

There are several advantages of line layout, and it should be used in preference to group layout wherever practicable. Line layout eliminates cross-handling of materials, conserves floor space, assures steady flow of production, improves co-ordination between operations, economizes the use of materials, reduces the cost and time of manufacture, and increases the volume of production. However, line layout has two defects. The possible breakdown of machines in open operation may stop the working of the entire plant. Furthermore, line layout is of inflexible type and cannot be adjusted to the requirement of manufacturing other parts or products. On the contrary, group layout is effective in job production under which a variety of products is manufactured in small quantities at irregular intervals and through a varying sequence of operations by the use of the same machines. Group layout imparts flexibility to the use of machines, facilitates the work of supervision and inspection, and reduces servicing charges for repairs and maintenance. But the defect of group layout lies in poor co-ordination between operations excessive materials handling and backtracking of work in-process. It also damages the machines and equipments because of their frequent resetting and readjustments. Briefly, it makes for a higher cost of production.

Plant Layout Tools and Techniques

1. Process charts
   (i) Operations Process Charts
   (ii) Flow process Chart
2. Process Flow Diagrams
3. Machine data cards
4. Visualization of Layout
   (i) Two-dimensional plan or Templates
   (ii) Three-dimensional Plan or machine models

Plant Location

Introduction to Production

The performance of an enterprise is considerably affected by its location. The location of an industry is as important as the choice is for the location of a business or a shop in a city or locality. Unscientific and unplanned industrialization is harmful not only to the industrial unit but also to the social and economic structure of the country as a whole.

Nearly sixty years before, much importance was not given to the selection of appropriate location and the decisions in this regard were mainly governed by the individual preferences of the entrepreneurs and social customs. This resulted in failure of any organization which otherwise could have been successful. Government also with the objective of establishing socialistic pattern of society became instrument all in the selection of site for various industries in undeveloped areas by providing various investment benefits and other incentives. All this encouraged a large number of industrialists to follow a more scientific and logical approach towards the selection of site for establishing their industries.

The degree of significance for the selection of location for any enterprise mainly depends on its size and nature. Sometimes, the nature of the product itself suggest some suitable location. A small scale industry mainly selects the site where in accordance with its capacity the local market for the product is available. It can easily shift to other place when there is any change in the market. But for large scales industries requiring huge amount of investment there are many considerations other than the local demand in the selection of proper plant location. These plants cannot be easily shifted to other place and an error of judgment in the selection of site can be very expensive to the organization.

Production Methods

One activity of the administrative side of production is concerned with finding and stating the one best way to do all jobs. No longer is this left to the skilled and interested operator, proceeding by trial and error, successive operators making the same, or sometimes a different result. As more machines, tools and equipment, some of them highly specialized, have been designed and become available, and new materials and process materials and process developed, it has become increasingly a skilled technical job to keep abreast of developments and always to know the up-to-date or best way to do a job. It would be quite impossible today for the craftsman at the bench or machine to keep himself so informed and do a job of producing. Skilled men are still required, but increasingly today they become setters, minders, or maintenance men.

The old type of foreman is apt to think that the appointment of a production engineer, process engineer, or chemist, reduces his usefulness, his value to the Company, or his status. It does nothing of the kind, of course. It is true that, before the development of production engineering, and the use of chemists in the works as well as in the analytical laboratory, the Work Manger and his foreman supplied the production "know-how", and decided how a job should be done. But it is now recognized that the training and supervising of person is a much more complex job than it once was, and to relive a foreman of a large amount of administrative work makes a higher general performance possible and his job more valuable, not less. It is essential to separate planning form doing, administration from execution.

When a new material is developed or a new product designed, the method of production is obviously either known or worked out. But form then onwards all is change. Better method of production are being discovered continually. Furthermore, in many factories, particularly those engaged in engineering, the detailed method of production for each part to be manufactured, the machines to be used and equipment required, is decided subsequent to design. The task of deciding the best method of production, of saying how a job shall be produced, and of finding new and better ways of doing so, should be the responsibility of a Method of Production Engineering Department. Similarly, in a company where the technical knowledge is supplied by chemists, production method would be the responsibility of the works laboratory.

In deciding the one best way of doing a job, the production engineer or chemist must have regard for the costs of production, and therefore for the time to do the job. He must have regard for the costs of production, and therefore for the time to do the job. He must have some say also in new tools or equipment required. These are the three divisions into which the activities of the production or methods engineer usually fall that is to say, work study or methods, work measurement or time study and tool design.

These three aspects all call for close collaboration with the designer and works departments. The design of jigs and tools might be thought to be a logical development of the Design or Drawing Office work and in some works it is done in the Drawing Office. But it cannot be effectively developed without detailed study of methods and work being done in the factory, and, as will be shown later, this study forms the basis of standards for time, and hence for payment by results, production planning and costs. This study work calls for a specialized technique and training quite different form Drawing Office work. The outlook required is different too. It is more successful in practice if it is recognized as a separate activity, and combined with the design of tools and equipment. To avid it becoming too remote from or independent of the Drawing Office, Design Department, or Technical Department, new drawings, designs, or technical developments should always be referred to, and discussed with, the production engineers before final issue.

The development of production engineering as a special skill and the extensive use of specially designed tools and equipment have contributed largely to the very much greater output per man-hour. There is no doubt that it is through such development, adding horse-power to man-power, and taking out the manual efforts from jobs, that the way lies to reduce man-hour requirements.

Because production engineers tend to get machine or gadget minded, they are apt to forget or neglect the human factor. Machines cannot yet operate without human agency, and men should not be made into robots. The foremen may have something to say if the division of labor, for example, is carried too far, or if new methods are forced on them without consultant. Continued and close co-operation between the production engineers and works departments is absolutely essential.

The function of the production Engineering or Methods Department is to determine, in collaboration with the Design and Works Departments, the most effective, economical and suitable method of production, today down standards for material and time, and to design special tools and equipment required.

2.2 Production Planning and Control

In any manufacturing enterprise production is the driving force to which most other functions react. This is particularly true with inventories; they exist because of the needs of production.

Objectives of Production Planning Control

The ultimate objective of production planning and control, like that of all other manufacturing controls, is to contribute to the profits of the enterprise. As with inventory management and control, this is accomplished by keeping the customers satisfied through the meeting of delivery schedules. Specific objectives of production planning and control are to establish routes and schedules for work that will ensure the optimum utilization of materials, workers, and machines and to provide the means for ensuring the operation of the plant in accordance with these plans.

2.3 Production Planning and Control Functions

All of the four basic phases of control of manufacture are easily identified in production planning and control. The plan for the processing of materials through the plant is established by the functions of process planning, loading, and scheduling. The function of dispatching puts the plan into effect; that is, operations are started in accordance with the plant. Actual performance is then compared to the planned performance, and, when required, corrective action is taken. In some instances re-planning is necessary to ensure the effective utilization of the manufacturing facilities and personnel.

Process Planning (Routing): The determination of where each operation on a component part, subassembly, or assembly is to be performed results in a route for the movement of a manufacturing lot through the factory. Prior determination of these routes is the job of the manufacturing engineering function.

Loading: Once the route has been established, the work required can be loaded against the selected machine or workstation. The total time required to perform the operation is computed by multiplying the unit operation times given on the standard process sheet by the number of parts to be processed. This total time is then added to the work already planned for the workstation. This is the function of loading, and it results in a tabulated list or chart showing the planned utilization of the machines or workstations in the plant.

Scheduling: Scheduling is the last of the planning functions. It determines when an operation is to be performed, or when work is to be completed; the difference lies in the detail of the scheduling procedure. In a centralized control situation - where all process planning, loading, and scheduling for the plant are done in a central office- the details of the schedule may specify the starting and finishing time for an operation. On the other hand, the central schedule may simply give a completion time for the work in a given department.

Combining Functions: While it is easy to define "where" as process planning, "how much work" as loading, and "when as scheduling, in actual operations these three functions are often combined and performed concurrently. How far in advance routes, loads, and schedules should be established always presents an interesting problem.

Obviously, it is desirable that a minimum of changes be made after schedules are established. This objective can be approached if the amount of work scheduled for the factory or department is equal to or slightly greater than the manufacturing cycle. For optimum control, it should never be less than the manufacturing cycle.

Dispatching: Authorizing the start of an operation on the shop floor is the function of dispatching. This function may be centralized or decentralized. Again using our machine-shop example, the departmental dispatcher would authorize the start of each of the three machine operations – three dispatch actions based on the foreman's routing and scheduling of the work through his department. This is decentralized dispatching.

Reporting or Follow – up: The manufacturing activity of a plant is said to be "in control" when the actual performance is within the objectives of the planned performance. When jobs are started and completed on schedule, there should be very little, if any, concern about the meeting of commitments. Optimum operation of the plant, however, is attained only if the original plan has been carefully prepared to utilize the manufacturing facilities fully and effectively.

Corrective Action: This is the keystone of any production planning and control activity. A plant in which all manufacturing activity runs on schedule in all probability is not being scheduled to its optimum productive capacity. With an optimum schedule, manufacturing delays are the rule, not the exception.

Re-planning: Re-planning is not corrective action. Re-planning revise routes, loads, and schedules; a new plan is developed. In manufacturing this is often required. Changes in market conditions, manufacturing methods, or many other factors affecting the plant will often indicate that a new manufacturing plan is needed.

Factors Affecting Production Planning and Control

The factors that affect the application of production planning and control to manufacturing are the same as the factors we have already discussed that affect inventory management and control.

Type of Product: Again, it is the complexity of the product that is important, not what the product is, except as this may in turn relate to the market being served. Production control procedures are much more complex and involve many more records in the manufacture of large steam turbine generator sets or locomotives to customer orders then in the production of large quantities of a standard product involving only a few component parts, such as electric blankets, steam irons, or similar small appliances.

Type of Manufacturing: This is probably the most influential factor in the control situation. For a large continuous manufacturing plant producing a standard product, we have already indicated that the routing was included in the planning of the plant layout.

2.4 Production Planning and Control Procedures

Planning and control practices will vary widely from plant to plant. Further the many ways in which of the functions might be carried out in practice. Though no production control function can be entirely eliminated, the least control that results in effective operation of the factory is the best control. It must be remembered that production planning and control systems should be tools of management. The objective is not an elaborate and detailed system of controls and records, but rather, the optimum operation of the plant for maximum profits.

Production Planning and Control Systems: Because production planning and control places an emphasis on the control of work-in-process, the system will in effect tie together all previous records and forms developed in all planning for the manufacture of the product.

Market forecast: Its value to production planning and control is that it will indicate future trends in demand for manufactured product. Work shift policies, plans for an increase or decrease in manufacturing activity, or possible plant expansions may often be based upon the market forecasts and in turn affect the planning of the production planning and control group.

Sales Order: This is the second of the five classes of orders. It is a rewrite of the customer' order specifying what has been purchased – product and quantity and authorizing shipment of the goods to the customer. Multiple copies are prepared and all interested functions are furnished a copy. Sales orders may be written by marketing, inventory control, or production control.

Stock Order: This third class of order is not always used. In the preceding paragraph we indicated how it may be used after sales order accumulate to an economical manufacturing lot. It is, of course, the principal order when manufacturing to stock. It will authorize production in anticipation of future sales.

Shop Order: This fourth class of order deals with the manufacture of component parts. Customer orders, sales orders, and stock orders are for the finished product. In the preceding chapters we discussed how, by product explosion, the requirements are established for component parts to build assembled products.

Standard Process sheet: This form is prepared by process engineering and it is the source of basic data as to the type of machine to be used, the time required for processing and the sequence of operations in the manufacture of the product. Routing and scheduling of shop orders, as well as loading of workstations in advance of scheduling, depend on up-to-date standard process sheets being available to the production planning and control group.

Engineering Specifications: Blueprints and bills of materials are used by production planning and control when they become a component part of the packaged instructions issued to the shop through the control office. One good planning procedure is to accumulate all necessary data for a shop order in a single package the standard process sheet, the blueprint, the bill of material (if an assembly operation is involved), the route sheet, and possibly the schedule for the production of the order.

Route Sheet: This is the form on which the route of a shop order is indicated. In practice, this form is generally combined with one of the other forms in the system. For example, the shop order, the standard process sheet, and the route sheet are often one piece of paper- usually called the shop order or the manufacturing order.

Load Charts: These charts are prepared to show the productive capacity that has been "sold" – and at the same time the available productive capacity. These charts may be prepared for each workstation or machine in the plant, cr they may be for groups of machines or departments.

Job Tickets: This is the fifth and last type of order in a manufacturing situation. Job tickets authorize the performance of individual operations in the manufacturing process.

Project Planning Methods: The production planning and control methods discussed thus far in this chapter deal primarily with the production of consumer or industrial products which could be considered to fall within the area of "repetitive manufacturing". The products to be produced are often manufactured in quantities of more than one, and their total processing time can be measured in hours, or at most, days.

The best –known methods that have been developed are CPM (for Critical Path Method) and PERT (for Program Evaluation and Review Technique). The original PERT technique is now considered, more accurately, PERT TIME, whereas a later development is known as PERT COST. From the optimistic, most likely, and pessimistic times, the expected elapsed time (te) can be obtained by statistical techniques.

Systems Analysis: As with other manufacturing control systems and procedures, production planning, and control lends itself to modern mechanization techniques such as machine accounting and use of computers. Careful study of the control system through procedure analysis will indicate the savings that may be effected by the utilization of modern equipment. These savings may be in the clerical help required in the administration of the system or in the advantages of quick compilation of data, which in turn results in up-to-date control data.

Production Planning and Control Organization

It should be obvious that there is no single pattern for the organization of the production planning and control activity. In many small plants the routing, loading, and scheduling functions may well be included in the duties of the operating line; the shop manager, superintended, and foremen. But it is difficult to combine day-to-day work with adequate planning, and as a result it is often more feasible to break away the production planning and control functions and assign them to qualified specialists. These groups should be organized as staff sections normally reporting to the top manufacturing executive.

Centralized Production Planning and Control: Centralization or decentralization of duties of the production control staff depends upon the design of the production planning and control system. In a completely centralized setup, determination of shipping promises; analysis of sales, stock, and shop orders; preparation of routes, load charts, and schedule charts; and dispatching of work to the shop complete with job tickets and all other necessary paper would be accomplished by a central production planning and control unit. In addition, as work is completed, a careful analysis of the actual performance would be made, and if corrective action were required, it would be initiated by this group.

Decentralized Production Planning and Control: We have discussed at great length that no matter how general the planning may be in a central office, the plan must eventually be developed into a detailed plan on the shop floor. Some companies are now endeavoring to make each foreman a manager of his own departmental operation. In these cases the foreman is furnished with a complete staff for the production planning and control of the activities in the department.

Planning Phase: We have already indicated in some details the duties involved in the production planning phase. Working from the basic data mentioned earlier, the personnel in this part of the activity routes and load and schedule charts.

Control Phase: The completed job ticket, or its equivalent, is the key to this phase of the production planning and control system. It is the means of reporting back from the shop floor that indicates that a job is completed; or if daily job tickets are turned in, the daily progress of a job can be determined.

Relation to Other Functions: Good relationships with all the other functions in the enterprise are essential to effective production planning and control. Full cooperation with the marketing group is necessary, particularly in view of the importance of market conditions and the goodwill of customers. Both product engineering and process engineering must keep production planning and control informed as to their plans to avoid the manufacture of goods either to incorrect specifications or by an improper method.

Measurement of Effectiveness

In determining the effectiveness of a production planning and control system, there are quite a few problems. The key criterion might well be whether or not shipping promises are being kept the percentage of the order shipped on time. This, however, would not be a true criterion if excessive overtime of expediting costs were involved in getting any of these orders shipped. The cost of the control system in relation to the value of goods shipped is another possibility.

Again, however, this may not be sound: if markets slump, a bad ratio will develop. Many good production planning and control systems have been discontinued because of "high costs" under these conditions- and have never revived after business picket up.

In a study of benefits and costs of computerized production planning and control systems, Schroeder et al. list the following performance criteria by which production planning and control systems might be judged:

1. Inventory turnover
2. Delivery lead time
3. Percent of time meeting delivery promises
4. Percent of orders requiring "splits" because of unavailable material.
5. Number of expeditors
6. Average unit cost

New Product Development

In business and engineering, **new product development** (NPD) is the term used to describe the complete process of bringing a new product or service to market. There are two parallel paths involved in the NPD process: one involves the idea generation, *product design* and detail engineering; the other involves market research and *marketing analysis*. Companies typically see new product development as the first stage in generating and commercializing new products within the overall strategic process of *product life cycle management* used to maintain or grow their market share.

The process

1. **Idea Generation** is often called the "fuzzy front end" of the NPD process
    - Ideas for new products can be obtained from basic research using a SWOT analysis (Strengths, Weaknesses, Opportunities & Threats), Market and consumer trends, company's R&D department, competitors, focus groups, employees, salespeople, corporate spies, trade shows, or Ethnographic discovery methods (searching for user patterns and habits) may also be used to got an insight into new product lines or product features.
    - Idea Generation or Brainstorming of new product, service, or store concepts - idea generation techniques can begin when you have done your OPPORTUNITY ANALYSIS to support your ideas in the **Idea Screening Phase**
2. **Idea Screening**
    - The object is to eliminate unsound concepts prior to devoting resources to them.
    - The screeners should ask several questions:

- Will the customer in the target market benefit from the product?
- What is the size and growth forecasts of the market segment/target market?
- What is the current or expected competitive pressure for the product idea?
- What are the industry sales and market trends the product idea is based on?
- Is it technically feasible to manufacture the product?
- Will the product be profitable when manufactured and delivered to the customer at the target price?

3. **Concept Development and Testing**
   - Develop the marketing and engineering details
     - Investigate *intellectual property* issues and search *patent* data bases
     - Who is the target market and who is the decision maker in the purchasing process?
     - What product features must the product incorporate?
     - What benefits will the product provide?
     - How will consumers react to the product?
     - How will the product be produced most cost effectively?
     - Prove feasibility through virtual computer aided rendering, and rapid prototyping
     - What will it cost to produce it?
   - *Testing the Concept* by asking a sample of prospective customers what they think of the idea. Usually via Choice Modelling.
4. **Business Analysis**
   - Estimate likely selling price based upon competition and customer feedback
   - Estimate sales volume based upon size of market and such tools as the *Fourt-Woodlock equation*
   - Estimate profitability and breakeven point
5. **Beta Testing and Market Testing**
   - Produce a physical prototype or mock-up
   - Test the product (and its packaging) in typical usage situations
   - Conduct focus group customer interviews or introduce at trade show

- Make adjustments where necessary
- Produce an initial run of the product and sell it in a test market area to determine customer acceptance

6. **Technical Implementation**
   - New program initiation
   - Finalize Quality management system
   - Resource estimation
   - Requirement publication
   - Publish technical communications such as *data sheets*
   - Engineering operations planning
   - Department scheduling
   - Supplier collaboration
   - Logistics plan
   - Resource plan publication
   - Program review and monitoring
   - Contingencies - what-if planning
7. **Commercialization** (often considered post-NPD)
   - Launch the product
   - Produce and place *advertisements* and other *promotions*
   - Fill the *distribution* pipeline with product
   - Critical path analysis is most useful at this stage
8. **New Product Pricing**
   - Impact of new product on the entire product portfolio
   - Value Analysis (internal and external)
   - Competition and alternative competitive technologies
   - Differing value segments (price, value, and need)
   - Product Costs (fixed and variable)
   - Forecast of unit volumes, revenue, and profit

These steps may be iterated as needed. Some steps may be eliminated. To reduce the time that the NPD process takes, many companies are completing several steps at the same time (referred to as **concurrent engineering** or **time to market**). Most industry leaders see new product development as a *proactive* process where resources are allocated to identify market changes and seize upon new product opportunities before they occur (in contrast to a *reactive strategy* in which nothing is done until problems occur or the competitor introduces an innovation). Many industry leaders see new product development as an ongoing process (referred to as *continuous development*) in which the entire organization is always looking for opportunities.

For the more innovative products indicated on the diagram above, great amounts of uncertainty and change may exist, which makes it difficult or impossible to plan the complete project before starting it. In this case, a more flexible approach may be advisable.

Because the NPD process typically requires both engineering and marketing expertise, cross-functional teams are a common way of organizing projects. The team is responsible for all aspects of the project, from initial idea generation to final commercialization, and they usually report to senior management (often to a vice president or Program Manager). In those industries where products are technically complex, development research is typically expensive, and product life cycles are relatively short, strategic alliances among several organizations helps to spread the costs, provide access to a wider skill set, and speeds the overall process.

Also, notice that because engineering and marketing expertise are usually both critical to the process, choosing an appropriate blend of the two is important. People respond to new products in different ways. The adoption of a new technology can be analyzed using a variety of diffusion theories such as the Diffusion of innovations theory.

A new product pricing process is important to reduce risk and increase confidence in the pricing and marketing decisions to be made. Bernstein and Macias describe an integrated process that breaks down the complex task of new product pricing into manageable elements

Fuzzy Front End

The Fuzzy Front End is the messy "getting started" period of new product development processes. It is in the front end where the organization formulates a concept of the product to be developed and decides whether or not to invest resources in the further development of an idea. It is the phase between first consideration of an opportunity and when it is judged ready to enter the structured development process It includes all activities from the search for new opportunities through the formation of a germ of an idea to the development of a precise concept. The Fuzzy Front End ends when an organization approves and begins formal development of the concept.

Although the Fuzzy Front End may not be an expensive part of product development, it can consume 50% of development time and it is where major commitments are typically made involving time, money, and the product's nature, thus setting the course for the entire project and final end product. Consequently, this phase should be considered as an essential part of development rather than something that happens "before development," and its cycle time should be included in the total development cycle time.

Koen et al.distinguish five different front-end elements (not necessarily in a particular order):

1. Opportunity Identification
2. Opportunity Analysis
3. Idea Genesis
4. Idea Selection
5. Concept and Technology Development

The first element is the opportunity identification. In this element, large or incremental business and technological chances are identified in a more or less structured way. Using the guidelines established here, resources will eventually be allocated to new projects.... which then lead to a structured NPPD (New Product & Process Development)strategy. The second element is the opportunity analysis. It is done to translate the identified opportunities into implications for the business and technology specific context of the company. Here extensive efforts may be made to align ideas to target customer groups and do market studies and/or technical trials and research. The third element is the idea genesis, which is described as evolutionary and iterative process progressing from birth to maturation of the opportunity into a tangible idea. The process of the idea genesis can be made internally or come from outside inputs, e.g. a supplier offering a new material/technology, or from a customer with an unusual request. The fourth element is the idea selection. Its purpose is to choose whether to pursue an idea by analyzing its potential business value. The fifth element is the concept and technology development. During this part of the front-end, the business case is developed based on estimates of the total available market, customer needs, investment requirements, competition analysis and project uncertainty. Some organizations consider this to be the first stage of the NPPD process (i.e., Stage 0).

The Fuzzy Front End is also described in literature as "Front End of Innovation", "Phase 0", "Stage 0" or "Pre-Project-Activities".

A universally acceptable definition for Fuzzy Front End or a dominant framework has not been developed so far.In a glossary of PDMA, it is mentioned that the Fuzzy Front End generally consists of three tasks: strategic planning, concept generation, and, especially, pre-technical evaluation. These activities are often chaotic, unpredictible, and unstructured. In comparison, the subsequent new product development process is typically structured, predictable, and formal. The term *Fuzzy Front End* was first popularized by Smith and Reinertsen .R.G.Cooper describes the early stages of NPPD as a four step process in which ideas are generated (I),subjected to a preliminary technical and market assessment(II) and merged to coherent product concepts(III) which are finally judged for their fit with existing product strategies and portfolios (IV). In a more recent paper, Cooper and Edgett affirm that vital predevelopment activities include:

1. Preliminary market assessment.
2. Technical assessment.
3. Source-of-supply-assessment:suppliers and partners or alliances.
4. Market research : market size and segmentation analysis,VoC (voice of customer) research.
5. Product concept testing
6. Value-to-the customer assessment
7. Product definition
8. Business and financial analysis.

These activities yield vital information to make a Go/No-Go to Development decision.

In the in-depth study by Khurana and Rosenthefront-end activities include:

- product strategy formulation and communication,
- opportunity identification and assessment,
- idea generation,
- product definition,
- project planning, and
- executive reviews.

Economical analysis, benchmarking of competitive products, and modeling and prototyping are also important activities during the front-end activities.

The outcomes of FFE are the

- mission statement
- customer needs
- details of the selected concept
- product definition and specifications
- economic analysis of the product
- development schedule
- project staffing and the budget, and a
- business plan aligned with corporate strategy.

In a paper by Husig, Kohn and Huskela proposed a conceptual model of Front-End Process which includes early Phases of Innovation Process. This model is structured in three phases and three gates:

- ***Phase 1:*** Environmental screening or opportunity identification stage in which external changes will be analysed and translated into potential business opportunities.
- ***Phase 2:*** Preliminary definition of an idea or concept.
- ***Phase 3:*** Detailed product, project or concept definition, and Business planning.

The gates are:

- Opportunity screening;
- Idea evaluation;
- Go/No-Go for development.

The final gate leads to a dedicated new product development project. Many professionals and academics consider that the general features of Fuzzy Front End (fuzziness, ambiguity, and uncertainty) make difficult to see the FFE as a structured process, but rather as a set of interdependent activities. However, Husig et al. argue that front-end not need to be fuzzy, but can be handled in a structured manner. Peter Koen argue that in the FFE for incremental, platform and radical projects, three separate strategies and processes are typically involved· The traditional Stage Gate (TM) process was designed for incremental product development, namely for a single product. The FFE for developing a new platform must start out with a strategic vision of where the company wants to develop products and this will lead to a family of products. Projects for breakthrough products start out with a similar strategic vision, but are associated with technologies which require new discoveries. It is worth mentioning what are incremental, platform and breakthrough products. *Incremental products* are considered to be cost reductions, improvements to existing product lines, additions to existing platforms and repositioning of existing products introduced in markets. *Breakthrough products* are new to the company or new to the world and offer a 5-10 times or greater improvement in performance combined with a 30-50% or greater reduction in costs. *Platform products* establish a basic architecture for a next generation product or process and are substantially larger in scope and resources than incremental projects.

2.5 Method Study and Work Statement

Work Study is the systemeatic examination of the methods of carrying out activities such as to improve the effective use of resources and to set up standards of performance for the activities carried out.

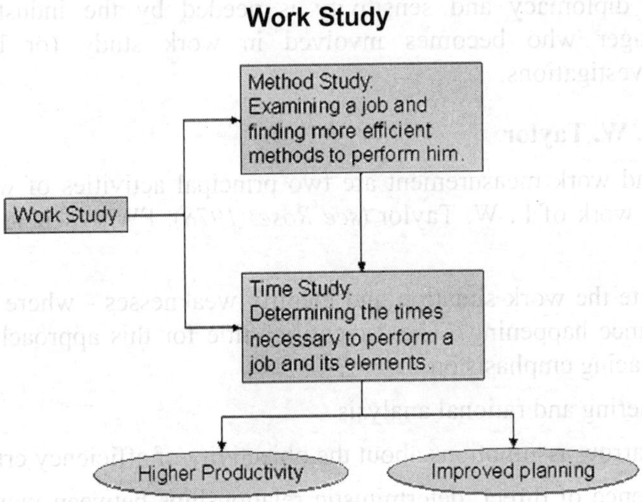

Components of Work Study

Another definition of **Work Study** could be: A generic term for those techniques, particularly method study and work measurement, which are used in the examination of human work in all its contexts, and which lead systematically to to the investigation of all the factors which affect the efficiency and economy of the situation being reviewed, in order to effect improvement'. This has to do with Productivity Improvement, but also improvement of Quality and Safety.

Managing people within operations involves actual design decisions about jobs, methods, relationships between jobs and machines and systems of control and communication. Work design involves complex "people" relationships between operative staff, supervisors and specialists e.g. engineering managers and staff who commission new machines and maintain them. Other specialists may co-ordinate health and safety systems or monitor performance and plan maintenance

People are not mere extensions to machines or horsepower to be switched on and off. A worker's performance may be better than a machine's capability - yet a machine may outstrip the human being for many tasks.

People can be *hurt/injured physically by operating environments* or trapped socially and psychologically in them/by them. How operational systems are designed and the jobs and performance relationships within them are of great operational, economic and social importance. In this context then work study is

a collection of techniques used to examine work - what is done and how it is done - so that there is systematic analysis of all the elements, factors, resources and relationships affecting the efficiency and effectiveness of the work being studied

Considerable diplomacy and sensitivity is needed by the industrial engineer or operations manager who becomes involved in work study (or business process improvement) investigations.

In the Path of F. W. Taylor

Method study and work measurement are two principal activities of work study which originated in the work of F. W. Taylor (*see Rose: 1978*). FW's "scientific management" imperatives are:

- investigate the work situation and identify weaknesses - where and why is poor performance happening? The "scientific" title for this approach to management means placing emphasis on
- data gathering and rational analysis
- certain narrow assumptions about the objectivity of efficiency criteria
- the existence of direct, deterministic relationships between worker performance and incentive payments and
- consideration of the worker to some extent as a machine. Thus we can evaluate and introduce improvements in operating methods. This includes type of equipment, its use, layout of operations, supply and use of materials, materials handling, work organization, effectiveness of planning procedures and so on.

Productivity improvement is the aim.

- we can select staff with characteristics that fit the job, train and reward them using payment schemes the offer particular economic incentive by linking payment to measured performance.

Such propositions are commonly the stuff of managerial populists and "how-to" texts on human resource management.

Methods Study

- is an analysis of ways of doing work. The mnemonic SREDIM (a common-sense heuristic or general problem-solving strategy) represents the method study stages

1. *select* the tasks to study
2. *record* the facts about it
3. *examine*
4. *develop* a new method
5. *install/implement* it
6. *maintain* it

Work Measurement

- involves assessing the time a job should take to do. Similar steps are involved as to method study

1. select the tasks
2. record the facts
3. analyze them
4. calculate basic and standard times for the task
5. *agree* the method and its related time

In the 1950's and 1960's the work study officer or O&M Person (organization and methods) gathered the data and gave advice. In the 1970's the titles evolved e.g. to that of management services officer. Work-study and methods study came within the scope of the industrial engineer. Today the techniques of method study are inclusive within the tool-kits and applications of the business systems analyst. The most modern application of some of the techniques of work study is the early 1990's managerial recipe; "*business process re-engineering*" i.e. re-designing business processes which have developed to the extent that they mismatch the needs of the situation today.

However -- having said this - the scope for work study definition and evaluation is useful for operations managers in a general sense. Such roles require data on operational capacities and effectiveness and the use of time and resources. Methods need regular re-evaluation. Some may have evolved and changed over time to become disjointed, patch works that no longer fully serve requirements. The case may need to be put for more staff or new methods and equipment. Such arguments call for data and measurement.

How many extra hours/people are needed? Why? What will the new method offer? Is it possible to change methods? What will be the costs/benefits?

Thus the techniques, assumptions and weaknesses of work study reflect important know-how for the operations manager generally - and not just those working in engineering or manufacturing environments. However the assumptions, difficulties and limitations of the claims must be understood.

Efficiency Indices

Using data on measured work, unmeasured work and idle time we can attempt to derive effectiveness indices. Constable and New exemplify efficiency and effectiveness indices

(a) **Efficiency:** while performing measured work (ratio of standard/measured hours of work produced and the actual time taken)

(b) **Effectiveness:** which includes accounting for work done for which no measured time exists. Such work is typically paid for by an agreed hourly/day rate i.e. there is no direct, measured relationship between pay and how much work is actually completed in that hour. Of course a supervisor may pass a judgment or state that the amount of work and its quality are inadequate. Recognition of possible idle time caused e.g. by management not allocating any work, supplier/materials delays, machine breakdowns etc.

Method Study

is an analysis of ways of doing work. The mnemonic SREDIM (a common-sense heuristic or general problem-solving strategy) represents the method study stages

select the tasks to study

record the facts about it

examine these

develop a new method

install/implement it

maintain it

Method study is the process of subjecting work to systematic, critical scrutiny to make it more effective and/or more efficient.

It was originally designed for the analysis and improvement of repetitive manual work but it can be used for all types of activity at all levels of an organization.

The process is often seen as a linear, described by its main steps of:

- Select (the work to be studied);
- Record (all relevant information about that work);
- Examine (the recorded information);
- Develop (an improved way of doing things);
- Install (the new method as standard practice);
- Maintain (the new standard proactive).

Although this linear representation shows the underlying simplicity of method study, in practice the process is much more one of repeated passes through the sequence of steps with each dominating at a different stage of the investigation.

The cyclic process often starts with a quick, rough pass in which preliminary data are collected and examined before subsequent passes provide and handle more comprehensive and more detailed data to obtain and analyze a more complete picture.

Select

Work selected for method study may be an identified problem area or an identified opportunity. It may be identified through a systematic review of available data, normal monitoring or control processes, high levels of dissatisfaction and complaint or as part of a change in management policy, practice, technology or location, and usually because it meets certain conditions of urgency and/or priority.

Define

Before any method study investigation is begun, it is necessary to establish clear terms of reference which define the aims, scale, scope and constraints of the investigation. This should also include an identification of who "owns" the problem or situation and ways in which such ownership is shared. This may lead to a debate on the aims of the project, on reporting mechanisms and frequencies, and on the measures of success. This process is sometimes introduced as a separate and distinct phase of method study, as the "Define" stage. It leads to a plan for the investigation which identifies appropriate techniques, personnel, and timescale.

Record

The Record stage of method study involves gathering sufficient data (in terms of both quality and quantity) to act as the basis of evaluation and examination. A wide range of techniques are available for recording; the choice depends on the nature of the investigation; the work being studied; and on the level of detail required. Many of the techniques are simple charts and diagrams, but these may be supplemented by photographic and video recording, and by computer based techniques.

Especially with "hard" (clearly defined) problems, method study often involves the construction and analysis of models, from simple charts and diagrams used to record and represent the situation to full, computerized simulations. Manipulation of and experimentation on the models leads to ideas for development.

Examine

The recorded data are subjected to examination and analysis; formalized versions of this process are critical examination and systems analysis. The aim is to identify, often through a structured, questioning process, those points of the overall system of work that require improvements or offer opportunity for beneficial change.

Develop

The Examine stage merges into the Develop stage of the investigation as more thorough analysis leads automatically to identified areas of change. The aim here is to identify possible actions for improvement and to subject these to evaluation in order to develop a preferred solution.

Sometimes it is necessary to identify short-term and long-term solutions so that improvements can be made (relatively) immediately, while longer-term changes are implemented and come to fruition.

Install

The success of any method study project is realized when actual change is made 'on the ground' - change that meets the originally specified terms of reference for the project. Thus, the Install phase is very important. Making theoretical change is easy; making real change demands careful planning - and handling of the people involved in the situation under review. They may need reassuring, retraining and supporting through the acquisition of new skills. Install, in some cases ,will require a parallel running of old and new systems, in others, it may need the build-up of buffer stocks, and other planning to manage the change. what matters is that the introduction of new working methods is successful. There is often only one chance to make change!

Maintain

Some time after the introduction of new working methods, it is necessary to check that the new method is working, that it is being properly followed, and that it has brought about the desired results. This is the Maintain phase. Method drift is common - when people either revert to old ways of work-in, or introduce new changes. Some of these may be helpful and should formally be incorporated; others may be inefficient or unsafe. A methods audit can be used to formally compare practice with the defined method and identify such irregularities.

Conclusion

In simple terms work study measures work and defines (some) performance standards. There are many uses for time estimates for tasks. Operations managers can guess or assume that a job is done in the correct time (whatever that is!) or they can be systematic and use time data gathered by a systematic technique which has reasonable accuracy. Whether or not the worker likes it - pushed hard in trying to complete a job with very tight measured work standards which don't anticipate the knotty problem encountered with a particular task - is another matter.

Work study/industrial engineers need time data to plan and evaluate production/transformation processes. Rewards systems need such data for performance related bonuses. Cost calculations need to incorporate operative and machine job times Costing systems reference work study data. Work study data contributes to:

Improved methods to raise output, quality, reduce wastage, enhance reliability and ensure safety.

Standard time data contributes to capacity planning, scheduling, control of staff, asset utilization and quality improvement. Service and after-sales method improvements may be obtained as well as process improvement and better raw materials usage.

Implementation planning for product/service and process design requires a detailed understanding of methods and timings. In a distribution/transport system we can evaluate logistical efficiencies.

We need to remember always that performance inefficiency may arise from many reasons outside of worker control - a cumbersome planning system, a slow computer system with heavy overheads, lack of investment or uninformed, disorganized management. It is crass to assume that the problems will only be due to staff inefficiencies or inappropriate methods.

2.6 Statistical Quality Control

Introduction

It has been the constant endeavor of Pharmacists to strive at higher and higher accuracy but absolute accuracy is unattainable. No two things can be made exactly alike. In Pharmaceutical production, no attempts are made to attain absolute perfection but to control the degree of variability of production so that the variation is within the prescribed statutory tolerance limits. There are two types of causes responsible for the variation of Pharmaceutical product manufactured.

(i) Inherent source of variation (Indeterminate or accidental variation)

(ii) Assignable causes of variation (determinate or constant variation)

Inherent Source of Variation

These variations or errors manifest themselves by the slight variations that occur in successive measurements by the same observer with the greatest care under as nearly identical conditions as possible. This natural variability can't be controlled and it occurs even under the best of methods and circumstances. These variations cannot be predicted and hence cannot be eliminated.

Assignable Causes of Variation

These are the variations which can be avoided or whose magnitude can be determined and hence can be checked and controlled. The assignable variations if present must be detected and corrected before defective results and products are produced. Some of the determinate errors are:

1. *Operational and personal errors* – mostly physical in nature. These errors are due to factors for which the individual is responsible and are not connected with the method or procedure. These errors may arise from the constitutional inability of an individual to make certain observations accurately. An example for this kind is some persons are unable to judge color changes sharply in visual titrations which may result in slight overlapping of the end point.
2. *Instrumental and reagent errors* – these variations arise due to defective instruments and improper chemicals.
3. *Errors of method or variations due to the process* – these arise from the incorrect sampling and from the incompleteness of the reaction.
4. *Additive and proportional variations* – the absolute value of an additive error is independent of the amount of the constituent present in the determination. Some examples of additive errors are loss in weight of a crucible in which a precipitate is ignited and errors in weights. The absolute value of a proportional error depends upon the amount of the constituents. An example of proportional error is impurity in a primary standard which leads to an incorrect value for the normality of a standard solution.

The science of quality control is largely statistical in nature. The statistical quality control technique is based on the theory of probability and sampling and is extensively used in Pharmaceutical industries and quality control labs. Quality control is a powerful productivity technique for effective diagnosis of lack of quality or conformity to settled standards in any of the materials, processes, machines or end products. Statistical quality control is a key factor in process validation and the manufacture of Pharmaceutical products. The technique attempts to locate the variability or error while the Pharmaceutical work is in process or progress.

In statistical quality control techniques, the actual physical measurements are first secured by inspection. Then the degree of variation among the measurements is analysed by statistical methods in terms of a standard value of variation among acceptable limits. By such comparisons, quality control is made to predict the significance of the variation analysed. This type of prediction can then be used to exert a positive influence over the control of product quality by studying the assignable causes. The quality control is thus directly associated with inspection and for statistical quality control, control charts are maintained. In order that things may be economical and quick, 100% inspection is not desirable. Rather 100% inspection leads to fatigue of human brain and faulty results are likely to be accepted. Control charts tell immediately whether the product is satisfactory or not.

The important objectives of statistical quality control in Pharmaceutical practice are as follows:

(i) Better quality level (ii) Better uniformity of quality (iii) Better utilization of raw materials (iv) Most efficient utilization of equipments. (v) Less scrap and rework (vi) Better inspection (vii) Improved producer consumer relations and (viii) Better specifications

Attributes and Variables

Attributes

Those measurements in which a quality characteristic is present or absent or falls into a limited number of discrete categories are referred to as attribute measurements. Here the examination leads to the result being satisfactory or unsatisfactory. Measurements by attributes are generally less expensive but many more measurements have to be taken in such cases as there is no way of telling to what extent an item fails to meet the desired quality level when it is rejected on a attribute basis.

Variability

Two things are said to be alike when the differences among them are so small that we do not care about them. But generally two things are considered to be identical vary from each other when sufficiently precise measuring equipment or process is available. Measurement by variable involved the use of a scale which can be theoretically subdivided infinitely and the results of the quality can be expressed quantitatively i.e. in numbers. The measures of size, weight, surface etc. are the examples of measurement by variables.

Control Charts

The statistical quality control is mainly classified into Process Control & Product Control. The aim of process control is to maintain satisfactory quality level in production. The process control should ensure that the product confirms to specified quality standards. The process control is achieved through the technique of control charts. Controlling the quality of product by critical examination at strategic points is known as product control and is achieved through sampling inspection plans. Random samples of work in process are taken and inspected data collected are then presented graphically in chart form and chart method is an essential part of quality control systems.

A control chart is a statistical device principally used for the study and control of repetitive processes. It is a device to measure the extent of variation or defects in a process and to identify where there is an assignable cause for the variation. Dr. Walter A. Shewhart, its originator suggested that control chart may serve, first to define the goal or standard for the process that the management might strive to attain and secondly it may be used as an instrument to attain that goal and thirdly it may serve as a means of judging whether the goal is being achieved. The charts provide a very simple but powerful graphic method or finding whether a process is in statistical control or not. The control charts are simple to construct and easy to interpret and they tell the manager at a glance whether the process is in control or not. It is a graphic device for presenting data so as to directly reveal the frequency and extent of variations from established standards of goals.

The control charts help to easily identify the assignable causes of quality variation and these should be controlled or eliminated economically whenever detected. In gathering data for preparation of control chats the following points should be borne in mind:

1. We should be sure that we are measuring the thing we want to measure.
2. Measuring equipment and computing equipment should be operated properly.
3. The operator should be properly trained and instructed and free from bias.
4. Transcription errors should be avoided by adequate checking.
5. At least 40 to 100 observations should be taken.

It is necessary that the control chart limits be based on only the variability that is inherent in the process. If the standard deviation is computed on the basis of individual measurements, it will include the determination of all the assignable causes as well as chance causes of variation.

Important Points to be Observed in Drawing the Quality Control Chart

As the quality control charts form important documents and have to be examined by senior personnel, these should be drawn in convenient manner and the following points should be considered:

1. The size of the chart should be handy one.
2. The chart should be as neat as possible.
3. There should be provision for accommodating additional information on the charts in future.
4. The chart should be labeled properly and sufficiently.
5. When it becomes necessary to draw revised control chart limits on the basis of additional data, they should not be drawn over the original limits but after these.
6. Plotted point should be legible.

7. The average lines are drawn by solid and control limits by dotted lines.
8. There should be minimum number of background lines on the graph paper selected for drawing the control charts. Such charts are often plotted on rectangular cross section paper. Some times profile paper may also be used. The vertical scale is used for the statistical measures and the horizontal scale is used for subgroup numbers, dates, hours or lot numbers etc.

Objectives of Control Charts

1. To determine whether a process can meet the specifications or to collect further information for establishing or changing the specifications.
2. To get information for changing the production procedures.
3. To get information for changing the inspection techniques or acceptance procedures.
4. Determination as to when to find causes of variation and take action to correct them and when to leave the process alone.
5. To take decision on acceptance or rejection of manufactured or purchased products.

Types of Quality Control Charts

Broadly speaking, control charts can be divided under tow heads:

(i) Control Charts for attributes

(ii) Control Charts for Variables

(i) ***Control Charts for attributes:*** Control charts for attributes can be used for quality characteristics which can be observed only as attributes by classifying an item as defective or non defective, i.e. confirming to specifications or not. The following are the three main attribute charts:

1. p-chart or chart for fraction defectives
2. np-chart or chart for number of defectives
3. c-chart or chart for number of defects per unit

(ii) ***Control Charts for variables:*** Control charts for variables are used for any quality characteristic that is measurable. Usually X and R charts used to control the mean (location) and standard deviation (dispersion) respectively of the quality characteristics.

(iii) Control Charts for attributes

1. *The Shewhart control chart for fraction defective*. This is also described as p-chart in technical language. In most of the routine inspection work (either

100% inspection or sampling inspection), the products are classified as either accepted or rejected. In such inspection it is a common practice to make a record of the number of items rejected. The ratio of the number of items rejected to the number of items rejected to the number of items inspected is the fraction of defective which is commonly expressed as a decimal fraction. The control limits of the chart which easily detect the presence of assignable and chance causes are set by simple statistical calculations. The p-chart is somewhat less sensitive than X and R charts and it does not have a great diagnostic value, but it serves to point out those situations needing diagnosis of trouble by the control chart for variables.

Nevertheless, it is an extremely useful and to production supervision in giving information as to when and where to exert pressure for quality improvement. It results in the reduction of the average fraction defective and in the improvement of inspection practices by disclosing erratic fluctuations in the quality of inspection. The p-chart serves as a very good tool in dealing with outside vendors by pointing our whether the vendors differ in quality level or in the variability of quality level.

2. The Shewart control chart for number of defectives. This chart is also described as np-chart or the chart for the number of defectives in the sample. The control chart for this is drawn by taking m samples, each of size n are drawn at regular intervals of time from a production process and for each sample the number of defectives d is found out. d follows the binomial distribution with parameters n and p, where n is total the total number of items in the sample and p is the fraction defectives of the sample.

The control limits for np-chart:

$$CL = n\,p$$

$$LCL = n\,p - 3\,[n\,p\,(1 - p)]^{½}$$

$$UCL = n\,p - 3\,[n\,p\,(1 - p)]^{½}$$

3. *The Shewhart control chart for defects per unit.* In technical language of the subject, it is described as c chart. This type of chart applies to a limited number of manufacturing situations involving quality, e.g., inspection of a fairly complex assembled unit in which there are a great many opportunities for occurrences of defects of various types, and the total number of defects or all types found by inspection are recorded for each unit.

In c-chart also, the control limits are set in a way to detect the presence or absence of assignable causes of variations; thereby telling when to take action on the process and when

(iv) Control Charts for variables ($\overline{X}$ Chart and R Chart): These charts help in trouble shooting of the manufacturing process by providing information on three matters all of which need to be known as a basis for action.

(a) Basis variability of the quality characteristic.

(b) Consistency of Performance.

(c) Average level of the quality characteristic.

No production process can produce identical objects. Some variability is unavoidable which depends upon the upon the various characteristics of the production process such as the machines, the materials, the operators. When both upper and lower values (e.g. dimensional tolerances) are specified and control chart shows that the process variability is great, then it is necessary to make change n the process or to take the trouble of sorting good product from bad. Sometimes it may be observed that tolerances are tighter than necessary for the functioning of the product and they can be widened instead of choosing a very precise and costly process.

The control limits on the charts are so placed as to disclose the presence or absence of the assignable causes. The control charts tell when to leave process alone and when to take action to correct trouble. The elimination of assignable causes of erratic fluctuation is described as bringing a process under control and is responsible for many of the cost savings resulting from statistical quality control.

In some instances the process variability is such that the natural tolerance range is narrower than the specified tolerance range, still the products are unsatisfactory because the average level of the quality characteristic is too high or too low. This will also be disclosed by control charts and correction of the average level can be taken by changing machine setting or taking some suitable action.

Once the control chart shows that a process is brought under control at a satisfactory level and with satisfactory limits of variability, one may feel confident that the product meets specifications. This suggests the possibility of basing acceptance procedures on the control charts and thereby result in substantial savings in costs related to inspection.

$\overline{X}$ chart is used to show the quality averages of the samples drawn from a given process. Let X denote the quality characteristic of a manufactured product. *m* samples each of size *n* are drawn form the production process at regular intervals of time.

Let $\overline{X}_i$ be the mean and R_i be the range of the ith sample, ($I = 1, 2, \ldots, n$).

Calculate $\overline{\overline{X}}$ and $\overline{R}$ using

$$\overline{\overline{X}} = \frac{\Sigma \overline{X}_i}{m} \quad \text{and} \quad \overline{R} = \frac{\Sigma \overline{R}_i}{m}$$

The control limits of $\overline{X}$ chart are set at

Central line (CL) = $\overline{X}$

Lower control limit (LCL) = $\overline{\overline{X}} - A_2 \overline{R}$

Upper control limit (UCL) = $\overline{\overline{X}} - A_2 \overline{R}$

The values of the constant A2 are computed and tabulated for different values of *n*.

The control limits for R – Chart are set at

Central line (CL) = $\overline{R}$

Lower control limit (LCL) = $D_3 \overline{R}$

Upper control limit (UCL) = $D_4 \overline{R}$

Here D_3 and D_4 are constants which depend on the sample size n.

For $\overline{X}$ chart the sample numbers are taken on the X – axis and the values of $\overline{X}$ are taken on the Y – axis. The central line and both the control limits are drawn parallel to the X – axis. The value of $\overline{X}$ for each sample is plotted on the graph paper. On joining these points in order, $\overline{X}$ chart is obtained.

For R – chart the sample numbers are taken on the X – axis and the values or R are taken on the Y – axis. The central line, LCL and UCL for R – chart are drawn parallel to the X – axis. The values of R obtained from each sample are plotted on the graph paper. On joining these points in order, R – chart is obtained.

Acceptance Sampling

Acceptance sampling is an important field of statistical quality control that was popularized by Dodge and Romig and originally applied by the U.S. military to the testing of bullets during World War II. If every bullet was tested in advance, no bullets would be left to ship. If, on the other hand, none were tested, malfunctions might occur in the field of battle, with potentially disastrous results

Dodge reasoned that a sample should be picked at random from the lot, and on the basis of information that was yielded by the sample, a decision should be made regarding the disposition of the lot. In general, the decision is either to accept or reject the lot. This process is called *Lot Acceptance Sampling* or just *Acceptance Sampling*

Acceptance sampling is "the middle of the road" approach between no inspection and 100% inspection. There are two major classifications of acceptance plans: by *attributes* ("go, no-go") and by *variables*. The attribute case is the most common for acceptance sampling, and will be assumed for the rest of this section.

A point to remember is that the main purpose of acceptance sampling is to decide whether or not the lot is likely to be acceptable, not to estimate the quality of the lot.

Acceptance sampling is employed when one or several of the following hold:

- Testing is destructive
- The cost of 100% inspection is very high
- 100% inspection takes too long

It was pointed out by Harold Dodge in 1969 that Acceptance Quality Control is not the same as Acceptance Sampling. The latter depends on specific sampling plans, which when implemented indicate the conditions for acceptance or rejection of the immediate lot that is being inspected. The former may be implemented in the form of an Acceptance Control Chart. The control limits for the Acceptance Control Chart are computed using the specification limits and the standard deviation of what is being monitored

In 1942, Dodge stated:

"....basically the "acceptance quality control" system that was developed encompasses the concept of protecting the consumer from getting unacceptable defective product, and encouraging the producer in the use of process quality control by: varying the quantity and severity of acceptance inspections in direct relation to the importance of the characteristics inspected, and in the inverse relation to the goodness of the quality level as indication by those inspections."

To reiterate the difference in these two approaches: acceptance sampling plans are one-shot deals, which essentially test short-run effects. Quality control is of the long-run variety, and is part of a well-designed system for lot acceptance.

An individual sampling plan has much the effect of a lone sniper, while the sampling plan scheme can provide a fusillade in the battle for quality improvement

According to the ISO standard on acceptance control charts *(ISO 7966, 1993)*, an acceptance control chart combines consideration of control implications with elements of acceptance sampling. It is an appropriate tool for helping to make decisions with respect to process acceptance. The difference between acceptance sampling approaches and acceptance control charts is the emphasis on process acceptability rather than on product disposition decisions.

According to the ISO standard on acceptance control charts *(ISO 7966, 1993)*, an acceptance control chart combines consideration of control implications with elements of acceptance sampling. It is an appropriate tool for helping to make decisions with respect to process acceptance. The difference between acceptance sampling approaches and acceptance control charts is the emphasis on process acceptability rather than on product disposition decisions.

LASPs fall into the following categories:

- ***Single sampling plans:*** One sample of items is selected at random from a lot and the disposition of the lot is determined from the resulting information. These plans are usually denoted as *(n,c)* plans for a sample size *n,* where the lot is rejected if there are more than *c* defectives. *These are the most common (and easiest) plans to use although not the most efficient in terms of average number of samples needed.*
- ***Double sampling plans:*** After the first sample is tested, there are three possibilities:
    1. Accept the lot
    2. Reject the lot
    3. No decision

    If the outcome is (3), and a second sample is taken, the procedure is to combine the results of both samples and make a final decision based on that information.
- ***Multiple sampling plans:*** This is an extension of the double sampling plans where more than two samples are needed to reach a conclusion. The advantage of multiple sampling is smaller sample sizes.
- ***Sequential sampling plans:*** This is the ultimate extension of multiple sampling where items are selected from a lot one at a time and after inspection of each item a decision is made to accept or reject the lot or select another unit.
- ***Skip lot sampling plans:*** Skip lot sampling means that only a fraction of the submitted lots are inspected.

Deriving a plan, within one of the categories listed above, is discussed in the pages that follow. All derivations depend on the properties you want the plan to have. These are described using the following terms:

- ***Acceptable Quality Level (AQL)***: The AQL is a percent defective that is the base line requirement for the quality of the producer's product. The producer would like to design a sampling plan such that there is a *high probability of accepting* a lot that has a defect level less than or equal to the AQL.
- ***Lot Tolerance Percent Defective (LTPD)***: The LTPD is a designated high defect level that would be unacceptable to the consumer. The consumer would like the sampling plan to have a *low probability of accepting* a lot with a defect level as high as the LTPD.
- ***Type I Error (Producer's Risk)***: This is the probability, for a given *(n,c)* sampling plan, of rejecting a lot that has a defect level equal to the AQL. The producer suffers when this occurs, because a lot with acceptable quality was rejected. The symbol α is commonly used for the Type I error and typical values for α range from 0.2 to 0.01.

- ***Type II Error (Consumer's Risk):*** This is the probability, for a given (n,c) sampling plan, of accepting a lot with a defect level equal to the LTPD. The consumer suffers when this occurs, because a lot with unacceptable quality was accepted. The symbol β is commonly used for the Type II error and typical values range from 0.2 to 0.01.
- ***Operating Characteristic (OC) Curve:*** This curve plots the probability of accepting the lot (Y-axis) versus the lot fraction or percent defectives (X-axis). *The OC curve is the primary tool for displaying and investigating the properties of a LASP.*
- ***Average Outgoing Quality (AOQ):*** A common procedure, when sampling and testing is non-destructive, is to 100% inspect rejected lots and replace all defectives with good units. In this case, all rejected lots are made perfect and the only defects left are those in lots that were accepted. *AOQ*'s refer to the long term defect level for this combined LASP and 100% inspection of rejected lots process. If all lots come in with a defect level of exactly p, and the OC curve for the chosen (n,c) LASP indicates a probability p_a of accepting such a lot, over the long run the *AOQ* can easily be shown to be:

  $$AOQ = \frac{p_a p(N-n)}{N}$$

  where N is the lot size.
- ***Average Outgoing Quality Level (AOQL):*** A plot of the *AOQ* (Y-axis) versus the incoming lot p (X-axis) will start at 0 for $p = 0$, and return to 0 for $p = 1$ (where every lot is 100% inspected and rectified). In between, it will rise to a maximum. This maximum, which is the worst possible long term *AOQ*, is called the *AOQL*.
- ***Average Total Inspection (ATI):*** When rejected lots are 100% inspected, it is easy to calculate the *ATI* if lots come consistently with a defect level of p. For a LASP (n,c) with a probability p_a of accepting a lot with defect level p, we have

  $$ATI = n + (1 - p_a)(N - n)$$

  where N is the lot size.
- ***Average Sample Number (ASN):*** For a single sampling LASP (n,c) we know each and every lot has a sample of size n taken and inspected or tested. For double, multiple and sequential LASP's, the amount of sampling varies depending on the number of defects observed. For any given double, multiple or sequential plan, a long term *ASN* can be calculated assuming all lots come in with a defect level of p. A plot of the *ASN*, versus the incoming defect level p, describes the sampling efficiency of a given LASP scheme.

Making a final choice between single or multiple sampling plans that have acceptable properties is a matter of deciding whether the average sampling savings gained by the various multiple sampling plans justifies the additional complexity of these plans and the uncertainty of not knowing how much sampling and inspection will be done on a day-by-day basis.

A single sampling plan, as *previously defined*, is specified by the pair of numbers (*n,c*). The sample size is *n,* and the lot is rejected if there are more than *c* defectives in the sample; otherwise the lot is accepted.

There are two widely used ways of picking (*n,c*):

1. Use tables (such as *MIL STD 105D*) that focus on either the AQL or the LTPD desired.
2. *Specify 2 desired points* on the *OC curve* and solve for the (*n,c*) that uniquely determines an OC curve going through these points.

The next two pages describe these methods in detail

Sampling plans are typically set up with reference to an acceptable quality level, or AQL . The *AQL* is the base line requirement for the quality of the producer's product. The producer would like to design a sampling plan such that the *OC curve* yields a high probability of acceptance at the *AQL.* On the other side of the OC curve, the consumer wishes to be protected from accepting poor quality from the producer. So the consumer establishes a criterion, the *lot tolerance percent defective* or LTPD . Here the idea is to only accept poor quality product with a very low probability. Mil. Std. plans have been used for over 50 years to achieve these goals.

Standard military sampling procedures for inspection by attributes were developed during World War II. Army Ordnance tables and procedures were generated in the early 1940's and these grew into the Army Service Forces tables. At the end of the war, the Navy also worked on a set of tables. In the meanwhile, the Statistical Research Group at Columbia University performed research and outputted many outstanding results on attribute sampling plans.

These three streams combined in 1950 into a standard called Mil. Std. 105A. It has since been modified from time to time and issued as 105B, 195C and 105D. Mil. Std. 105D was issued by the U.S. government in 1963. It was adopted in 1971 by the American National Standards Institute as ANSI Standard Z1.4 and in 1974 it was adopted (with minor changes) by the International Organization for Standardization as ISO Std. 2859. The latest revision is Mil. Std 105E and was issued in 1989.

These three similar standards are continuously being updated and revised, but the basic tables remain the same. Thus the discussion that follows of the germane aspects of Mil. Std. 105E also applies to the other two standards.

This document is essentially a set of individual plans, organized in a system of sampling schemes. A sampling scheme consists of a combination of a normal sampling plan, a tightened sampling plan, and a reduced sampling plan plus rules for switching from one to the other

The foundation of the Standard is the acceptable quality level or *AQL*. In the following scenario, a certain military agency, called the Consumer from here on, wants to purchase a particular product from a supplier, called the Producer from here on.

In applying the Mil. Std. 105D it is expected that there is perfect agreement between Producer and Consumer regarding what the *AQL* is for a given product characteristic. It is understood by both parties that the Producer will be submitting for inspection a number of lots whose quality level is typically as good as specified by the Consumer. Continued quality is assured by the acceptance or rejection of lots following a particular sampling plan and also by providing for a shift to another, tighter sampling plan, when there is evidence that the Producer's product does not meet the agreed-upon *AQL*.

Mil. Std. 105E offers three types of sampling plans: single, double and multiple plans. The choice is, in general, up to the inspectors.

Because of the three possible selections, the standard does not give a sample size, but rather a sample code letter. This, together with the decision of the type of plan yields the specific sampling plan to be used.

In addition to an initial decision on an *AQL* it is also necessary to decide on an "inspection level". This determines the relationship between the lot size and the sample size. The standard offers three general and four special levels.

The steps in the use of the standard can be summarized as follows.

1. Decide on the *AQL*.
2. Decide on the inspection level.
3. Determine the lot size.
4. Enter the table to find sample size code letter.
5. Decide on type of sampling to be used.
6. Enter proper table to find the plan to be used.
7. Begin with normal inspection, follow the switching rules and the rule for stopping the inspection (if needed).

We start by looking at a typical *OC curve*. The OC curve for a (52 ,3) sampling plan is shown below.

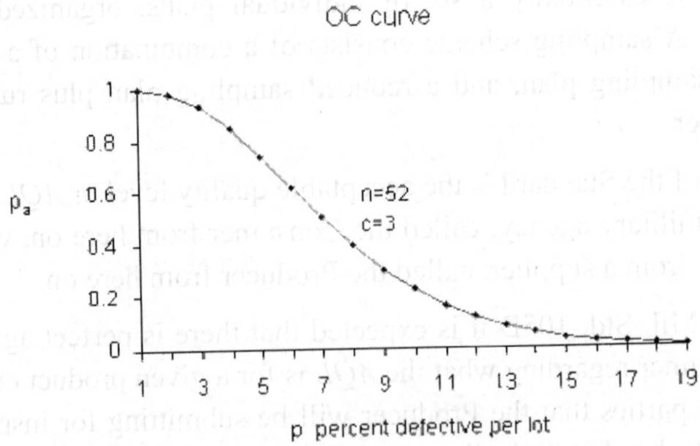

It is instructive to show how the points on this curve are obtained, once we have a sampling plan (*n,c*) - later we will demonstrate how a sampling plan (*n,c*) is obtained.

We assume that the lot size *N* is very large, as compared to the sample size *n*, so that removing the sample doesn't significantly change the remainder of the lot, no matter how many defects are in the sample. Then the distribution of the number of defectives, *d*, in a random sample of *n* items is approximately binomial with parameters *n* and *p*, where *p* is the fraction of defectives per lot.

The probability of observing exactly *d* defectives is given by

$$P(d) = f(d) = \frac{n!}{d!(n-d)!} p^d (1-p)^{n-d}$$

The probability of acceptance is the probability that *d*, the number of defectives, is less than or equal to *c*, the accept number. This means that

$$P_a = P\{d \le c\} = \sum_{d-0}^{c} \frac{n!}{d!(n-d)!} p^d (1-p)^{n-d}$$

Using this formula with $n = 52$ and $c=3$ and $p = .01, .02, ...,.12$ we find

P_a	P_d
.998	.01
.980	.02
.930	.03
.845	.04
.739	.05

.620	.06
.502	.07
.394	.08
.300	.09
.223	.10
.162	.11
.115	.12

Solving for (*n,c*)

In order to design a sampling plan with a specified OC curve one needs two designated points. Let us design a sampling plan such that the probability of acceptance is 1-α for lots with fraction defective p_1 and the probability of acceptance is β for lots with fraction defective p_2. Typical choices for these points are: p_1 is the AQL, p_2 is the LTPD and α, β are the *Producer's Risk (Type I error)* and *Consumer's Risk (Type II error)*, respectively.

If we are willing to assume that binomial sampling is valid, then the sample size *n*, and the acceptance number *c* are the solution to

$$1-\alpha=\sum_{d-0}^{c}\frac{n!}{d!(n-d)!}p_1^d(1-p_1)^{n-d}$$

$$\beta=\sum_{d-0}^{c}\frac{n!}{d!(n-d)!}p_2^d(1-p_2)^{n-d}$$

These two simultaneous equations are nonlinear so there is no simple, direct solution. There are however a number of iterative techniques available that give approximate solutions so that composition of a computer program poses few problems.

Average Outgoing Quality (AOQ)

We can also calculate the AOQ for a (*n,c*) sampling plan, provided rejected lots are 100% inspected and defectives are replaced with good parts.

Assume all lots come in with exactly a p_0 proportion of defectives. After screening a rejected lot, the final fraction defectives will be zero for that lot. However, accepted lots have fraction defectivep_0. Therefore, the outgoing lots from the inspection stations are a mixture of lots with fractions defective p_0 and 0. Assuming the lot size is *N*, we have.

$$AOQ=\frac{P_a p(N-n)}{N}$$

For example, let $N = 10000$, $n = 52$, $c = 3$, and p, the quality of incoming lots, = 0.03. Now at $p = 0.03$, we glean from the OC curve table that $p_a = 0.930$ and

$AOQ = (.930)(.03)(10000\text{-}52) / 10000 = 0.02775$

Setting $p = .01, .02, ..., .12$, we can generate the following table

AOQ	p
.0010	.01
.0196	.02
.0278	.03
.0338	.04
.0369	.05
.0372	.06
.0351	.07
.0315	.08
.0270	.09
.0223	.10
.0178	.11
.0138	.12

A plot of the *AOQ* versus *p* is given below.

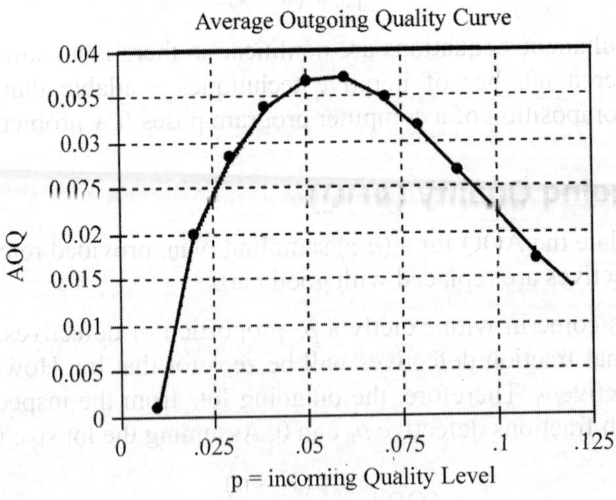

From examining this curve we observe that when the incoming quality is very good (very small fraction of defectives coming in), then the outgoing quality is also very good (very small fraction of defectives going out). When the incoming lot quality is very bad, most of the lots are rejected and then inspected. The "duds" are eliminated or replaced by good ones, so that the quality of the outgoing lots, the *AOQ*, becomes very good. In between these extremes, the *AOQ* rises, reaches a maximum, and then drops.

The maximum ordinate on the *AOQ* curve represents the worst possible quality that results from the rectifying inspection program. It is called the **average outgoing quality limit, (AOQL)**.

From the table we see that the $AOQL = 0.0372$ at $p = .06$ for the above example.

One final remark: if $N >> n$, then the $AOQ \sim p_a p$.

What is the total amount of inspection when rejected lots are screened?

If all lots contain zero defectives, no lot will be rejected.

If all items are defective, all lots will be inspected, and the amount to be inspected is *N*.

Finally, if the lot quality is $0 < p < 1$, the average amount of inspection per lot will vary between the sample size *n*, and the lot size *N*.

Let the quality of the lot be *p* and the probability of lot acceptance be p_a, then the *ATI* per lot is

$$ATI = n + (1 - p_a)\ (N - n)$$

For example, let $N = 10000$, $n = 52$, $c = 3$, and $p = .03$ We know from the OC table that $p_a = 0.930$. Then $ATI = 52 + (1\text{-}.930)\ (10000 - 52) = 753$. (Note that while 0.930 was rounded to three decimal places, 753 was obtained using more decimal places.)

Setting p= .01, .02, ...14 generates the following table

ATI	P
70	.01
253	.02
753	.03
1584	.04
2655	.05
3836	.06
5007	.07

⋮

6083	.08
7012	.09
7779	.10
8388	.11
8854	.12
9201	.13
9453	.14

A plot of *ATI* versus *p,* the Incoming Lot Quality (*ILQ*) is given below.

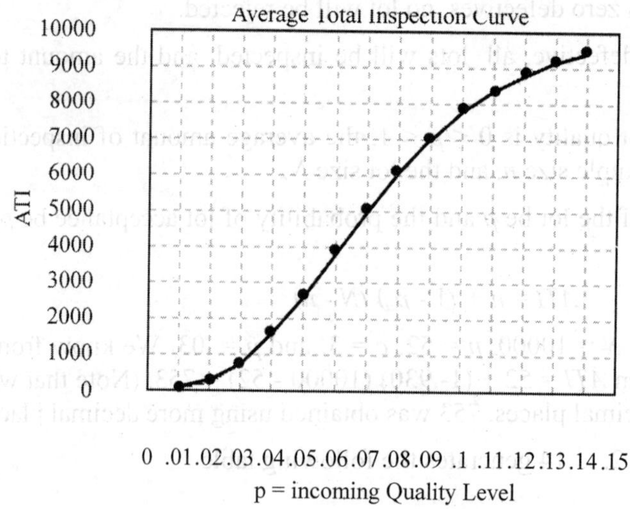

Double and multiple sampling plans were invented to give a questionable lot another chance. For example, if in double sampling the results of the first sample are not conclusive with regard to accepting or rejecting, a second sample is taken. Application of double sampling requires that a first sample of size n_1 is taken at random from the (large) lot. The number of defectives is then counted and compared to the first sample's acceptance number a_1 and rejection number r_1. Denote the number of defectives in sample 1 by d_1 and in sample 2 by d_2, then:

If $d_1 \leq a_1$, the lot is accepted.

If $d_1 \geq r_1$, the lot is rejected.

If $a_1 < d_1 < r_1$, a second sample is taken.

If a second sample of size n_2 is taken, the number of defectives, d_2, is counted. The total number of defectives is $D_2 = d_1 + d_2$. Now this is compared to the acceptance number a_2 and the rejection number r_2 of sample 2. In double sampling, $r_2 = a_2 + 1$ to ensure a decision on the sample.

If $D_2 \leq a_2$, the lot is accepted.

If $D_2 \geq r_2$, the lot is rejected.

The parameters required to construct the OC curve are similar to the single sample case. The two points of interest are (p_1, 1-α) and (p_2, β, where p_1 is the lot fraction defective for plan 1 and p_2 is the lot fraction defective for plan 2. As far as the respective sample sizes are concerned, the second sample size must be equal to, or an even multiple of, the first sample size.

There exist a variety of tables that assist the user in constructing double and multiple sampling plans. The index to these tables is the p_2/p_1 ratio, where $p_2 > p_1$. One set of tables, taken from the *Army Chemical Corps* Engineering Agency for $\alpha = .05$ and $\beta = .10$, is given below:

Tables for $n_1 = n_2$

$R =$	Accept numbers		Approximation values of pn_1 for	
p_2/p_1	c_1	c_2	P = .95	P = .10
11.90	0	1	0.21	2.50
7.54	1	2	0.52	3.92
6.79	0	2	0.43	2.96
5.39	1	3	0.76	4.11
4.65	2	4	1.16	5.39
4.25	1	4	1.04	4.42
3.88	2	5	1.43	5.55
3.63	3	6	1.87	6.78
3.38	2	6	1.72	5.82
3.21	3	7	2.15	6.91
3.09	4	8	2.62	8.10

Tables for $n_1 = n_2$

R = p_2/p_1	Accept numbers c_1	c_2	Approximation values of pn_1 for P = .95	P = .10
2.85	4	9	2.90	8.26
2.60	5	11	3.68	9.56
2.44	5	12	4.00	9.77
2.32	5	13	4.35	10.08
2.22	5	14	4.70	10.45
2.12	5	16	5.39	11.41

Tables for $n_2 = 2n_1$

R = p_2/p_1	accept numbers c_1	c_2	approximation values of pn_1 for P = .95	P = .10
14.50	0	1	0.16	2.32
8.07	0	2	0.30	2.42
6.48	1	3	0.60	3.89
5.39	0	3	0.49	2.64
5.09	0	4	0.77	3.92
4.31	1	4	0.68	2.93
4.19	0	5	0.96	4.02
3.60	1	6	1.16	4.17
3.26	1	8	1.68	5.47
2.96	2	10	2.27	6.72
2.77	3	11	2.46	6.82

Tables for $n_2 = 2n_1$

R =	accept numbers		approximation values of pn_1 for	
p_2/p_1	c_1	c_2	P = .95	P = .10
2.62	4	13	3.07	8.05
2.46	4	14	3.29	8.11
2.21	3	15	3.41	7.55
1.97	4	20	4.75	9.35
1.74	6	30	7.45	12.96

We wish to construct a double sampling plan according to

$$p_1 = 0.01 \quad \alpha = 0.05 \quad p_2 = 0.05 \quad \beta = 0.10 \quad \text{and} \quad n_1 = n_2$$

The plans in the corresponding table are indexed on the ratio

$$R = p_2/p_1 = 5$$

We find the row whose R is closet to 5. This is the 5th row ($R = 4.65$). This gives $c_1 = 2$ and $c_2 = 4$. The value of n_1 is determined from either of the two columns labeled pn_1.

The left holds α constant at 0.05 ($P = 0.95 = 1 - \alpha$) and the right holds β constant at 0.10. ($P = 0.10$). Then holding α constant we find $pn_1 = 1.16$ so $n_1 = 1.16/p_1 = 116$. And, holding β constant we find $pn_1 = 5.39$, so $n_1 = 5.39/p_2 = 108$. Thus the desired sampling plan is

$$n_1 = 108 \quad c_1 = 2 \quad n_2 = 108 \quad c_2 = 4$$

If we opt for $n_2 = 2n_1$, and follow the same procedure using the appropriate table, the plan is:

$$n_1 = 77 \quad c_1 = 1 \quad n_2 = 154 \quad c_2 = 4$$

The first plan needs less samples if the number of defectives in sample 1 is greater than 2, while the second plan needs less samples if the number of defectives in sample 1 is less than 2.

ASN Curve for a Double Sampling Plan

Since when using a double sampling plan the sample size depends on whether or not a second sample is required, an important consideration for this kind of sampling is the Average Sample Number (ASN) curve. This curve plots the ASN versus p', the true fraction defective in an incoming lot.

We will illustrate how to calculate the *ASN* curve with an example. Consider a double-sampling plan $n_1 = 50$, $c_1 = 2$, $n_2 = 100$, $c_2 = 6$, where n_1 is the sample size for plan 1, with accept number c_1, and n_2, c_2, are the sample size and accept number, respectively, for plan 2.

Let $p' = .06$. Then the probability of acceptance on the first sample, which is the chance of getting two or less defectives, is .416 (using binomial tables). The probability of rejection on the second sample, which is the chance of getting more than six defectives, is (1-.971) = .029. The probability of making a decision on the first sample is .445, equal to the sum of .416 and .029. With complete inspection of the second sample, the *average* size sample is equal to the size of the first sample times the probability that there will be only one sample plus the size of the combined samples times the probability that a second sample will be necessary. For the sampling plan under consideration, the *ASN* with complete inspection of the second sample for a p' of .06 is

$$50(.445) + 150(.555) = 106$$

The general formula for an average sample number curve of a double-sampling plan with complete inspection of the second sample is

$$ASN = n_1P_1 + (n_1 + n_2)(1 - P_1) = n_1 + n_2(1 - P_1)$$

where P_1 is the probability of a decision on the first sample. The graph below shows a plot of the *ASN* versus

P_1 is the probability of a decision on the first sample. The graph below shows a plot of the *ASN* versus p'.

The ASN curve for a double sampling plan

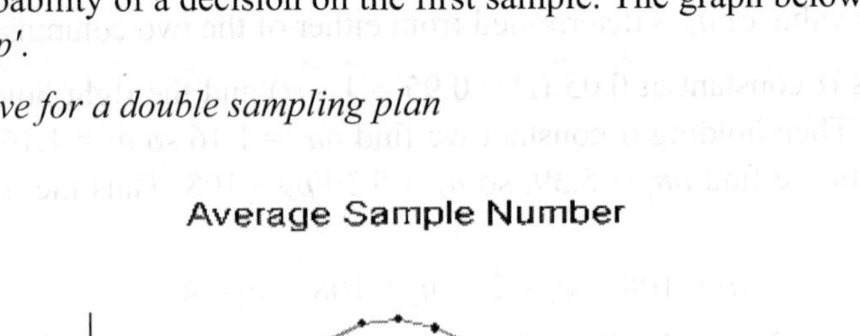

Multiple sampling is an extension of double sampling. It involves inspection of 1 to k successive samples as required to reach an ultimate decision.

Mil-Std 105D suggests $k = 7$ is a good number. Multiple sampling plans are usually presented in tabular form

The procedure commences with taking a random sample of size n_1 from a large lot of size N and counting the number of defectives, d_1.

if $d_1 \le a_1$ the lot is accepted.

if $d_1 \ge r_1$ the lot is rejected.

if $a_1 < d_1 < r_1$, another sample is taken.

If subsequent samples are required, the first sample procedure is repeated sample by sample. For each sample, the total number of defectives found at any stage, say stage i, is

$$D_i - \sum_{j=1}^{i} d_j$$

This is compared with the acceptance number a_i and the rejection number r_i for that stage until a decision is made. Sometimes acceptance is not allowed at the early stages of multiple sampling; however, rejection can occur at any stage.

Efficiency for a multiple sampling scheme is measured by the *average sample number* (ASN) required for a given *Type I* and *Type II* set of errors. The number of samples needed when following a multiple sampling scheme may vary from trial to trial, and the *ASN* represents the average of what might happen over many trials with a fixed incoming defect level.

Sequential sampling is different from single, double or multiple sampling. Here one takes a sequence of samples from a lot. How many total samples looked at is a function of the results of the sampling process.

The sequence can be one sample at a time, and then the sampling process is usually called *item-by-item* sequential sampling. One can also select sample sizes greater than one, in which case the process is referred to as *group* sequential sampling. Item-by-item is more popular so we concentrate on it. The operation of such a plan is illustrated below:

Sampling. Item-by-item is more popular so we concentrate on it. The operation of such a plan is illustrated below:

Diagram of item-by-item sampling

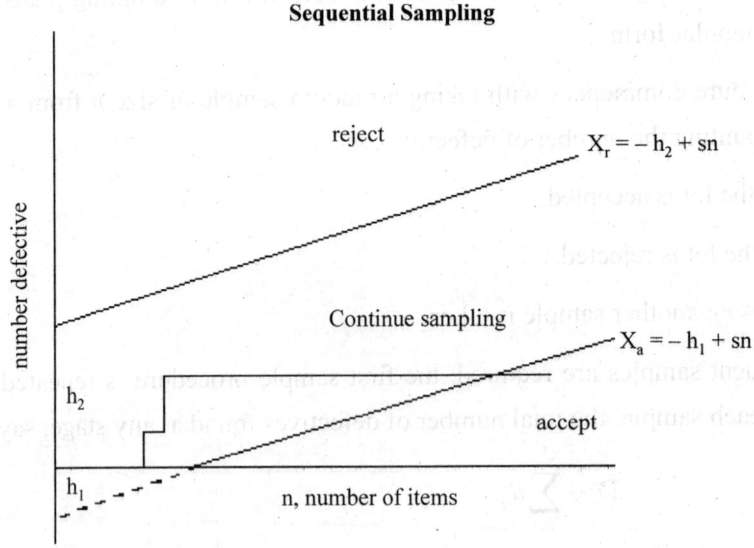

The cumulative observed number of defectives is plotted on the graph. For each point, the x-axis is the total number of items thus far selected, and the y-axis is the total number of observed defectives. If the plotted point falls within the parallel lines the process continues by drawing another sample. As soon as a point falls on or above the upper line, the lot is rejected. And when a point falls on or below the lower line, the lot is accepted. The process can theoretically last until the lot is 100% inspected. However, as a rule of thumb, sequential-sampling plans are truncated after the number inspected reaches three times the number that would have been inspected using a corresponding single sampling plan.

The equations for the two limit lines are functions of the parameters p_1, α, p_2, and β.

$x_a = - h_1 + sn$ (acceptance line)

$x_r = h_2 + sn$ (rejection line)

where

$$h_1 = \left(\log \frac{1-\alpha}{\beta}\right) \Big/ k_i$$

$$h_2 = \left(\log \frac{1-\beta}{\alpha}\right) \Big/ k_i$$

$$k_i = \log \frac{p_2(1-p_1)}{p_1(1-p_2)}$$

$$s = \left(\log \left[\frac{1-p_1}{1-p_2} \right] \right) \Big/ k$$

Instead of using the graph to determine the fate of the lot, one can resort to generating tables (with the help of a computer program

As an example, let $p_1 = .01$, $p_2 = .10$, $\alpha = .05$, $\beta = .10$. The resulting equations are

$$x_a = -0.939 + 0.04n$$

$$x_r = 1.205 + 0.04n$$

Both acceptance numbers and rejection numbers must be integers. The acceptance number is the next integer less than or equal to x_a and the rejection number is the next integer greater than or equal to x_r. Thus for $n = 1$, the acceptance number = -1, which is impossible, and the rejection number = 2, which is also impossible. For $n = 24$, the acceptance number is 0 and the rejection number = 3.

The results for n =1, 2, 3... 26 are tabulated below.

n inspect	n accept	n reject	n inspect	n accept	n reject
1	x	x	14	x	2
2	x	2	15	x	2
3	x	2	16	x	3
4	x	2	17	x	3
5	x	2	18	x	3
6	x	2	19	x	3
7	x	2	20	x	3
8	x	2	21	x	3
9	x	2	22	x	3
10	x	2	23	x	3
11	x	2	24	0	3
12	x	2	25	0	3
13	x	2	26	0	3

So, for n = 24 the acceptance number is 0 and the rejection number is 3. The "x" means that acceptance or rejection is not possible.

Other sequential plans are given below.

n inspect	*n* accept	*n* reject
49	1	3
58	1	4
74	2	4
83	2	5
100	3	5
109	3	6

The corresponding single sampling plan is (52,2) and double sampling plan is (21,0), (21,1). for a sequential sampling scheme is measured by the *average sample number (*ASN*)* required for a given *Type I* and *Type II* set of errors. The number of samples needed when following a sequential sampling scheme may vary from trial to trial, and the *ASN* represents the average of what might happen over many trials with a fixed incoming defect level. Good software for designing sequential sampling schemes will calculate the *ASN* curve as a function of the incoming defect level.

Skip Lot sampling means that only a fraction of the submitted lots are inspected. This mode of sampling is of the cost-saving variety in terms of time and effort. However skip-lot sampling should only be used when it has been demonstrated that the quality of the submitted product is very good

A skip-lot sampling plan is implemented as follows:

1. *Design a single sampling plan* by specifying the alpha and beta risks and the consumer/producer's risks. This plan is called "the reference sampling plan".
2. Start with normal lot-by-lot inspection, using the reference plan.
3. When a pre-specified number, *i*, of consecutive lots are accepted, switch to inspecting only a fraction *f* of the lots. The selection of the members of that fraction is done at random.
4. When a lot is rejected return to normal inspection.

The parameters *f* and *i* are essential to calculating the probability of acceptance for a skip-lot sampling plan. In this scheme, *i*, called the *clearance number,* is a positive integer and the sampling fraction *f* is such that $0 < f < 1$. Hence, when $f = 1$ there is no longer skip-lot sampling. The calculation of the acceptance probability for the skip-lot sampling plan is performed via the following formula

$$P_a(f,i) = \frac{fP + (1-f)P^i}{f + (1-f)P^i}$$

where P is the probability of accepting a lot with a given proportion of incoming defectives p, from the *OC curve* of the single sampling plan.

The following relationships hold:

for a given i, the smaller is f, the greater is P_a for a given f, the smaller is i, the greater is P_a

An illustration of a a skip-lot sampling plan is given below.

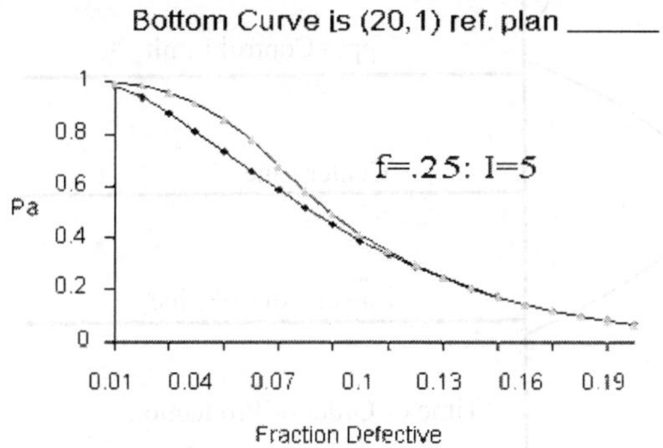

An important property of skip-lot sampling plans is the average sample number (ASN). The *ASN* of a skip-lot sampling plan is

$$ASN_{skip\text{-}lot} = (F)(ASN_{reference})$$

where F is defined by

$$F = \frac{f}{(1-f)P^i + f}$$

Therefore, since $0 < F < 1$, it follows that the *ASN* of skip-lot sampling is smaller than the *ASN* of the reference sampling plan.

In summary, skip-lot sampling is preferred when the quality of the submitted lots is excellent and the supplier can demonstrate a proven track record.

Control charts are used to routinely monitor quality. Depending on the number of process characteristics to be monitored, there are two basic types of control charts. The first, referred to as a univariate control chart, is a graphical display (chart) of one quality characteristic. The second, referred to as a multivariate control chart, is a graphical display of a statistic that summarizes or represents more than one quality characteristic.

A single quality characteristic has been measured or computed from a sample, the control chart shows the value of the quality characteristic versus the sample number or versus time. In general, the chart contains a center line that represents the mean value for the in-control process. Two other horizontal lines, called the upper control limit (UCL) and the lower control limit (LCL), are also shown on the chart. These control limits are chosen so that almost all of the data points will fall within these limits as long as the process remains in-control. The figure below illustrates this.

Demonstrating basis of control chart

Theoretical Basis for a Control Chart

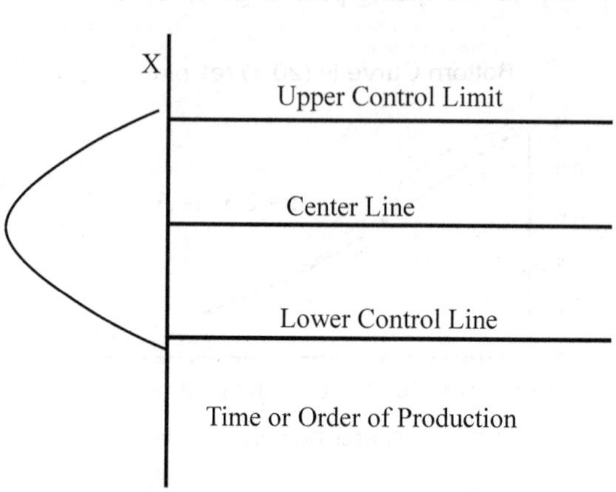

The control limits as pictured in the graph might be .001 *probability* limits. If so, and if chance causes alone were present, the probability of a point falling above the upper limit would be one out of a thousand, and similarly, a point falling below the lower limit would be one out of a thousand. We would be searching for an assignable cause if a point would fall outside these limits. Where we put these limits will determine the risk of undertaking such a search when in reality there is no assignable cause for variation.

Since two out of a thousand is a very small risk, the 0.001 limits may be said to give practical assurances that, if a point falls outside these limits, the variation was caused be an assignable cause. It must be noted that two out of one thousand is a purely arbitrary number. There is no reason why it could not have been set to one out a hundred or even larger. The decision would depend on the amount of risk the management of the quality control program is willing to take. In general (in the world of quality control) it is customary to use limits that approximate the 0.002 standard.

Letting *X* denote the value of a process characteristic, if the system of chance causes generates a variation in *X* that follows the normal distribution, the 0.001 probability limits will be very close to the 3σ limits. From normal tables we glean that the 3σ in one direction is 0.00135, or in both directions 0.0027. For normal distributions, therefore, the 3σ limits are the practical equivalent of 0.001 probability limits.

In the U.S., whether X is normally distributed or not, it is an acceptable practice to base the control limits upon a multiple of the standard deviation. Usually this multiple is 3 and thus the limits are called 3-sigma limits. This term is used whether the standard deviation is the universe or population parameter, or some estimate thereof, or simply a "standard value" for control chart purposes. It should be inferred from the context what standard deviation is involved. (Note that in the U.K., statisticians generally prefer to adhere to probability limits.)

If the underlying distribution is skewed, say in the positive direction, the 3-sigma limit will fall short of the upper 0.001 limit, while the lower 3-sigma limit will fall below the 0.001 limit. This situation means that the risk of looking for assignable causes of positive variation when none exists will be greater than one out of a thousand. But the risk of searching for an assignable cause of negative variation, when none exists, will be reduced. The net result, however, will be an increase in the risk of a chance variation beyond the control limits. How much this risk will be increased will depend on the degree of skewness.

If variation in quality follows a Poisson distribution, for example, for which $np = .8$, the risk of exceeding the upper limit by chance would be raised by the use of 3-sigma limits from 0.001 to 0.009 and the lower limit reduces from 0.001 to 0. For a Poisson distribution the mean and variance both equal np. Hence the upper 3-sigma limit is 0.8 + 3 *sqrt*(.8) = 3.48 and the lower limit = 0 (here *sqrt* denotes "square root"). For $np = .8$ the probability of getting more than 3 successes = 0.009.

If a data point falls outside the control limits, we assume that the process is probably out of control and that an investigation is warranted to find and eliminate the cause or causes.

Does this mean that when all points fall within the limits, the process is in control? Not necessarily. If the plot looks non-random, that is, if the points exhibit some form of systematic behavior, there is still something wrong. For example, if the first 25 of 30 points fall above the center line and the last 5 fall below the center line, we would wish to know why this is so. Statistical methods to detect sequences or nonrandom patterns can be applied to the interpretation of control charts. To be sure, "in control" implies that all points are between the control limits and they form a random pattern.

During the 1920's, Dr. Walter A. Shewhart proposed a general model for control charts as follows:

Shewhart Control Charts for variables

Let w be a sample statistic that measures some continuously varying quality characteristic of interest (e.g., thickness), and suppose that the mean of w is μ_w, with a standard deviation of σ_w. Then the center line, the UCL and the LCL are

$$\text{UCL} = \mu_w + k\sigma_w$$

$$\text{Center Line} = \mu_w$$

$$\text{LCL} = \mu_w - k\sigma_w$$

where k is the distance of the control limits from the center line, expressed in terms of standard deviation units. When k is set to 3, we speak of 3-sigma control charts.

Historically, k = 3 has become an accepted standard in industry.

The centerline is the process mean, which in general is unknown. We replace it with a *target* or the average of all the data. The quantity that we plot is the sample average, $\overline{X}$. The chart is called the $\overline{X}$ chart.

We also have to deal with the fact that σ is, in general, unknown. Here we replace σ_w with a given standard value, or we estimate it by a function of the *average standard deviation*. This is obtained by averaging the individual standard deviations that we calculated from each of *m* preliminary (or present) samples, each of size *n*. This function will be discussed shortly.

It is equally important to examine the standard deviations in ascertaining whether the process is in control. There is, unfortunately, a slight problem involved when we work with the usual estimator of σ. The following discussion will illustrate this

If σ^2 is the unknown variance of a probability distribution, then an unbiased estimator of σ^2 is the sample variance

$$s^2 = \frac{\sum_{i-1}^{n}\left(x_i - \overline{x}\right)^2}{n-1}$$

However, s, the sample standard deviation is *not* an unbiased estimator of σ. If the underlying distribution is normal, then s actually estimates $c_4\,\sigma$, where c_4 is a constant that depends on the sample size n. This constant is tabulated in most text books on statistical quality control and may be calculated using

C_4 factor

$$c_4 = \sqrt{\frac{2}{n-1}}\,\frac{\left(\frac{n}{2}-1\right)!}{\left(\frac{n-1}{2}-1\right)!}$$

To compute this we need a *non-integer factorial,* which is defined for $n/2$ as follows:

So the mean or expected value of the sample standard deviation is $c_4\,\sigma$.

The standard deviation of the sample standard deviation is

$$\sigma_s = \sigma\sqrt{1-c_4^2}$$

What are the differences between control limits and specification limits?

Control Limits are used to determine if the process is in a state of statistical control (i.e., is producing consistent output).

Specification Limits are used to determine if the product will function in the intended fashion.

How many data points are needed to set up a control chart?

Shewhart gave the following rule of thumb:

"It has also been observed that a person would seldom if ever be justified in concluding that a state of statistical control of a given repetitive operation or production process has been reached until he had obtained, under presumably the same essential conditions, a sequence of not less than twenty five samples of size four that are in control."

It is important to note that control chart properties, such as false alarm probabilities, are generally given under the assumption that the parameters, such as μ and σ, are known. When the control limits are not computed from a large amount of data, the actual properties might be quite different from what is assumed (see, e.g., *Quesenberry, 1993*).

When do we recalculate control limits?

Since a control chart "compares" the current performance of the process characteristic to the past performance of this characteristic, changing the control limits frequently would negate any usefulness.

So, only change your control limits if you have a valid, compelling reason for doing so. Some examples of reasons:

When you have at least 30 more data points to add to the chart and there have been no known changes to the process

- you get a better estimate of the variability

If a major process change occurs and affects the way your process runs.

If a known, preventable act changes the way the tool or process would behave (power goes out, consumable is corrupted or bad quality, etc.)

What are the WECO rules for signaling "Out of Control"?

General rules for detecting out of control or non-random situations

WECO stands for Western Electric Company Rules

Any Point Above +3 Sigma

--- +3 σ LIMIT

2 Out of the Last 3 Points Above +2 Sigma

-- +2 σ LIMIT

4 Out of the Last 5 Points Above +1 Sigma

-- +1 σ LIMIT

8 Consecutive Points on This Side of Control Line

== CENTER LINE

8 Consecutive Points on This Side of Control Line

-- – 1 σ LIMIT

4 Out of the Last 5 Points Below – 1 Sigma

-- – 2 σ LIMIT

2 Out of the Last 3 Points Below – 2 Sigma

-- – 3 σ LIMIT

Any Point Below -3 Sigma

Trend Rules

6 in a row trending up or down. 14 in a row alternating up and down

The WECO rules are based on probability. We know that, for a normal distribution, the probability of encountering a point outside $\pm$ 3σ is 0.3%. This is a rare event. Therefore, if we observe a point outside the control limits, we conclude the process has shifted and is unstable. Similarly, we can identify other events that are equally rare and use them as flags for instability. The probability of observing two points out of three in a row between 2σ and 3σ and the probability of observing four points out of five in a row between 1σ and 2σ are also about 0.3%.

Note: While the WECO rules increase a Shewhart chart's sensitivity to trends or drifts in the mean, there is a severe downside to adding the WECO rules to an ordinary Shewhart control chart that the user should understand. When following the standard Shewhart "out of control" rule (i.e., signal if and only if you see a point beyond the plus or minus 3 sigma control limits) you will have "false alarms" every 371 points on the average (see the description of *Average Run Length or ARL* on the next page). Adding the WECO rules increases the frequency of false alarms to about once in every 91.75 points, on the average (see *Champ and Woodall, 1987*). The user has to decide whether this price is worth paying (some users add the WECO rules, but take them "less seriously" in terms of the effort put into troubleshooting activities when out of control signals occur).

With this background, the next page will describe how to construct Shewhart variables control charts.

Samples are Individual Measurements

Moving range used to derive upper and lower limits

Control charts for individual measurements, e.g., the sample size = 1, use the *moving range* of two successive observations to measure the process variability.

The moving range is defined as

$$MR_i = |x_i - x_{i-1}|$$

which is the absolute value of the first difference (e.g., the difference between two consecutive data points) of the data. Analogous to the Shewhart control chart, one can plot both the data (which are the individuals) and the moving range.

For the control chart for individual measurements, the lines plotted are:

$$\text{UCL} = \bar{x} + 3\frac{\overline{MR}}{1.128}$$

$$\text{Centre line} = \bar{x}$$

$$\text{LCL} = \bar{\text{x}} - 3\frac{\overline{MR}}{1.128}$$

where $\overline{\text{X}}$ is the average of all the individuals and $\overline{MR}$ is the average of all the moving ranges of two observations. Keep in mind that either or both averages may be replaced by a standard or target, if available. (Note that 1.128 is the value of d_2 for $n = 2$).

The following example illustrates the control chart for individual observations. A new process was studied in order to monitor flow rate. The first 10 batches resulted in

Batch Number	Flowrate x	Moving Range MR
1	49.6	
2	47.6	2.0
3	49.9	2.3
4	51.3	14
5	47.8	3.5
6	51.2	3.4
7	52.6	1.4
8	52.4	0.2
9	53.6	1.2
10	52.1	1.5
	$\overline{\text{X}} = 50.81$	$\overline{MR} = 1.8778$

This yields the parameters below.

$$UCL = \bar{x} + 3\frac{\overline{MR}}{1.128} = 50.81 + 3\frac{1.8778}{1.128} = 55.8041$$

$$\text{Centre line } \bar{x} = 50.81$$

$$LCL = \bar{x} - 3\frac{\overline{MR}}{1.128} = 50.81 - 3\frac{1.8778}{1.128} = 45.8159$$

The control chart is given below

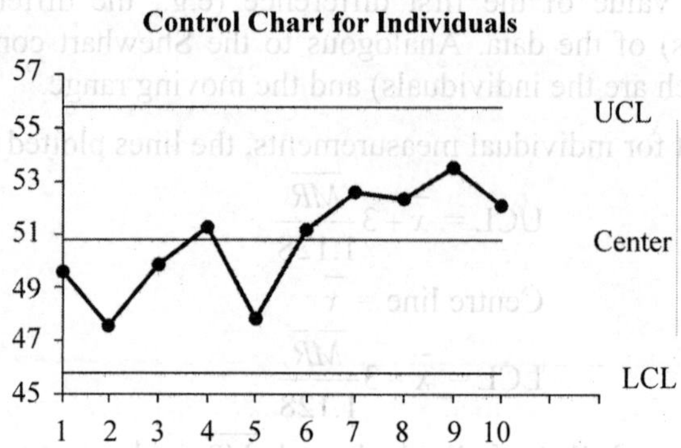

The process is in control, since none of the plotted points fall outside either the *UCL* or *LCL*.

Alternative for constructing individuals control chart

Note: Another way to construct the individuals chart is by using the standard deviation. Then we can obtain the chart from

$$\bar{x} \pm 3s / c_4$$

It is preferable to have the limits computed this way for the start of Phase 2.

Dr W. Edward Deming's 14 Principles – Deming's principles of quality improvement

Constancy of purpose: Create constancy of purpose for continual improvement of products and service to society, allocating resources to provide for long range needs rather than only short term profitability, with a plan to become competitive, to stay in business, and to provide jobs.

1. ***The new philosophy:*** Adopt the new philosophy. We are in a new economic age, created in Japan. We can no longer live with commonly accepted levels of delays, mistakes, defective materials and defective workmanship. Transformation of Western management style is necessary to halt the continued decline of business and industry.

2. ***Cease dependence on mass inspection:*** Eliminate the need for mass inspection as the way of life to achieve quality by building quality into the product in the first place. Require statistical evidence of built in quality in both manufacturing and purchasing functions.
3. ***End lowest tender contracts:*** End the practice of awarding business solely on the basis of price tag. Instead require meaningful measures of quality along with price. Reduce the number of suppliers for the same item by eliminating those that do not qualify with statistical and other evidence of quality. The aim is to minimize total cost, not merely initial cost, by minimizing variation. This may be achieved by moving toward a single supplier for any one item, on a long term relationship of loyalty and trust. Purchasing managers have a new job, and must learn it.
4. ***Improve every process:*** Improve constantly and forever every process for planning, production, and service. Search continually for problems in order to improve every activity in the company, to improve quality and productivity, and thus to constantly decrease costs. Institute innovation and constant improvement of product, service, and process. It is management's job to work continually on the system (design, incoming materials, maintenance, improvement of machines, supervision, training, retraining).
5. ***Institute training on the job:*** Institute modern methods of training on the job for all, including management, to make better use of every employee. New skills are required to keep up with changes in materials, methods, product and service design, machinery, techniques, and service.
6. ***Institute leadership:*** Adopt and institute leadership aimed at helping people do a better job. The responsibility of managers and supervisors must be changed from sheer numbers to quality. Improvement of quality will automatically improve productivity. Management must ensure that immediate action is taken on reports of inherited defects, maintenance requirements, poor tools, fuzzy operational definitions, and all conditions detrimental to quality.
7. Drive out fear: Encourage effective two way communication and other means to drive out fear throughout the organization so that everybody may work effectively and more productively for the company.
8. ***Break down barriers:*** Break down barriers between departments and staff areas. People in different areas, such as Leasing, Maintenance, Administration, must work in teams to tackle problems that may be encountered with products or service.
9. ***Eliminate exhortations:*** Eliminate the use of slogans, posters and exhortations for the work force, demanding Zero Defects and new levels of productivity, without providing methods. Such exhortations only create adversarial relationships; the bulk of the causes of low quality and low productivity belong to the system, and thus lie beyond the power of the work force.

10. ***Eliminate arbitrary numerical targets:*** Eliminate work standards that prescribe quotas for the work force and numerical goals for people in management. Substitute aids and helpful leadership in order to achieve continual improvement of quality and productivity.
11. ***Permit pride of workmanship:*** Remove the barriers that rob hourly workers, and people in management, of their right to pride of workmanship. This implies, among other things, abolition of the annual merit rating (appraisal of performance) and of Management by Objective. Again, the responsibility of managers, supervisors, foremen must be changed from sheer numbers to quality.
12. ***Encourage education:*** Institute a vigorous program of education, and encourage self improvement for everyone. What an organization needs is not just good people; it needs people that are improving with education. Advances in competitive position will have their roots in knowledge.
13. ***Top management commitment and action:*** Clearly define top management's permanent commitment to ever improving quality and productivity, and their obligation to implement all of these principles. Indeed, it is not enough that top management commit themselves for life to quality and productivity. They must know what it is that they are committed to-that is, what they must do. Create a structure in top management that will push every day on the preceding 13 Points, and take action in order to accomplish the transformation. Support is not enough: action is required

PDCA Cycle

From problem-faced to problem-solved

The PDCA Cycle is a checklist of the four stages which you must go through to get from `problem-faced' to `problem solved'. The four stages are Plan-Do-Check-Act, and they are carried out in the cycle illustrated below.

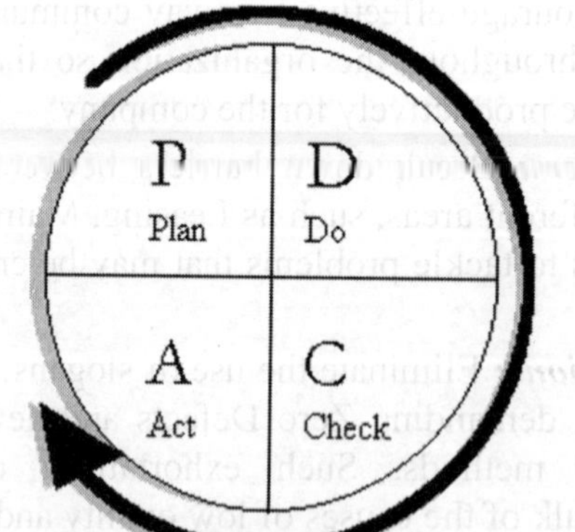

The concept of the PDCA Cycle was originally developed by Walter Shewhart, the pioneering statistician who developed statistical process control in the Bell Laboratories in the US during the 1930's. It is often referred to as `the Shewhart Cycle'. It was taken up and promoted very effectively from the 1950s on by the famous Quality Management authority, W. Edwards Deming, and is consequently known by many as `the Deming Wheel'.

Use the PDCA Cycle to coordinate your continuous improvement efforts. It both emphasises and demonstrates that improvement programs must start with careful planning, must result in effective action, and must move on again to careful planning in a continuous cycle.

Also use the PDCA Cycle diagram in team meetings to take stock of what stage improvement initiatives are at, and to choose the appropriate tools to see each stage through to successful completion.

Plan-Do-Check-Act

Here is what you do for each stage of the Cycle:

Plan to improve your operations first by finding out what things are going wrong (that is identify the problems faced), and come up with ideas for solving these problems.

Do changes designed to solve the problems on a small or experimental scale first. This minimises disruption to routine activity while testing whether the changes will work or not.

Check whether the small scale or experimental changes are achieving the desired result or not. Also, continuously Check nominated key activities (regardless of any experimentation going on) to ensure that you know what the quality of the output is at all times to identify any new problems when they crop up.

Act to implement changes on a larger scale if the experiment is successful. This means making the changes a routine part of your activity. Also Act to involve other persons (other departments, suppliers, or customers) affected by the changes and whose cooperation you need to implement them on a larger scale, or those who may simply benefit from what you have learned (you may, of course, already have involved these people in the Do or trial stage).

You have now completed the cycle to arrive at `problem solved'. Go back to the Plan stage to identify the next `problem faced'.

If the experiment was not successful, skip the Act stage and go back to the Plan stage to come up with some new ideas for solving the problem and go through the cycle again. Plan-Do-Check-Act describes the overall stages of improvement activity, but how is each stage carried out? This is where other specific quality management, or continuous improvement, tools and techniques come into play. The diagram below lists the tools and techniques which can be used to complete each stage of the PDCA Cycle.

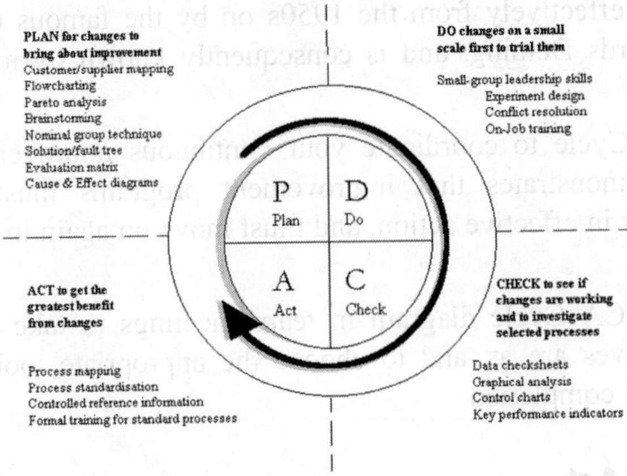

This classification of tools into sections of the PDCA Cycle is not meant to be strictly applied, but it is a useful prompt to help you choose what to do at each critical stage of your improvement efforts.

Questions

1. Explain the concept: manufacturing management?
2. Explain manufacturing and production with suitable examples?
3. Discuss the steps involved in the production control?
4. What are the different components of facility location planning?
5. Explain the different methods of production?
6. What is production planning and control? Discuss its significance in the context of manufacturing management?
7. Explain the various factors to be taken into consideration while taking a decision on factory location?
8. What do you understand by statistical quality control?
9. Explain Edward deming's 14 points of improving quality?
10. What is control chart? Explain the different types of control charts?
11. Describe deming's pdca cycle and state its significance?
12. Define work study, method study and work measurement? Explain their significance?
13. State the applications of work study? Describe the procedure for work study?

Chapter - 3

Social use of Drugs – Drug Addiction

It can be difficult deciding between something which is used on a casual basis or has become an addiction.

That odd glass of wine or two

The old saying 'everything in moderation' still holds true and it is the case that a small amount of something, for example alcohol or a couple of cups of coffee per week is not likely to cause any harm. In fact it may do you some good. One example of this is red wine which is considered to be good for your heart.

If we take this further, there is the case of the 'French Paradox'. This expression arose from a research study carried out in 1992 which reported upon the fact that the French diet was high in fats yet they had a relatively low rate of heart disease.

Types of Addictions - Drug Addiction

There are a whole range of things that we can become addicted to which include gambling, exercise, 'retail therapy' (shopping), sex, food, alcohol, the Internet, the list goes on and on.

Alcohol

Nicotine (smoking)

Drugs (cocaine, heroin, amphetamines etc)

Caffeine (coffee, chocolate etc)

When we think of 'drug addiction', many of us probably have a mental picture of a pale, skinny individual with needle marks down their arms who lives in a squat and commits crime to feed their habit.

This is a stereotype but like all stereotypes, it contains an element of truth. There are addicts who look and behave in this way, but, there are also a great many addicts who do not. There are people who hide their signs of their addiction so well that no one is aware that they have a problem.

As we know addiction is no respecter of person. It doesn't matter whether you are working class or middle class; young or old; male or female, or married or single. Addictions can affect anyone of us and the way they do so varies between individuals.

Alcohol

Some addictions appear to be more 'socially acceptable' than others, for example alcohol. Many people enjoy a drink and are able to control how much they consume. But there others who find that alcohol becomes more than a pleasant social activity.

Alcohol Addiction, Abuse and Dependency

Alcohol is consumed by a great many people who see it as a pleasant way of unwinding after a long, hard day at work or as an enjoyable aspect of socializing with others. Alcohol helps us to relax: it gives us confidence in an unfamiliar situation, enables us to interact with others or is a means of celebrating an occasion.

A moderate amount of alcohol is good for your health and as long as you don't overdo it is unlikely to cause any problems. We know about the French diet, which includes red wine and yet they have some of the lowest rates of heart disease in the world. Their rates are lower than those in the UK.

Plus there is some research which suggests that there is a substance present in red wine which helps to protect against heart disease, although this is still open to debate.

These are the positive aspects of alcohol use. But, it is when you overdo it on a regular basis or find it increasingly difficult to manage without a drink that the situation changes from social use to an addiction. In other words you have crossed the line into 'alcoholism'.

What is alcohol?

If you ask someone to describe alcohol then they are likely to say that it is something you drink such as beer, wine or spirits. They may also add that it can get you drunk if you consume enough of it! But alcohol is actually the name given to a group of chemicals which are found in a wide variety of products such as mouthwashes, deodorants, body cleansers and of course, beer, wine and spirits.

There are four groups of alcohol which are as follows:

Grain alcohol: also known as ethanol. This is made from the fermentation of sugars and starches and is the type of alcohol you find in drinks such as beer, wine and spirits.

Aromatic alcohol: a form of alcohol which is found in health products or cosmetics.

Denatured alcohol: this is similar to grain alcohol but with one difference - it contains addictives which means that it is unfit for human consumption. Usually found in cosmetics, mouthwashes, moisturizing creams and deodorants.

Fatty alcohol: this is also found in cosmetics. It is used as a lubricant to bind oil and water together in the production of skin creams.

We talk about alcohol we mean grain alcohol (ethanol) which is present in all types of drinks, such as beer and wine.

Alcohol is a Depressant Drug

Alcohol is classed as a depressant drug. Now you may think that this seems strange as a great many people find that having a drink makes them feel happy. But the first part of this term - 'depressant' is used to describe processes in which alcohol shuts down those areas of the brain which are responsible for our physical, mental and emotional behavior. The second part - 'drug' refers to the fact that it directly affects the physical and mental state of the drinker and excessive use can lead to an addiction.

It is true that alcohol causes some people to become talkative, outgoing and upbeat but equally there other people who find that it makes them feel aggressive or depressed. It can be the case that if you are feeling low then having a few drinks will worsen that feeling. What confuses most people is what is considered a 'safe' amount to drink? Why are some people able to consume more alcohol than others but without any ill-effects? Also why is it such a major problem?

Units of Alcohol

The NHS has information on what are considered 'safe' levels of alcohol. These are measured in units and differ between men and women. It is difficult to be exact about a 'safe' level of drinking as everyone is different in this aspect. But there are guidelines on the recommended levels of alcohol consumption which are measured in units.

A unit is equivalent to:

Half a pint of cider, beer or lager

A small measure of spirits

A small glass of wine (125 ml)

A standard measure of sherry or port

If you are buying alcohol to drink at home then a good way of understanding about units is to look at the amount of pure alcohol contained in a drink. This is called 'ABV' or 'alcohol by volume'. In the UK a single unit of alcohol contains 10ml (8g) of pure alcohol. If you want to check the number of units of pure alcohol in a drink then multiple its volume (ml) by the ABV (its strength), and then divide this figure by 1,000. As you might imagine a higher ABV means a stronger drink with a higher concentration or alcohol.

The NHS advises men to drink no more than four units a day and women no more than two units a day. Men should have no more than fourteen units of alcohol in a week and women no more than nine units per week. Avoid drinking all of these units in a single go as a 'binge drinking' session.

Sticking to the recommended units doesn't mean a completely safe level of drinking but it does put you in a low risk group. Units of alcohol and risk levels are categorised as follows:

Low risk: men who drink three to four units of alcohol a day and women who drink one to two units of alcohol a day.

Medium risk: people who drink more than these units, also called 'increased risk drinkers'.

High risk: men who drink more than eight units a day or fifty units in a week and women who drink more than six units a day or thirty five units in a week.

Gender and Alcohol

The reason why the number of units is higher for men is because generally, men have a higher level of tolerance than women and metabolise (break down) alcohol more quickly than women. Women have higher levels of body fat and less water in their bodies than men which means that alcohol is not easily diluted and so remains in the body much longer than for men. This is why women often become drunker more quickly or are unable to consume as much alcohol as men although there are exceptions. Men are bigger and heavier which is why they are able to consume larger amounts where as women are smaller and lighter.

But like we say there are exceptions to this and many women are drinking as much if not more than men. Evidence of this can be seen in town and city centres across the UK. Alcohol tends to be removed from the body at the rate of one unit per hour. This is why it helps to space your drinks out or to drink water or non-alcoholic drinks in between. Note: Pregnant women or those women trying to start a family should avoid alcohol.

Underestimation of Units

One thing many of us are good at is underestimating the amount we drink. It is very easy to assume that you have drank only a certain amount when in fact you have more than your recommended units in a week. The units do add up and it is easy to forget how much you have had, especially if you are at a party or out at the weekend. This is something that alcoholics do when trying to defend the amount they have had to drink. They will engage in self-denial or lie about the amount of alcohol they have consumed, citing a lower amount than is really the case.

So what it is about alcohol that we like?

Effects of alcohol

The effects of alcohol vary according to your gender, age, weight, height and other similar factors. A state of drunkenness includes slurring of one's words, staggering or difficulty walking upright, double vision and poor muscle control. Extreme drunkenness involves vomiting, an inability to stand, a coma state and incapability to communicate. It is the case that some appear less affected than others although excessive use can affect anyone.

The manner in which alcohol affects you depends upon the following:

Your sensitivity to alcohol

Whether you have eaten or not

If you have eaten then the type of food and the amount

How much you drink

How often you drink

The amount of time you have been drinking (period of time)

Your environment at that time

If you have taken drugs, e.g. cannabis at the same time

You may find that a few drinks may release your inhibitions, making you feel confident and self-assured. On the other hand alcohol may make you feel depressed or angry or possibly suicidal.

Women are generally more sensitive to these effects than men but this affects both sexes equally as they get older. Signs of alcohol intoxication include a flushed, reddened face, slower reactions and reduced inhibitions. If a person experiences extreme drunkenness then there is a great risk that they may vomit in their sleep and choke on this vomit. Overindulging on a few occasions, for example at a friend's birthday, is unlikely to cause any long term effects but damage to health will occur if it becomes a regular habit.

There is also an unpleasant reminder of your overindulgence known as a 'hangover'. A hangover is your body's reaction to intoxication and is partly caused by dehydration and the production of a toxic chemical as alcohol is broken down by your liver. Symptoms of a hangover include headaches, nausea and possibly vomiting; shakiness, tiredness and thirst. The effects will have disappeared by either the end of the day or the next. But it is when this crosses the line from an occasional event to a regular event that signals a drinking problem.

Alcohol Addiction

Alcoholism (alcohol addiction/abuse) is the consumption of or preoccupation with alcoholic beverages to the extent that this behavior interferes with the alcoholic's normal personal, family, social, or work life. The chronic alcohol consumption caused by alcoholism can result in psychological and physiological disorders.

The primary effect of alcoholism is to encourage the sufferer to drink at times and in amounts that are damaging. The secondary damage caused by an inability to control one's drinking manifests in many ways. It is common for a person suffering from alcoholism to drink well after physical health effects start to manifest. The physical health effects associated with alcohol consumption include cirrhosis of the liver, pancreatitis, polyneuropathy, alcoholic dementia, heart disease, increased chance of cancer, nutritional deficiencies, sexual dysfunction, and death from many sources.

Why do some people become alcoholics?

There is no easy answer for this. Why do some people drive too fast? Why do some people smoke or take drugs? Why do some people enjoy adrenaline sports? We are all different and make choices in our lives - some good some not so good which are the result of various factors. These include our background, family upbringing, lifestyle, genetics, environment etc. There may be family history of alcoholism. If for example either of your parents or grandparents was an alcoholic then this is a risk factor.

If you suffer from a mental illness such as anxiety, depression or manic depression then you may use alcohol as a way of coping with your illness. It can also be a form of escapism. If you work in an environment which has a 'drinking culture' then this is another risk factor. Also, stressful life events such as divorce, bereavement or moving house can all trigger alcohol abuse. It is difficult to say when social drinking becomes a problem which eventually leads to an addiction (alcoholism). However the first step for these people is recognizing that their drinking is out of control.

The signs of a drinking problem or 'alcohol abuse' are:

Unable to stick to one drink

Guilt or feeling ashamed about your drinking

Lying to family and/or friends about your drinking

Having a need to drink in order to relax or feel confident

Finding that you drink more than is good for you

Experiencing 'blackouts' or forgetting what you did when drunk

Your family and friends are worried about your drinking

Need a drink to get through the day or to cope with your illness

The journey from problem drinking to full blown alcoholism happens over a period of time. However if detected at an early stage then it can be prevented. Having a problem with alcohol doesn't mean that you will automatically become an alcoholic but it does increase the risk of that happening. What happens is that you develop a tolerance to alcohol over a period of time, which is a sign that your body is becoming used to alcohol and demands it in order for you to function normally. It can start off by a few drinks several times a week, then drinking every day or 'binge drinking' which can result in alcoholism.

Alcohol abuse is a self-destructive condition and one that many people consider to be alcoholism, but there is a minor difference between the two. Someone who abuses alcohol is causing damage to both their mental and physical health but they still retain the ability to curb their drinking. However this is likely to be dependent upon their mood at the time. Alcoholism doesn't happen overnight: it is a gradual process in which the drinker passes through three stages to get to this point. The three stages of alcoholism are:

Stage one: no obvious signs of damage yet. The drinker is still in control but is gradually developing a tolerance to alcohol.

Stage two: problems have started to occur. The drinker is experiencing physical and mental effects of their habit and has developed alcohol abuse.

Stage three: this is the final stage in the journey. The drinker has become a full blown alcoholic and is unable to stop drinking.

There are warning signs of alcoholism which include an increased tolerance; finding that you can drink more than your friends or colleagues; drinking to ease withdrawal symptoms such as shakiness or anxiety and denying or attempting to justify your drinking to family, friends and colleagues.

Physical Signs of Alcohol Addiction

So what does excess alcohol do to our bodies? Alcoholism causes damage to many areas of the body which include the liver, stomach, pancreas, throat and the brain. The physical effects of alcoholism include:

Cirrhosis of the liver

Halitosis (bad breath)

Slurred speech

Menstrual problems

Stomach ulcer

Jaundice

Pancreatitis

Gallstones

Vitamin and mineral deficiencies

Loss of appetite

Increased risk of breast, stomach and liver cancer

Impotence

Numbness in fingers and toes

In some cases these can be fatal.

Psychological signs of alcohol addiction

Alcoholism affects the brain as much as the body. The psychological signs of alcoholism include:

Poor personal hygiene

Lack of interest in one's appearance

Lack of concentration or focus

Slow reactions

Impaired judgment

Hallucinations

Anxiety/panic attacks

Depression/increased risk of suicide

Difficulties with balance

Consuming alcohol in dangerous or difficult situations

Neglecting work, family, friends etc

Committing an offence under the influence of alcohol, e.g. drink driving

Possibly early onset of dementia

Social effects of alcohol addiction

The social problems arising from alcoholism can be significant. Being drunk or hung over during work hours can result in loss of employment, which can lead to financial problems including the loss of living quarters. Drinking at inappropriate times, and behavior caused by reduced judgment, can lead to legal consequences, such as criminal charges for drunk driving or public disorder, or civil penalties for tortuous behavior. An alcoholic's behavior and mental impairment while drunk can profoundly impact surrounding family and friends, possibly leading to marital conflict and divorce, or contributing to domestic violence. This can contribute to lasting damage to the emotional development of the alcoholic's children, even after they reach adulthood. The alcoholic could suffer from loss of respect from others who may see the problem as self-inflicted and easily avoided.

Alcohol Withdrawal

Alcohol withdrawal differs significantly from withdrawal from other drugs in that it can be directly fatal. While it is possible for heroin addicts, for instance, to die from other health problems made worse by the strain of withdrawal, an otherwise healthy alcoholic can die from the direct effects of withdrawal if it is not properly managed. Heavy consumption of alcohol reduces the production of GABA, which is a neuro-inhibitor. An abrupt stop of alcohol consumption can induce a condition where neither alcohol nor GABA exists in the system in adequate quantities, causing uncontrolled firing of the synapses. This manifests as hallucinations, shakes, convulsions, seizures, and possible heart failure, all of which are collectively referred to as delirium tremens.

Treatments for Alcohol Addiction

Before you seek treatment the first and most important part of the process is that of admitting that you have a problem. Once you have done so then the next step is help and support.

Beating an alcohol addiction is a long and painful process. It requires much more than sheer willpower: it requires you to make changes to every aspect of your life and some of that can be more difficult to do than others. But help and support is available so you don't need to do this on your own.

Treatments for alcohol addiction are quite varied because there are multiple perspectives for the condition itself. Those who approach alcoholism as a medical condition or disease recommend differing treatments than, for instance, those who approach the condition as one of social choice.

Most treatments focus on helping people discontinue their alcohol intake, followed up with life training and/or social support in order to help them resist a return to alcohol use.

Since alcoholism involves multiple factors which encourage a person to continue drinking, they must all be addressed in order to successfully prevent a relapse. An example of this kind of treatment is detoxification followed by a combination of supportive therapy, attendance at self-help groups, and ongoing development of coping mechanisms. The treatment community for alcoholism typically supports an abstinence-based zero tolerance approach; however, there are some who promote a harm-reduction approach as well.

The effectiveness of alcohol addiction treatments varies widely. When considering the effectiveness of treatment options, one must consider the success rate based on those who enter a program, not just those who complete it. Since completion of a program is the qualification for success, success among those who complete a program is generally near 100%. It is also important to consider not just the rate of those reaching treatment goals but the rate of those relapsing. Results should also be compared to the roughly 5% rate at which people will quit on their own.

Detoxification

Detoxification or 'detox' for alcoholics is an abrupt stop of alcohol drinking coupled with the substitution of drugs that have similar effects to offset the withdrawal symptoms. Benzodiazepines are the most common family of drugs used for this, followed by barbiturates.

Detoxes are performed in multiple ways. The first takes into consideration the varying degrees of tolerance. In it, a standard dose of the benzodiazepine is given every half hour until light sedation is reached. Once a baseline dose is determined, the medication is tapered over the ensuing 3-10 days. Another option is to give a standard dose of benzodiazepine based on history and adjust based on withdrawal phenomenon. A third option is to defer treatment until symptoms occur, which is safe only with relatively mild alcohol users.

Detoxification treats the physical effects of prolonged use of alcohol, but does not actually treat alcoholism. After detox is complete, relapse is likely without further treatment. These rehabilitations (or 'rehabs') may take place in an inpatient or outpatient setting. Detoxification may or may not be necessary depending upon an individual's age, medical status, and history of alcohol intake. For example, a young man who binge drinks and seeks treatment one week after his last use of alcohol may not require detoxification before beginning treatment for alcoholism.

Group Therapy and Psychotherapy for Alcohol Addiction

After detoxification, various forms of group therapy or psychotherapy can be used to deal with underlying psychological issues that are related to alcohol addiction, as well as provide relapse prevention skills. The mutual-help group-counseling approach is one of the most common ways of helping alcoholics maintain sobriety. Many organizations have been formed to provide this service, including Alcoholics Anonymous, Life Ring Secular Recovery, Rational Recovery, Smart Recovery, and Women For Sobriety.

Rationing and Moderation for Alcohol Addiction

Rationing and moderation programs do not mandate complete abstinence. Since one of the effects of alcohol is to reduce a person's judgment, each drink makes it more difficult to decide that the next drink is a bad idea. Additionally, for those who are predisposed towards alcoholism, drinking in moderation can result in the strengthening of the endorphin-based addiction.

While most alcoholics are unable to limit their drinking in this way, moderate drinking works for some people, and it may avoid the physical, financial, and social costs of other treatments - particularly in the early phase of recovery. Professional help can be sought for rationing from programs such as Moderation Management.

Medications for Treating Alcohol Addiction

Although not necessary for treatment of alcoholism, a variety of medications may be prescribed as part of treatment. Some may ease the transition to sobriety, while others cause physical hardship to result from the use of alcohol. In most cases, the desired effect is to have an alcoholic abstain from drinking.

Antabuse (disulfiram) prevents the elimination of (acetaldehyde), a chemical the body produces when breaking down ethanol. Acetaldehyde itself is the cause of many hangs over symptoms from alcohol use. The overall effect is severe discomfort when alcohol is ingested: an extremely fast acting and long lasting uncomfortable hang over. This discourages an alcoholic from drinking in significant amounts while they take the medicine. Heavy drinking while on antabuse can cause severe illness and death.

Naltrexone is a competitive antagonist for opioid receptors, effectively blocking our ability to use endorphins and opiates. It also appears to act on glutamate neurotransmission. Naltrexone is used in two very different forms of treatment. The first treatment uses naltrexone to decrease cravings for alcohol and encourage abstinence. The other treatment, called pharmacological extinction, combines naltrexone with normal drinking habits in order to reverse the endorphin conditioning that causes alcohol addiction. Naltrexone comes in two forms. Oral naltrexone, originally but no longer available as the brand ReVia, is a pill form and must be taken daily to be effective. Vivitrol is a time-release formulation that is injected in the buttocks once a month.

Acamprosate (also known as Campral) is thought to stabilize the chemical balance of the brain that would otherwise be disrupted by alcoholism. Campral is thought to act on the brain pathways related to alcohol abuse in maintaining abstinence for a short period of time. While effective alone, it is often paired with other medication treatments like naltrexone with great success. Acamprosate reduces glutamate release.

Sodium oxybate is the sodium salt of gamma-hydroxybutyric acid (GHB). It is used for both acute alcohol withdrawal and medium to long-term detoxification. This drug enhances GABA neurotransmission and reduces glutamate levels. It is used in Italy in small amounts under the trade name Alcover.

Baclofen has been shown in animal studies and in small human studies to enhance detoxification. This drug acts as a GABA B receptor agonist and this may be beneficial.

Pharmacological Extinction

Pharmacological extinction is the use of opioid antagonists like naltrexone combined with normal drinking habits to eliminate the craving for alcohol. This technique is sometimes referred to as the Sinclair Method.

While standard naltrexone treatment uses the drug to curb craving and enforce abstinence, pharmacological extinction targets the endorphin-based neurological conditioning. Our behaviours become conditioned when our neurons are bathed in endorphins following that action. Conversely, we receive negative reinforcement when we perform that action and yet do not get our endorphins. By having the alcoholic go about their normal drinking habits (limited only by safety concerns), and while preventing the endorphins from being released by the alcohol, the pull to drink is eliminated over a period of about three months.

This allows an alcoholic to give up drinking as being sensibly unbeneficial. The effects persist after the drug is discontinued, but the addiction can return if the person drinks without first taking the drug. This treatment is also highly unusual in that it works better if the patient does not go through detoxification before starting it. Clinical studies have shown this treatment to allow 78-87% of inductees to reduce their drinking below levels dangerous to health, and allow 25% of inductees to achieve complete abstinence. Follow-up studies indicate an overall 50% relapse rate over five years, and 2% relapse rate for those who continue to take naltrexone before drinking.

There is a lot of professional resistance to this treatment for two reasons. Studies have demonstrated that controlled drinking for alcoholics was not a useful treatment technique. Other studies have also shown naltrexone to be of questionable value in supporting abstinence alone. The individual failure of these two separate treatments suggests that their use in combination is equally ineffective. This would be the case if the two treatments were merely additive, as for two people pushing a car. Experimental evidence indicates that the presence of naltrexone causes the drinking of alcohol to have a reverse effect on alcoholism, decreasing the alcoholic's attachment to alcohol consumption when they drink instead of increasing it.

Nutritional Therapy for Alcohol Addiction

Preventative treatment of alcohol complications includes long-term use of a multivitamin as well as such specific vitamins as B12 and folate.

While nutritional therapy is not a treatment of alcoholism itself, it treats the difficulties that can arise after years of heavy alcohol use. Many alcohol dependents have insulin resistance syndrome, a metabolic disorder where the body's difficulty in processing sugars causes an unsteady supply to the blood stream. While the disorder can be diminished by a hypoglycemic diet, this can affect behaviour and emotions, side-effects often seen among alcohol dependents in treatment. The metabolic aspects of such dependence are often overlooked, causing poor treatment outcomes.

Nicotine

Nicotine which is present in cigarette smoke is a highly addictive substance and is very difficult to break away from. There are people who state that they became addicted after their first cigarette although smoking experts tend to disprove this.

It may take only a few cigarettes for someone to become addicted to the 'high' experienced as nicotine affects every area of your body and brain.

Once you are addicted you find that your body craves more and more nicotine which is why there is no such thing as 'social smoking'. Your body adjusts to a certain level but then requires ever increasing amounts of this to satisfy the urges which mean that you smoke more and more cigarettes.

Whereas someone can enjoy a single drink but not feel as if they must increase this in order to experience the same level of enjoyment.

Smoking - Drug Addiction

Smoking is a popular activity for many people who continue to enjoy it even though they are well aware of the health risks.

The main reason for this is nicotine addiction. Tobacco contains nicotine - a stimulant which affects both the mind and the body. It increases heart rate and breathing and causes a surge of adrenaline which gives that 'buzz' that smokers enjoy.

Psychologically, it causes the smoker to feel relaxed as well as stimulated which is due to the production of a chemical called Dopamine. Dopamine is released into the blood stream which causes feelings of pleasure and well being.

Your body becomes accustomed to these effects and its tolerance increases. This means that you require larger amounts or in this case, smoke more cigarettes in order to have the same effects.

This is why it is very difficult to give up smoking.

What does it look like and how is it used?

The main ingredient is tobacco which is made from dried leaves of the tobacco plant. Tobacco contains nicotine which is responsible for people's addiction to smoking. It is an intensely powerful stimulant which many smokers find difficult to beat.

Tobacco is found in cigarettes, pipes and cigars and snuff (sniffed up the nose). There is a form of tobacco called 'chewing tobacco' which is also popular.

Lose tobacco is used in 'roll ups' and is often mixed with cannabis or a herbal mixture such as Spice then smoked as a 'joint'.

What is its street name?

Smoking is also known by the following names:

Ciggies

Fags

Smokes

Who smokes?

All sorts of people are smokers. Young people are attracted to smoking as they see it is a sign of being grown up or a statement of being cool and sophisticated. Others do it as a form of rebellion or to fit in with their peer group.

Smoking is also popular with adults, some of whom started when they were young and are still smoking well into middle age or older.

Effects of smoking

Smokers claim that it helps them to relax or gives them an energy boost or 'rush'. They argue that it relieves stress, increases concentration and in the case of women, reduces their appetite and helps them to lose weight.

This is why female smokers claim that stopping smoking would lead to weight gain. Hence this is one of the reasons why they continue to do so. It's as if the risks of smoking are preferable to putting on weight.

Many smokers find that the first time they smoke they feel sick, dizzy or get a headache.

Tobacco smoke contains nicotine, tar, carbon monoxide and other chemicals which when inhaled, increases heart rate, blood pressure and respiration. It causes a surge in energy which is due to the release of adrenaline. This causes that energy boost and also acts upon insulin production which smokers believe suppresses their appetite.

Other physical effects include a dry mouth, a decrease in urine production and dizziness.

Psychological effects include a feeling of relaxation and generally being in a good mood. Some smokers find that it calms their nerves or energizes them, especially if they smoke first thing in the morning.

Is it easy to become addicted to smoking?

Yes, very. Cigarette smoke contains a substance called nicotine which is extremely powerful and addictive. It is possible to become addicted after just smoking a few cigarettes.

What happens then is that you become used to the effects of smoking and experience cravings or unpleasant withdrawal symptoms when you don't. So, you light up again in order to prevent these symptoms.

Your mind and body develop a tolerance to the effects of nicotine which means that you need to smoke more and more cigarettes to get these effects as well as stopping any cravings. It can get to the point where you are constantly smoking throughout the day.

If you go for a certain period of time without a cigarette then you will find that you are anxious, restless and literally, 'gasping' for a smoke.

It is not the type of habit in which you can have the occasional cigarette. Most people find that they either smoke heavily or not at all.

The withdrawal symptoms include:

Mood swings

Irritability

Anxiety

Edginess

Constant hunger

Headaches

Poor concentration

Dizziness

Tiredness

Some people find that they generally feel unwell when not smoking.

What are the risks of smoking?

The risks are well documented and can be fatal. Smoking causes lung cancer, heart disease, bronchitis, poor circulation, reduces fertility (both men and women) and increases the risks of many other diseases.

These include:

Chronic Obstructive Pulmonary Disease (COPD)

Cancers of the nose, throat, kidney, pancreas, larynx, bladder and cervix.

Sexual problems such as impotence

Risk of infertility in both sexes

Ageing

Peripheral vascular disease (poor circulation)

Diabetes

Chest Infections

Hyperthyroidism

Age-related macular degeneration (AMD)

Osteoporosis

Dental problems such as gum disease

Asthma

There are particular problems for women who smoke during pregnancy which include risk of miscarriage, stillbirth, birth defects, low birth weight and poor development in the child.

If you have children there is the risk of them inhaling 'second hand smoke' which causes health problems such as asthma and ear, nose and throat infections. They may also go on to be smokers themselves when they are older.

Second hand smoke or 'passive smoking' is another issue which is open to debate. There are arguments for and against this but it is claimed that there are health risks from inhaling someone's cigarette smoke.

Smoking is expensive, stains your teeth and clothes, dulls your taste buds and sense of smell and overall, is considered socially unacceptable.

3.1 Drugs

This includes both 'hard' and 'soft' drugs, and examples of these include marijuana, ecstasy, crack cocaine and heroin. There are also hallucinogenic drugs such as LSD, solvents such as glue or 'poppers' and prescription drugs such as anti-depressants or tranquillisers.

Another category of drugs are they which are often used to improve athletic performance - anabolic steroids.

Drug Addiction

A neutral, uncritical approach

We are not here to pass judgment on anyone or to criticize a mode of behavior. An addiction can happen to anyone and it is a case of 'there but for the grace of god' in this situation. An addiction can develop from the most unlikely source or in someone you might have assumed is the last person on this earth to become dependent so a rational approach is called for here.

Types of addiction ...its not just drugs

There are numerous forms of addiction which include gambling, shopping, coffee and computer usage.

Drug addiction is a major problem which is caused by a variety of factors. Heroin, cocaine, cannabis and ecstasy, these are just a few of the many substances which are misused on a regular basis. These are also the substances which have a high profile and seen as a contributor to many of the problems in the society today.

But there are other less obvious forms of drug addiction, for example 'legal drugs' such as alcohol, cigarettes and caffeine. These are used by many people on a recreational basis and in the case of alcohol and caffeine are seen as socially acceptable.

Yet they can have far reaching effects. Misuse can cause serious, long term damage both mentally and physically, not to mention the social and emotional consequences as well.

Drug Addiction is a Major Problem

This is one of the major forms of addiction which causes untold misery to many people. It doesn't just affect the addict: it also encompasses their families, friends, colleagues and the authorities.

All drugs have their problems- whether they are classed as 'hard' drugs or 'soft' drugs but addiction can be broken-as long as the addict wants to give up.

And that's the most difficult part. There are many drug addicts who either deny that they have an addiction, hide the signs of it or flatly refuse to get any help. As with any addiction the first step is usually the most important: this is recognizing that you have an addiction and want to do something about it.

It is easy to feel embarrassed or ashamed about your habit but don't be. Many people are in the same position as you and feel the same way but it can be beaten.

This means going into 'rehab' for a drug treatment Programme and attending support groups and/or networks. Very few people can beat their addiction on their own so help and support from family and friends is vital.

It takes a great deal of willpower, determination and persistence to break a drug addiction. Many people suffer from relapses and several sessions of treatment are required before they can be said to have 'kicked their habit'.

Learning more about these types of drugs can help you to better understand your addiction and how it might be dealt with.

Drug addiction affects us all

Sad but true. Most if not all of us have come into contact with drugs or know someone who takes drugs. Many drugs are easy to obtain - legally or illegally and a habit can start from what might be considered an unlikely source e.g. prescription drugs.

Drug addiction can start for a variety of reasons which include experimentation, escapism, and dependency on prescription drugs or a need to relax. It can also develop from a desire to 'fit in' either at work or school or from doing competitive sport.

What is important to remember is that it is a highly complex condition which occurs for a variety of reasons with no easy ways of dealing with it.

Why are drugs so addictive?

Drug addicts are controlled by their habit. Everything they do is geared towards satisfying their need. This need is uncontrollable which often leads addicts to turn to crime to pay for their habit

Addicts will persist in taking drugs even though they are fully aware of the consequences.

But why you might be asking? Why continue to take something which could kill you? Also why is it so difficult to give up?

The answer to these is that drugs have a dramatic impact upon your physical and mental health. They alter the structure and function of the brain to the extent that it behaves in an irrational and unpredictable manner. Concentration, judgement, rational thinking, empathy and self-discipline are all affected and these plus other changes are what cause the cravings and desire for drugs impossible to resist.

The problem is that the first few times you take a drug there appears to be no ill-effects. You find that it is a pleasurable experience and something you are likely to repeat.

However there are some drugs which can cause an addiction the first time they are taken. But what happens is that as you take the drug over time your body becomes used to it. It develops a tolerance and you require larger doses in order to feel the same effects. If you don't then withdrawal symptoms occur and these are so unpleasant that you take more drugs to ease them. You feel as if you can't cope without the drug or that life is too difficult to manage unless you have your fix.

The effects of drug addiction

Each drug affects a person in a particular way so the effects of heroin will differ from solvents or amphetamines. But the one thing that is common to them all is the power to change the chemistry of the brain so that it develops uncontrollable cravings for that drug.

Your addiction will mean more to you than your partner/spouse, family, friends, career and even your health.

So why take drugs?

There is no simple answer to this. Some people start by experimenting with friends whilst still at school. Others started when they attended a party or socialised with colleagues after work.

Others developed an addiction to prescription drugs over a period of time.

There are people who use drugs in order to boost their confidence and self-esteem. Others use them to relax or wind down at the end of a stressful week.

There is also the fact that some people appear to be vulnerable to drug addiction. They have what is called an 'addictive personality' and find it difficult to resist the temptation.

Signs of Drug Addiction

Each drug has its own physical and psychological effects but the signs of addiction are usually the same whatever the substance.

Drug addiction can be a process in which you start with casual drug use which leads to dependency and finally addiction. The problem here is that when you have reached the stage of dependency then you may also be at that point in which self-denial has set in. You may not be aware of the hold that drug has over you or the damage it is doing to you and others around you.

Common indicators of drug dependency and/or addiction include:

Have developed a tolerance to the drug so require ever increasing amounts to feel the same effects.

Have started to neglect or evade your responsibilities to your family, work colleagues or your boss.

Taking a drug in a dangerous situation such as combining it with another substance or using a dirty needle.

Withdrawing from your family and friends. Acting in a secretive manner or being mysterious about any new friends you have acquired.

Stealing or lying to others. Committing crime to pay for your addiction.

Giving up all your hobbies, sports, interests etc as a result of your addiction.

Losing control of your drug addiction.

Spending every minute of the day thinking about drugs and your addiction.

Continuing to use drugs even though you are suffering from ill effects such as blackouts or even an overdose.

Any drug has the potential to be abused even something relatively innocuous as sleeping pills.

Physical Signs of Drug Addiction

Drug addicts will often try and hide the signs of their habit, for example by wearing a long sleeved top to hide needle tracks on their arms, even on a hot day.

But if you are concerned then look for the following:

Sudden, unexplained weight loss

Bloodshot eyes

Dilated pupils or black rimmed eyes

Spots around the nose and mouth

Pale skin

Facial skin in a poor condition (spots, blotches etc)

Shakes

Loss of appetite

Unkempt appearance

Needle marks on arms and legs

Psychological signs of drug addiction

There are also psychological indicators of drug addiction which include:

Paranoia

Secretive behavior

Mood swings

Outbursts

Irritability

Extremes of behavior ('highs' and 'lows')

Anxiety

Depression

Agitation

Change in personality

There are also social aspects to this as well which include poor performance at work or school; stealing money from family or friends or begging for money; furtive behavior; getting into trouble with the police and dropping old friends, hobbies and interests.

If you are the parent of a teenager then it can be even harder to detect if he/she is taking drugs as some of the social indicators of addiction could be normal teenage behavior.

No-one likes to think of themselves as a drug addict as the picture it conjures up is not a pleasant one. Drug addicts are not seen in a favorable light in our society and generally public opinion is negative towards them.

With this in mind it is very easy to deny that you have a problem or may have become an addict. Plus there is the fact that you may find it difficult to believe that you have developed an addiction so it must be a sign of a weakness in your character or that you are a 'bad' person.

Added to this is the fact that you cannot break your habit.

If you suspect that you may have a problem with drugs then ask yourself any of the following:

Do you lie about your drug addiction to other people?

Do you feel a sense of guilt or shame about your drug addiction?

Do you take drugs to cope with everyday life, to reduce stress or to relax?

Do you feel helpless or unable to stop taking drugs?

Have you ever committed a crime to pay for addiction?

Have you spent money you cannot afford on your drug habit?

Have you used more than one drug?

If you find that you have answered 'yes' to more than one of these questions then that suggests that you may have a problem. It also means that you are prepared to face up to your addiction which is far harder than people realize.

However you need to talk about this with someone you can trust, for example your GP or contact a drugs helpline.

Help with drug addiction

To start with it's important to enlist the help and support of family and friends rather than try to go it alone. Trying to break an addiction on willpower alone is extremely difficult and only a few people can manage to do so.

You are better seeking help via a drug treatment Programme or go for counseling.

This also means that you have to make changes, such as your lifestyle, circle of friends, environment and your own behavior. That can mean changing the way you deal with a problem or stress, or in the way you interact with other people.

In order for you to succeed in beating this addiction, it means making changes on a permanent basis. If you are concerned about drug addiction then this section contains individual pages which cover each drug in turn, what it does, the effects and the consequences. It is important to note that no two people are affected in the same way by taking the same drug. There are other factors involved which need to be taken into account, such as sex, age, height, genetics etc.

List of Addiction Forming Drugs

Amphetamines

Anabolic Steroids

Barbiturates

Cannabis

Codeine

Cocaine

Ecstasy

Gammahydroxybutrate

Hallucinogens

Heroin

Ketamine

'Legal high' drugs

Marijuana

Methadone

Morphine

Prescription drugs

Solvents

Tranquilisers

Amphetamines

These drugs act as a stimulant on the body and are designed to increase energy. They also enable you to stay awake and alert.

They are either inhaled (snorted), smoked, taken as pills or injected.

Anabolic Steroids

A synthetic derivative of the male hormone testosterone: these drugs are popular with bodybuilders and athletes who use them to build muscle mass and strength.

Street names include 'roids' and 'gear'.

These drugs can be injected or taken as pills.

Barbiturates

These drugs were routinely prescribed to treat anxiety, depression and insomnia. But this has been largely curtailed due to the risk of an accidental overdose. They are only prescribed, if at all, for severe insomnia.

Street names include 'barbies', 'blue devils' and 'blue bullets'.

They are usually taken as pills or injected.

Cannabis

A naturally occurring drug (cannabis plant), that is also known as marijuana. It is usually mixed with loose tobacco to form a cigarette ('joint') or smoked through a pipe ('bong'.

Some people choose to mix it with food or add it to drinks

Codeine

Many popular forms of painkillers contain codeine - a type of opiate which is used in these medications to help relieve pain. This opiate is found in the seed pod of the poppy although other opiates are synthetically produced. They come in a variety of forms such as pills, capsules, suppositories and syrups.

Cocaine

This stimulant increases energy and alertness as well as giving a feeling of euphoria ('high'). It increases heart rate, breathing and body temperature and makes the user feel more confident and assured.

It takes the form of a white powder which can be inhaled (sniffed) or injected. It can also be made into a solid rock called 'crack' which is then smoked or prepared for injecting. Cocaine can also be mixed with other drugs, e.g. heroin. '.

Ecstasy

A popular drug often used by clubbers in order to be able to dance for hours on end. It became the drug of choice during the 'acid house' scene of the 1990's.

It is artificially produced in laboratories and is usually a combination of other drugs as well.

It comes in tablet form although the powder form is increasingly being used. This powder is either inhaled (snorted) or in a few rare cases, prepared for injecting.

Gammahydroxybutrate (GHB)

This is a synthetic chemical, available in liquid form which is often found in paint strippers and stain removers. It comes in small bottles or capsules and when consumed using a teaspoon, causes euphoria and uninhibited behaviour.

This is a high risk drug which is even more dangerous if combined with other substances such as alcohol or other recreational drugs.

Hallucinogens

These types of drugs are often referred to as 'psychedelic drugs' and affect the senses in a variety of ways. People who use these drugs report that they are able to see, smell, hear or touch things which in reality, don't exist.

They can have a good experience - a 'good trip' or an unpleasant one - a 'bad trip'.

Some hallucinogens come in natural plant forms whereas others are produced artificially in laboratories.

Heroin

This is another opiate, produced from morphine (derived from poppies) which was originally designed as a painkiller. However this highly addictive Class A drug is used by all sorts of people.

Pure heroin comes as a white powder but other versions are sold on the street, e.g. brown as many of these are mixed or 'cut' with other substances.

It can be inhaled, smoked, snorted or injected. Injecting is the most popular form of use as this tends to give an instant 'hit'.

Ketamine

This hallucinogenic drug was originally designed for veterinary purposes, mainly as an anaesthetic during animal surgery but has been appropriated for recreational use in clubs.

It comes in liquid form although a powder is also available and can be injected, added to drinks or smoked with tobacco. It causes intense hallucinations and feelings of weightlessness.

It can also act as a sedative and has been referred to recently as a 'date rape' drug.

Street names include 'special K', 'vitamin K' and 'K'.

'Legal High' drugs

The term 'legal high' refers to drugs which are legally available for personal use. These drugs cause users to experience a 'high' in the same way as taking an illegal drug. Examples of these drugs include herbal smoking mixtures e.g. 'Spice', caffeine powders, salvia and mephedrone.

However, many of these drugs have been banned (or are about to be banned) as they have a range of dangerous side effects which in some cases have proven to be fatal.

Methadone

This is a drug from the opiates family which is commonly used to treat heroin withdrawal symptoms. But people who use this can develop a tolerance to it which means that they require increased amounts to achieve the same effect.

Methadone acts as a sedative and causes users to feel safe and relaxed. It also reduces anxiety. It is usually available in liquid form although it can be taken as a tablet or injected.

Morphine

This is another drug from the opiates family which is designed to ease chronic or acute pain. However it is a highly addictive substance which affects both the mind and body and is comparable to heroin.

People can become addicted to morphine very quickly and because of this, it is very difficult to break this addiction. This drug has the highest rate of relapse than any others.

Morphine can be injected or taken orally.

Prescription Drugs

These include drugs such as anti-depressants, tranquilisers and sleeping pills. These drugs are prescribed to treat a range of conditions such as anxiety, depression, ADHD and insomnia. They are successful at doing so but it is easy to develop a tolerance to these drugs which can result in dependence.

Solvents

This group includes lighter fuels, glue, aerosols, dry cleaning fluids and air fresheners. They are easy to obtain and use but were designed for everyday use and not as recreational drugs.

Their accessibility means that they are popular with children and young people who find that they can experience an instant 'buzz' from them.

These substances are inhaled, sniffed or directly squirted into the back of the throat.

Background to Drug Addiction

There are people who appear to have 'addictive personalities' in that they are particularly susceptible to developing an addiction. They have behavior traits which appear to predispose them towards dependency. The issue here is whether this can be used as an explanation for an addiction or whether it is a convenient excuse for personal actions and behavior?

Deciding whether someone has an addiction or not involves a variety of factors such as genetic predisposition, their environment; their response to external triggers, e.g. stress and their relationship with family and friends.

Teenagers and young people like to experiment with drugs and other substances for several reasons which include peer pressure, home environment or as a form of rebellion.

However it's important that these are dealt with when they are still young as they may lead to a lifelong dependency.

Once an addiction has been diagnosed then the next step is treating that addiction. This has to start with awareness on the part of the person concerned that they have an addiction and want to beat that addiction. There is help available to do so which includes support groups, counseling, rehabilitation, detoxification and drug control therapies.

3.2 Prescription Dug Abuse

Introduction

Prescription drug abuse means taking a prescription medication that is not prescribed for you, or taking it for reasons or in dosages other than as prescribed. Abuse of prescription drugs can produce serious health effects, including addiction. Commonly abused classes of prescription medications include opioids (for pain), central nervous system depressants (for anxiety and sleep disorders), and stimulants. Opioids include hydrocodone, oxycodone, propoxyphene, hydromorphone, meperidine and diphenoxylate. Central nervous system depressants include barbiturates such as pentobarbital sodium and benzodiazepines such as diazepam and alprazolam, Stimulants include dextroamphetamine and methylphenidate.

Long-term use of opioids or central nervous system depressants can lead to physical dependence and addiction. Opioids can produce drowsiness, constipation and, depending on amount taken, can depress breathing. Central nervous system depressants slow down brain function; if combined with other medications that cause drowsiness or with alcohol, heart rate and respiration can slow down dangerously. Taken repeatedly or in high doses, stimulants can cause anxiety, paranoia, dangerously high body temperatures, irregular heartbeat, or seizures.

Painkillers

Painkillers are drugs commonly prescribed for pain and are only legally available by prescription.

Painkiller abuse can be dangerous, even deadly, with too high a dose or when taken with other drugs, like alcohol. Short-term effects of painkiller abuse may include lack of energy, inability to concentrate, nausea and vomiting, and apathy. Significant doses of painkillers can cause breathing problems. When abused, painkillers can be addictive.

Depressants

Depressants, or downers, are prescribed to treat a variety of health conditions including anxiety and panic attacks, tension, severe stress reactions, and sleep disorders. Also referred to as sedatives and tranquilizers, depressants can slow normal brain function.

Health risks related to ***depressant abuse*** include loss of coordination, respiratory depression, dizziness due to lowered blood pressure, slurred speech, poor concentration, feelings of confusion, and in extreme cases, coma and possible death.

Stimulants

Stimulants, or uppers, are most commonly prescribed for attention deficit/hyperactivity disorder (ADHD), but they are also used to treat a variety of conditions such as asthma, respiratory problems, obesity, and sleep disorders such as narcolepsy. When taken in higher doses, these drugs can produce euphoric effects and counteract sluggish feelings.

Health risks related to ***stimulant abuse*** include increased heart and respiratory rates, excessive sweating, vomiting, tremors, anxiety, hostility and aggression, and in severe abuse, suicidal/homicidal tendencies, convulsions, and cardiovascular collapse

Steroids are used to medically treat people with abnormally low testosterone levels or symptoms of body wasting, as is the case with cancer patients

Abuse of steroids is often related to physical appearance, such as a desire to build muscle or change body shape.

While health effects vary by individual, they can include liver cysts and cancer, kidney cancer, jaundice, severe acne, and hair loss.

The History of Prescription Drug abuse

Drug abuse is as old as the use of medications to cure illnesses. But it was the 19th century that brought about the modern issues of prescription drug abuse. At first a totally unregulated industry, prescription medications became tightly controlled by the government. Despite this, the incidences of prescription drug abuse are on the rise.

Unregulated

In the 19th century, active substances in drugs were first extracted. These included morphine, laudanum and cocaine. The sale and use of the drugs was largely unregulated by the law. Physicians were not aware of their addictive properties and prescribed them liberally for all types of ailments. They were available for sale by traveling vendors, in drugstores and through mail order. The easy access and lack of knowledge quickly led to rampant drug addiction. Sigmund Freud treated many who were addicted to cocaine, a drug that was first used as a local anesthetic during surgery.

Civil War

The Civil War brought widespread use of morphine; those wounded in battle were often prescribed the drug for pain management. Veterans of the war returned home with an addiction along with their drug of choice and hypodermic needles for its delivery. At the same time, cocaine and heroin were readily available without a prescription and were used as treatments for all types of illness. The use of opium as a recreational drug began to flourish, and by the early 20th century, according to the National Drug and Alcohol Abuse Hotline, the United States had upwards of 250,000 addicts.

Late 19th Century

With the end of the 19th century came recognition of the issue of drug addiction. In 1875, the first laws against drug abuse were passed, and opium dens were outlawed. In 1906, the Pure Food and Drug Act was passed; it required that medications containing opium and other narcotics be properly labeled. In 1914, the Harrison Narcotic Act was passed; it required the sale of larger doses of narcotics be made only by licensed physicians or pharmacists.

Early 20th Century

By the 1930s, states began requiring schools to provide anti-drug education to students. However, fear that education would lead to students trying drugs caused most of these early anti-drug programs to be stopped. The U.S. wasn't the only country to struggle with addiction to newly developed *pr*escription drugs. According to the National Drug and Alcohol Abuse Hotline, in 1928 it was estimated that one in every 100 German physicians was addicted to morphine. By 1938, in the United States, 25,000 physicians had been charged with narcotics crimes under the provisions of the Harrison Act, and 3,000 had served time in prison.

Early 21st Century

The use of prescription *pain* relievers,stimulants, sedatives and tranquilizers in an abusive manner continues. Current trends show younger people, including teenagers, are becoming addicted to these prescription medications, as well as elderly patients. According to the National Institute on Drug Abuse, the number of people abusing prescription drugs increased from just fewer than 600,000 in 1990 to 2.5 million in 2000. According to the Drug Enforcement Administration, the street value of prescription drugs sold illegally is likely greater than that from the sale of heroin and marijuana combined

Signs, Symptoms, and Help for Drug Problems and Substance Abuse

Addiction is a complex disorder characterized by compulsive drug use. People who are addicted feel an overwhelming, uncontrollable need for drugs or alcohol, even in the face of negative consequences. This self-destructive behavior can be hard to understand. Why continue doing something that's hurting you? Why is it so hard to stop?

The answer lies in the brain. Repeated drug use alters the brain—causing long-lasting changes to the way it looks and functions. These brain changes interfere with your ability to think clearly, exercise good judgment, control your behavior, and feel normal without drugs. These changes are also responsible, in large part, for the drug cravings and compulsion to use that make addiction so powerful.

How addiction develops

The path to drug addiction starts with experimentation. You or your loved one may have tried drugs out of curiosity, because friends were doing it, or in an effort to erase another problem. At first, the substance seems to solve the problem or make life better, so you use the drug more and more.

But as the addiction progresses, getting and using the drug becomes more and more important and your ability to stop using is compromised. What begins as a voluntary choice turns into a physical and psychological need. The good news is that drug addiction is treatable. With treatment and support, you can counteract the disruptive effects of addiction and regain control of your life.

Myths about Drug Addiction and Substance Abuse

MYTH 1: Overcoming addiction is a simply a matter of willpower. You can stop using drugs if you really want to. Prolonged exposure to drugs alters the brain in ways that result in powerful cravings and a compulsion to use. These brain changes make it extremely difficult to quit by sheer force of will.

MYTH 2: Addiction is a disease; there's nothing you can do about it. Most experts agree that addiction is a brain disease, but that doesn't mean you're a helpless victim. The brain changes associated with addiction can be treated and reversed through therapy, medication, exercise, and other treatments

MYTH 3: Addicts have to hit rock bottom before they can get better. Recovery can begin at any point in the addiction process—and the earlier, the better. The longer drug abuse continues, the stronger the addiction becomes and the harder it is to treat. Don't wait to intervene until the addict has lost it all.

MYTH 4: You can't force someone into treatment; they have to want help. Treatment doesn't have to be voluntary to be successful. People who are pressured into treatment by their family, employer, or the legal system are just as likely to benefit as those who choose to enter treatment on their own. As they sober up and their thinking clears, many formerly resistant addicts decide they want to change.

MYTH 5: Treatment didn't work before, so there's no point trying again; some cases are hopeless. Recovery from drug addiction is a long process that often involves setbacks. Relapse doesn't mean that treatment has failed or that you're a lost cause. Rather, it's a signal to get back on track, either by going back to treatment or adjusting the treatment approach.

The far-reaching effects of drug abuse and drug addiction

While each drug of abuse produces different physical effects, all abused substances share one thing in common. They hijack the brain's normal "reward" pathways and alter the areas of the brain responsible for self-control, judgment, emotional regulation, motivation, memory, and learning.

Whether you're addicted to nicotine, alcohol, heroin, Xanax, speed, or Vicodin, the effect on the brain is the same: an uncontrollable craving to use that is more important than anything else, including family, friends, career, and even your own health and happiness.

Using drugs as an escape: A short-term fix with long-term consequences

Many people use drugs in order to escape physical and emotional discomfort. Maybe you started drinking to numb feelings of depression, smoking pot to deal with stress at home or school, relying on cocaine to boost your energy and confidence, using sleeping pills to cope with panic attacks, or taking prescription painkillers to relieve chronic back pain.

But while drugs might make you feel better in the short-term, attempts to self-medicate ultimately backfire. Instead of treating the underlying problem, drug use simply masks the symptoms. Take the drug away and the problem is still there, whether it be low self-esteem, anxiety, loneliness, or an unhappy family life. Furthermore, prolonged drug use eventually brings its own host of problems, including major disruptions to normal, daily functioning. Unfortunately, the psychological, physical, and social consequences of drug abuse and addiction become worse than the original problem you were trying to cope with or avoid.

Why do some drug users become addicted, while others don't?

As with many other conditions and diseases, vulnerability to addiction differs from person to person. Your genes, age when you started taking drugs, and family and social environment all play a role in addiction. Risk factors that increase your vulnerability include:

- Family history of addiction
- Abuse, neglect, or other traumatic experiences in childhood
- Mental disorders such as depression and anxiety
- Early use of drugs

Signs and symptoms of drug abuse and drug addiction

Although different drugs have different physical effects, the symptoms of addiction are the same no matter the substance. The more drugs begin to affect and control your life, the more likely it is that you've crossed the line from drug use to abuse and drug addiction. Unfortunately, when you're in the middle of it, you may be in denial about the magnitude of the problem or the negative impact it's had on your life. See if you recognize yourself in the following signs and symptoms of substance abuse and addiction. If so, consider talking to someone about your drug use. You're on a dangerous road, and the sooner you get help, the better.

Common signs and symptoms of drug abuse

- **You're neglecting your responsibilities** at school, work, or home (e.g. flunking classes, skipping work, neglecting your children) because of your drug use.
- **You're using drugs under dangerous conditions or taking risks while high**, such as driving while on drugs, using dirty needles, or having unprotected sex.
- **Your drug use is getting you into legal trouble,** such as arrests for disorderly conduct, driving under the influence, or stealing to support a drug habit.
- **Your drug use is causing problems in your relationships,** such as fights with your partner or family members, an unhappy boss, or the loss of old friends.

Common signs and symptoms of drug addiction

- **You've built up a drug tolerance.** You need to use more of the drug to experience the same effects you used to with smaller amounts.
- **You take drugs to avoid or relieve withdrawal symptoms.** If you go too long without drugs, you experience symptoms such as nausea, restlessness, insomnia, depression, sweating, shaking, and anxiety.
- **You've lost control over your drug use.** You often do drugs or use more than you planned, even though you told yourself you wouldn't. You may want to stop using, but you feel powerless.
- **Your life revolves around drug use.** You spend a lot of time using and thinking about drugs, figuring out how to get them, and recovering from the drug's effects.
- **You've abandoned activities you used to enjoy,** such as hobbies, sports, and socializing, because of your drug use.
- **You continue to use drugs, despite knowing it's hurting you.** It's causing major problems in your life—blackouts, infections, mood swings, depression, paranoia—but you use anyway.

What drugs are most commonly abused and what are the signs and symptoms?

Almost all drugs have the potential for addiction and abuse, from caffeine to prescription medication. However, the majority of non-alcohol related addictions are due to a short list of drugs including sleeping pills, painkillers, cocaine, marijuana, methamphetamine, and heroin.

Physical warning signs of drug abuse

- Bloodshot eyes or pupils that are larger or smaller than usual.
- Changes in appetite or sleep patterns. Sudden weight loss or weight gain.
- Deterioration of physical appearance and personal grooming habits.
- Unusual smells on breath, body, or clothing.
- Tremors, slurred speech, or impaired coordination.

Behavioral signs of drug abuse

- Drop in attendance and performance at work or school.
- Unexplained need for money or financial problems. May borrow or steal to get it.
- Engaging in secretive or suspicious behaviors.
- Sudden change in friends, favorite hangouts, and hobbies.
- Frequently getting into trouble (fights, accidents, illegal activities).

Psychological warning signs of drug abuse

- Unexplained change in personality or attitude.
- Sudden mood swings, irritability, or angry outbursts.
- Periods of unusual hyperactivity, agitation, or giddiness.
- Lack of motivation; appears lethargic or "spaced out."
- Appears fearful, anxious, or paranoid, with no reason.

Warning Signs of Teen Drug Use

There are many warning signs of drug use and abuse in teenagers. The challenge for parents is to distinguish between the normal, sometimes volatile, ups and downs of the teen years and the red flags of substance abuse.

- Being secretive about friends, possessions, and activities.

- New interest in clothing, music, and other items that highlight drug use.
- Demanding more privacy; locking doors; avoiding eye contact; sneaking around.
- Skipping class; declining grades; suddenly getting into trouble at school.
- Missing money, valuables, or prescriptions.
- Acting uncharacteristically isolated, withdrawn, or depressed.
- Using incense, perfume, or air freshener to hide the smell of smoke or drugs.
- Using eyedrops to mask bloodshot eyes or dilated pupils.

Drug addiction and Denial

One of the most dangerous effects of drug abuse and addiction is denial. The urge to use is so strong that the mind finds many ways to rationalize the addiction. You may drastically underestimate the quantity of drugs you're taking, how much it impacts your life, and the level of control you have over your drug use.

Denial is an unconscious defense mechanism. Minimizing and rationalizing the addiction is less scary than admitting that your drug use is dangerously out of control. But the cost of denial can be extremely high—including the loss of important relationships, your job, financial security, and your physical and mental health.

Do you have a substance abuse problem?

- Do you feel like you can't stop, even if you wanted to?
- Do you ever feel bad or guilty about your drug use?
- Do you need to use drugs to relax or feel better?
- Do your friends or family members complain or worry about your drug use?
- Do you hide or lie about your drug use?
- Have you ever done anything illegal in order to obtain drugs?
- Do you spend money on drugs that you really can't afford?
- Do you ever use more than one recreational drug at a time?

Support is essential to addiction recovery

Don't try to go it alone; it's all too easy to get discouraged and rationalize "just one more" hit or pill. Whether you choose to go to rehab, rely on self-help programs, get therapy, or take a self-directed treatment approach, support is essential. Recovering from drug addiction is much easier when you have people you can lean on for encouragement, comfort, and guidance.

Support can come from:

- family members
- close friends
- therapists or counselors
- other recovering addicts
- healthcare providers
- people from your faith community

Recovering from drug addiction

Addiction is a complex problem that affects every aspect of your life. Overcoming it requires making major changes to the way you live, deal with problems, and relate to others. It's not just a matter of willpower or simply wanting to quit. Getting off drugs for good is difficult without treatment and ongoing support. The good news is that there are many tools that can help you on your journey to sobriety.

If you suspect that a friend or family member has a drug problem, here are a few things you can do:

- **Speak up.** Talk to the person about your concerns, and offer your help and support. The earlier addiction is treated, the better. Don't wait for your loved one to hit bottom! Be prepared for excuses and denial with specific examples of behavior that has you worried.
- **Take care of yourself**. Don't get so caught up in someone else's drug problem that you neglect your own needs. Make sure you have people you can talk to and lean on for support. And stay safe. Don't put yourself in dangerous situations.
- **Don't cover for the drug user**. Don't make excuses or try to hide the problem. It's natural to want to help a loved one in need, but protecting them from the negative consequences of their choices may keep them from getting the help they need.
- **Avoid self-blame**. You can support a person with a substance abuse problem and encourage treatment, but you can't force an addict to change. You can't control your loved one's decisions. Let the person accept responsibility for his or her actions, an essential step along the way to recovery for drug addiction.

3.3 Behavioral Pharmacy

With the emergence of clinical pharmacy in the late 1960s ,the role of pharmacist has expanded to include other functions like monitoring , of patients on medications for chronic disorders , pharmacokinetic consultation , drug information dissemination to health professionals and patients , consultation with physicians on therapeutic decisions in hospitals , nursing homes , clinics and community settings , teaching drug therapy and monitoring health professionals , counseling patients on medication and health management in institutional and community settings and working with other members of health care teams to increase the overall quality of healthcare.

The above expanded roles require that the pharmacist becomes 1. A drug expert and 2. Communicates with patients and health professionals. To carry out these new roles pharmacists require knowledge of new technical information on drugs and their effect on the body and also an understanding of the social , political and economic contexts of pharmaceutical care within the broader health care system.

As these new functions require identification of problems and solutions to them and also professional interactions with patients and other health professionals , some basic social / behavioral skills are also required e.g. 1) .the ability to understand human behavior , thoughts , feelings , beliefs and values. 2).To identify and solve problems of human and organizational systems and 3). To communicate effectively

The pharmacist is now expected to think beyond the concepts, principles and theories of natural science and be prepared to know, understand, analyze, synthesize, evaluate and apply concepts, principles and theories of the social, behavioral sciences to the practice of pharmacy.

Compliance and adherence to medications

In medicine, **compliance** (also **adherence** or **concordance**) describes the degree to which a patient correctly follows medical advice. Most commonly, it refers to medication or drug compliance, but may also mean use of medical appliances such as compression stockings, chronic wound care, self-directed physiotherapy exercises, or attending counseling or other courses of therapy. Both the patient and the health-care provider affect compliance, and a positive physician-patient relationship is the most important factor in improving compliance although the high cost of prescription medication also plays a major role

Non-compliance is a major obstacle to the effective delivery of health care. Estimates from the World Health Organization *i*ndicate that only about 50% of patients with chronic diseases living in developed countries follow treatment recommendations. In particular, low rates of adherence to therapies for asthma, diabetes, and hypertension are thought to contribute substantially to the human and economic burden of those conditions. Compliance rates may be overestimated in the medical literature, as compliance is often high in the setting of a formal clinical trial but drops off in a "real-world" setting.

Major barriers to compliance are thought to include the complexity of modern medication regimens, poor "health literacy" and lack of comprehension of treatment benefits, the occurrence of undiscussed side effects, the cost of prescription medicine, and poor communication or lack of trust between the patient and his or her health-care provider. Efforts to improve compliance have been aimed at simplifying medication packaging, providing effective medication reminders, improving patient education, and limiting the number of medications prescribed simultaneously

An estimated half of those for whom treatment regimens are prescribed do not follow them as directed Until recently, this was termed "non-compliance", which was sometimes regarded as meaning that not following the directions for treatment was due to irrational behavior or willful ignoring of instructions. Today, health care professionals more commonly use the terms "**adherence**" to or "**concordance**" with a regimen rather than "**compliance**", because these terms are thought to more accurately reflect the diverse reasons for patients not following treatment directions in part or in full. However, the preferred terminology remains a matter of debate. In some cases, concordance is used to refer specifically to patient adherence to a treatment regimen that is designed collaboratively by the patient and physician, to differentiate it from adherence to a physician only prescribed treatment regimen.

Concordance also refers to a initiative to involve the patient in the treatment process to improve compliance.In this context, the patient is informed about their condition and treatment options. They are involved with the treatment team in the decision as to which course of action to take, and partially responsible for monitoring and reporting back to the team. Compliance with treatment is improved by:

- Only recommending treatments that are effective in circumstances when they are required
- Selecting treatments with lower levels of side effect or fewer concerns for long-term use
- Prescribing the minimum number of different medications, e.g., prescribing a single antibiotic that addresses two concurrent infections (though risking contributing to antibiotic resistant species development)
- Simplifying dosage regimen by selecting a different drug or using a sustained release preparation that needs fewer doses during the day.
- Discussing possible side effects, and whether it is important to continue medication regardless of those effects
- Advice on minimizing or coping with side effects, e.g., whether to take a particular drug on an empty stomach or with food
- Developing trust so patients don't fear embarrassment or anger if unable to take a particular drug, allowing the doctor to try a better tolerated alternative

Societal Impact

A WHO study estimates that only 50% of patients suffering from chronic diseases in developed countries follow treatment recommendations. This may affect patient health, and affect the wider society when it causes complications from chronic diseases, formation of resistant infections, or untreated psychiatric illness. Compliance rates during closely monitored studies are usually far higher than in later real-world situations. For example, one study reported a 97% compliance rate at the beginning of treatment with statins, but only about 50% of patients were still compliant after six months

Compliance issues

Prescription Fill Rates

While a health care provider visit with a patient may result in a the patient leaving with a prescription for medication, not all patients will fill the prescription at a pharmacy. In india, 20-30% of prescriptions are never filled at the pharmacy. There are many reasons patients do not fill prescriptions including the cost of the medication, doubting the need for medication, or preference for self-care measures other than medication. Cost is the most significant barrier to prescription drug adherence. An Indian nationwide survey of 1,010 adults in 2001 found that 22% chose not to fill prescriptions because of the price, which is similar to the 20-30% overall rate of unfilled prescriptions.

Course completion

Once started, patients seldom follow treatment regimens as directed, and seldom complete the course of treatment.Cost and poor understanding of the directions for the treatment (referred to as 'health literacy') are major barriers to completing treatments. As mentioend previously, the World Health Organization (WHO) has estimates that only 50% of people complete long-term therapy for chronic illnesses as they were prescribed, which puts patient health at risk.

A wide variety of packaging approaches have been proposed to help patient's complete prescribed treatments. These approaches include formats that increase the ease of remembering the dosage regimen as well as different labels for increasing patient understanding of directions. For example, medications are sometimes packed with reminder systems for the day and/or time of the week to take the medicine

The failure to complete treatment regimens as prescribed has significant negative health impacts world wide Examples of the rate and consequences of non-compliance for selected medical disorders is as follows:

- Diabetes non-compliance is the principal cause of complications related to diabetes including nerve damage and kidney failure
- Hypertension non-compliance is the main cause of uncontrolled hypertension-associated heart attack and stroke
- Asthma non-compliance increase the risk of severe asthma attacks requiring hospitalization

Pharmacoeconomics refers to the scientific discipline that compares the value of one pharmaceutical drug or drug therapy to another. It is a sub-discipline of Health economics. A pharmacoeconomic study evaluates the cost (expressed in monetary terms) and effects (expressed in terms of monetary value, efficacy or enhanced quality of life) of a pharmaceutical product. We can distinguish several types of pharmacoeconomic evaluation:cost-minimization analysis, cost-benefit analysis, cost-effectiveness analysis and cost-utility analysis. Pharmacoeconomic studies serve to guide optimal healthcare resource allocation, in a standardized and scientifically grounded manner.

One important consideration in a pharmacoeconomic evaluation is to decide the perspective from which the analysis should be conducted (such as institutional or societal).

Cost-minimization is the simplest of the pharmacoeconomics tools and is applied when comparing two drugs of equal efficacy and equal tolerability

Therapeutic equivalence must be referenced by the author conducting the study and should have been done prior to the cost-minimization work. Since equal efficacy and equal tolerability is already demonstrated, there is no requirement to find a common efficacy denominator as would be the case when conducting a cost-effectiveness study. The author is not precluded from doing so through the use of "cost/cure" or "cost/year of life gained". If efficacy and tolerability is demonstrated, however, then a simple comparison of "cost/course of treatment" can suffice for the purpose of comparing two or more therapeutically equivalent treatment alternatives.

However when doing so you do run the risk of confusing possible target markets due to the issue of severity of possible deaths occurring. This was the case in New York in 2004 with the well known case 'Murpheys Law' which is now a well known case study for cost minisation. This was all due to severe cost cutting leading to 'Murphcys' death due to a large back lash from his employees resulting in his death! Cost minimisation should be carefully considered before being implemented.

When conducting a cost-minimization study, one needs to measure all costs (resource expenditures) inherent to the delivery of the therapeutic intervention and that are relevant to the pharmacoeconomic perspective.

Cost-effectiveness analysis (CEA) is a form of economic analysis that compares the relative costs and outcomes (effects) of two or more courses of action. Cost-effectiveness analysis is distinct from cost-benefit analysis, which assigns a monetary value to the measure of effect. Cost-effectiveness analysis is often used in the field of health services, where it may be inappropriate to monetize health effect. Typically the CEA is expressed in terms of a ratio where the denominator is a gain in health from a measure (years of life, premature births averted, sight-years gained) and the numerator is the cost associated with the health gain. The most commonly used outcome measure is quality-adjusted life years (QALY). Cost-utility analysis is similar to cost-effectiveness analysis

General application

The concept of cost effectiveness is applied to the planning and management of many types of organized activity. In the acquisition of military *tanks*, for example, competing designs are compared not only for purchase price, but also for such factors as their operating radius, top speed, rate of fire, armor protection, and caliber and armor penetration of their guns. If a tank's performance in these areas is equal or even slightly inferior to its competitor, but substantially less expensive and easier to produce, military planners may select it as more cost effective than the competitor. Conversely, if the difference in price is near zero, but the more costly competitor would convey an enormous battlefield advantage through special ammunition, radar fire control and laser range finding, enabling it to destroy enemy tanks accurately at extreme ranges, military planners may choose it instead—based on the same cost effectiveness principle.

Cost effectiveness analysis is also applied to many other areas of human activity, including the economics of automobile usage.

CEA in pharmacoeconomics

In the context of pharmacoeconomics, the cost-effectiveness of a therapeutic or preventive intervention is the ratio of the cost of the intervention to a relevant measure of its effect. Cost refers to the resource expended for the intervention, usually measured in monetary terms such as dollars or pounds. The measure of effects depends on the intervention being considered. Examples include the number of people cured of a disease, the mm Hg reduction in diastolic blood pressure and the number of symptom-free days experienced by a patient. The selection of the appropriate effect measure should be based on clinical judgment in the context of the intervention being considered.

A special case of CEA is cost-utility analysis, where the effects are measured in terms of years of full health lived, using a measure such as quality-adjusted life years or disability-adjusted life years.

Cost-effectiveness is typically expressed as an incremental cost-effectiveness ratio (ICER), the ratio of change in costs to the change in effects.

A 1995 study of the cost-effectiveness of over 500 life-saving medical interventions found that the median cost per intervention was $42,000 per life-year saved. A 2006 systematic review found that industry-funded studies often concluded with cost effective ratios below $20,000 per QALY and low quality studies and those conducted outside the US and EU were less likely to be below this threshold. While the two conclusions may indicate that industry-funded ICER measures are lower methodological quality than those by non-industry sources, there is also a possibility that, due to the nature of retrospective or other non-public work, bias may exist rather than methodology biases. There may be incentive for an organization not to develop or publish an analysis that does not demonstrate the value of their product.

Cost-benefit analysis is a term that refers both to:

- helping to appraise, or assess, the case for a *project*, programme or policy proposal;
- an approach to making economic decisions of any kind.

Under both definitions the process involves, whether explicitly or implicitly, weighing the total expected costs against the total expected benefits of one or more actions in order to choose the best or most profitable option. The formal process is often referred to as either CBA (Cost-Benefit Analysis) or BCA (Benefit-Cost Analysis).

Benefits and costs are often expressed in money terms, and are adjusted for the *time value of money*, so that all flows of benefits and flows of project costs over time (which tend to occur at different points in time) are expressed on a common basis in terms of their "present value." Closely related, but slightly different, formal techniques include *cost-effectiveness* analysis, *economic impact analysis*, fiscal impact analysis and *Social Return on Investment* (SROI) analysis. The latter builds upon the logic of cost-benefit analysis, but differs in that it is explicitly designed to inform the practical decision-making of enterprise managers and investors focused on optimizing their social and environmental impacts. Cost-benefit Analysis is also used in *Decision Architecture* to justify investment

Theory

Cost–benefit analysis is typically used by governments to evaluate the desirability of a given intervention. It is heavily used in today's government. It is an analysis of the cost effectiveness of different alternatives in order to see whether the benefits outweigh the costs. The aim is to gauge the efficiency of the intervention relative to the status quo. The costs and benefits of the impacts of an intervention are evaluated in terms of the public's willingness to pay for them (benefits) or willingness to pay to avoid them (costs). Inputs are typically measured in terms of *opportunity costs* - the value in their best alternative use. The guiding principle is to list all parties affected by an intervention and place a monetary value of the effect it has on their welfare as it would be valued by them.

The process involves monetary value of initial and ongoing expenses vs. expected return. Constructing plausible measures of the costs and benefits of specific actions is often very difficult. In practice, analysts try to estimate costs and benefits either by using survey methods or by drawing inferences from market behavior. For example, a product manager may compare manufacturing and marketing expenses with projected sales for a proposed product and decide to produce it only if he expects the revenues to eventually recoup the costs. Cost–benefit analysis attempts to put all relevant costs and benefits on a common temporal footing. A discount rate is chosen, which is then used to compute all relevant future costs and benefits in present-value terms. Most commonly, the discount rate used for present-value calculations is an interest rate taken from financial markets

(R.H. Frank 2000). This can be very controversial; for example, a high discount rate implies a very low value on the welfare of future generations, which may have a huge impact on the desirability of interventions to help the environment. Empirical studies suggest that in reality, people's discount rates *do* decline over time. Because cost–benefit analysis aims to measure the public's true willingness to pay, this feature is typically built into studies.

During cost–benefit analysis, monetary values may also be assigned to less tangible effects such as the various risks that could contribute to partial or total project failure, such as loss of reputation, *market penetration*, or long-term enterprise strategy alignments. This is especially true when governments use the technique, for instance to decide whether to introduce business *regulation*, build a new road, or offer a new drug through the state *healthcare* system. In this case, a value must be put on human life or the *environment*, often causing great controversy. For example, the cost–benefit principle says that we should install a guardrail on a dangerous stretch of mountain road if the dollar cost of doing so is less than the implicit dollar value of the injuries, deaths, and property damage thus prevented.

Cost–benefit calculations typically involve using *time value of money* formulas. This is usually done by converting the future expected streams of costs and benefits into a *present value* amount.

Application and History

Cost–benefit analysis is used mainly to assess the monetary value of very large private and public sector projects. This is because such projects tend to include costs and benefits that are less amenable to being expressed in financial or monetary terms (e.g., environmental damage), as well as those that can be expressed in monetary terms. Private sector organizations tend to make much more use of other project appraisal techniques, such as *rate of return*, where feasible.

The practice of cost–benefit analysis differs between countries and between sectors (e.g., *transport, health*) within countries. Some of the main differences include the types of impacts that are included as costs and benefits within appraisals, the extent to which impacts are expressed in monetary terms, and differences in the *discount rate* between countries. Agencies across the world rely on a basic set of key cost–benefit indicators, including the following:

- NPV (net present value)
- PVB (present value of benefits)
- PVC (present value of costs)
- BCR (*benefit cost ratio* = PVB / PVC)

- Net benefit (= PVB - PVC)
- NPV/k (where k is the level of funds available)

The concept of CBA dates back to an 1848 article by Dupuit and was formalized in subsequent works by *Alfred Marshall*. The practical application of CBA was initiated in the US by the *Corps of Engineers*, after the *Federal Navigation Act of 1936* effectively required cost–benefit analysis for proposed federal waterway infrastructure. The *Flood Control Act of 1939* was instrumental in establishing CBA as federal policy. It specified the standard that "the benefits to whomever they accrue [be] in excess of the estimated costs.

Subsequently, cost–benefit techniques were applied to the development of highway and motorway investments in the US and UK in the 1950s and 1960s. An early and often-quoted, more developed application of the technique was made to *London Underground*'s *Victoria Line*. Over the last 40 years, cost–benefit techniques have gradually developed to the extent that substantial guidance now exists on how transport projects should be appraised in many countries around the world.

In the UK, the *New Approach to Appraisal* (NATA) was introduced by the then *Department for Transport, Environment and the Regions*. This brought together cost–benefit results with those from detailed *environmental impact assessments* and presented them in a balanced way. NATA was first applied to national road schemes in the 1998 Roads Review but subsequently rolled out to all modes of transport. It is now a cornerstone of transport appraisal in the UK and is maintained and developed by the Department for Transport.

The *EU*'s 'Developing Harmonised European Approaches for Transport Costing and Project Assessment' (HEATCO) project, part of its *Sixth Framework Programme*, has reviewed transport appraisal guidance across EU member states and found that significant differences exist between countries. HEATCO's aim is to develop guidelines to harmonise transport appraisal practice across the EU.

Accuracy Problems

The *accuracy* of the outcome of a cost–benefit analysis depends on how accurately *costs* and benefits have been *estimated*. A *peer-reviewed* study of the accuracy of cost *estimates* in transportation *infrastructure planning* found that for *rail* projects actual costs turned out to be on average 44.7 percent higher than estimated costs, and for *roads* 20.4 percent higher (Flyvbjerg, Holm, and Buhl, 2002). For benefits, another peer-reviewed study found that actual rail *ridership* was on average 51.4 percent lower than estimated ridership; for roads it was found that for half of all projects estimated *traffic* was wrong by more than 20 percent (Flyvbjerg, Holm, and Buhl, 2005). Comparative studies indicate that similar inaccuracies apply to fields other than transportation. These studies indicate that the outcomes of cost–benefit analyses should be treated with caution because they may be highly *inaccurate*. In fact, inaccurate cost–benefit analyses may be argued to be a substantial *risk* in *planning*, because inaccuracies of the size documented are likely to lead to *inefficient* decisions, as defined by *Pareto* and *Kaldor-H.cks efficiency*.

These outcomes (almost always tending to underestimation *unless significant new approaches are overlooked*) are to be expected because such estimates:

1. Rely heavily on past like projects (often differing markedly in function or size and certainly in the skill levels of the team members)
2. Rely heavily on the project's members to identify (*remember* from their collective past experiences) the significant cost drivers
3. Rely on very crude heuristics to estimate the money cost of the intangible elements
4. Are unable to completely dispel the usually unconscious biases of the team members (who often have a vested interest in a decision to go ahead) and the natural psychological tendency to *"think positive"* (whatever that involves)

Another challenge to cost–benefit analysis comes from determining which costs should be included in an analysis (the significant cost drivers). This is often controversial because organizations or interest groups may think that some costs should be included or excluded from a study.

In the field of health economics, some analysts think cost–benefit analysis can be an inadequate measure because willingness-to-pay methods of determining the value of human life can be subject to bias according to income inequity. They support use of variants such as *cost-utility analysis* and *quality-adjusted life year* to analyze the effects of health policies

Pharmacoeconomic Perspective

Perspective in *pharmacoeconomics* refers to the economic vantage point that is being taken in a pharmacoeconomic analysis, such as a *cost-effectiveness analysis* or *cost-utility analysis*. This will affect the types of costs (resource expenditures) and benefits that will be considered relevant to the analysis.

Five general perspectives that are often cited in pharmacoeconomics include: institutional, third party, *patient*, *governmental* and *societal*. The author must state the perspective and then insure that costs and valuations remain consistent with it throughout the study.

If, for example, a pharmacoeconomic study is done from the institutional perspective, the medication cost would be relevant to the resource expenditures involved in the delivery of the therapy. Since the institution (e.g. *hospital*) incurs this expense, then it would be included. Other relevant costs might include: inventory carrying cost, pharmacy time to compound or dispense, nursing time to administer, disposables (e.g. medication cups or intraveous tubing) and even allocated hospital overhead costs.

The next component of perspective that needs to be addressed under perspective is valuation. Valuation defines the currency reference that will be used to represent the resource expenditure associated with a given cost. When it comes time to determine the actual "dollar amount" to be attributed to the medication, it needs to be consistent with the perspective as well. Average wholesaler price (AWP) might NOT be considered an appropriate valuation of medication cost from an institutional perspective, if it does not represent the true cost to the institution. Average acquisition cost would be more relevant as a medication cost valuation.

More complex perspectives may require broader stables of resource expenditures (costs) and more intricate valuations. For example, in the "societal" perspective, it is necessary for the author to consider additional costs that would not be relevant to a given institutional perspective. One such example includes "lost productivity". Lost wages from work due to illness would not be relevant to an insitutional perspective, since these do not represent expenditures an average institution (e.g. hospital) will incur. From a societal perspective, they would need to be included. Lost productivity due to illness has an impact on society at large and must therefore be included and properly valued.

Pharmaceutical Outcomes (Quality Of Life Concepts)

Introduction

Pharmaceuticals are among the most widely used interventions in health care today. They are used in both the prevention and treatment of disease and amelioration of symptoms to improve patient outcomes. The relative importance of pharmaceuticals in health care is growing in most industrialized nations, as the percentage of health care expenditures for pharmaceuticals continues to increase. Spending on prescription drugs in the United States is increasing at a rate of 12% annually and will continue to increase approximately 10% per year over the next 8 years.

Not all outcomes from the use of pharmaceuticals are positive. Adverse drug reactions are the fourth to sixth leading cause of death and in the United States, medication errors are the largest category of the 44,000-98,000 deaths each year due to medical errors. The total annual cost of drug-related morbidity and mortality in the ambulatory setting in the United States has more than doubled in 5 years, increasing from $76.7 billion in 1995 to $177.4 billion in 2000.

Many drug-related adverse outcomes are preventable. For example, a significant percentage of hospital admissions are due to drug-related morbidity and approximately one-half of these admissions are preventable. Preventable adverse outcomes related to drug use—often referred to as preventable drug-related morbidities (PDRMs)—are typically not due to the inherent pharmacological properties of medicines, but rather to problems such as a lack of systematic approach to monitoring of patients receiving drug therapy by health professionals. .

One framework for looking at pharmaceutical outcomes—whether these outcomes are positive or negative—is the ECHO (Economic, Clinical, and Humanistic Outcomes) model, proposed by Kozma, Reeder and Schulz. According to this model, three main types of health-related outcomes should be considered: economic (drug-related and non-drug-related), clinical (clinical events, physiologic and metabolic measures), and humanistic outcomes [such as patient satisfaction and health-related quality of life (HRQoL)]. Economic and clinical (and fairly often humanistic) outcomes are incorporated into pharmacoeconomic evaluations.

Patient satisfaction is growing in importance and has become a key part of most health care report cards. Perceived satisfaction with medical treatment is key in determining the overall well-being and health of patients, and is recognized as being one of the main components of quality. HRQoL relates to those aspects of a patient's life dominated by personal health. Although differing opinions exist, there is some consensus that there are four main dimensions (or domains) constituting "health": a physical dimension, a functional dimension, a psychological dimension, and a social dimension.Increasingly, HRQoL is being used in clinical drug trials and in pharmacy program evaluations, and to monitor patients.

Quality of Life

Quality of Working Life is a term that had been used to describe the broader job-related experience an individual has.

Whilst there has, for many years, been much research into job satisfaction and, more recently, an interest has arisen into the broader concepts of stress and subjective well-being, the precise nature of the relationship between these concepts has still been little explored. Stress at work is often considered in isolation, wherein it is assessed on the basis that attention to an individual's stress management skills or the sources of stress will prove to provide a good enough basis for effective intervention. Alternatively, job satisfaction may be assessed, so that action can be taken which will enhance an individual's performance. Somewhere in all this, there is often an awareness of the greater context, whereupon the home-work context is considered, for example, and other factors, such as an individual's personal characteristics, and the broader economic or cultural climate, might be seen as relevant. In this context, subjective well-being is seen as drawing upon both work and non-work aspects of life.

However, more complex models of an individuals experience in the workplace often appear to be set aside in an Endeavour to simplify the process of trying to measuring "stress" or some similarly apparently discrete entity. It may be, however, that the consideration of the bigger, more complex picture is essential, if targeted, effective action is to be taken to address quality of working life or any of it's sub-components in such a way as to produce real benefits, be they for the individual or the organization.

Quality of working life has been differentiated from the broader concept of Quality of Life. To some degree, this may be overly simplistic, as Elizur and Shye,(1990) concluded that quality of work performance is affected by Quality of Life as well as Quality of working life.

It is argued that the whole is greater than the sum of the parts as regards Quality of working Life, and, therefore, the failure to attend to the bigger picture may lead to the failure of interventions which tackle only one aspect. A clearer understanding of the inter-relationship of the various facets of quality of working life offers the opportunity for improved analysis of cause and effect in the workplace.

This consideration of Quality of working Life as the greater context for various factors in the workplace, such as job satisfaction and stress, may offer opportunity for more cost-effective interventions in the workplace. The effective targeting of stress reduction, for example, may otherwise prove a hopeless task for employers pressured to take action to meet governmental requirements.

History of pharmaceutical outcomes movement

Various authors and researchers have proposed models of Quality of working life which include a wide range of factors. Selected models are reviewed below.

Hackman and Oldham (1976) drew attention to what they described as psychological growth needs as relevant to the consideration of Quality of working life. Several such needs were identified; Skill variety, Task Identity, Task significance, Autonomy and Feedback. They suggested that such needs have to be addressed if employees are to experience high quality of working life.

In contrast to such theory based models, Taylor (1979) more pragmatically identified the essential components of Quality of working life as; basic extrinsic job factors of wages, hours and working conditions, and the intrinsic job notions of the nature of the work itself. He suggested that a number of other aspects could be added, including; individual power, employee participation in the management, fairness and equity, social support, use of one's present skills, self development, a meaningful future at work, social relevance of the work or product, effect on extra work activities. Taylor suggested that relevant Quality of working life concepts may vary according to organisation and employee group.

Warr and colleagues (1979), in an investigation of Quality of working life, considered a range of apparently relevant factors, including work involvement, intrinsic job motivation, higher order need strength, perceived intrinsic job characteristics, job satisfaction, life satisfaction, happiness, and self-rated anxiety. They discussed a range of correlations derived from their work, such as those between work involvement and job satisfaction, intrinsic job motivation and job satisfaction, and perceived intrinsic job characteristics and job satisfaction. In particular, Warr et al. found evidence for a moderate association between total job satisfaction and total life satisfaction and happiness, with a less strong, but significant association with self-rated anxiety.

Thus, whilst some authors have emphasised the workplace aspects in Quality of working life, others have identified the relevance of personality factors, psychological well being, and broader concepts of happiness and life satisfaction.

Factors more obviously and directly affecting work have, however, served as the main focus of attention, as researchers have tried to tease out the important influences on Quality of working life in the workplace.

Mirvis and Lawler (1984)suggested that Quality of working life was associated with satisfaction with wages, hours and working conditions, describing the "basic elements of a good quality of work life" as; safe work environment, equitable wages, equal employment opportunities and opportunities for advancement.

Baba and Jamal (1991) listed what they described as typical indicators of quality of working life, including: job satisfaction, job involvement, work role ambiguity, work role conflict, work role overload, job stress, organisational commitment and turn-over intentions. Baba and Jamal also explored routinisation of job content, suggesting that this facet should be investigated as part of the concept of quality of working life.

Some have argued that quality of working life might vary between groups of workers. For example, Ellis and Pompli (2002) identified a number of factors contributing to job dissatisfaction and quality of working life in nurses, including: Poor working environments, Resident aggression, Workload, Unable to deliver quality of care preferred, Balance of work and family, Shiftwork, Lack of involvement in decision making, Professional isolation, Lack of recognition, Poor relationships with supervisor/peers, Role conflict, Lack of opportunity to learn new skills.

The key factors in quality of working life are: Need satisfaction based on job requirements, Need satisfaction based on Work environment, Need satisfaction based on Supervisory behaviour, Need satisfaction based on Ancillary programmes, Organizational commitment. They defined quality of working life as satisfaction of these key needs through resources, activities, and outcomes stemming from participation in the workplace. Maslow's needs were seen as relevant in underpinning this model, covering Health & safety, Economic and family, Social, Esteem, Actualisation, Knowledge and Aesthetics, although the relevance of non-work aspects is play down as attention is focussed on quality of work life rather than the broader concept of quality of life.

These attempts at defining quality of working life have included theoretical approaches, lists of identified factors, correlational analyses, with opinions varying as to whether such definitions and explanations can be both global, or need to be specific to each work setting.

Bearfield, (2003) used 16 questions to examine quality of working life, and distinguished between causes of dissatisfaction in professionals, intermediate clerical, sales and service workers, indicating that different concerns might have to be addressed for different groups.

The distinction made between job satisfaction and dissatisfaction in quality of working life reflects the influence of job satisfaction theories. Herzberg at al., (1959) used "Hygiene factors" and "Motivator factors" to distinguish between the separate causes of job satisfaction and job dissatisfaction. It has been suggested that Motivator factors are intrinsic to the job, that is; job content, the work itself, responsibility and advancement. The Hygiene factors or dissatisfaction-avoidance factors include aspects of the job environment such as interpersonal relationships, salary, working conditions and security. Of these latter, the most common cause of job dissatisfaction can be company policy and administration, whilst achievement can be the greatest source of extreme satisfaction.

An individual's experience of satisfaction or dissatisfaction can be substantially rooted in their perception, rather than simply reflecting their "real world". Further, an individual's perception can be affected by relative comparison – am I paid as much as that person - and comparisons of internalised ideals, aspirations, and expectations, for example, with the individual's current state (Lawler and Porter, 1966)..

In summary, where it has been considered, authors differ in their views on the core constituents of Quality of Working Life (e.g. Sirgy, Efraty, Siegel & Lee, 2001 and Warr, Cook & Wall, 1979).

It has generally been agreed however that Quality of Working Life is conceptually similar to well-being of employees but differs from job satisfaction which solely represents the workplace domain (Lawler, 1982).

Quality of Working Life is not a unitary concept, but has been seen as incorporating a hierarchy of perspectives that not only include work-based factors such as job satisfaction, satisfaction with pay and relationships with work colleagues, but also factors that broadly reflect life satisfaction and general feelings of well-being (Danna & Griffin, 1999). More recently, work-related stress and the relationship between work and non-work life domains (Loscocco & Roschelle, 1991) have also been identified as factors that should conceptually be included in Quality of Working Life.

Measurement

There are few recognised measures of quality of working life, and of those that exist few have evidence of validity and reliability, that is, there is a very limited literature based on peer reviewed evbaluations of available assessments. A recent statistical analysis of a new measure, the Work-Related Quality of Life scale (WRQoL), indicates that this assessment device should prove to be a useful instrument, although further evaluation would be useful. The WRQoWL measure uses 6 core factors to explain most of the variation in an individuals quality of working life: Job and Career Satisfaction; Working Conditions; General Well-Being; Home-Work Interface; Stress at Work and Control at Work.

The Job and Career Satisfaction Job and Career satisfaction (JCS)scale of the the Work-Related Quality of Life scale (WRQoL) is said to reflect an employee's feelings about, or evaluation of, their satisfaction or contentment with their job and career and the training they receive to do it. Within the WRQoL measure, JCS is reflected by questions asking how satisfied people feel about their work. It has been proposed that this Positive Job Satisfaction factor is influenced by various issues including clarity of goals and role ambiguity, appraisal, recognition and reward, personal development career benefits and enhancement and training needs.

The General well-being (GWB)scale of the Work-Related Quality of Life scale (WRQoL), aims to assess the extent to which an individual feels good or content in themselves, in a way which may be independent of their work situation. It is suggested that general well-being both influences, and is influenced by work. Mental health problems, predominantly depression and anxiety disorders, are common, and may have a major impact on the general well-being of the population. The WRQoL GWB factor assesses issues of mood, depression and anxiety, life satisfaction, general quality of life, optimism and happiness.

The WRQoL Stress at Work sub-scale (SAW) reflects the extent to which an individual perceives they have excessive pressures, and feel stressed at work. The WRQoL SAW factor is assessed through items dealing with demand and perception of stress and actual demand overload. Whilst it is possible to be pressured at work and not be stressed at work, in general, high stress is associated with high pressure.

The Control at Work (CAW) subsacle of the WRQoL scale addresses how much employees feel they can control their work through the freedom to express their opinions and being involved in decisions at work. Perceived control at work as measureed by the Work-Related Quality of Life scale (WRQoL)is recognized as a central concept in the understanding of relationships between stressful experiences, behaviour and health. Control at work, within the theoretical model underpinning the WRQoL, is influenced by issues of communication at work, decision making and decision control.

The WRQoL Home-Work Interface scale (HWI) measures the extent to which an employer is perceived to support the family and home life of employees. This factor explores the interrelationship between home and work life domains. Issues that appear to influence employee HWI include adequate facilities at work, flexibile working hours and the understanding of managers.

The Working Conditions scale of the WRQoL assesses the extent to which the employee is satisfied with the fundamental resources, working conditions and security necessary to do their job effectively. Physical working conditions influence employee health and safety and thus employee Quality of working life. This scale also taps into satisfaction with the resources provided to help people do their jobs.

Applications

Regular assessment of Quality of Working Life can potentially provide organisations with important information about the welfare of their employees, such as job satisfaction, general well-being, work-related stress and the home-work interface. Studies in the UK University sector have shown a valid measure of Quality of Working Life exists and can be used as a basis for effective interventions.

Worrall and Cooper (2006) recently reported that a low level of well-being at work is estimated to cost about 5-10% of Gross National Product per annum, yet Quality of Working Life as a theoretical construct remains relatively unexplored and unexplained within the organisational psychology research literature.

A large chunk of most peoples' lives will be spent at work. Most people recognise the importance of sleeping well, and actively try to enjoy the leisure time that they can snatch. But all too often, people tend to see work as something they just have to put up with, or even something they don't even expect to enjoy.

Some of the factors used to measure quality of working life pick up on things that don't actually make people feel good, but which seem to make people feel bad about work if those things are absent. For example, noise – if the place where someone works is too noisy, they might get frequent headaches, or find they can not concentrate, and so feel dissatisfied. But when it is quiet enough they don't feel pleased or happy - they just don't feel bad. This can apply to a range of factors that affect someone's working conditions.

Other things seem to be more likely to make people feel good about work and themselves once the basics are OK at work. Challenging work (not too little, not too much) can make them feel good. Similarly, opportunities for career progression and using their abilities can contribute to someone's quality of working life.

The recent publication of National Institute of Clinical Excellence (NICE) public health guidance; Promoting mental wellbeing through productive and healthy working conditions , emphasises the core role of assessment and understanding of the way working environments pose risks for psychological wellbeing through lack of control and excessive demand. The emphasis placed by NICE on assessment and monitoring wellbeing springs from the fact that these processes are the key first step in identifying areas for improveming quality of working life and addressing risks at work.

3.4 Pharmacovigilence

Introduction

Pharmacovigilance (PV or PVG) is the science associated with detection, assessment, understanding and prevention of adverse effects of drugs. According to the Pharmacovigilence definition given by WHO, it is "the science and activities relating to the detection, assessment, understanding and prevention of adverse effects or any other possible drug-related problems. Recently, its concerns have been widened to include herbals, traditional and complementary medicines, blood products, biologicals, medical devices and vaccines

Pharmacovigilance System

Pharmacovigilence studies the long term and short term adverse drug reaction or simply stated- side effects of medicines. Pharmacovigilance system involves collection, monitoring, researching upon, assessing and evaluating information received from health care workers such as doctors, dentists, pharmacists, nurses and other health professionals for understanding the adverse drug reaction. Pharmacovigilance definition includes monitoring of all pharmaceutical drugs and also other medical products including vaccines, X-ray contrast media, traditional and herbal remedies etc. especially when the reaction is unusual, potentially serious or clinically significant.

Report of Suspected Adverse Drug Reaction Including Birth Defects

Drug Control Authority

Note: Identities of reporter, patient and institution will remain confidential

PARTICULARS OF PATIENT

Patient Initials or Record No.: ______________________ Sex: ______________

Date of Birth (DD-MM-YYYY) or age: ______________________ Weight in kg: ______________

DETAIL OF ADVERSE DRUG REACTION

________ Headache	________ Shock/anaphylaxis	________ Skin rash
________ Diarrhoea	________ Nausea or Vomiting	________ Others

Description of reaction (if possible) ....

....

Date reaction started → ______/______/______

Date reaction stopped (if known) → ______/______/______

Other relevant information: e.g. medical history, allergies, pregnancy, smoking, alcohol use, etc. **Please enclose any relevant laboratory results including dates (*if done*)** ....

....

....

III. DETAILS OF SUSPECTED DRUG (S) AND ALL OTHER DRUGS USED

Name of suspected drug(s) (Please specify brand name if known)	Dosage	Frequency	Route	Therapy Date		Batch No. & Expiry date (if known)	Reason for use
				Start	Stop		
Other drugs (including herbal medicines consumed at same time and or 1 month before)							

IV. MANAGEMENT OF ADVERSE REACTION

Reaction subsided after stopping the suspected drug/reducing the dose: ______ Yes No Unknown

Reaction reappeared after reintroducing drug: Yes No Not applicable

Do You consider the reaction to be serious? Yes No

If Yes, please indicate why the reaction is considered to be serious (Please tick all that apply):

_______ Pateint dies due to reaction _______ Required or Prolonged hospitalization

_______ Is life threatening _______ Causes irreversible disability or incapacity

_______ Causes a congenital anomaly _______ Others, please give details……………………….

Treatment of adverse reaction ______ Yes ______ No (if yes please specify): …………………………………

………

………

Outcome of the reaction ______ Not yet recovered ______ Recovered

______ Fatal (Date of death): _____/_____/_______

V. PARTICULARS OF REPORTER (HEALTH CARE PROVIDER)

Name: ______________ Profession: ______________

Contact Phone No: __________ E-mail: ______________

Signature: ______________ Date of report: ____/____/______

______ Please tick if you wish to receive information about other local reports associated with the suspected drug(s)

Name and Address of the health facility: ______________

Thank You for Your cooperation	Submission of an ADR case repot does not discredit the competence of the reporter.	Ref No. (for official Use)

-- First Fold --

Guide to filling the Form

How to report?

- Dully fill in the form as required
- Use a separate form for each patient.
- Report direct to TFDA through the addresses.

An Adverse drug reaction (ADR) is defined as a reaction which is noxious and unintended, and which occurs at doses normally used in human for prophylaxis, diagnosis, or therapy of a disease, or for the modification of physiological function.

What to report?

Please report all undesirable patient effect suspected to be associated with drugs, cosmetics or medical devices use.

Report even if:

- You`re not sure that the product caused the event.
- You don't have all the details.

When to report?

As soon as possible

Submission of follow-up reports:

Any follow-up information for an ADR that has already been reported can be sent on another ADR form or it can be communicated directly to TFDA by telephone, fax or e-mail. Please indicate that it is a follow-up report. It is very important that follow-up reports are identified and linked to the original report.

---Second Fold ---

POSTAGE WILL
BE PAID BY
LICENCEE

No postage stamp required
If posted in India

BUSINESS REPLY SERVICE
LICENCE No. BRS 01

TO: THE DIRECTOR GENERAL OF HEALTH SERVICES

NEW DELHI

Pharmacovigilance in Different Countries/ Regions

All the regions of the world have their own particular pharmacovigilance system, though based on WHO guidelines.

Pharmacovigilance in Europe- Pharmacovigilance system in Europe is coordinated by the European Medicines Agency (EMA) and conducted by the National Competent Authorities (NCAs). The EMA maintains and develops the pharmacovigilance database comprising all suspected serious adverse drug reactions observed in the European region. Here, the pharmacovigilance system is called EudraVigilance and contains separate but similar databases of human and veterinary reactions.

Pharmacovigilance in United States- Here pharmacovigilance has a multi faceted approach. Three branches of pharmacovigilance in the USA can be defined as the FDA; the pharmaceutical manufacturers; and the academic/non-profit organizations like RADAR and Public Citizen. The US Food and Drug Administration (FDA) receives reports about adverse drug reaction and takes appropriate actions for drug safety.

Pharmacovigilance in India- The Central Drugs Standard Control Organization (CDSCO), Ministry of Health and Family Welfare, Govt. of India launched the National Pharmacovigilance Programme (NPP) in November, 2004 based on the WHO recommendations made in the document titled "Safety Monitoring of Medicinal Products – Guidelines for Setting Up and Running a Pharmacovigilance Centre". The whole country is divided into zones and regions for operational efficiency. CDSCO, New Delhi is at the top of the hierarchy followed by two zonal pharmacovigilance centers viz, Seth GS Medical College, Mumbai and AIIMS, New Delhi.

To summarize the basic knowledge about pharmacovigilance, it can be said that the information obtained from reports about adverse drug reactions promote drug safety on a local and national level. These reports are entered into the national adverse drug reaction database and analyzed by expert reviewers justifying the whole pharmacovigilance system.

Why is Pharmacovigilance important?

When a medicine is released onto the market there is still a great deal that is unknown about the safety of the product. Once marketed the medicines are used by patients who have many different diseases, who are using several other drugs and who have different traditions and diets which may affect the way in which they react to a medicine. Different brands of medicines may differ in the manner in which they are produced and the ingredients that are used. The adverse drug reactions and poisonings associated with traditional and herbal remedies also need to be monitored in each country.

The information we receive on the adverse effects of drugs in other countries may not be relevant or applicable to citizens. In some cases, adverse effects to certain drugs may only occur in citizens. In order to prevent unnecessary suffering by patients and to decrease the financial loss sustained by the patient due to the inappropriate or unsafe use of medicines, it is essential that a monitoring system for the safety of medicines is supported by doctors, pharmacists, nurses and other health professionals in the country.

The *{Drug Regulatory Authority}* and the Department of Health's Essential Drug Programme are committed to improving drug safety through adverse drug reaction monitoring. Through the *{Drug Regulatory Authority}'s* national pharmacovigilance programme, adverse reactions should be reported on a daily basis.

What is the Size or Severity of the ADR Problem in INDIA ?

While no studies have comprehensively assessed the burden of adverse drug reactions on health care, it is likely that the problem is considerable in *india.*

Studies conducted in developed countries have consistently shown that approximately 5% of hospitalised patients are admitted into hospital as a result of an ADR and 6-10% of in-patients will experience a serious ADR during hospitalisation. Even these startling figures don't represent the whole picture. These studies generally excluded ADRs caused by overdose, drug abuse, or therapeutic failures. The cost to most countries for managing adverse drug reactions is considerable.

Who should report Adverse Drug Reactions?

All health care workers, including doctors, dentists, pharmacists, nurses and other health professionals are requested to report all suspected adverse reactions to drugs (including vaccines, X-ray contrast media, traditional and herbal remedies), especially when the reaction is unusual, potentially serious or clinically significant. It is vital to report an adverse drug reaction to the *{Drug Regulatory Authority}'s* Pharmacovigilance programme **even if you do not have all the facts or are uncertain that the medicine is definitely responsible for causing the reaction**.

What will happen to my Adverse Drug Reaction or Product Quality Report?

The information obtained from your reported reactions promotes the safe use of medicines on a local and national level. Your reported case will be entered into the national adverse drug reaction database and analysed by expert reviewers. A wellcompleted adverse drug reaction/product quality form submitted by you could result in any of the following:

- additional investigations into the use of the medication in India.
- educational initiatives to improve the safe use of the medication.
- appropriate package insert changes to include the potential for the reaction
- reported by you
- changes in the scheduling or manufacture of the medicine to make the medicine safer Therefore, the purpose of ADR reporting is to reduce the risks associated with drug prescribing and administration and to ultimately improve patient care and safety.

What are the benefits of these reports for me and for my patients?

Will reporting have any negative consequences on the health worker or the patient?
This adverse drug reaction report does not constitute an admission that you or any other health professional contributed to the event in any way. The outcome of the report, together with any important or relevant information relating to the reaction you have reported, will be sent back to you as appropriate. The details of your report will be stored in a confidential database. The names of the reporter or any other health professionals named on a report and the patient will be removed before any details about a specific adverse drug reaction are used or communicated to others. The information obtained from your report will not be used for commercial purposes. The information is only meant to improve our understanding of the medicines we use in the country.

How do I know if a patient's condition is an ADR?

1. **Take a Proper History and do a proper examination**
   - A full drug and medical history should be done
   - Can this adverse be explained by other causes e.g. patient's underlying disease, other drug/s, over-the-counter medicines or traditional medicines; toxins or foods
   - It is essential that the patient is thoroughly investigated to decide what the actual cause of any new medical problem is. A drug related cause should be considered, especially when other causes do not explain the patient's condition
2. **Establish time relationships**
   - some reactions occur immediately after being given a medicine while other reactions take time to develop)
   - The time from the start of therapy to the time of onset of the suspected reaction must be logical.
3. **Do a thorough physical examination with appropriate laboratory investigations**
   - Few drug produce distinctive physical signs
   - Exceptions include fixed drug eruptions, steroid-induced dermal atrophy, acute extrapyramidal reactions
   - Lab tests are especially important if the drug is considered essential in improving patient care or of the lab test results will improve management of the patient

- *try to describe the reaction as clearly as possible and where possible provide an accurate diagnosis*

4. **Effect of Dechallenge and Rechallenge should be determined. (when necessary)**

   Dechallenge = withdraw of drug

   - resolution of suspected ADR when the drug is withdrawn is a strong, although not conclusive indication of drug-induced disease.
   - In cases where a withdrawal reaction is experienced, a dechallenge is when the drug is again given to the patient.
   - "Positive" dechallenge = improvement of reaction when dechallenge occurs Rechallenge = reintroducing the drug after a dechallenge.
   - this is only justifiable when the benefit of re-introducing the drug to the patient outweighs the risk of recurrence of the reaction. This is rare. In some cases the reaction may be more severe on repeat exposure.

5. **Check the known pharmacology of the Medicine.**

   - Is the reaction known to occur with the particular drug as stated in the package insert or other reference?
   - If the reaction is not documented in the package insert, it does not mean that the reaction cannot occur with that particular medicine.)

Causality Classification

In order to assess the likelihood that the suspected adverse reaction is actually due to the medicine, the WHO has provided a list of causality assessment criteria for deciding on the contribution of the medicine towards the adverse event. These criteria are defined as follows:

WHO Definitions for Causality Assessment Certain:

- Clinical event, lab test abnormality with plausible time relationship to drug intake
- Cannot be explained by concurrent disease or other drugs /chemicals
- Response to dechallenge- plausible
- Event must be definitive pharmacologically / immunologically
- Positive rechallenges (if performed).

Probable/ Likely:

- Clinical event, lab test abnormality with reasonable time relationship to drug intake

- Unlikely to be to concurrent disease, drugs / chemicals
- Clinically reasonable response to withdrawal (dechallenge)
- Rechallenge not required

Possible

- Clinical event lab test abnormality with reasonable time relationship to drug intake
- Could also be explained by concurrent disease or other drugs or chemicals
- Information on drug withdrawal may be lacking or unclear

Unlikely

- Clinical event , lab test with improbable time relationship to drug intake
- Other drugs , chemicals or underlying disease provide plausible explanations

Inaccessible /unclassifiable

- Insufficient /contradictory evidence which cannot be supplemented or verified

Conditional / unclassified

- More data is essential for proper assessment or additional data are under

Examination in most cases there is some level of uncertainty as to whether the drug is directly responsible for the reaction. Many of the questions above may remain unanswered or may be contradictory, however this should not dissuade you, from reporting the reaction to the *{National Pharmacovigilance Programme}*. A well-documented report which includes information about all the above-mentioned questions can provide us with the first signal of a previously unknown problem.

What types of reactions should be reported to the {Drug Regulatory Authority}'s Pharmacoviglance Programme?

Report adverse drug reactions such as:

- all ADRs to newly marketed drugs or new drugs added to the Essential Drugs List
- all serious reactions and interactions
- ADRs which are not clearly stated in the package insert.
- unusual or interesting adverse drug reactions
- all adverse reactions or poisonings to traditional or herbal remedies

What Product Quality Problems should I report?

Report Product Quality Problems such as:

- suspected contamination
- questionable stability
- defective components
- poor packaging or labelling
- therapeutic failures

What should I know about the *{Drug Regulatory Authority}*'s Pharmacovigilance Programme?

The *{Drug Regulatory Authority}* has a responsibility to ensure the safety, efficacy and quality of all medicines used by the public. Therefore it is the responsibility of the MCC to monitor the performance of these medicines once they are marketed. Essential drugs are particularly important as they are used by a large percentage of the population.

The national pharmacovigilance programme, which is co-ordinated by the *{Drug Regulatory Authority}* offices, presently has one national pharmacovigilance centre in *every state of India.*. The *state Pharmacovigilance Programme}* housed within *the state* is responsible for monitoring the safety of all registered medicines in the state.

These units are responsible for collecting, evaluating and communicating the findings of ADR reports to the *{National Pharmacovigilance Committee}*. This committee advises the Council on how to prevent or minimise the risk of these adverse reactions in *India.*. The *{Drug Regulatory Authority}* may communicate their findings and recommendations to the appropriate organisations or individuals. These include but are not limited to health professionals, pharmaceutical manufacturers, the Essential Drugs Programme or other directorates within the Department of Health, other public health institutions, the media and the public.

How can I prevent ADRs from occurring in my patients?

Some ADRs are unavoidable and cannot be prevented. However, most ADRs can be prevented by following the basic principles of rational use of medicines that are described as follows:

Some ADRs are unavoidable and cannot be prevented. However, most ADRs can be prevented by following the basic principles of rational use of medicines as follows:

1. *Use few drugs, whenever possible*
2. *Use drug that you know well*
3. *Do not change therapy from known drugs to unfamiliar one without good reasons.*

4. *Use text books and other reference material providing information on drug reactions and interactions.*
5. *Take extra care when you prescribe drugs known to exhibit a large variety of interactions and adverse reactions (anticoagulants, hypoglycemic, and drug affecting the CNS) with careful monitoring of patients with such reactions.*
6. *Beware of the interaction of drugs with certain food stuffs, alcohol and even with house hold chemicals.*
7. *Review all the drug used by your patients regularly, taking special notice with those bought without prescription .(Over the counter, herbal preparations).*
8. *Be particularly careful when prescribing to children, the elderly, the pregnant and nursing women, the seriously ill and patients with hepatic and renal diseases. Careful ongoing monitoring is also essential in these patients is essential.*
9. *If your patients show signs or symptoms not clearly explained by the course of their illness, think of adverse drug reaction.*
10. *If you suspect an adverse reaction, consider stopping the drug or reduce the dosage as soon possible and please notify the adverse drug reaction to {Pharmacovigilence Programme Co-coordinator} at the {drug regulatory authority}.*

Adverse Drug Reactions, Reporting of Adverse Drug Reactions and Formats for Reporting the Reactions

Adverse Drug Reactions monitoring is a process of continuously monitoring of undesirable effect suspected to be associated with use of medicinal products. It facilitates collection of unbiased safety data observed during clinical practice in 'real life' circumstances.

The guidelines have been developed to assist health care professionals on understanding the importance of ADRs monitoring, procedures of reporting an ADR and the four essential components of an ADRs case report to improve drug safety. The essential components include information about the patient, description of the adverse drug reactions, the suspected drug(s) and the reporter.

Public health programmes, such as Malaria, Human Immuno Deficiency Virus/Acquired Immuno Deficiency Syndrome (HIV/AIDS), Tuberculosis (TB) and Leprosy, Parasitic infections and vaccines should introduce ADR reporting in their programmes. This should include sensitizing health workers during seminars and trainings to report adverse drug reactions. Close collaboration between TFDA and these programmes is necessary.

It is mandatory for pharmaceutical manufacturers or product registrants to monitor their products in the market and report any suspected undesirable effects to TFDA. ADR reporting covers all pharmaceutical products, biological, herbal drugs, cosmetics and medical devices circulating in the Indian market. For those conducting clinical trials phase I – IV it is mandatory to report all adverse event encountered to the Authority.

The current Indian system of ADR notification is a modified model of WHO. This system is a long established, cost effective and useful method for detecting signals by identifying previously unknown adverse reactions to medicinal products or changes in the patterns of known adverse effects which aim at ensuring that patient obtain safe and efficacious medicinal products and other pharmaceutical products. Where necessary, epidemiological studies may be conducted in collaboration with research institutions to substantiate generated signals.

In addition, drug monitoring is important in detection of lack of efficacy, detection and prevention of counterfeit and substandard products in clinical practice. It is essential that the ADR monitoring program for safety of medicinal product be supported by health care professionals

All adverse reactions should be considered reportable according to the requirements outlined in these guidelines and key players to this activity are all health care professionals, preferably those directly associated with the care of patients/consumers

Disadvantage of not reporting may result in deleterious effects of a medicinal product not being noticeable for a long time or the association became clear worldwide e.g. Aspirin in the Gastro-intestinal tract, amydopyrine in agranulocytosis, phocomelia with thalidomide. For the same reason it may take too long before it is recognized that prolonged abuse of a medicinal product can produce deliberate health effects e.g. Phenacetin in renal papillary necrosis

Therefore, proper implementation of these guidelines will help to reduce the harmful effects resulting from use of medicinal products by early detection of drug safety problems in patients, assessing the risk benefit in an individual and the population, improving the selection, rational use of drugs through provision of timely warning to healthcare professionals.

Objectives of Adverse Drug Reactions Monitoring

Rationale for ADRs Monitoring

Information on safety and efficacy of a pharmaceutical product once it is marketed is limited to premarketing evaluation, clinical trials (phase I, II and III), animal tests and other factors in the product development process.

1. Phase I trial – Single dose studies in healthy volunteers, using low doses of the drug. Subsequently, larger doses and multiple sequences, the pharmacological and pharmacokinetics properties of a drug are evaluated
2. Phase II trial – Efficacy is the primary objective of this phase, but safety is also continuously monitored and evaluated.
3. Phase III trial – Evaluation of safety in a group of patients with the disease.

Each phase involves increasing number of patients and by the end of full pre-marketing clinical trial about 5,000 patients would have taken the drug. However, there is a problem of whether clinical trial involving 5,000 people provides enough information to extrapolate the safety of new drug to millions of people.

Therefore, premarketing safety evaluation of pharmaceutical products at the time of registration is inherently limited due to the following three reasons:

1. The population in phase III clinical trials is very selective and limited. Many types of patients with different characteristics are often excluded from studies, such as patients in certain age groups and pregnant women, patients with diseases other than the one being treated and patients using other drugs concomitantly. This often prevents the identification of side effects caused by interaction of more than one drug given at the same time. Statistically, reactions with an incidence of less than 1% are frequently not identified.
2. The duration of clinical trial is too short. Such studies do not allow the detection of adverse effects that appear after long periods of use or exposure, especially with chronic medication e.g. oral contraceptives.
3. Differences between countries which lead to variation in patient factors, variation in drug utilization among health care professionals, variation in drug manufacturing processes used which influence pharmaceutical quality and composition of locally produced products and those imported outside the country

Post Marketing Surveillance

It is not possible to identify all safety-related problems that may exist with drug during premarketing test and evaluation.

For these reasons, it is obvious that safety monitoring of a drug is carried out through the life cycle of each medicinal product. Pharmaceutical product registrants and health care professionals are responsible for post-marketing surveillance of these products. One of the most common methods of Post Marketing Surveillance is ADRs monitoring

Objectives of ADRs Monitoring

To detect the nature and frequency of ADRs including periodic re-evaluation of the benefit-risk ratio of medicinal products in order to assist the drug regulatory authority, public health programs, scientists and consumer society take appropriate action to minimise risks of ADRs to consumers by:

(i) Providing updated drug safety information to health care professionals and other stakeholders including WHO ADRs Monitoring Centres

(ii) Upgrading package insert, design appropriate package insert information and dissemination of information which may constitute institution of recall or withdrawal of the product in the market or restrictions for marketing

(iii) Dissemination of information by designing proper education program to consumers and other users

(iv) Initiation of further studies for education value. For example benefit of the drug especially in long term for prevention of relapse or study of new indication, overuse, possible mechanism underlying the adverse reaction observed or misuse (utilisation pattern)

1. To identify risk factors that may predispose, induce or influence the development, severity and incidence of adverse reactions in the population of Tanzania, examples;

(i) Patient factors: genetics, racial differences, diets, diseases, prescribing practices, culture of drug use and traditions of the people e.g. high carbohydrate, fat diet etc.

(ii) Drug interactions, drug distribution, storage and use including indications, dose, availability and other underlying conditions.

The Pharmacological Basis of Adverse Drug Reactions and Interactions

ADR is an unexpected consequence of drug usage and its risk of occurrence can not be predetermined. Almost all effective drugs, no matter how skilfully used, may cause adverse reactions. The fact that an adverse reaction has occurred does not reflect in any way discreditably on the health care professional who prescribed, dispensed or sold the drug.

2. **Classification of ADRs (etiological basis)**

In many cases no specific reason can be given as to why a particular patient develops an adverse drug reaction, while another patient does not. With some relatively toxic drugs, adverse reactions are the rule rather than the exception. Four special etiological factors can however be defined. They comprise of inherent anomalies in patient response (allergic or idiosyncratic), acquired patient anomalies, anomalies of drug presentation and administration, and interactions.

Inherent anomalies in patient response (allergic or idiosyncratic)

(a) ***Drug allergy (hypersensitivity):*** Reactions are due to genetic factors and physiological variables such as age, sex and pregnancy. Drug allergy is mediated by immunological mechanisms. Characteristics of allergic reactions;

(i) are not correlated with the known pharmacological effects

(ii) can be precipitated by small amounts of drugs

(iii) repeated exposure will cause recurrence of reactions

(iv) often include skin rash, angioneurotic oedema, serum sickness and anaphylaxis or asthma.

Factors affecting the incidence of allergic reactions are the drug, the patient and the disease for which the drug is given.

(b) ***Genetically determined ADRs (idiosyncrous):*** The major genetically determined ADRs can be divided into two types;

(i) Reactions due to altered pharmacokinetic handling of the drug in the body

(ii) Reactions due to altered tissue responsiveness.

Acquired patient anomalies

These reactions are due to the presence of intercurrent illness, which may unmask pharmacological effects that are not apparent in normal individuals. For examples, haemorrhage or perforation of the peptic ulcers due to aspirin or corticosteroids. Liver disease may impair drug detoxification and renal disease which impairs glomerular filtration leading to reduced elimination of drugs that undergo renal excretion.

Anomalies of drug presentation and administration

These reactions may be a consequence of excessive response, alterations in bioavailability or an inappropriate method of administration. There are three main potential sources of ADRs in this class. They include decomposition of active constituents, effects of by-products of the active constituents derived from chemical synthesis and effects of additives, solubilizing, stabilizing, colouring agents and excipients commonly incorporated in pharmaceutical preparations. Therefore, alteration in production methods may have marked adverse effects consequences.

Drug interactions

These are ADRs resulting from interactions of more than one drug given at the same time and are likely to be proportional to the number of drugs given. However, some drug interactions may have both unwanted consequences and certain benefits (e.g. potentiation). The frequency of adverse drug interactions in clinical practice makes it mandatory for health care professionals to know the principle drugs and mechanisms of interactions involved.

Predisposing factors of ADRs and the mechanisms of drug interaction many reactions occur early in the course of treatment (such as anaphylaxis after penicillin injection); some other reactions may develop over a prolonged period of treatment (such as osteoporosis with oral steroids); the other reactions may appear long after the drug is discontinued (such as vaginal adenocarcinoma due to diethylstilbestrol given to the mother).

The following are predisposing factors of ADRs:-

Age

The incidence of adverse drug reaction appears to be highest in the very young and very old people. In these two extreme periods of life, there is poorly developed and altered physiological function respectively. Therefore, metabolism and elimination of some drugs may be delayed.

Pathophysiological conditions

Intercurrent diseases may alter the pharmacokinetic handling of a drug, its tissue sensitivity or the response to a drug. That is, diseases can alter drug absorption, metabolism, elimination and the body's response to drugs.

Amount of drug administered

An excessive response to drug or prolonged therapy may be a predisposing factor for ADRs. Over dosage is often relative rather than absolute because the individual response to a drug varies.

Sex

Several studies have shown that for some drugs women are more likely to suffer from ADRs than men. This is due to pharmacokinetic and or pharmacodynamic sex-related factors.

Previous history of allergy

Patients who have previously suffered an allergic drug reaction appear to be more susceptible than others to allergic ADRs in general. Heredity may make some people more susceptible to the toxic effects of certain drugs.

Racial or Genetic Factors

There may be racial differences in the incidence of some type of ADRs or some individuals have a genetically determined response to development of ADRs. e. g. ethinopharmacological difference such as glucose 6-phosphate dehydrogenase deficiency, which predisposes to some drug induced haemolytic anaemia, is commoner amongst Africans, Kurdish and Iraqi Jews, some Mediterranean people and Filipinos and is relatively infrequent amongst other races.

Multiple Drug Therapy (Polypharmacy)

The incidence of ADRs increases with the number of drugs given due to risk of interactions. Interaction between prescribed drugs is therefore an area, which is of concern to every health care professional.

The following are the mechanisms of drug interactions:

(a) Direct physical or chemical interactions of more than one drug given concomitantly.

(b) Altered gastrointestinal absorption, competition for protein binding sites or receptors.

(c) Increased or decreased metabolism of a drug by induction, activation or inhibition of drug metabolizing enzymes.

(d) Alteration of acid-base equilibrium thereby influencing drug distribution and renal clearance.

(e) Alteration of haemodynamics or renal function that influences rates of renal excretion.

Procedure for Reporting Adverse Drug Reaction

Health care professional should bear in mind when reporting an ADR that ADR reports are, for the most part, only suspected associations that a drug has caused a particular adverse event. Reporting an ADR does not imply a causal association between the drug and the adverse reaction. However, in a doubtful case it is better to report than not to report.

1. WHAT TO REPORT

Any undesirable adverse event suspected to be associated with use of drug, biological (including blood products), herbal drugs, cosmetics or medical devices should be reported. They should include;

1. All ADRs as a result of prescription and non-prescription
2. All suspected adverse drug reactions regardless of whether or not the product was used in accordance with the product information provided by the company marketing the product

3. Unexpected reaction, regardless of their nature or severity, whether not consistent with product information or labelling
4. An observed increase in frequency of a given reaction
5. A serious reaction, whether expected or not
6. All suspected ADRs associated with drug-drug, drug-food or drug-food supplements interactions
7. ADRs in special field of interest such as drug abuse and drug use in pregnancy and during lactation
8. ADRs occurring from overdose or medication error
9. Unusual lack of efficacy or when suspected pharmaceutical defects are observed

What information is required for an ADR case report?

The minimal standard information to be provided for proper assessment of the ADR case report are;

1. Patient information
2. Adverse reactions description (include laboratory results if available)
3. Information related to the suspected drug(s)
4. Information on management of the adverse reactions
5. **Information about the reporter**

I. Patient information

1. *Patient identity:* indicate initials or record number of the patient in hospital, medical institution, dispensary, clinic or pharmacy.
2. *Birth dates or age:* indicate date, month and year
3. *Sex:* Male or Female
4. *Weight:* should be in Kilograms

II. Adverse reaction(s)

1. *Brief description of the ADR(s):* It indicates the adverse(s) reaction by marking X in the appropriate box. Preferably describe briefly the nature of the adverse reaction being reported but as clearly as possible, including the body site and severity.

2. *Time/date of onset of the adverse reactions:* State the time of onset or the occurrence of the adverse reaction in relation to the administration of the drug. Indicate the date of onset in the following order; day, month and year. For example, did the drug reaction appear immediately following drug administration or there was temporal or spatial correlation with administration.

3. *Other relevant information:*

   (i) Patient medical history or laboratory data including dates if available, considered relevant to the case or the adverse reaction being reported should be entered.

(ii) Mention appropriate laboratory tests done to the patient and results to confirm the adverse reaction.

(iii) State this concisely but clearly.

III. Suspected drug(s)

1. *Name of the suspected drug (s):* trade name should preferably be used, if trade name not available, generic name may be used. Strength of the drug (s) should be stated

2. *Dosage, frequency and route of administration* should be clearly notified.

For example;

(i) Dosage (specify dosage form; tablet, capsules, syrup, injection, cream, eye drops, etc. including total amount of drugs).

(ii) Frequency: specify unit first i.e. mg, ml, mg/kg and number of time given e.g. 4 times daily or q.i.d.

(iii) Route of administration by which the drug was administered. This should be entered in full term or abbreviated using the World Health Organisation (WHO) codes as follows:

ROUTES CODES	ROUTES CODES
Buccal BU	Intrathecal IT
Conjuctival CO	Intratracheal TR
Dental DE	Intrauterine IU
Implant MP	Intravenous IV
Inhalation IH	Intravesical IB
Insufflation IS	Per oral PO
Intra-arterial IA	Per rectal PR
Intra-articular IR	Subcutaneous SC
Intra-cardiac IC	Sublingual SL
Intradermal ID	Systemic (if route is not Specified) SY
Intramuscular IM	Topical (external) TO
Intranasal IN	Transmammary transfer TM

3. *Therapy date:* the dates of beginning and termination of the administration of each drug should be stated, and preferably recorded as follows:- date, month and year. If dates are not available, record duration of treatment. If drug administration has not been terminated at the time of reporting, state 'Continuing'

4. *Batch number and expiry date:* provide these information if are available

5. *Reason for use:* state indication or condition for which the drug(s) was given for.

6. *Particular of concurrently drugs(or other treatment)*: state particulars of other drug (s) administered by the patient concurrently with the suspected drug, including drug administration for at least 1 month back with dosage, route of administration, duration of administration and indications.

7. *Provide relevant information on medical devices*

IV. Management of the adverse reaction

1. *Confirmation of the ADRs:* indicate what assisted in confirming the suspected adverse reactions. For example:
   (i) Drug reactions confirmed by disappearance of the reaction after stopping administration of the drug or reducing the doses.
   (ii) Recovery on withdrawal of suspected drug(s) if no other drug is withdrawn and no therapy given.
   (iii) Recovery follows treatment of the reaction in addition to withdrawal of drug.
2. *Mention the criteria* for regarding the reaction as serious
3. *Mention any treatment given* to the patient after experiencing the ADRs.
4. *Outcome*: indicate the outcome of the adverse reaction by marking X in the appropriate box with dates in case of fatal outcome.

Reporter information

Details on reporter of an ADR: mention your particulars:-name, address of the health facility (hospital, institution, dispensary, clinic, company, pharmacy or maternity home). E-mail address (optional), signature, telephone number and date of reporting the reaction (indicate date, month and year)

2. WHO SHOULD REPORT

Submission of a report does not constitute an admission that a health care professional or the drug or the product caused or contributed to the ADR in any way as all reports are termed as suspected.

Reporters should bear in mind that any information related to the reporter and patient identities shall be kept confidential.

The following should provide reports of any case of suspected ADRs when encountered to the patient as part of their professional responsibility:-

1. All health care professionals including specialists, doctors, dentists, pharmacists, nurses, assistant medical officers, clinical officers, pharmaceutical technicians, pharmaceutical assistants, traditional medicine practitioners and others health care providers

2. Manufacturers or Product registrants: They should develop system for ADR follow-up within their company and assessment of impact of notification of significant safety data on their products.
3. All government hospitals, private hospitals, health centres, dispensaries private clinics, private pharmacies and private nursing homes have obligation to report all ADR cases encountered or reported to them by the patients.

Incharge of the following facilities; government and private hospitals, health centres and dispensaries they are required to nominate a focal person who will coordinate the ADRs collection and reporting within the facility.

This person will be a link between the institution and the government.

It is vital to report an ADR even if you are doubtful about the precise relationship with the given medication or you do not have all the facts. What is required is to report all SUSPECTED ADRs.

Collection of reports from several healthcare providers in different parts of the country assists in making associations (strengthening of signal) between a particular drug and the adverse reaction.

Therefore, you must ensure that all necessary information for submission of ADR reports are obtained and reported through the reporting forms.

3. When to Report

Any suspected ADR should be reported as soon as possible. Delay in reporting will make reporting inaccurate and unreliable. If possible, report while the patient is still in the health facility this gives a chance to reporter to clear any ambiguity by re-questioning or examining the patient

4. How to Report

1. Send your report in a standardised form for reporting ADRs. The reporting form is self adhesive postage paid form
2. Dully fill in the ADRs reporting form (annexed) when encountering an ADR to the patient.
3. Use a separate form for each patient (refer to filling guides)
4. A completed ADRs case report form should immediately be sealed and mailed preferably directly within three days or through other reporting centres for onward transmission.
5. Reports can also be submitted online by going to the website and clicking on "adverse drug reaction reporting" on the bottom-right
6. Reports may be sent by e-mail also.
7. ADR reports may be faxed in cases of perceived urgency

8. Any follow-up information for an ADR case that has already been reported can be sent on another ADR form, or communicated by telephone, fax or e-mail. To enable this information be matched with the original report it is very important that follow-up reports are identified and the following should be indicated in the report;
   (i) that it is a follow-up information,
   (ii) the date of the original report and
   (iii) the patient identities.

Basic principles of efficient reporting

1. Report the adverse reaction immediately after it occurs.
2. If possible, take the decision to report whilst the patient is still with you, so that the details can be filled in at once on the reporting form.
3. Think about any other factors which may contribute in causing the event such as other prescribed drugs, self-medication, herbal products, food, chemicals, ask the patient particularly about other medicines taken.
4. If you get any supplementary data later, e.g. if the same patient develops the effect again or if something happens which increases your suspicion or seem to exclude the reaction, please send in a supplementary note immediately using ADRs reporting form with the patient identifiers.
5. All reports must have the following four data elements
   (i) An identifiable patient
   (ii) A suspected adverse effect
   (iii) A named suspected drug (s)
   (iv) An identifiable reporter
6. Always write legibly.

5. Where to Report

1. Report any suspected ADRs for pharmaceutical products to the ministry of health, govt. of India Preferably directly by post or online
2. Via Zonal Drug Information Centres at every state head quarter.
3. Via a focal person in the following health facility; government hospitals, private hospitals, health centres, dispensaries for onward transmission to ministry of health.

How to obtain the reporting form?

The ADR reporting form is obtained free of charge from;

1. ministry of health offices

2. The website of ministry
3. Zonal Drug Information Centres.
4. Regional hospital, district hospitals and ADRs focal persons in hospitals, health centres, clinics and dispensaries.

Processing of Collected Adverse Drug Reaction Data

1. Assessment of ADR Case Reports

Assessment of case report aim at identifying national drug safety problems and respond to these through communication and or scientific risk/benefit assessment.

Ministry of health is responsible with continuous collection, assessment and storage of reports of, suspected adverse reaction to medicinal products marketed in the country.

Reports are initially separated according to their source. All case reports will be individually assessed and the following shall be considered: -

1. Quality of documentation in respect to completeness on the four elements of a case report as possible, integrity of data, quality of diagnosis and follow-up.
2. Analysis; this shall be based on the temporal relationship between the reaction and the drug, whether there was positive dechallenge/rechallenge, the seriousness of the reaction, whether the current labelling lists the reaction and whether the reaction is reported on the medical literature.
3. Clinical relevance in respect to detection of new reaction especially for new drugs, unknown reactions or serious. If similar cases are found, the report becomes a monitored adverse drug reaction.
4. Quality control in respect to identification of duplicate reports. Certain characteristics of a case report for example; sex, date of birth or age, name of the suspected drug, dates of drug exposure etc. shall be used to identify duplicate reporting or follow up report.
5. Causality assessment and transmission of the assessed reports in suitable format to the WHO database of International Drug Monitoring at Uppsala Monitoring Centre (UMC) shall be done monthly.

   The causality assessment and ADR coding shall be based on WHO causality categories. The categories are based on four considerations:-

   (i) The association in time between drug administration and event

   (ii) Pharmacology (including current knowledge of nature and frequency of adverse reactions)

(iii) Medical or pharmacological plausibility (signs and symptoms, laboratory tests, pathological findings, mechanism)

(iv) Likelihood or exclusion of other causes

The Coding; drug names shall be entered in a systemic way by using the WHO Drug Dictionary and preferably the trade name of the suspected product shall be used. Diseases will be classified based on International Classification of Diseases (ICD) developed by WHO. The adverse events description shall be entered based on the WHO Adverse Reaction Terminology (WHO-ART).

6. Generation of hypotheses or the identification of signals. This activity shall be strengthened by a search from the cumulative data in the global WHO database for similar report.
7. Presentation of analyzed case reports to the Drug Committee. This committee of experts shall be responsible for evaluation and interpretation of the compiled coded case reports and giving advice on appropriate interventions.
8. Receipt and communication of appropriate safety information resulting from analysis of local reports, from UMC, other national Centre, regulatory agencies and literature.

2. Handling of ADR Data

An acknowledgement letter or note will be sent to the reporter for every ADR report received with an additional reporting form. the ADR reports shall be stored in a confidential database at ministry of health and analyzed report sent to the WHO database of International Programme on safety monitoring of drugs to which all case reports received by the National centers are sent.

The names of reporter and the patient will be removed before any details about a specific adverse drug reaction are used or communicated to others. Publications will not disclose trade name of products unless regulatory actions have been taken. In this regard information obtained from spontaneous ADR monitoring system will not be used for commercial purposes. The information is only meant to improve our understanding on use of medicinal products by reducing the risks associated with drug prescribing and administration and to ultimately improve patient care, safety and treatment outcome. In the same way suspected ADR reports cannot be used in a court of law under any circumstances.

Ministry is responsible for providing reporting forms, collecting, analyzing and communicating the findings and evaluation reports. The government shall use the finding from the reporter for making regulatory decisions on how to prevent or minimize the risk of ADRs from the use of pharmaceutical products circulating in the country.

Health ministry may communicate the findings, recommendations and directives to appropriate organizations or individuals. These include, healthcare professionals, pharmaceutical manufacturers, public health programmes within the country, other public and private health institutions, the media and the public.

Provision of feedback to reporters

The outcome of the report, together with any important or relevant information relating to the reaction reported, will be communicated to the reporters and other parties as appropriate.

After a significant ADR is detected and a decision on the course of action determined, the information shall be communicated rapidly and systematically to healthcare providers and product registrant.

In addition, healthcare professionals will have an increased advantage of access to feed back information on reaction to drug within the same pharmacological class reported within the country and internationally and availability of additional database for further investigation.

3. Utilisation of ADR Data

Data collected will be used for provision of timely advice to health-care professionals and consumers on drug safety issues at facility level, national and international level. A well-documented adverse drug reaction case could result in one or more of the following;

1. Further investigation of signals. For example, identifying `at risk' group, a dose range which might be more suspected, suggesting a pharmaceutical group effect, pharmacological mechanisms, lack of effect by a particular drug or investigation into the use of a drug in the country
2. Drug regulation and dissemination of information of current importance
3. Education and training initiatives to improve the safe use of the medication and other health promotion interventions as the situation may warrant including change in supply status or withdrawal Report on drug problems from healthcare provider can prevent new drugs tragedies or can reduce suffering and save lives of thousands of patients

3.5 Irrational Drug Combinations

Prescribing fixed dose drug combinations has become the "in thing" in medical practice. Using the excuse of better patient compliance, many doctors, both in private as well as government prescribe irrational fixed dose drug combinations. Quite a few infectious diseases are becoming resistant to treatment with a single drug. With the escalating cost of drugs, there is poor drug compliance, which further magnifies the problem, both for the prescriber as well the patient. Manufacturers of drugs having quickly tuned in to the potential golden egg, are marketing fixed dose drug formulations for various diseases.

Even though use of combinations of drugs is common practice, the selection of optimal dose and optimal combination has remained largely a matter of trial and error. The basis of many fixed dose drug combinations being taught to the undergraduate medical students and also being prescribed popularly, appears to be irrational to pharmacologists.

CIMS lists more than 100 irrational combinations which are not approved in any developed country but are being marketed in India. This fact has to be taught to undergraduate medical students in their formative years of learning so that once they address medical ailments like malaria, tuberculosis, AIDS, hypertension, etc. they should be more logical in selecting appropriate drug combinations and should not be swayed by marketing tricks and false claims made by the pharmaceutical industry. The pharmacological basis of combining each ingredient in the formulation should be taught. Selection of P drugs, rational drug use, use of rational drug combinations and ethical laboratory practices should be inculcated in the student's curriculum during their clinical training.

Fourteenth WHO model list of essential medicines (March 2005) contains only 18 approved drug combinations, whereas in India, there are innumerable examples of irrational drug combinations, which are easily available and can be bought without necessarily giving a prescription. [Table 3.1] This issue has to be urgently addressed by us, pharmacologists, as the magnitude of the problem is increasing.

Table 3.1 Some irrational fixed dose drug combinations available in the Indian market.

Combinations	Irrationality
1. Norfloxacin + Metronidazole; Norfloxacin + Tinidazole; Norfloxacin + Tinidazole + Loperamide; Norfloxacin + Tinidazole + Dicyclomine; Norfloxacin + Ornidazole; Ciprofloxacin + Tinidazole; Ofloxacin + Tinidazole; Ofloxacin + Metronidazole; Ofloxacin + Ornidazole; Gatifloxacin + Ornidazole.	Though claimed to be broad spectrum, combining (antiamoebic) with fluoroquinolone (antibacterial) is irrational because patient suffers only from one type of diarrhoea. Using this combination adds to cost, adverse effects and may encourage resistance.
2. Nimesulide + Diclofenac; Nimesulide + Dicyclomine + Simethicone; Nimesulide + Paracetamol; Nimesulide + Cetirizine + Pseudoephedrine; Nimesulide + Paracetamol + Tizanidine.	Nimesulide a controversial drug, has been banned in many countries. It is a sorry state of affairs that its combinations are readily available over the counter. Combining two NSAIDs may increase the side effects of both the NSAIDs. There is little documentary evidence that a preparation containing more than one analgesic is more effective than a single ingredient preparation.
3. Amoxycillin + Cloxacillin	Amoxycillin is inactive against staphylococcus, as most strains produce ß-lactamase and cloxacillin is not so active against streptococci. For any given infection, one of the components is useless but adds to cost and adverse effect. Since amount of each drug is halved, efficacy is reduced and chances of selecting resistant strains is increased.

Contd....

Combinations Irrationality

4. Domperidone + Rabeprazole; Domperidone + Esomeprazole Increased incidence of rhabdomyolysis.
5. Simvastatin + Nicotinic acid; Atorvastatin + Nicotinic acid Probability of myopathy is increased.
6. Roxithromycin + Ambroxol; Ciprofloxacin + Ambroxol; Gatifloxacin + Many trials have failed to show superior efficacy of the combination over use of Ambroxol; Cefadroxil + Ambroxol; Cefixime + Ambroxol + Lactobacillus ambroxol alone in respiratory tract infection. Gatifloxacin is withdrawn.
7. Fluconazole + Tinidazole; Doxycycline + Tinidazole; Tetracycline + Combining two antimicrobial agents to increase the spectrum of activity is Metronidazole irrational, as the patient may need only one drug. The keypoint is to make a correct diagnosis.
8. Enalapril + Losartan Combining two drugs affecting the same pathway is irrational; it doesn't add to efficacy.
9. Cetirizine + Phenylpropanolamine + Dextromethorpan Phenylpropanolamine is a banned drug; yet it is a part of many cough and cold Cetirizine + Phenylpropanolamine + Paracetamol; Levocetirizine + remedies. Besides its potential to cause stroke (more so in hypertensives), it Paracetamol + Phenylpropanolamine. can aggravate diabetes, glaucoma and prostate enlargement.
10. Diazepam + Dried aluminium hydroxide gel + Aluminium glycinate + Antacids raise the gastric pH and reduce the absorption of benzodiazepines. Oxyphenonium; Diazepam + Magaldrate + Oxyphenonium; Diazepam + Dried aluminium hydroxide gel + Magnesium trisilicate + Dimethylpolysiloxane.
11. Cisapride + Omeprazole; Mosapride + Pantoprazole ; In patients with gastroesophageal reflux disease, the use of this combination Ondansetron + Pantoprazole. has shown no benefit due to the addition of prokinetic drugs.

What needs to be done?

The hit and trial method of combining drugs should be replaced by a rational and logical basis for bringing out a fixed dose drug formulation. Operational, statistical and mathematical models constitute a highly versatile framework for mechanism based modeling (pharmacokinetic/ pharmacodynamic) by taking signal transduction properties of the drug combination into account. Sound scientific research should underlie the development and production of drug combinations.

There is a need to carefully monitor and censor misleading claims by the pharmaceutical industry. Some degree of irresponsibility on the part of the pharmaceutical industry and lack of vigilance of government agencies underlies the increased popularity of irrational drug combinations. Most advertisements in many of the medical journals published from India fail to mention important details pertaining to correct usage of drug combinations. Clinical pharmacists can play an important role in guiding and imparting knowledge to the public.

There is a need to strengthen the mechanism for continuing professional development of practitioners to ensure that they have the necessary knowledge and skills to prescribe rationally. Perhaps the insistence that prescribers, especially those in private practice should undergo a continuing medical education (CME) course once in two years on newer drug combinations, new drug molecules introduced into the market and adversc drug reactions will go a long way in curbing irrational prescribing.

ADR reporting should be made mandatory as they are in developed countries. Pharmacovigilence should be more effective.

Hospitals should constitute drugs and therapeutics review committees to rationalize prescribing.

Finally, medical schools and postgraduate colleges must take the responsibility of training students and young doctors how to assess new drug combinations more logically. Unless we encourage our students to think rationally and independently this menace will continue to grow. We cannot complacently offload all blame onto the industry and government regulators; the onus of responsibility lies heavily on the shoulders of academicians too.

3.6 List of Drugs Banned by Government of India and Other State Governments

1. Amidopyrine.
2. Fixed dose combinations of vitamins with anti-inflammatory agents and tranquilizers.
3. Fixed dose combinations of Atropine in Analgesics and Antipyretics.
4. Fixed dose combinations of Strychnine and Caffeine in tonics.
5. Fixed dose combinations of Yohimbine and Strychnine with Testosterone and Vitamins.
6. Fixed dose combinations of Iron with Strychnine, Arsenic and Yohimbine.
7. Fixed dose combinations of Sodium Bromide/chloral hydrate with other drugs.
8. Phenacetin.
9. Fixed dose combinations of antihistaminic with anti-diarrhoeals.
10. Fixed dose combinations of Penicillin with Sulphonamides.
11. Fixed dose combinations of Vitamins with Analgesics.
12. Fixed dose combinations of any other Tetracycline with Vitamin C.
13. Fixed dose combinations of Hydroxyquinoline group of drugs with any other drug except for preparations meant for external use.
14. Fixed dose combinations of Corticosteroids with any other drug for internal use.
15. Fixed dose combinations of Chloramphenicol with any other drug for internal use.

16. Fixed dose combinations of crude Ergot preparations except those containing Ergotamine, Caffeine, analgesics, antihistamines for the treatment of migraine, headaches.
17. Fixed dose combinations of Vitamins with Anti TB drugs except combination of Isoniazid with Pyridoxine Hydrochloride (Vitamin B6).
18. Penicillin skin/eye Ointment.
19. Tetracycline Liquid Oral preparations.
20. Nialamide.
21. Practolol.
22. Methapyrilene, its salts.
23. Methaqualone.
24. Oxytetracycline Liquid Oral preparations.
25. Demeclocycline Liquid Oral preparations.
26. Combination of anabolic Steroids with other drugs.
27. Fixed dose combination of Oestrogen and Progestin (other than oral contraceptive) containing per tablet estrogen content of more than 50 mcg (equivalent to Ethinyl Estradiol) and progestin content of more than 3 mg (equivalent to Norethisterone Acetate) and all fixed dose combination injectable preparations containing synthetic Oestrogen and Progesterone. (Subs. By Noti. No. 743 (E) dt 10-08-1989)
28. Fixed dose combination of Sedatives/ hypnotics/anxiolytics with analgesics-antipyretics.
29. Fixed dose combination of Rifampicin, isoniazid and Pyrazinamide, except those which provide daily adult dose given below:

Drugs	Minimum	Maximum
Rifampicin	450 mg	600 mg
Isoniazid	300 mg	400 mg
Pyrazinamide	1000mg	1500 mg

30. Fixed dose combination of Histamine H-2 receptor antagonists with antacids except for those combinations approved by Drugs Controller, India.
31. The patent and proprietary medicines of fixed dose combinations of essential oils with alcohol having percentage higher than 20% proof except preparations given in the Indian Pharmacopoeia.
32. All Pharmaceutical preparations containing Chloroform exceeding 0.5% w/w or v/v whichever is appropriate.
33. Fixed dose combination of Ethambutol with INH other than the following: INH Ethambutol 200 mg. 600 mg. 300 mg. 800 mg.
34. Fixed dose combination containing more than one antihistamine.

35. Fixed dose combination of any anthelmintic with cathartic/purgative except for piperazine/Santonim.
36. Fixed dose combination of Salbutamol or any other drug having primarily bronchodilatory activity with centrally acting anti-tussive and/or antihistamine.
37. Fixed dose combination of laxatives and/or anti-spasmodic drugs in enzyme preparations.
38. Fixed dose combination of Metoclopramide with systemically absorbed drugs except fixed dose combination of metoclopramide with aspirin/paracetamol
39. Fixed dose combination of centrally acting, antitussive with antihistamine, having high atropine like activity in expectorants.
40. Preparations claiming to combat cough associated with asthma containing centrally acting antitussive and/ or an antihistamine.
41. Liquid oral tonic preparations containing glycerophosphates and/or other phosphates and / or central nervous system stimulant and such preparations containing alcohol more than 20% proof.
42. .Fixed dose combination containing Pectin and/or Kaolin with any drug which is systemically absorbed from GI tract except for combinations of Pectin and/or Kaolin with drugs not systemically absorbed.
43. Chloral Hydrate as a drug.
44. Dovers Powder I.P.
45. Dover's Powder Tablets I.P.
46. Antidiarrhoeal formulations containing Kaolin or Pectin or Attapulgite or Activated Charcoal.
47. Antidiarrhoeal formulations containing Phthalyl Sulphathiazole or Sulphaguanidine or Succinyl Sulphathiazole.
48. Antidiarrhoeal formulations containing Neomycin or Streptomycin or Dihydrostreptomycin including their respective salts or esters.
49. Liquid Oral antidiarrhoeals or any other dosage form for pediatric use containing Diphenoxylate Lorloperamide or Atropine or Belladona including their salts or esters or metabolites Hyoscyamine or their extracts or their alkaloids.
50. Liquid Oral antidiarrhoeals or any other dosage form for pediatric use containing halogenated hydroxyquinolines.
51. Fixed dose combination of antidiarrhoeals with electrolytes.
52. Patent and Proprietary Oral Rehydration Salts other than those conforming to the
53. Fixed dose combination of Oxyphenbutazone or Phenylbutazone with any other drug.
54. Fixed dose combination of Analgin with any other drug.
55. Fixed dose combination of dextropropoxyphene with any other drug other than anti-spasmodics and/or non-steriodal anti-inflammatory drugs (NSAIDS).

56. Fixed dose combination of a drug, standards of which are prescribed in the Second Schedule to the said Act with an Ayurvedic, Siddha or Unani drug.
57. Mepacrine Hydrochloride (Quinacrine and its salts) in any dosage form for use for female sterilization or contraception.
58. Fenfluramine and Dexfenfluramine.
59. Fixed dose combination of Diazepam and Diphenhydramine Hydrochloride .
60. Rimonabant.

List of Drugs Prohibited for Import

1. Nialamide
2. Practolol
3. Amidopyrine
4. Phenacetin
5. Methapyrilene and its salts
6. Methaqualone
7. Chloral Hydrate as a drug
8. Mepacrine Hydrochloride (Quinacrine and its Salts) in any dosage form for use for female sterilization or contraception.
9. Fenfluramine and Dexfenfluramine
10. Rimonabant

Drugs Prohibited for Manufacture , Sale and Distribution In India (Drugs and Formulations)

1. Cosmetics Licensed as toothpaste/tooth powder containing tobacco.
2. Parenteal Preparations fixed dose combination of streptomycin with Pencillin
3. Fixed dose combination of Vitamin B1, Vitamin B6 and Vitamin B12 for human use
4. Fixed dose combination of haemoglobin in any form (natural or synthetic).
5. Fixed dose combination of Pancreatin or Pancrelipase containing amylase, protease and lipase with any other enzyme.
6. Fixed dose combination of Nitrofurantoin and trimethoprim.
7. Fixed dose combination of Phenobarbitone with any anti-asthmatic drugs.
8. Fixed dose combination of Phenobarbitone with Hyoscin and/or Hyoscyamine
9. Fixed dose combination of Phenobarbitone with Ergotamine and/or Belladona
10. Fixed dose combination of Haloperidol with any anti-cholinergic agent including Propantheline Bromide.

11. Fixed dose combination of Nalidixic Acid with any anti-amoebic including Metronidazole.
12. Fixed dose combination of Loperamide Hydrochloride with Furazolidone
13. Fixed dose combination of Cyproheptadine with Lysine or Peptone.
14. Astemizole
15. Terfinadine
16. Fenformin
17. Rafecoxib
18. Valdecoxib and its formulation
19. Diclofenac and its formulations for animal use

Questions

1. Explain the concept of irrational drug combinations and give the list of irrational drug combinations notified by the health agencies?
2. Explain the concept of pharmaceutical outcomes movement in India?
3. Explain the following concepts and their relevance (a) list of drugs banned by govt.of India (b) pharmaco epidemiology.
4. What is pharmacoeconomics? explain its significance in Pharma health care practice?
5. What is the present status of pharmacovigilence in India? Exp[lain the role of central and state govts. in taking measures for pharmacovigilence?
6. Explain in detail about social abuse of drugs and measures to be taken to control the abuse?
7. Explain the following: (a) alcohol de-addiction program (b) abuse of NSAIDS.
8. What are the legal, social and family consequences of social abuse of drugs?
9. Explain in detail the steps to be taken to eradicate the practice of drug abuse?
10. Explain the following: (a) comparative cost effectiveness ratio
    (b) cost benefit ratio of medicines?

Chapter - 4

Organisation of Distribution and Marketing

4.1 Marketing and Functions of Marketing

What is Marketing?

Marketing is defined as the process of determining the needs and wants of consumers and being able to deliver products that satisfy those needs and wants. Marketing includes all of the activities necessary to move a product from the producer to the consumer. *Think of marketing as a bridge from the producer to the consumer.*

Marketing starts with market research, a learning process in which marketers get to know everything they can about the needs and wants of consumers, and it ends when somebody buys something. Many companies feel that services provided to customers after the purchase also are an important part of marketing. All of these enterprises -- production, advertising, transportation, processing, packaging, and selling -- are included in the marketing process.

The Nine Functions of Marketing

In order for the marketing bridge to work correctly -- providing consumers with opportunities to purchase the products and services they need -- the marketing process must accomplish nine important functions.

The functions are:

Buying - people have the opportunity to buy products that they want.

Selling - producers function within a free market to sell products to consumers.

Financing - banks and other financial institutions provide money for the production and marketing of products.

Storage - products must be stored and protect ed until they are needed. This function is especially important for perishable products such as fruits and vegetables.

Transportation -products must be physically relocated to the locations where consumers can buy them. This is a very important function. Transportation includes rail road, ship, airplane, truck, and telecommunications for non-tangible products such as market information.

Processing - processing involves turning a raw product, like wheat, into something the consumer can use -- for example, bread.

Risk-Taking - insurance companies provide coverage to protect producers and marketers from loss due to fire, theft, or natural disasters

Market Information - information from around the world about market conditions, weather, price movements, and political changes, can affect the marketing process. Market information is provided by all forms of telecommunication, such as television, the internet, and phone.

Grading and Standardizing - Many products are graded in order to conform to previously determined standards of quality. For example, when you purchase No. 1Potatoes, you know you are buying the best potatoes on the market.

The Four Utilities of Marketing

The marketing process must also add "utility" to the products consumers want. Utility is the use or satisfaction a person gets from a product. If you purchase a chain saw you anticipate that you will receive a certain amount of utility from it. You will be able to use the saw to cut fire wood, prune trees, and take care of a variety of jobs around your home. There are four types of utility.

Form Utility - a product must be processed into a form that the customer wants or needs. For example, wheat is processed into bread, trees are processed into lumber, and potatoes are processed into french fries. If you ordered french fries with your lunch and the waiter brought you a raw potato, you probably wouldn't be too happy.

An example of ***Form Utility.*** involves transporting products to the location where consumers can buy them. If you live in HYDERABAD, you certainly wouldn't want to have to drive to kurnool to buy oranges. Thanks to our modern transportation systems you don't have to; you simply drive to the local grocery store and oranges are there ready to add to your shopping cart -- place utility.

Trucking is one form of transportation that helps add **Place Utility** to products.

Possession Utility - possession utility establishes legal ownership of a product. When you purchase something you normally receive a receipt; this provides legal ownership and the right to use the product. Some products, computer software, for example, also provide a user license. A license of this kind gives you the right to use the product within certain guidelines. *Stock certificates are proof of ownership.*

Stocks prove that you own part of a company. This is an example of **Possession Utility.**

Time Utility - this could be described as being in the right place at the right time when a customer is ready to purchase a product. Creating and keeping customers means having products available for when they want them, and often this requires some type of storage facility. Wheat is one example of a commodity that must be stored after it is harvested. It is stored in silos until processors are ready to convert it into food products such as bread or cereals.

Silo is used to store grain products like wheat. This allows the product to be used by people when they need it; an example of ***Time Utility.***

4.2 Marketing Mix

Introduction

The basic task of marketing is the delivery of product(s) to consumers so that their needs are fulfilled and organisational objectives are also achieved. This involves several important decisions, e.g. deciding about the product or products which should be offered for sale, price of the product, markets where products may sell and the means of communication with the consumer for the sale of the product. All these decisions form part of marketing-mix.

Concept and Characteristics of Marketing Mix

The process of marketing or distribution of goods require particular attention of management of business because production has no relevance unless products are sold. Marketing mix, simply stated, is the process of designing and integrating various elements of marketing in such a way as to ensure the achievement of enterprise objectives

The elements of marketing mix have been classified under four heads - product, price, place and promotion. That is why marketing mix is said to be a combination of 4 P's.

Decisions relating to the product include product designing, packaging and labelling and varieties of the product. Decision on 'Price' is very important because sales depend to a large extent on product pricing. Whether uniform price will be charged or different prices will be charged for the same product in different markets are examples of decision pertaining to the price of the product.

The third important element is 'place', which refers to decision regarding the market where products will be offered for sale. 'Promotion' involves decisions bearing on the ways and means of increasing sales.

Different tools or methods may be adopted for this purpose. The relative importance to be attached to the various methods is decided while concentrating on the element of 'promotion' in marketing mix, lastly, the marketing manager has to take into account the impact of external factors like consumer behaviour, competitors' strategy, and Government policy on each element of marketing mix.

In short, marketing mix involves decisions regarding products to the made available, the price to be charged for the same, the incentives to be provided to the consumers in the markets where products would be made available for sale. These decision are taken keeping in view the influence of marketing forces outside the organisation.

Characteristics of Marketing Mix

(i) ***Marketing-mix is the crux of marketing process:*** Marketing mix involves many crucial decisions relating to each element of the mix. The impact of the mix would be the best when proper weightage is assigned to each element and they are integrated so that the combined effect leads to the best results.

(ii) Marketing mix has to be reviewed constantly in order to meet the changing requirements :

(iii) The marketing manager is required to constantly review the mix and conditions of the market, and make necessary changes in the marketing mix according to changes in the conditions and complexion of the market.

(iv) Changes in external environment necessitate alterations in the mix:

(v) Changes keep on taking place in the external environment. For many industries, customer is the most fluctuating variable of environment. Customers' tastes and prefrances change very fast. Brand loyalty and purchasing power too change over a period of time. The marketing manager has to carry out market analysis constantly to make necessary changes in the marketing mix.

(vi) Changes taking place within the firm too necessitate changes in marketing mix:

(vii) Changes within the firm may take place due to technological changes, or changes in the product line, or changes in the size and scale of operation. Such changes call for correspondent changes in the marketing mix.

(viii) Marketing mix should be so planned that it fulfills the needs of the consumer as well as the organisation.

Elements of Marketing Mix

As mentioned earlier the elements or constituents of marketing mix may be grouped broadly under four heads :

(i) Product

(ii) Price

(iii) Place
(iv) Promotion

Product

Product refers to a physical product or a service or an idea which a consumer needs and for which he is ready to pay. Physical products include tangible goods like grocery items, garments etc. Services are intangible products which are offered and purchased by consumers. Services may involve also an innovative idea on any aspect of operation.

Products is the key element of any marketing mix. The decisions concerning product may relate to -

(a) Product attributes
(b) Branding
(c) Packaging and labelling
(d) Product support service
(e) Product mix.

Product attributes refer to the quality, features and design of the product. A product should serve the purpose for which it is made, in terms of utility and quality. In a competitive market, products are differentiated on the basis of certain features or design. For example, in the whirlpool washing machine. 'Agitate wash' is the distinctive feature.

Branding is a crucial decision. In a competitive market, many products are sold by brand names. You might have come across Indian brand names, like Maruti, HMT, Godrej, TATA. Amongst foreign brand names Sony, Samsung are well known. Brand is an identification of product. It plays an important role in creation of demand while branding a product, it should be ensured that the name is simple, easy to read and pronounce and if possible, it should have an appeal.

Packaging and labelling of product are quite important decisions Packaging means putting the products in suitable containers or packets such as tin, plastic jar or card board box, etc. Packaging should be such that product is protected and easily handled. Sometimes, the container may have its own usefulness. For instance Baidyanath chyawanprash (pack) is available in a plastic jar which can be reused after consuming the chyawanprash. Certain polythene and plastic are not considered good as packaging material from the environment point of view. Their usage should be avoided.

Labelling serves the purpose of indicating the contents, weight or measure, instructions for use, price, name of the producer, date of manufacture and expiry, etc. The information on the label is essential for various reasons. For example, the date of expiry in case of medicines, and date of manufacture in the case of eatables prevent the sale of products which may prove harmful.

Product support service is another important element of product decision. It includes decision pertaining to the type of service and availability of the service. Service may be by way of installation service, training in product use, after sale service, credit and financing service, etc. It should be decided whether services would be provided free or against separate charge. Secondly, how the services would be made available by the producers or agencies, are also important decisions to be made particularly with respect to durable consumer goods like TV, washing machines electric fans, etc.

The markets in which products will be offered is yet another important decision. A company may decide to a single or a variety of products, add new products, or withdraw certain products. Relevant decisions are made keeping in view the scope of marketing. Such decisions are called product line or product mix decisions. Product life cycle is a guiding factor while decisions are made.

Product Life Cycle

Product life cycle denotes different stages through which the sale of any product changes over a period of time. Generally, there are four stages in the life of each product– introductory stage, growth stage, maturity stage, and declining stage. When any product is introduced in the market, heavy expenditure is incurred on advertising and other methods of increasing the sale. This is known as introductory stage.

During the growth period, sale of the product increases fast and cost of production comes down due to increase in scale of production. Profits earned increase substantially. During the maturity stage, the growth in sale of the product slows down. Profits also start declining. After the maturity stage there is a stage of decline, when the product starts losing its acceptance. There is a pressure for price cut. Firms generally start withdrawing the product after maturity stage. Some firms start preparing for introducing alternative product at the end of growth stage. Product life cycle, thus, helps in deciding about the product or products which should be offered in different markets.

Price

Price is the amount charged for a product or service. It is the consideration paid by consumers for the benefit of using any product or service. Price fixation is an important aspect of marketing. Pricing decisions of a company are affected by both internal as well as external factors.

Internal Factors External Factors

- Cost of the product – Nature of market
- Marketing objectives Pricing or demand for product
- Marketing mix strategy Decision – Competitors' costs and strategy price offers.
- Organisation for pricing – Other environmental factors like economy, government's policies, etc.

Internal factors

Internal factors, affecting the price of a product, are many. Cost of the product sets the floor. Any company would like to charge a price which covers the cost of the product and a fair rate of return. Cost of the product means total cost i.e., fixed plus variable costs. Fixed costs do not change with the change in volume of production upto a certain level. Variable costs change proportionately. In the period of recession, companies continue to supply at a rate which covers variable costs and as much of costs as possible.

The Company's marketing objective is yet another important variable for price fixation. If it is survival, the company would stay in the market as long as it covers variable costs fully and fixed costs partly. In case it is market leadership, a low price will be fixed initially. After wards prices may be enhanced. 'Surf Excel' is an example. At the time of introduction, its price was just equal to other close substitutes, but today it has its own market. It is bought by consumers without comparing its price with other substitutes.

The relative importance of pricing decision in marketing mix, also affects price fixation. Sometimes pricing decision is the control decision and all other decisions are taken afterwards. It may also happen that other variables of marketing mix like promotion become more important. Price is fixed after considering other variables. Who will fix the price is yet another important decision. In small organisations, top management sets the price. In large companies, product line managers perform this job. For industrial markets, sales managers are permitted to negotiate prices within a specified range. These days many companies set up a separate department to handle pricing decision.

External factors

Besides internal factors, external factors also influence the pricing decision of a company. These factors are called environmental factors. Nature of demand, competitors' costs, price offers and government policy are very important factors to be considered while fixing prices. The relationship between price and demand should be analysed properly. No company can ignore the costs, prices and offers of substitute items from competitiors. Economic factors, like rate of interest, state of industry (boom or recession), inflation, etc. affect the price-fixing decision. In case of certain products, e.g. products which fulfil basic needs, government may impose price control. Thus, it would also affect price of the product.

There may be two methods of price-fixation:

Business Studies

1. Cost-based approach
2. Competition-based approach

Cost-based approach: This is the simplest method of pricing. Generally companies add a certain percentage of Profit, to the total cost of the product. The total cost of the product is calculated after taking all types of costs into consideration. While following this approach, no other factors e.g. prices of substitute goods, nature of demand, etc. are considered.

Competition-based approach: In competitive market, cost-based approach is not always practicable. The prices are determined on the basis of conditions in the market. Companies may follow any one of the following three approaches.

(a) Price-in-line

(b) Market-plus

(c) Market-minus

Price-in-line means prices fixed nearly equal to the prices of close alternatives. Generally this happens under free market conditions i.e. when the number of buyers and sellers is so large that they cannot affect the prices. Prices are decided by the market forces of demand and supply.

When companies charge (fix up) a price which is more than the price of existing substitutes, it is called market plus pricing. This approach is adopted when the quality of a product is better, or it has a popular brand name, or its packaging is attractive and useful. Consumers will pay more only when they find distinctive differences in the product and its substitutes.

Sometimes business enterprises get ready to supply products at a price lower than the market price. It may be adopted to grab a larger market share or to make a newly introduced product more popular. This approach is called market-minus approach. Companies having shorter channels of distributions or direct selling facilities can afford to fix a price lower than the prevailing market price.

Promotion

Promotion refers to using methods of communication with two objectives : (i) informing the existing and potential consumers about a product, and (2) to persuade consumers to buy the product. It is an important element of marketing mix. In the absence of communication, consumers may not be aware of the product and its potential to satisfy their needs and desires. Various tools of communication form part of promotion mix. Companies must decide which tool(s) should be used for larger sales and in what proportion. The tools should be combined. These decisions are known as promotion-mix decisions.

There are four components of promotion-mix i.e., advertising, personal selling, sales promotion and public relations. Thus, promotion mix is a company's total communication programs which consists of different blends of its components and which is used to achieve the company's marketing objectives.

Tools of Promotion-mix

Advertising, personal selling, sales promotion and publicity are the major tools. The marketing manager must recognise the characteristics of each tool and costs involved while deciding on the promotion-mix.

Advertising

Advertising is an impersonal form of communication for which the seller pays in order to promote a physical product or service. It may be in print form as in newspapers and magazines, or in audio form as on the radio and other similiar methods, or in audio-visual forms as on the Television, cinema screen, etc.

The merits of advertising is that it reaches a larger number of people, the message can be repeated, its cost is not high, and with the development of art and computer graphics, simple statements can be transformed into forceful messages.

The other side of advertising is that it doesnot provide any feed back, it is not as forceful as personal selling, it is not flexible, and good advertisements cost a lot.

Personal selling

Personal selling is a personal communication with one or more prospective buyers for the purpose of selling a product or service.

These days, personal selling is considered to be the most effective tool because of various characteristics which are listed below:

- it involves personal interaction, hence feed back is received immediately;
- it is quite flexible, salesman can adjust communication according to the level of customer's under-standing.
- it is more persuasive; buyers can be convinced about the utility of the product;
- impressive salesman leaves an impression on the prospective buyer; it may increase sales in the future.

Personal selling suffers from a few drawbacks too. It is the most expensive tool of promotion. Secondly, it requires too much dependence on sales force.

Sales Promotion

Sales promotion means the use of short-term incentives which are designed to encourage immediate purchase of a product or service by the buyer. It may includes offer of discounts, free gifts, free sample, coupons, demonstration, store display, etc. One tooth brush free with one 100gm. Close-up dental cream is an example of sales promotion.

Generally this tool supplements the efforts made through personal selling and advertisement. Most of the sales promotion activities come in the form of some incentive for the buyer; hence sales generally increase immediately. Big business enterprises use sales promotion tools while introducing a new product. It adds to the effectiveness of total promotional efforts of a company.

Sales promotion has certain demerits e.g. it does not leave a lasting effect. Some customers also feel that sales promotion schemes are launched to clear old stocks.

Publicity

Publicity takes place when a favourable presentation is made through mass media about a product or service. People believe more on such news than in advertising. It covers people who do not entertain personal selling and sales promotion approaches. It is a non-paid form of communication but sometimes it is not regarded as a promotional tool within the reach of a company. Very few products or services are covered by publicity.

Packaging is also considered as a powerful sales promotion tool these days. It immediately attracts the buyer and makes him buy the product. This tool has produced good results in case of consumer goods. To some extend, packaging has replaced the counter salesman.

You have now learnt about the various tools of promotion. Each tool has certain merits and demerits. It is very important that promotion mix is so devised that it achieves marketing objectives optimally. It is not an easy task. There are no hard and fast rules of promotion mix.

Hence every factor should be paid due attention while deciding on the promotion mix.

Factors governing Promotion-mix

1. ***Nature of product:*** Different types of products require different promotion mix. In case of consumer goods, advertisement is considered to be the most important because the goods are non-technical and produced on a large scale. But for industrial goods personal selling is regarded as the most important tool because the products are technical in nature, costly and persuasion is considered essential for their sale.
2. ***Type of the market:*** If the number of customers is quite large and they are spread over a vast area, advertisement is more helpful because it can reach people everywhere. However if number of customers is not very large and they are concentrated geographically, personal selling and sales promotion may be more effective.
3. ***Stage of the product life cycle:*** The promotional mix depends upon the stage of the product in product life cycle. During introduction, heavy expenditure is incurred on

advertisement followed by personal selling and sales promotion. During the growth stage, customers are aware of the benefits of product. Hence advertisement alongwith personal selling will be more effective. At the maturity stage, competition is more intense. Sales promotion becomes the most important tool to boost sales.

4. ***Budget:*** Funds available for promotion also decide promotion mix, e.g. advertisement is a costly tool. If sufficient funds are not available this tool may not be adopted. Personal selling involves continuous spending. Thus, budget is a deciding factor for promotion-mix.
5. ***Push vs. Pull Strategy:*** When the firm pushes the product to the middlemen they in turn push it to the consumers, it is known as 'push' strategy. In this case, personal selling or display should be more effective.

Pull strategy refers to the policy of a company to strive to build up consumer demand without recourse to middlemen. Generally advertising is considered more important in case of pull strategy.

To sum up, it may be said that all promotional tools are complementary and not competitive. The degree of emphasis on each tools will differ depending upon the influence of certain factors. A proper combination of promotional tools should be designed to attain better results.

Place

Place is another important element of marketing mix. Once the goods are manufactured, packaged, priced and promoted, they must be made available to the consumers. Activities related to placing the products are covered under this element of marketing-mix. It consists of decisions relating to channels of distribution and physical distribution. Channels of distribution refer to the individuals and organisations which facilitate moving the goods from manufactures to consumers. It is important that regular and smooth flow of goods is maintained so that products are not spoiled and supplies are not delayed. To ensure this, various facilitating services need to be arranged like transportation, warehousing, inventory control, and order processing. These are known as components of physical distribution. Let us now study the two sub-elements of 'place'-

(a) Channels of distribution

(b) Physical distribution

(a) ***Channels of Distribution:*** Channel of distribution denotes the intermediaries involved in the process whereby a product passes from the manufacturer to consumers. It is very important for the producers to involve middlemen in order to reach consumers. Middlemen reduce the problems of both producers and consumers. Secondly, middlemen help in distributing the products over a large area. Middlemen also supply useful market information to the producer for improving the product. Involvement of middlemen adds to the convenience of consumers because they are able to lay many items from a single store. Some people feel that by involving more middlemen in the process of distribution, the final price of a products is considerably raised which is ultimately paid by the consumer. Therefore the number of middlemen involved should be limited, if at all necessary: There can be various levels of channel. It is for the producer to decide which level would suit the sale of his product.

Number of Channel Levels

Distribution channel starts from the producer and ends with the consumer. Each layer of middleman that performs some work in bringing the product closer to the final layer is a channel level. The diagram given below shows the various channel levels.

Channel 1 Manufacturer-Consumer

Channel 2 Manufacturer-Retailer-Consumer

Channel 3 Manufacturer-Wholesaler-Retailer-Consumer

Channel 4 Manufacturer-Wholesalers-Jobers-Retailer-Consumer.

Channel 1 is called a direct marketing channel. It has no intermediary level. Producers sell products directly to the consumers. Channel 2 includes one intermediary which is generally a retailer. Retailers buy products directly from the manufacturer and sell these to the consumers. Generally electronic goods like televisions, computers, are sold through this channel level. Channel 3 consists of two levels, typically a wholesaler and a retailer. This channel is often used by small manufacturers of food items, and other products. Channel 4 contains three middlemen levels. Jobbers usually come between wholesalers and retailers. They buy from wholesaler and sell to small retailers who generally are not served by wholesalers. There can be even more levels in distribution channel but from producers point of view, greater number of levels means less control and greater complexity of channel.

Choice of channel of distribution

There are a number of factors which govern the choice regarding channel of distribution. These are listed below:-

(i) ***Nature of product:*** For perishable goods, shorter channel is preferred whereas for durable goods channel 3 is more popular. If goods are made to order, direct selling may be effected. For technical products and costly products, manufacturers generally go for direct selling through agents specially hired for this purpose.

(ii) ***Nature of market:*** If the market is concentrated and not scattered, producers may go for direct selling but for scattered market, middlemen are involved. If there are more buyers, there may be a need to include more middleman. For consumer product market retailers are essential but in case of industrial products a shorter channel is preferred, hence middlemen may be eliminated.

(iii) ***Middlemen:*** Middlemen who can provide desired marketing services are given preference. The availability of middlemen also affect channel decision. The middlemen must be co-operative and honest. The channel which generates largest sales volume at lower unit cost will be given priority.

(iv) ***Size and Policy of the Company:*** There are many factors related to company which influence channel decision. A big size company with broader product line can afford to have shorter channel. New companies heavily rely on middlemen. A company with sufficient financial resources can spend heavily on advertisement and its own outlets. Hence need for middleman is reduced. Companies desiring efficient control over channel members will always prefer shorter channel.

(v) ***Marketing Environment:*** During recession or depression shorter channels are preferred because of being less costly. In times of prosperity a wide choice is available. Technological inventions also have an impact e.g., distribution of perishable goods to distant places has become possible due to cold storage facilities in warehousing and transporting. Such facilities have expanded the role of intermediaries.

(vi) ***Competitors:*** Channels of distribution used by competitors also influence this decision. Some organisation may like to follow the same chains as used by competitors. On the other hand, some organization may avoid channels already customary. They may have their own decisions.

Thus after visualising the impact of the factors mentioned above a company adopts the best channel from among the available alternatives.

(b) Physical Distribution: Physical distribution comprises all those activities which deliver customer satisfaction by supplying right type of products at right place and at right time regularly. Economical and satisfactory customer service is the primary goal of physical distribution. Providing the right type of goal at right place and at right time is the ultimate goal of any marketing department. These goals may be conflicting, sometimes, e.g., for meeting sudden and unforeseen demand for goods, maintenance of large inventory is suggested but this involves cost as well as risk. This means that a proper balance between the cost and service should be achieved.

Components of physical distribution :-

(i) ***Order Processing:*** Physical distribution begins with customers' order. Both the company and customer are benefitted if order processing is carried out quickly and accurately. These days computers are used which establish a link between retailers and producers. Producers keep a watch on the stock position at retailers' place retailers may also place orders through computer. This facility speeds up the process.

(ii) ***Warehousing:*** Every company must store goods to maintain a proper flow. Storage facilities are important because production and consumption cycles generally do not match. Companies need to decide the number, space and location of warehouses. The cost of these should be in balance with customer service. Companies may own warehouses or take them on rent.

4.3 Product Life Cycle

The Product Life Cycle (PLC) is based upon the biological life cycle. For example, a seed is planted (introduction); it begins to sprout (growth); it shoots out leaves and puts down roots as it becomes an adult (maturity); after a long period as an adult the plant begins to shrink and die out (decline).

In theory it's the same for a product. After a period of development it is introduced or launched into the market; it gains more and more customers as it grows; eventually the market stabilises and the product becomes mature; then after a period of time the product is overtaken by development and the introduction of superior competitors, it goes into decline and is eventually withdrawn.

However, most products fail in the introduction phase. Others have very cyclical maturity phases where declines see the product promoted to regain customers.

The product Life Cycle (PLC)

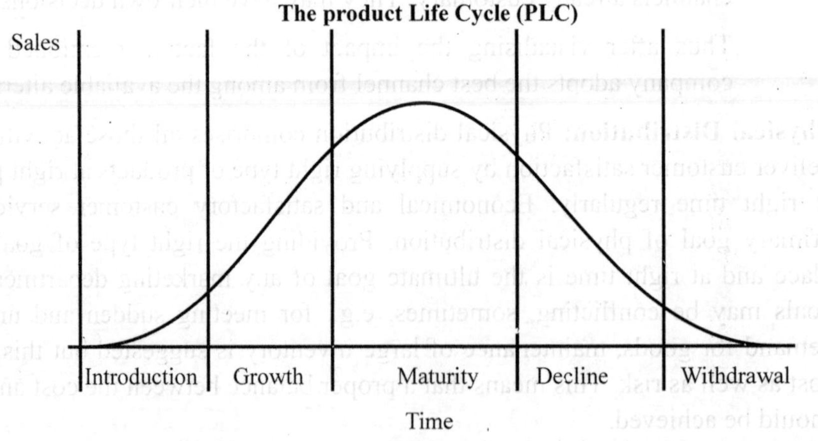

Strategies for the different stages of the Product Life Cycle

Introduction

The need for immediate profit is not a pressure. The product is promoted to create awareness. If the product has no or few competitors, a skimming price strategy is employed. Limited numbers of product are available in few channels of distribution.

Growth

Competitors are attracted into the market with very similar offerings. Products become more profitable and companies form alliances, joint ventures and take each other over. Advertising spend is high and focuses upon building brand. Market share tends to stabilise.

Maturity

Those products that survive the earlier stages tend to spend longest in this phase. Sales grow at a decreasing rate and then stabilise. Producers attempt to differentiate products and brands are key to this. Price wars and intense competition occur. At this point the market reaches saturation. Producers begin to leave the market due to poor margins. Promotion becomes more widespread and use a greater variety of media.

Decline

At this point there is a downturn in the market. For example more innovative products are introduced or consumer tastes have changed. There is intense price-cutting and many more products are withdrawn from the market. Profits can be improved by reducing marketing spend and cost cutting.

Problems with Product Life Cycle

In reality very few products follow such a prescriptive cycle. The length of each stage varies enormously. The decisions of marketers can change the stage, for example from maturity to decline by price-cutting. Not all products go through each stage. Some go from introduction to decline. It is not easy to tell which stage the product is in. Remember that PLC is like all other tools. Use it to inform your gut feeling.

4.4 Product Life Cycle – Stages

There are 4 stages in a product's life cycle. :

Stage	Characteristics
1. Market introduction stage	costs are high slow sales volumes to start little or no competition demand has to be created customers have to be prompted to try the product makes no money at this stage
2. Growth stage	Costs reduced due to economies of scale sales volume increases significantly profitability begins to rise public awareness increases competition begins to increase with a few new players in establishing market increased competition leads to price decreases
3. Maturity stage	Costs are lowered as a result of production volumes increasing and experience curve effects sales volume peaks and market saturation is reached increase in competitors entering the market prices tend to drop due to the proliferation of competing products brand differentiation and feature diversification is emphasized to maintain or increase market share Industrial profits go down
4. Saturation and decline stage	Costs become counter-optimal sales volume decline or stabilize prices, profitability diminish profit becomes more a challenge of production/distribution efficiency than increased sales

Request for deviation

In the process of building a product following defined procedure, an RFD is a request for authorization, granted **prior** to the manufacture of an item, to depart from a particular performance or design requirement of a specification, drawing or other document, for a specific number of units or a specific period of time.

Market identification

A "micro-market" can be used to describe a *Walkman,* more portable, as well as individually and privately recordable; and then Compact Discs ("CDs") brought increased capacity and CD-R offered individual private recording...and so the process goes. The "technology lifecycle" is a most appropriate concept in this context.

In short, termination is not always the end of the cycle; it can be the end of a micro-entrant within the grander scope of a macro-environment. The auto industry, fast-food industry, petro-chemical industry, are just a few that demonstrate a macro-environment that overall has not terminated even while micro-entrants over time have come and gone.

Lessons of the product life cycle (PLC)

It is claimed that every product has a life period, it is launched, it grows, and at some point, may die. A fair comment is that - at least in the short term - not all products or services die. Jeans may die, but clothes probably will not. Legal services or medical services may die, but depending on the social and political climate, probably will not.

Even though its validity is questionable, it can offer a useful *'model'* for managers to keep at the back of their mind. Indeed, if their products are in the introductory or growth phases, or in that of decline, it perhaps should be at the front of their mind; for the predominant features of these phases may be those revolving around such life and death. Between these two extremes, it is salutary for them to have that vision of mortality in front of them.

However, the most important aspect of product life-cycles is that, even under normal conditions, to all practical intents and purposes they often do not exist (hence, there needs to be more emphasis on model/reality mappings). In most markets the majority of the major brands have held their position for at least two decades. The dominant product life-cycle, that of the brand leaders which almost monopolize many markets, is therefore one of continuity.

In the criticism of the product life cycle, Dhalla & Yuspeh state:

...clearly, the PLC is a dependent variable which is determined by market actions; it is not an independent variable to which companies should adapt their marketing programs. Marketing management itself can alter the shape and duration of a brand's life cycle.[1]

Thus, the life cycle may be useful as a description, but not as a *predictor*; and usually should be firmly under the control of the marketer. The important point is that in many markets the product or brand life cycle is significantly longer than the planning cycle of the organisations involved. Thus, it offers little practical value for most marketers. Even if the PLC (and the related PLM support) exists for them, their plans will be based just upon that piece of the curve where they currently reside (most probably in the 'mature' stage); and their view of that part of it will almost certainly be *'linear'* (and limited), and will not encompass the whole range from growth to decline.

Limitations

The PLC model is of some degree of usefulness to marketing managers, in that it is based on factual assumptions. Nevertheless, it is difficult for marketing management to gauge accurately where a product is on its PLC graph. A rise in sales *per se* is not necessarily evidence of growth. A fall in sales *per se* does not typify decline. Furthermore, some products do not (or to date, at the least, have not) experienced a decline. *Coca Cola* and *Pepsi* are examples of two products that have existed for many decades, but are still popular products all over the world. Both modes of cola have been in maturity for some years.

Another factor is that differing products would possess different PLC "shapes". A fad product would hold a steep sloped growth stage, a short maturity stage, and a steep sloped decline stage. A product such as Coca Cola and Pepsi would experience growth, but also a constant level of sales over a number of decades. It can probably be said that a given product (or products collectively within an industry) may hold a unique PLC shape, and the typical PLC model can only be used as a rough guide for marketing management. This is why its called the product life cycle.

4.5 Channels of Distribution

Introduction

As you know, the primary objective of all business enterprises is toearn profit by selling goods and services to ultimate consumers or users. In order to bring goods from the place of manufacture to the place of consumers, the goods have to follow a path or route which is known as channel of distribution or trade channel. A trade or marketing channel consists of producer, middlemen, and consumers or users. The channel serves as a link between the producer and consumers. In the present lesson we shall discuss the various aspects of channels of distribution.

Direct Sale

Retailer

Wholesaler Retailer

Agent Retailer

Agent Wholesaler Retailer

Agent/dealer Retailer

Agent/dealer Wholesaler Retailer

Channel of distribution – importance

A channel of distribution or trade channel is the path or route along which goods move from producers to ultimate consumers or industrial users. In other words, it is the distribution network through which a producer puts his product in the hands of actual users. The channel of distribution includes the original producer, the final buyer and any middlemen-either wholesaler or retailer. The term middleman refers to any institution or individual in the channel which either acquires title to the goods or negotiates or sells in the capacity of an agent or broker. But facilitating agencies who perform or assist in marketing function are not included as middlemen in the channel of distribution. This is because they neither acquire title to the goods nor negotiate purchase or sale. Such facilitating agencies include banks, railways, roadways, warehouses, insurance companies, advertising agencies, e middleman. But that is very rare.

The producer may sell goods to retailer who may then sell the same to consumers. The producer may sell goods to wholesalers who may in turn sell to retailers and the retailer may sell to consumers. The fourth alternative channel of distribution is when any agent/dealer intervenes between the producer and retailers and acts as a middlemen. The agent is appointed by the producer for the sale of goods to the retailers. Another alternative channel is there when producer's agent sells goods to wholesalers who sell to retailers. Agent/dealer is an independent person/firm buying goods and selling them to retailers. Agent/dealer may also sell to wholesalers who may then sell to retailers and goods are thus made available to consumers. In the channel of distribution there may be more than one agent/dealer and wholesaler.

Role of middlemen in the distribution of goods

The middlemen perform the following marketing functions which are listed in sequence.

(i) Searching out buyers and sellers (contacting & Merchandising), matching goods to the requirements of market.

(ii) Offering goods in the form of assortments or packages.

(iii) Persuading and influencing the prospective buyers to favor a certain product and its maker (personal selling/sales promotion).

(iv) Implementing pricing policies in such a manner that would be acceptable to buyers and ensure effective distribution.

(v) Providing feed back information, marketing intelligence and sales forecasting services for the regions to their suppliers.

(vi) Looking after the process of distribution where necessary.

(vii) Participating actively in the creation and establishment of a market for a new product.

(viii) Offering pre and after sale services to consumers.

(ix) Communicating the use of technique of the product to the users.

(x) Offering credit to retailers and consumers.

(xi) Risk bearing with reference to stock hoarding/transport.

Desirability of eliminating the middlemen

You have already learnt the role of middlemen above, which indicates the significance of middlemen in the channel of distribution. Indeed without the existence of middlemen goods produced on a mass scale could not have reached the consumers at right time and place. However the existence of middlemen may lead to several short comings. The elimination of middlemen is based on the following grounds.

(i) ***Excessive number:*** Often there are too many middlemen between the manufacturers and consumers. As every middleman charges some commission or profit, the ultimate consumer has to pay a very high price for goods. They are social parasites thriving at the cost of the consumer and their ultimate elimination will reduce prices and burden on consumers.

(ii) ***Superfluous:*** Most middlemen do not render any useful service in lieu of profit or commission. They act as only transfer agents and unnecessarily cause delay in the flow of goods. Their elimination will result in quick and smooth flow of goods.

(iii) ***Limited risk taking:*** Middlemen do not bear the producers' risk such as loss due to strikes, lockouts, depression and change in fashions and habits, etc.

(iv) ***Anti-social activities:*** They take undue advantage of adverse conditions in business. Some businessmen (middlemen) indulge in anti-social activities like hoarding and adulteration to earn huge amount to profits.

(v) ***Limiting consumers' choice:*** The middlemen often promote products which are inferior in quality and get high margin of profit. Thus they exploit consumers and limit their choice.

Role of wholesaler and retailer in distribution of goods

Role of Wholesaler: Wholesaler acts as a middlemen in the channel of distribution as he buys goods in large quantity from the manufacturer and sells these to retailers in small quantities. His role in distribution of goods is discussed below:

(i) ***Buying and assembling:*** A wholesaler forecasts the demand for goods and assembles different varieties of goods from several manufacturers. Some wholesalers also import goods from foreign countries.

(ii) ***Selling and dispersing:*** A wholesaler breaks the bulk so that retailers and users can buy them in small lots. His representatives egularly call on retailers and industrial users/buyers to distribute the goods among widely scattered people.

(iii) ***Transportation:*** A wholesaler arranges transportation of goods from producers to his godowns and from there to retailers.

Sometimes he has his own transport arrangement for this purpose.

(iv) ***Storage:*** He holds large stocks and serves as a reservoir and supplies to retailers. He helps in stablising prices by adjusting supply of goods to their demand.

(v) ***Packing and grading:*** A wholesaler packs and repacks goods in convenient lots. He sorts out goods in different grades. He also gives brand names to the products packed and graded by him.

(vi) ***Advertising and sales promotion:*** A wholesaler performs advertising and sales promotion activities to increase the sale of products. He also takes the services of experts for this purpose.

(vii) ***Financing:*** Sometimes the wholesaler buys goods on cash basis from manufacturers and sells them on credit to retailers. In this way he provides financial help both to the producers and retailers. If necessary, the wholesaler also provide financial help by way of advance payment to producers.

(viii) ***Risk-taking:*** A wholesaler bears risks of changes in demand and prices, bad debts and damage to goods in the course of transportation and storage. By undertaking various risks he simplifies the process of distribution.

Role of Retailers

Retailers buys goods from wholesaler and sells them directly to consumers. Thus he acts as a direct link between the wholesaler and consumers. His role in distribution of goods is enumerated below:

(i) ***Wide choice to consumers:*** The retailer anticipates needs of consumers. He assembles goods from different sources and stocks different varieties of products. Thus, he offers a wide choice to consumers. They can buy according to their purchasing power and requirements.

(ii) Availability of goods in small quantities and at convenient locations: A retailer provides ready supply of goods so that consumers can buy conveniently and quickly in small lots without any inconvenience of placing advance orders and waiting for supplies. By ensuring uninterrupted and fresh supply of goods, he saves consumers from the botheration of buying goods in bulk and storing them.

(iii) ***Home delivery:*** A retailer transports goods from wholesalers to ultimate consumers. Some retailers provide free home delivery service to their consumers. Thus they create place utility.

(iv) ***Assurance of regular supply:*** He maintains adequate supply of goods so that consumers are sure of getting regular supply at the time of their need.

(v) ***Credit facility:*** Although retailers mostly sell goods for cash, they also supply goods on credit to their regular customers.

(vi) ***Close interaction with customers:*** A retailer brings new products to the notice of customers and educates them in their uses. A retailer thus, acts as a friend and guide to his customers. Indeed his interaction with customers is of intimate personal nature and thus he is able to provide feed back to wholesalers and manufacturers about consumers' preferences.

Role of specialized retail outlets e.g., departmental stores, multiple shops and mail order business house

A retailer is the final link in the distribution channel between a manufacturer and the consumers. He is directly and continuously in touch with people of varied tastes and preferences. Reta.lers may be divided into two categories, namely institutional and non-institutional. The institutional retailers (retail outlets) include departmental stores, multiple shops and mail order houses. Non-institutional retailers include the floating population of street sellers, pedlars, and hawkers.

(a) ***Departmental Stores:*** A departmental Store is a big retail store with many departments under one roof. It offers a wide range of products so as to suit different consumer tastes and preferences. All the departments are centrally controlled but each department forms a complete sales unit in itself. The examples of such stores in metropolitan cities are Akbarally's and Sahakari Bhandar in Bombay and Spencers in Madras.

(b) ***Multiple shops or chain stores:*** Manufacturers often use their own retail shops for direct sale of their products to consumers. These retail shops are established as multiple shops operating in the same city or different parts of the country. These shops have identical product display. Bata India Ltd and DCM provide typical examples of multiple shops system. In this type of retail selling manufacturers have control over distribution channel and have first hand information regarding customers' preferences.

(c) ***Mail-order business:*** These are retail outlets which sell goods by mail only. The mail order house centrally procures products, advertises them and expect perspective buyers to send offers/orders. The products are sent through value-payable post. Mail Order Sales Ltd, Bombay, the seller of 'Bull worker' health aid, is a typical example of such mail order business in India. It is through these retail outlets that manufacturers often by pass the wholesalers in trade route or path.

Choice of a channel of distribution

The factors to be considered before choosing a suitable channel of distribution are listed below:

1. ***Product considerations:*** The nature and type of product have an important bearing on the choice of distribution channels. For examples, perishable goods

need speedy movements and hence shorter channel or route of distribution; For durable goods, longer and diversified channels may be used; Similarly, for technical products requiring specialized selling and serving talents, the shortest channel should be used.

2. ***Market considerations:*** The nature and type of customers and size of market are important considerations in the choice of a channel of distribution. For example, if the market size is large, there may be long channels, whereas in a small market direct selling may be profitable. The nature and type of consumers include factors such as desire for credit, preference for the stop shopping, demand for personal services, amount of time and effort the customer is willing to spend. It also includes factors like age, income group, sex, and religion of customers.

3. ***Company considerations:*** The nature, size and objectives of the business firm also play an important role in the selection of distribution channel. It includes financial resources, market standing, volume of production, desire for control of channel, services provided by manufacturers', etc. For example a company with substantial financial resources need not rely too much on the middlemen and can afford to reduce the levels of distribution. Similarly a company desiring to exercise greater control over channel will prefer a shorter channel.

4. ***Middlemen considerations:*** The cost and efficiency of distribution depend largely on the nature and type of middlemen. It includes characteristics of middlemen such as availability, attitudes, services, sales potential, costs etc. For example, if the terms and conditions of engaging wholesalers are unfavorable, a manufacturer may like to channelise his products through wholesalers or retailers, thereby, bypassing wholesalers. However, the determining factor would be the differential advantage involved in the choice.

To conclude, the channel generating the largest sales volume at lower unit cost will be given top priority. This will minimize distribution costs

4.6 Sales Promotion

Sales promotion is one of the four aspects of *promotional mix*. (The other three parts of the *promotional mix* are *advertising, personal selling*, and *publicity/public relations*.) Media and non-media marketing communication are employed for a pre-determined, limited time to increase consumer demand, stimulate market demand or improve product availability. Examples include:

- *contests*
- point of purchase displays
- *rebate (marketing)*
- free travel, such as free flights

Sales promotions can be directed at either the *customer*, sales staff, or *distribution* channel members (such as *retailers*). Sales promotions targeted at the *consumer* are called **consumer sales promotions**. Sales promotions targeted at retailers and *wholesale* are called **trade sales promotions**. Some sale promotions, particularly ones with unusual methods, are considered *gimmick* by many.

Consumer sales promotion techniques

- Price deal: A temporary reduction in the price, such as *happy hour*
- Loyal Reward Program: Consumers collect points, miles, or credits for purchases and redeem them for rewards. Two famous examples are *Pepsi Stuff* and *AAdvantage*.
- Cents-off deal: Offers a brand at a lower price. Price reduction may be a percentage marked on the package.
- Price-pack deal: The packaging offers a consumer a certain percentage more of the product for the same price (for example, 25 percent extra).
- Coupons: coupons have become a standard mechanism for sales promotions.
- *Loss leader:* the price of a popular product is temporarily reduced in order to stimulate other profitable sales
- Free-standing insert (FSI): A coupon booklet is inserted into the local newspaper for delivery.
- On-shelf couponing: Coupons are present at the shelf where the product is available.
- Checkout dispensers: On checkout the customer is given a coupon based on products purchased.
- On-line couponing: Coupons are available on line. Consumers print them out and take them to the store.
- Mobile couponing: Coupons are available on a mobile phone. Consumers show the offer on a mobile phone to a salesperson for redemption.
- Online interactive promotion game: Consumers play an interactive game associated with the promoted product. See an example of the *Interactive Internet Ad* for tomato ketchup.
- *Rebates:* Consumers are offered money back if the receipt and *barcode* are mailed to the producer.
- Contests/sweepstakes/games: The consumer is automatically entered into the event by purchasing the product.
- Point-of-sale displays:-
    - Aisle interrupter: A sign that juts into the aisle from the shelf.

  - Dangler: A sign that sways when a consumer walks by it.
  - Dump bin: A bin full of products dumped inside.
  - Glorifier: A small stage that elevates a product above other products.
  - Wobbler: A sign that jiggles.
  - Lipstick Board: A board on which messages are written in crayon.
  - Necker: A coupon placed on the 'neck' of a bottle.
  - YES unit: "your extra salesperson" is a pull-out *fact sheet*.
- Kids eat free specials: Offers a discount on the total dining bill by offering 1 free kids meal with each regular meal purchased.

Trade sales promotion techniques

- Trade allowances: short term incentive offered to induce a retailer to stock up on a product.
- Dealer loader: An incentive given to induce a retailer to purchase and display a product.
- Trade contest: A contest to reward retailers that sell the most product.
- Point-of-purchase displays: Extra sales tools given to retailers to boost sales.
- Training programs: dealer employees are trained in selling the product.
- Push money: also known as "spiffs". An extra commission paid to retail employees to push products.

Trade discounts (also called functional discounts): These are payments to distribution channel members for performing some function

4.7 Pharma Marketing Process and Its Challenges

Introduction

The pharmaceutical industry is the world's largest industry due to worldwide revenues of approximately US$2.8 trillion. Pharma industry has seen major changes in the recent years that place new demands on payers, providers and manufacturers. Customers now demand the same choice and convenience from pharma industry that they find in other segment. Indian Pharmaceutical Industry is poised for high consistent growth over the next few years, driven by a multitude of factors. Top Indian Companies like **Ranbaxy, DRL, CIPLA** and **Dabur** have already established their presence. The pharmaceutical industry is a knowledge driven industry and is heavily dependent on Research and Development for new products and growth. However, basic research (discovering new molecules) is a time consuming and expensive process and is thus, dominated by large global multinationals.

Indian companies have only recently entered the area. The Indian pharmaceutical industry came into existence in 1901, when Bengal Chemical & Pharmaceutical Company started its maiden operation in Calcutta. The next few decades saw the pharmaceutical industry moving through several phases, largely in accordance with government policies. Commencing with repackaging and preparation of formulations from imported bulk drugs, the Indian industry has moved on to become a net foreign exchange earner, and has been able to underline its presence in the global pharmaceutical arena as one of the top 35 drug producers worldwide. Currently, there are more than 2,400 registered pharmaceutical producers in India. There are 24,000 licensed pharmaceutical companies. Of the 465 bulk drugs used in India, approximately 425 are manufactured here. India has more drug-manufacturing facilities that have been approved by the U.S. Food and Drug Administration than any country other than the US. Indian generics companies supply 84% of the AIDS drugs that Doctors without Borders uses to treat 60,000 patients in more than 30 countries.

Therapeutic Area wise Total Pharma Market

Category Value Market Share%

Anti-Infective 16.4

Gastrointestinal 10.9

Cardiac 10.3

Respiratory 10.2

Vit./Minerals/Nutrient 9.6

Pain/Analgesics 9.5

Dermatologics 5.4

Gynecology 5.3

Neuro psychiatry 5.3

Ant diabetics 4.4

Opthologicals 1.7

Others 11.0

Total 100.00

It is very much evident that chronic therapy area (Gastro Cardiac, Respiratory, Neuro Psychiatry and Ant diabetics) is dominating the market in long run.

Pharma Marketing Process and its Challenges

While many pharmaceutical companies have successfully deployed a plethora of strategies to target the various customer types, recent business and customer trends are creating new challenges and opportunities for increasing profitability. In the pharmaceutical and healthcare industries, a complex web of decision-makers determines the nature of the transaction (prescription) for which direct customer (doctor) of Pharma industry is responsible. Essentially, the end-user (patient) consumes a product and pays the cost.

Use of medical representatives for marketing products to physicians and to exert some influence over others in the hierarchy of decision makers has been a time-tested tradition. Typically, sales force expense comprises an estimated 15 percent to 20 percent of annual product revenues, the largest line item on the balance sheet. Despite this other expense, the industry is still plagued with some very serious strategic and operational level issues.

From **organizational perspective** the most prominent performance related issues are enlisted below:

(a) Increased competition and unethical practices adopted by some of the propaganda base companies.

(b) Low level of customer knowledge (Doctors, Retailers, Wholesalers).

(c) Poor customer (both external & internal) acquisition, development and retention strategies

(d) Varying customer perception.

(e) The number and the quality of medical representatives

(f) Very high territory development costs.

(g) High training and re-training costs of sales personnel.

(h) Very high attrition rate of the sales personnel.

(i) Busy doctors giving less time for sales calls.

(j) Poor territory knowledge in terms of business value at medical representative level.

(k) Unclear value of prescription from **each doctor** in the list of **each sales person**.

(l) Unknown value of revenue from each retailer in the territory

(m) Absence of ideal mechanism of sales forecasting from field sales level, leading

(n) to huge deviations

(o) Absence of analysis on the amount of time invested on profitable and not so profitable customers and lack of time-share planning towards developing customer base for future and un-tapped markets.

Patents

Patents are a vital aspect of the global Pharma industry. Patent protection is essential to spur basic R&D and make it commercially viable. But, only the developed nations endorse product patents. Most third world countries have patent laws but enforcement is totally lax.

New Drug Approval (NDA)

Prior to launching its products in any country, a Pharma company undertakes patent registration to protect its own interests. To protect the interests of the consumers, it is necessary that the product be approved by the drug authorities in that country. Mostly the process for seeking approval is initiated alongside the patent registration process.

WTO

Due to pressure from the developed countries, across the world uniformity in patent laws is being implemented under WTO (World Trade Organization - earlier GATT i.e. General Agreement on Tariffs & Trade). Presently, different countries have different patent types and life period. WTO has decided upon a product patent life of 20 years in all countries.

Research and Development (R & D)

The pharmaceutical industry is characterized by heavy R&D expenditure. It is only the large pharmaceutical companies who can allocate significant resources for R&D to introduce new products. As the products are an outcome of significant R&D expenditures incurred by these companies, they have their products patented. The patent allows the companies concerned to wield immense pricing power for their new products.

The Competition

The level of competition on day-to-day basis in very **high** in **Acute segment,** however the degree of competition is not as much as high in **Chronic therapy** area. As doctor has to prescribe drug for a long time in chronic cases and patient is suppose to consume it without any change of brand. While in acute cases doctor is changing brands on day to day basis. In acute area however there is a large competition from local and propaganda companies.

Pharmaceutical Company Business Strategies

What's the secret behind successes? For one, the company operates in niche formulations **(chronic)** segments such as psychiatry, cardiovascular, gastroenterology and neurology.

While most of the top Indian companies have focused on antibiotics and anti–invectives (**acute**), Sun Pharma focused on therapeutic areas such as depression, hypertension and cancer. The company has introduced the entire range of products and has gained leadership position in each of these areas. Being a specialty company insulates Sun Pharma from the industry growth. The first quarter results for FY02 explain this to some extent. While the industry was affected to a large extent by a slowdown in the domestic formulations market, Sun Pharma logged a growth of 26% in revenues. Over the years Sun has also used the strategy of acquisitions and mergers to grow quickly. It acquired Knoll Pharma's bulk drug facility, Gujarat Lyka Organics, 51.5% in M. J. Pharma, merged TamilNadu Dadha Pharma & Milmet Labs and acquired Natco's brands. Post Merger with TamilNadu Dadha Pharma the company gained presence in gynecology and oncology segments.

The bases of marketing strategies can be best described in these two models in both acute and chronic segments:

(i) **Super Core Model** involving the search for, and distribution of a small number of drugs from **Chronic Therapy Area** that achieve substantial global sales. The success of this model depends on achieving large returns from a small number of drugs in order to pay for the high cost of the drug discovery and development process for a large number of patients. Total revenues are highly dependant on sales from a small number of drugs. This model incorporates highly specialized approach in all the manner. Initially the competition is seems more at entry level but since growth is stable and more in this area; every company is striving very hard to enter in this area. The major strategy in this model involves right focus to highly specialized customer by well trained team.

(ii) **Core Model** in which a larger number of drugs from **Acute Therapy Area** are marketed to big diversified markets. The advantage of this model is that its success is not dependant on sales of a small number of drugs. Here presenting a large number of product and taking the advantage of opportunity cost is one of the important strategy.

Marketing approaches of Super Core Model

In pharmaceutical market there has been a significant shift from Acute towards Chronic Therapy area. Chronic segments are driving the growth of the market as leading prescribes in these segments are specialists as opposed to general practioners. This is evident from high growth rates achieved by firms like Sun Pharma, Dr.Reddy

Laboratories and Dabur Pharma Ltd. Who have focused on these segments The doctor's prescription has become just the starting point in determining what drug the retailer dispenses. During last five years Pharma companies have started identifying the hidden potential of oncological market also. A number of drugs have been launched into the oncological market by pharmaceutical companies, including new biological drugs and drugs that can be used as a support for patients undergoing cytotoxic chemotherapy. As a matter of fact, pharmaceutical companies are merging, and, through the merging process, the portfolio of the new companies changes.

Medical representatives are rearranged throughout the new companies. Some of the sales representatives are now afraid of losing their job, due to the changing scenario and the possible lay offs. On the other hand, the new, bigger, pharmaceutical companies are competing more and more with one another, and, in order to stress their products, might adopt a more aggressive sales strategy. For example, sometimes in the same geographical area there are eight to ten representatives for just one company, or different representatives for the same drug in different settings. As a result of the new, aggressive strategy, the aggressiveness of representatives has also been increasing, since the larger stress exerted by their companies might affect their stay in the company. Therefore, they tend to have more frequent visits to encourage doctors to prescribe drugs and thus increase sales.

In this model medical representatives are the key actors for example in a small cardiology unit almost 40 sales representatives interacting with doctors, and most of them are coming for a visit on a regular once-a-month basis as this is the restriction put by doctors of meeting only once in a month that to on a fix time only, in order to stress the usefulness of their products and push clinicians towards the use of their drugs. This means that, basically, there are at least two representatives every day in busy clinic asking for a 'short' meeting to support their product.

Pharmaceutical marketing is a specialized field where medical representatives form the backbone of entire marketing effort. Pharmaceutical companies also appoint medical representatives and assign them defined territories. Medical representatives meet doctors, chemists and stockiest as per company norms. Medical representatives try to influence prescription pattern of doctors in favor of their brands.

The pharmaceutical distribution channel is indirect with usually three channel members i.e. depot/C&F, stockiest and chemist. Pharmaceutical companies appoint one company depot or C&F agent usually in each state and authorized stockist(s) in each district across the country. Company depot/C&F sends stocks to authorized stockists as per the requirement. Retail chemists buy medicines on daily or weekly basis from authorized stockiest as per demand. Patients visit chemists for buying medicines either prescribed by a doctor or advertised in the media. Here patient is end customer and doctor is direct customer for any pharmaceutical company. But for doctor customer (patient) is more important so he wants an effective supply chain management from prescribed company. And for pharmaceutical companies their customer that is doctor is more important that's why they emphasize more on supply chain management. Ultimately end customer is benefited out of this.

For marketing of these type of products companies require more and more skilled field force to develop good rapport with their direct customer (doctor). Moreover field force should have good product knowledge and USP of their products over other so as to convince doctors and **PULL** the demand for their products i.e. from Doctor to Retailer to Stockist to CFA to company.

CORE CUSTOMER

(Doctor)

END-CUSTOMER

(Patient)

NONCORE

CUSTOMER

(Retailer)

CUSTOMER

(Stockist)

CUSTOMER

(C & FA)

Marketing & Sales

Team

In this system, doctors are the core customers and the major thrust is given to build and retain these customer because they are pulling the demand for products hence companies also give main emphasis in building and retaining these customers. All efforts are being put for generating **secondary sales i.e.** from stockist to retailer. Ensuring of auto demand with limited availability and maximum liquidation of the products is the main characteristic of this approach.

For retaining and developing customers, the companies normally provide gifts like sponsorship for various conferences like RSSDI, FOGSI, APICON, UPCON etc. For example Dabur having PASS (Professional Academic and Scientific Services) activities for promoting its chronic therapy range.

Also it is interesting to note that since this is a pull system demand is being pulled in to the market so generally representatives calculate product orders i.e. **primary sales** from their stockist on the basis of following formula:

Normally there are absolutely no chances of dumping of goods at stockist and retailer level is yet reported also payment recovery of companies is also very good.

Marketing Approaches of Core Model

In present scenario companies are focusing more and more on the availability of products so as to enjoy good image in their customer's (doctors) chamber. Many companies such as Glaxo, Pfizer, Dabur, FDC, Aventies, and Cipla etc. are known for their availability of products.

For marketing of these types of products companies require more and more field force to remind their products on daily basis to their direct customer (doctor). Moreover field force should have good knowledge of product schemes and offers. Also field force is required to have a good rapport with retailers. Field force also required to ensure good availability of their products to convince doctors and **PUSH** their products i.e. from to Stockist to Retailer to Doctor.

It has been observed that sometimes there are more than fifteen or sixteen representatives in a day are meeting with their customer and requesting for same type of products. Although field force visits are important for an update on drugs and their use. The doctors are, in general, sneaking away, trying to hide from sales representatives, since there are too many and they are too pushy and there is too little time, and the representatives probably have noticed that the reluctant doctors have always less time for short meetings and less interest and tend to reduce the time of the visit.

SECONDARY SALES * 2 – OPENING STOCK= ORDER

The relationship between clinicians and representatives has always been good and pharmaceutical companies have provided, and still provide, the major economical support for customers' continuous medical education. Something needs to be done to find a solution to this problem that takes into account the needs of both pharmaceutical companies and their representatives on one side and physicians on the other, for a better professional interaction.

Push System Working in Acute Therapy Segment

In this system, doctors and retailers are the core customers and the major thrust is given to build and retain these customers. Here retailers are also core customer as most of the times they are substituting the products based on their own discretion.

For retaining and developing customers, the companies normally provide utility gifts to remind the products on daily basis.

Also it is interesting to note that since this is a push system products are being pushed in to the market so generally representatives place product orders from their stockist on the basis of SKUs sold and schemes. In this pumping the goods in the market and ensuring

CORE CUSTOMER
(Doctor)
END-CUSTOMER
(Patient)
CORE CUSTOMER
(Retailer)
CORE
CUSTOMER
(Stockist)
Marketing & Sales
Team more and more **primary sales i.e. from CFA to Stockist and availability of goods are major strategies.**

Normally the chances of dumping of goods at stockist and retailer level are reported also payment recovery of companies is also not very good.

Here the role of supply chain managers can be to provide considerable value to their companies by understanding the customers' delivery requirements. A very powerful tool for understanding these requirements is account segmentation. A company can use account segmentation to identify market segments Such as Acute & Chronic therapy market. which is well positioned to serve and then organize its product range and even SKU's and service in a superior way.

Companies are fighting (for customers) like never before and if anything is certain then it is further intensification of this war, and because of this companies are increasingly looking at Logistics, as a weapon to gain Competitive Advantage and it is true that Logistics has the potential to do so. and corporate cases associated with them are given below:

Conclusion

There can be various ways through which a business organization can achieve success in the market, but all those ways can be comprised into as above, then it can be rightly said that it revolves specifically around three parties or more; the triangular linkages or the relationship between these three parties (company, customers and competitors) determine the success and failure of business organization. In the medium to long run, the domestic pharmaceutical market will be largely driven by the increasing prevalence of chronic segment. The domestic industry is principally being driven by the chronic segment which has grown by **17.8%** this year. Against the backdrop up- take of acute segments has been slow and has grown by **10.1%** only. The basis of success in any competitive context can be, at the most, elemental level commercial success; and commercial success can be derived either from a cost advantage or a value advantage or ideally from a combination of both. In other words, the organization with Competitive Advantage tends to be the cost leader in the industry or a seller of most differentiated products amongst all the players. At last the role of supply chain is very prominent in both the phases (in acute as well as in chronic). But the successes of any pharmaceutical industry; when a company changes its concentration from "Acute" to "Chronic" therapy market depend on competitiveness of supply chain. Supply Chain Managers can provide considerable value to their companies by understanding the customers' delivery requirements. A very powerful tool for understanding these requirements is account segmentation. A company can use account segmentation to identify market segments Such as Acute & Chronic therapy market. which is well positioned to serve and then organize its product range and even SKU's and service in a superior way. The company must tailor its supply chain offerings to meet the needs of each of the market segment it serves. For example, **Dabur Pharma** has started launching of its products which were G.P.(**Acute Threapy**) oriented latter it enter in to specialists oriented (**Chronic Threapy**) products.

Questions

1. Define sales promotion? Explain the different methods of sales promotion?
2. What is product life cycle? Explain strategies to extend the product life cycle with examples?
3. What is sales organization"? What are the different types of sales organization available in the marketing process?
4. Explain marketing mix? What significance does marketing mix has in Pharma. Industry?
5. Explain the concepts 'market" and 'marketing' with suitable examples? add a note on social marketing and multi level marketing?
6. What are channels of distribution and explain its importance in market building?
7. Add note on the following: (a) window display (b) e-marketing.
8. What are the different factors to be considered while deciding about a suitable channel of distribution?
9. Explain the major differences between general marketing and Pharma marketing?
10. Explain the various functions of marketing?

Chapter - 5

Pharmaceutical Industry

5.1 Indian pharmaceutical industry

Introduction

The **Indian Pharmaceutical Industry** today is in the front rank of India's science-based industries with wide ranging capabilities in the complex field of drug manufacture and technology. A highly organized sector, the Indian Pharma Industry is estimated to be worth $ 4.5 billion, growing at about 8 to 9 percent annually. It ranks very high in the third world, in terms of technology, quality and range of medicines manufactured. From simple headache pills to sophisticated antibiotics and complex cardiaç compounds, almost every type of medicine is now made indigenously.

Playing a key role in promoting and sustaining development in the vital field of medicines, **Indian Pharma Industry** boasts of quality producers and many units approved by regulatory authorities in USA and UK. International companies associated with this sector have stimulated, assisted and spearheaded this dynamic development in the past 53 years and helped to put India on the pharmaceutical map of the world.

The Indian Pharmaceutical sector is highly fragmented with more than 20,000 registered units. It has expanded drastically in the last two decades. The leading 250 pharmaceutical companies control 70% of the market with market leader holding nearly 7% of the market share. It is an extremely fragmented market with severe price competition and government price control.

The pharmaceutical industry in India meets around 70% of the country's demand for bulk drugs, drug intermediates, pharmaceutical formulations, chemicals, tablets, capsules, orals and injectibles. There are about 250 large units and about 8000 Small Scale Units, which form the core of the pharmaceutical industry in India (including 5 Central Public Sector Units). These units produce the complete range of pharmaceutical formulations, i.e., medicines ready for consumption by patients and about 350 bulk drugs, i.e., chemicals having therapeutic value and used for production of pharmaceutical formulations.

Following the de-licensing of the pharmaceutical industry, industrial licensing for most of the drugs and pharmaceutical products has been done away with. Manufacturers are free to produce any drug duly approved by the Drug Control Authority. Technologically strong and totally self-reliant, the pharmaceutical industry in India has low costs of production, low R&D costs, innovative scientific manpower, strength of national laboratories and an increasing balance of trade. The Pharmaceutical Industry, with its rich scientific talents and research capabilities, supported by Intellectual Property Protection regime is well set to take on the international market.

Advantage India – Current Status and its Role in National Economy

Competent workforce: India has a pool of personnel with high managerial and technical competence as also skilled workforce. It has an educated work force and English is commonly used. Professional services are easily available.

Cost-effective chemical synthesis: Its track record of development, particularly in the area of improved cost-beneficial chemical synthesis for various drug molecules is excellent. It provides a wide variety of bulk drugs and exports sophisticated bulk drugs.

Legal and Financial Framework: India has a 53 year old democracy and hence has a solid legal framework and strong financial markets. There is already an established international industry and business community.

Information and Technology: It has a good network of world-class educational institutions and established strengths in Information Technology.

Globalization: The country is committed to a free market economy and globalization. Above all, it has a 70 million middle class market, which is continuously growing.

Consolidation: For the first time in many years, the international pharmaceutical industry is finding great opportunities in India. The process of consolidation, which has become a generalized phenomenon in the world pharmaceutical industry, has started taking place in India.

The Growth Scenario

India's US$ 3.1 billion pharmaceutical industry is growing at the rate of 14 percent per year. It is one of the largest and most advanced among the developing countries.

Over 20,000 registered pharmaceutical manufacturers exist in the country. The domestic pharmaceuticals industry output is expected to exceed Rs260 billion in the financial year 2002, which accounts for merely 1.3% of the global pharmaceutical sector. Of this, bulk drugs will account for Rs 54 billion (21%) and formulations, the remaining Rs 210 billion (79%). In financial year 2001, imports were Rs 20 billion while exports were Rs87 billion.

As per WTO, from the year 2005, India will grant product patent recognition to all new chemical entities (NCEs) i.e., bulk drugs developed then onwards. The Indian Government's decision to allow 100 percent foreign direct investment into the drugs and pharmaceutical industry is expected to aid the growth of contract research in the country. Technology transfer to 100 percent Indian subsidiaries of MNCs is expected only in 2005.

Indian pharmaceutical interests in making a mark on the global scene got a boost when Dr Reddy's licensed two of its anti-diabetic molecules to Novo Nordisk and when Ranbaxy licensed its Novel Drug Delivery System (NDDS) of ciprofloxacin to Bayer. MNCs in India faced the problem of having a very high DPCO coverage, weakening their bottom lines as well as hindering their growth through the launch of new products. DPCO coverage is expected to be diluted further in the near future benefiting the MNCs. New legislation is also expected in the OTC segment increasing the number of brands in the Over the Counter (OTC) segment.

The Indian pharmaceutical industry is also getting increasingly U.S. FDA compliant to harness the growth opportunities in areas of contract manufacturing and research. Indian companies such as Ranbaxy, Sun Pharma, and Dr. Reddy's are increasingly focusing on tapping the U.S. generic market, projected to be around $180 billion by 2012

Steps to Strengthen the Industry

Indian companies need to attain the right product-mix for sustained future growth. Core competencies will play an important role in determining the future of many Indian pharmaceutical companies in the post product-patent regime after 2005. Indian companies, in an effort to consolidate their position, will have to increasingly look at merger and acquisition options of either companies or products. This would help them to offset loss of new product options, improve their R&D efforts and improve distribution to penetrate markets.

Research and development has always taken the back seat amongst Indian pharmaceutical companies. In order to stay competitive in the future, Indian companies will have to refocus and invest heavily in R&D.

The Indian pharmaceutical industry also needs to take advantage of the recent advances in biotechnology and information technology. The future of the industry will be determined by how well it markets its products to several regions and distributes risks, its forward and backward integration capabilities, its R&D, its consolidation through mergers and acquisitions, co-marketing and licensing agreements.

Research and Development is the key to the future of pharmaceutical industry. The pharmaceutical advances for considerable improvement in life expectancy and health all over the world are the result of a steadily increasing investment in research. There is considerable scope for collaborative R & D in India. India can offer several strengths to the international R & D community. These strengths relate to availability of excellent scientific talents who can develop combinatorial chemistry, new synthetic molecules and plant derived candidate drugs.

R & D in the pharmaceutical industry in India is critical to find answers for some of the diseases peculiar to a tropical country like India and also for finding solutions for unmet medical needs. Industrial R & D groups can carry out limited primary screening to identify lead molecules or even candidate drugs for further in vivo screening, pre-clinical pharmacology, toxicology, animal and human pharmacokinetics and metabolic studies before taking them up for human trials. In such collaborations, harmonized standards of screening can be assured following established good laboratory practices. The R & D expenditure by the Indian pharmaceutical industry is around 1.9% of the industry's turnover. This obviously, is very low when compared to the investment on R & D by foreign research-based Pharma companies. They spend 10 - 16% of the turnover on R & D. However, now that India is entering into the Patent protection area, many companies are spending relatively more on R & D.

When it comes to clinical evaluation at the time of multi-center trials, India would provide a strong base considering the real availability of clinical materials in diverse therapeutic areas. Such active collaboration will be mutually beneficial to both partners. According to a survey by the Pharmaceutical Outsourcing Management Association and Bio/Pharmaceutical Outsourcing Report, pharmaceutical companies are utilizing substantially the services of Contract Research Organizations (CROs).

Indian Pharmaceutical Industry, with its rich scientific talents, provides cost-effective clinical trial research. It has an excellent record of development of improved, cost-beneficial chemical syntheses for various drug molecules. Some MNCs are already sourcing these services from their Indian affiliates.

The Pharmaceutical and Biotechnology Industry is eligible for weight deduction for R&D expense upto 150%. These R&D companies will also enjoy tax holiday for 10 years. A promotional research and development fund of Rs.150 crores is set up by the Government to promote research and development in the pharmaceutical sector. The Indian pharmaceutical industry is highly regulated. The Government controls prices of a large number of bulk drugs and formulations. Profit margins of players vary widely in both domestic and export sales due to many factors.

Domestic Trade

More than 85% of the formulations produced in the country are sold in the domestic market. India is largely self-sufficient in case of formulations. Some life saving, new generation under-patent formulations continue to be imported, especially by MNCs, which then market them in India. Overall, the size of the domestic formulations market is around Rs160bn and it is growing at 10% p.a.

Exports

Over 60% of India's bulk drug production is exported. The balance is sold locally to other formulators. India's pharmaceutical exports are to the tune of Rs87bn, of which formulations contribute nearly 55% and the rest 45% comes from bulk drugs. In financial year 200, exports grew by 21%. India's pharmaceuticals imports were to the tune of Rs20.3billion in FY2001. Imports have registered a CAGR of only 2% in the past 5 years. Import of bulk drugs have slowed down in the recent years.

5.2 Indian Pharma research and development - Challenges

Pharmaceutical R&D management is braving unprecedented challenges. Drug Research and Development (R&D) costs have rocketed 23 fold in 28 years, touching an all time high of $1.25 billion per new molecular entity (NME). Drug development time has gone up from 11.6 years in the 1970s to 14.9 years in 2001 reducing patent protected market life and shaving billions off potential revenues. And the output does not justify the increasing time and cost. The pharmaceutical R&D pipeline is thinning, with more blockbusters set to go off patent than to emerge from the R&D pipeline. Blockbusters are now not only desirable for success, but essential for survival. However future blockbusters are more likely to emerge from outside traditional chemistry based pharmaceutical industries (Pharma) or from innovative small biotech startups scattered around the world. As a result, Big Pharma companies historic high valuation is being questioned – it was based on steady and measurable income from patent protected drugs and rich R&D pipelines with potential blockbusters.

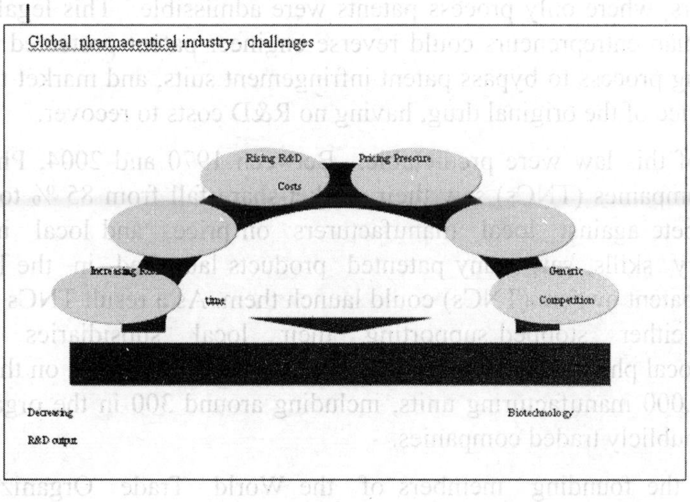

Background

"India meets Doha, a white paper from Deloitte, focused on the recent strengthening of the patent laws in India (Indian Patent (Amendment) Act 200) and mentioned several new opportunities for one of the most Intellectual Property (IP) sensitive industries of our time - the pharmaceutical industry – emphasizing increased R&D productivity by outsourcing drug research and development to India. This paper, as a sequel, presents an overview of the Indian pharmaceutical landscape, and studies the opportunities for outsourcing clinical trials - the most cost and time intensive phase of the R&D process today.

Indian Patents and TRIPS

India could not have stepped into the limelight at a more opportune time. From January 2005, the country became TRIPS compliant and formally recognized product patents. Patent protection in India is now on levels comparable to developed nations (caveat). For any Intellectual Property (IP) sensitive industry India is now a destination to be considered – both as a market and for manufacturing and research & development (R&D).

Patent Progress

The Indian Patents & Designs Act (1911) recognized product patents but the goals of patent protection – to promote and protect innovation – did not materialize. To encourage investments and promote development The Indian Patent Act, 1970 (with amendments) removed product patents in pharmaceutical, agro-chemical and food processing sectors, where only process patents were admissible. This legalized copycat drug making Indian entrepreneurs could reverse engineer patent protected drugs, tweak the manufacturing process to bypass patent infringement suits, and market the drugs at a fraction of the price of the original drug, having no R&D costs to recover.

The effects of this law were predictable. Between 1970 and 2004, Pharmaceutical Transnational companies (TNCs) saw their market-share fall from 85 % to 15%. TNCs could not compete against local manufacturers on price, and local ingenuity and process chemistry skills saw many patented products launched in the local markets even before the patent owners (TNCs) could launch them. As a result TNCs lost interest in India and either stopped supporting their local subsidiaries or withdrew altogether. The local pharmaceutical (Pharma) manufacturing industry, on the other hand, grew to over 20,000 manufacturing units, including around 300 in the organized sector and a few large publicly traded companies.

As one of the founding members of the World Trade Organization, India committed to bring its patent protection laws to internationally acceptable minimum

TRIPS levels in 10 years. Accordingly, from January 01, 2005, product patent was recognized in the pharmaceutical sector and the patent period increased from the earlier seven years to 20 years.

Indian Pharmaceutical Landscape – Post TRIPS

The Indian pharmaceutical industry is the worlds 13th largest in terms of value and the 4th largest in terms of volume. With over 60,000 brands in over 60 therapeutic categories, the total market size is approximately USD 5 billion. India has world class facilities and expertise in manufacturing with the largest number of US FDA approved manufacturing units in the world outside the US. Ancillary industries are well developed with support available locally. Quality bulk drugs at competitive prices are assured. In R&D, basic research and biology skills are weak, a legacy of the lax patent regime where basic research was neglected. But process chemistry skills – honed over decades of reverse-engineering – are strong. The Indian pharmaceutical industry accounts for at least 35% of bulk drug filings in the US.

Post-TRIPS, the Indian pharmaceutical landscape is set to change permanently. Local pharmaceutical majors are moving up the international value chain, focusing on generics marketing in Europe and the US to complement their already-strong presence in bulk active pharmaceutical ingredient (API) supply, and to capitalize on the record number of drugs set to go off-patent over the next five years.

To leverage their experience in manufacturing, local companies are scouting for contract manufacturing opportunities. And to leverage their country-wide network of skilled marketing personnel they are actively seeking in-licensing and marketing opportunities.

Local pharmaceutical majors do not have the finances to take a product to market. With annual sales of a billion - less than the R&D budgets of Big Pharma companies – they are out licensing their NME innovation , and focusing on cheaper Abbreviated New Drug Applications (ANDAs). And to 'learn and earn', they are positioning themselves as willing partners in global pharmaceutical knowledge networks. With cost and process skills working to their advantage, local companies are also scouting to grab a share of the international R&D outsourcing market.

Of all the opportunities for global pharmaceutical companies in this scenario, outsourcing the clinical development phase of the R&D process appears the most promising. With a large population and world class medical skills, this outsourçing service segment is developing rapidly and with patent protection no longer a hurdle, a fresh look at this segment is warranted. Including India in the clinical development outsourcing network presents a four fold benefit – it is the most immediate opportunity with the greatest potential benefit in the shortest possible time addressing the most pressing issue today.

Clinical Trials

Clinical studies take up between 30 to 50% of the time spent in R&D, and within this, a third of the time (in clinical trials) is taken in patient recruitment. With patent protection being limited to 20 years including the R&D stage, every year saved here can bring in additional revenues of a billion dollars for a blockbuster. As drugs targeting smaller segments of therapeutics are discovered, the clinical development stage can present a serious bottleneck. It is conceivably difficult to find the adequate study population in time, particularly in smaller geographies with small population densities, particularly in the west, with highly treatment experienced patients causing a delay in 80% of clinical trials.

Advantage - India

The duration of clinical trials can be greatly reduced in India. India is the second most populous country in the world with a large pool of naïve patients and the fourth largest pool of medical professionals in the world. Rapidly improving support industries such as labs and hospitals, and a world respected IT industry capable of picking up domain expertise to support R&D and clinical trials are further advantages. Pharma giants are also attracted by the heterogeneity of the billion plus population, the fact that the country offers nearly 700,000 specialty hospital beds at about a tenth of the price in developed nations, 221 medical colleges and skilled English-speaking medical personnel. In India, the contract research and clinical business in India during FY 2003 - 04 was USD 59.4 million (INR 275 crores) as against USD 29.16 million (INR 135 crore) in the previous year, a growth of 104 percent, and is projected to grow 8-10 times by 2010 to $ 250-300 million .

Optimistic estimates put the figure between $500 million and $1 billion by 2010.University and other diploma courses in biotechnology, bioinformatics, and clinical trials are beginning to become fashionable just as IT was in the 1990s and a reverse brain drain from the west is beginning and can help greatly in scientific and accurate clinical trials. It is easier to do multi-centric large-scale trials in India for many diseases, since the patients' enrollment rate for phase III studies can be up to six times higher in India than US or Europe. Because of the god-like status traditionally accorded to doctors, patient compliance and commitment is extremely high.

But the size of the industry is very small by global standards. In the US, for example, the number of GCP trials is 60,000 and the number of GCP trained investigators is over 40,000. According to Center Watch 2.8 million US subjects completed initial screening in 1999, of which 5 per cent (140,000) completed the trial and 2005 projections for screening are19.8 million subjects. In comparison, the estimated number of ICH-GCP clinical studies was 40-50 and the number of GCP trained investigators was 200-250. Most studies are carried out in 20-25 major public hospitals in capital cities. However, because of global pressures on industry to recruit patients faster and make the trials economic, large numbers of clinical trials are likely to be placed in countries like India. This is expected to explode the Indian clinical trials market over next 5 years.

Disadvantage - India

However, India faces quite a few challenges, before it can claim to be the world class status like the IT industry. Unlike IT, healthcare requires more specialized, less transferable competencies. Furthermore, the IT industry in India flourished, it can be argued, because it was under-regulated and did not hamper entrepreneurship, in contrast to the overregulated pharmaceutical industry. Pharmaceutical products and services from India may also be stonewalled in other overregulated markets, all these are probable barriers to entry and growth. Though the doctors have excellent skills and patient coverage, their lack of experience in GCP trials is undeniable. Furthermore, it is unclear whether an international company cannot carry out concurrent phase I trial. After submission of phase I data generated outside India, sponsors may be permitted to repeat phase I trials. Phase II, III, and IV trials can be concurrently done with other global trials for that drug.

Imports of body fluids/ test samples from India have been another bottleneck hampering the industry. Companies that have global testing labs for sample testing have had failures in the entire outsourcing strategy due to this and a lack of world class GLP labs further incapacitated these companies from successfully completing their trials.

Ethical trials are another issue that is hard to ignore. There are instances of litigation for unethical trials without requisite permissions, or on ill-informed patients. A recent survey of 200 health researchers globally that was commissioned by the former US National Bioethics Advisory Commission and published in February's edition of the Journal of Medical Ethics revealed that a quarter of clinical trials conducted in developing countries did not undergo ethical review.

Local disinformation campaigns can also mar clinical studies and damage company reputation. A TNC runs the risk of being labeled an exploiter of local poverty or ignorance for carrying out cheap clinical trials.

Current Scenario

There has been an overall positive effect of India complying with TRIPS norms on product patents. Even before January 2005, a number of MNCs have set up R&D centers in India. Around 25 contract research organizations (CROs) and almost all multinational pharmaceuticals companies have started full-fledged clinical trials there in the last three years. This move accelerated from up to January 2005 and afterwards. To prepare for the opportunity, reputed institutions for training such as the Academy for Clinical Excellence and Institute of Clinical Research have been established over the last decade to train physicians in ICH- GCP guidelines and ethical trial requirements. The Clinical Data Interchange Standards Consortium (CDISC), USA, an NPO committed to the development of clinical research organizations' standards the world over, is looking at setting up a chapter in India. The Indian Society for Clinical Research launched in August 2005, aims to bring world-class clinical research organizations in India together, advise the government on clinical trials issues and foster the highest levels of ethics in the industry.

The Bottom-line

Outsourcing clinical development to India generates benefits in terms of time and cost savings that are too significant to be ignored. Some estimates we made to analyze the dollar benefits of outsourcing showed that the average saving per commercialized drug can be up to an optimal $ 363 million to a desirable first target of $40 million.

Conclusion

Of the several new opportunities created by India's compliance with WTO levels of patent protection, clinical research outsourcing has the most significant impact. Moreover clinical trials outsourcing fits the classic requirements of outsourcing a process – it is standard, increases efficiencies of time and costs, and improves organizational flexibility. Finally, India has country specific factors that favor outsourcing of this part of the R&D process. From this year, patent protection is no longer a barrier to outsourcing and the way is clear for global pharmaceutical companies to include Indian clinical research organizations in the global R&D network.

While there seems to be an exciting time ahead, a few challenges still remain. As in all cases of successful outsourcing, three things are necessary – commitment, compliance and quality. The right partner selection can eliminate the hazards of outsourcing and the potential pitfalls of a well intentioned venture.

From the host country perspective, the government initiatives need to be clear cut and quick and more educational institutions need to offer specialized courses to tackle the impending shortage of ICH-GCP trained doctors. On the other hand Indian CROs need to be more aggressive in their marketing of their skills externally, and combat potential disinformation campaigns internally. If high ethical standards are adhered to, clinical research studies help the poor in the country by giving them free access to the newest drugs and the highest levels of health care that even the middle class cannot afford to have access to. This should always be remembered and portrayed.

Two approaches can be taken to estimate the savings by time and cost by outsourcing clinical trials to India.

In the first approach widely accepted estimates that a clinical trial costs an average $ 30,000 a day and lasts an average 6.6 years, and that outsourcing to India could save half the time and cost.

In the second approach a more generic view that bringing a molecule to market has crossed a billion dollars in recent times, and that overall half the costs of clinical trials can be saved by outsourcing to India.

The calculation table is presented below.

Row	calculation	PHASE - CLINICAL TRIALS Method – I	US$	Source
		Present Clinical trials costs		
a		Cost per day	30,000	
b		Average Duration	2,409	Tufts Center for the study
c	(a*b)	Total Costs	72,270,000	of drug Development 2001
		Clinical trials costs in India		
d	(a/2)	Cost per day	15,000	
e	(b/2)	Average Duration	1,205	
f	(d*e)	Total Costs	18,067,500	
g	(f*10%)	Add offshoring costs	1,806,750	
h	(f+g)	Total costs of outsourced trials	19,874,250	
i	(c-h)	Direct Savings	52,395,750	
j	(b-e)*20%	dded Margins (20%)	316,783,500	CenterWatch (assuming avg. annual sales of $480mn)
i		TOTAL IMPACT	369,179,250	
		If only 25% of the work outsourced	92,294,813	

Row	calculation	Method – II	US$mn	Source
a		Cost of Drug R&D	1,000	PhRMA
b	(a*32%)	Clinical Trials phase	320	Business Insights
c	(b*50%)	Overview of 50% savings	160	Interviews, Reports
d	(c*50%)	If only 25% of the work outsourced	40	Conservative outsourced

5.3 Globalization and its Impact on the Indian Pharmaceutical Industry

Globalization is a process which involves economic inter-dependence of countries world-wide removing all barriers for economic integration as if the whole world is a single village. Obviously, in this process, the rich nations with their superior financial power, control the scenario and the poor and the developing nations are forced to integrate surrendering their economic independence knowing fully well what they are forced to accept is really prejudicial to their own interest. In this process the world financial institutions like the World Bank, IMF and now the WTO advance the interest of the rich countries alone. The draconian policies of the World Bank and the IMF under the structural adjustment Programme resulted in the net transfer of $178 billion between 1984 and 1990 from the poor countries to the commercial banks of rich nations. (UNDP Human Development Report, 1994). The Transnational Corporations (TNCs) of the rich nations are practically controlling the world finances. Today, the whole world is colonized by global finance and the TNCs supported by the neo-colonial structure including the World Bank, IMF and WTO are controlling the financial situation world-wide. The governments of third world countries are powerless against global finance and are unable to control its movement within their own national boundaries.

The situation of the world drug industry is no different. 'Operating at the behest of the Pharmaceutical Research and Manufacturers' Association (PhRMA) for a decade and a half, the U.S.Government has waged a ruthless crusade to force third world countries to adopt strait jacketing intellectual property rules at the expense of protecting public health', says the editorial comment in the June 1998 issue of *Multinational Monitor*, a journal published from Washington.

The structural adjustment Programme introduced by the government of India at the behest of the IMF, World Bank and WTO created a serious impact on India's drug industry, health care system, on the workers engaged in the industry and ultimately on the people of the country. These reform policies are mainly the reduced role of the Government, cut in subsidy in the social sector, increase in administered prices, liberalization of trade by increasing tariff rates providing incentives for foreign investment, privatization of the public sector, equating foreign companies with Indian companies, de-regulating the labor market etc. This is aimed at the withdrawal of the state initiative from the social and welfare sectors like health, education, public distribution etc.

Drug industry situation prior to the Indian Patent Act, 1970

At the time of independence, the total drug production in our country was around Rs. 10 *crores*. At that time the MNCs taking the help of the colonial Patent and Designs Act, 1911 exploited the drug market of our country. They were engaged mainly in the import of drugs from their country of origin. Between 1947-57, 99% of the 1704 drugs and pharmaceutical patents in India were held by foreign MNCs. During that time the MNCs who were controlling 80% of the market did not come forward with financial investment and technological help to establish drug production centres in India. Drug prices in India were amongst the highest in the world. In 1954, the first public sector drug company Hindustan Antibiotic Ltd. (HAL) was established with the help of WHO and UNICEF. The Indian Drugs and Pharmaceutical Limited (IDPL) was established in 1961 with help from the Soviet Union. The establishment of these two public sector units and the coming into force of the Drug Policy of 1978 had been mainly responsible for the availability of drugs and medicines at relatively lower prices in India. The country became almost self-sufficient in the production of drugs.

Indian Patent Act 1970

The Patent Bill was first introduced in Parliament in 1967, but the Patent Act, 1970 came into force only in 1972. The Indian Patent Act 1970 which is in operation in our country does not allow product patents on medicines, agricultural products and atomic energy. This is the most suitable patent act for the developing world. Here, process patents are allowed for 5-7 years. Mainly with the help of the Indian Patent Act 1970 India is today self-sufficient in the production of basic drugs covering various groups of drugs. Indian scientists developed new processes for 107 drugs. Indian companies are now among the world leaders in the production of bulk drugs from basic stages. At present, the prices of drugs in India are comparatively cheaper than many other countries. As per UNIDO, India is identified to produce its own drug needs with its own technology and manpower indigenously. After 1970, many new drug firms were established by Indian businessmen. At present, around 23 thousand small, big, and medium factories are producing drugs in India.

Attempts to change the Indian Patent Act 1970 are a part of this globalization Programme. The imposition of an unequal trade treaty like the World Trade Organization (WTO) is a step towards globalization in favor of the MNCs of rich nations. With its help, the market of the developing nations is forced open for the developed countries. Most of the developing countries were forced to sign the WTO agreement without realizing its implication: as a result, the developed countries are the gainers. Already, at the dictates of the IMF, World Bank and WTO, the Government of India is slackening all checks and controls to invite the MNCs in all industries including the pharmaceutical industry. FERA and MRTP Acts have been amended. Customs duties and corporate taxes have been lowered. Relief, concessions and facilities have been extended to the MNCs as to Indian companies. All these, already, had an adverse impact on the indigenous drug industry. As per the requirement of WTO guidelines for the product patent regime, the availability of new drugs in our country may be delayed depending on the desire of the patent holders. As per the guidelines, a product patent is granted for 20 years and a process patent for another 20 years. At present, newer drugs are made available in our country within a 4-6 years period. Prices of drugs will go up by 5 to 10 times as it is evident from the prices of drugs in India and other countries like Pakistan, U.K. and U.S.A. where product patents are in force. Ranitidine is sold by Glaxo in India at Rs. 7.20. The same product is sold by the same company in Pakistan at Rs. 65 and in the U.S.A. at Rs. 545. Similarly, the anti-viral drug Aciclovir costs Rs. 33.75 in India while the same drug is sold in Pakistan at Rs. 363. There are many such examples. The drug prices in the U.S.A., U.K. and other developed countries have gone up so high that the health care expenditure in those countries is predominantly funded by insurance companies at a very high premium. In those countries people cannot think of treatment without insurance coverage. Product patent regime will definitely hamper India's drugs exports as countries will be forced to purchase from patent holders only.

Dilution of Drug Policy and Drug Price Increase

Unlike consumer goods, drugs are not purchased by the preference of a person, but on a doctors' prescription. Consumers have no choice of their own on this matter.

Prices of drugs are increasing by leaps and bounds along with the prices of other commodities in recent times. The drug manufacturers are flouting the Drug Price Control Order (DPCO). The DPCO was first introduced in 1970. In 1970 most of the drugs were under price control. In 1987 this was diluted and the number of drugs which were restricted declined to 347, in 1987 it was brought down to 163 drugs and in 1994 only 73 drugs were under DPCO. Even then industry is not happy; they want the control to be abolished totally. They have already demanded decontrol of 17 bulk drugs and further recommended full decontrol within 3 years time . Many developed countries of Europe control drug prices directly. In the U.K., the government determines the profit level of drugs supplied by individual companies. A company has to reimburse excess profits to the Department of Health.

A recent study shows that the prices of many life-saving bulk drugs have gone up steeply. Drugs policies in our country are decided not by the need of our people, the pattern of diseases or by the purchasing capacity of the people, but by the profit motive of the industry and the Central Government is playing the role of a silent onlooker.

The prices of twelve essential drugs before the liberal decontrol of DPCO in 1995 and today are given below.

Table 5.1

Name of drug	For treatment	Packing	Price 1995	1998	Percentage increase
Diazepam	Depression	10	3.13	9.50	204%
Ampicillin	Antibiotic	4	12.85	23.15	80%
Cephalexin	Antibiotic	10	45.07	113.15	151%
Ethambutol	Anti T.B.drugs	10	5.92	33.00	457%
Rifampicin	-do-	10	24.00	64.00	167%
Pirazinamide	-do-	10	17.01	46.95	176%
Lignocaine Hcl	Anaesthetic	30 ml.	4.16	12.40	198%
Promethaxine Hcl	Anti allergic	10	1.25	3.23	158%
Antacid liq.	Gastritis	200 ml.	13.00	23.00	77%
Oxyfedrine Hcl	Angina pectoris	10	10.44	21.41	105%
Discopyramide Phosphate	Cardiac problems	10	16.50	50.46	206%
Dipyridamole	Anti angina	10	2.00	4.73	137%

The above list is only indicative. Hundreds of such examples can be given.

Further, under the WTO agreement and the imposition of a products patent regime, the prices of all new drugs (patented) will go up without any control of domestic law. The DPCO will become further irrelevant and Indian people's accessibility to newer drugs will be restricted only to the rich of the country. Given below are the high prices of some of the new drugs introduced in 1997 in the Indian market.

Table 5.2

Drug	Company	Strength	Pack	Price
Sporanox	Ethnor	100 mg	4 tablets	173.00
Lumicil	Novertis	250 mg	14 capsules	1247.00
Spariex	Sun Pharma	200 mg	6 tablets	154.00
Rispid	Panacea	50 ml	1 mg/ml capsule	141.00
Livial	Infar		28 tablets	1225.00
Pipracil	Cyanamid	2 G	Vial	215.78
Amate	Mesco Pharma	50 mg	12 tablets	180.00
Adnoject	Inca	3 mg	2 ml. vial	210.00
Roxisara	Sarabhai	300 mg	6 tablets	165.00
Celex	Glaxo	250 mg	4 tablets	140.00

World-wide concern has been expressed about the sharp rise of drug prices. The WHO's goal of Health for All by 2000 AD will remain a distant dream.

Moreover, with the rapid development in technology, a greater number of new drugs are being introduced. Experts say that very few of them are having therapeutic advantages over the existing drugs. 'Out of 348 new drugs introduced by 25 big US companies during 1981 to 1988 only 3 per cent made important potential contribution while 84 percent made little or no potential contribution' said the US federal authority. Hence the introduction of new costly drugs should be properly monitored by the central government.

Mass Ending of Jobs

With the reduction of the customs duties on foreign imports many drugs manufactured in India have become unviable compared to the foreign goods in the Indian market. As a result, the owner of these factories are closing down their units and throwing the workers out of employment. Messrs. Boehringer Mannheim, and Parks Davis who were the lone producers of Chloramphenicol in India stopped their production as its prices in the international market were cheaper than the cost of production in India. M/s. Sarabhai Chemicals closed their Vitamin 'C' plant for a similar reason. Like Chloramphenicol and vitamin 'C' many other drugs like paracetamol, metronidazole, ampicillin, amoxycillin etc. are available at a cheaper price in our country from abroad because of the lowering of the customs duties so that Indian factories have closed and workers are on the streets. For the above drugs our country has became dependent on foreign supply.

In their attempt to shift the production to the third party manufacturing already, Hindustan Ciba Geigy, Roche, Abbot, Boehringer Mannheim, Boots, Park Davis, Unichem etc. have closed their factories and offered a voluntary retiring scheme to workers and they have sold the land of their factory premises at a premium price. Apart from these closures, Pfizer, Rhone Poulenc, Hoechst, Glaxo etc. have reduced their work force. *Crores* of rupees have been spent to give VRS. These companies are manufacturing their products with the help of loan licenses. Some of the companies have opened new smaller factories in new places and appointed workers with lower wages and more workload. More casual workers are being appointed. In the last two years in the Mumbai Thane region of Maharashtra around 30,000 workers have lost their jobs in the pharmaceutical industry.

Apart from the factory workers the distribution workers are gradually being replaced by Cost and Freight agency system. In this system, the original company does not have any responsibility for the workers. They are employed by agents with more workload and lower wages. In the last decade around 15 thousand distribution workers have lost their jobs in the pharmaceutical industry. Moreover, through the agency system the Government is deprived of sales tax.

In marketing also the field workers or the sales promotion employees are facing tremendous attacks in the name of franchise, co-marketing, appointment of communicators etc. many permanent sales promotion employees are losing their jobs. Many others are appointed in the name of so-called executives to remove them from the fold of the union. More casual and contractual workers are being recruited.

Table 5.3

Company	Year	Reduction of work force
Glaxo	1995	1564
Hoechst	1996	1049
Knoll Pharma (Boots)	1995	600 (All workers)
Smith Kline Beecham	1995	208
E. Merck	1995	194
Rhone Poulenc	1996	700
Hindusthan Ciba Geigy	1993	907
Duphar Interfran	1996	154
Bayer	1996	590
Abbott	1996	All workers
Roche	1996	All 320 workers
Boehringer Mannheim	1997	All 335 workers
Park Davis	1997	All 650 workers
Pfizer	1995	215
Unichem	1997	All workers

(Source : Annual reports of respective companies and interaction with the office bearers of Unions).

Thus, the total payment on voluntary retirement schemes by firms like Glaxo, Hoechst, Pfizer, Knoll Pharma, Rhone Poulenc, Park Davis, Smith Kline Beecham, Duphar, Bayer etc. are more than Rs. 200 crores in the last three financial years. The main important thing is that employment opportunities in these units have been reduced for ever.

Impact on Public Sector

With the reduced role of the state under globalization the public sector drug companies are faced with serious problems including imminent closures. Public sector drug companies like Indian Drugs and Pharmaceuticals Ltd. (IDPL), Hindustan Antibiotics Ltd. (HAL), Bengal Chemicals and Pharmaceuticals Ltd. (BCPL), Bengal Immunity (BI) and Smith Stanistreet Pharmaceuticals Ltd. (SSPL) played an important role in the production of essential drugs at affordable prices. Under the globalization process the role of the public sector has been marginalized and they have been made sick. Attempts have been made to either privatize or close them. The Penicillin Plant in HAL, the biggest in the country, has been handed over to private hands. Its Streptomycin plant also has been leased to a private company for manufacture of other drugs. IDPL which is having the biggest pharmaceutical plant in Asia is closed from 1996 for want of proper financial assistance from the government. The public sector drug companies used to supply raw materials to the small scale sector companies. Now, these companies are facing difficulties in procuring raw materials. Similar is the fate of BCPL, B.I. and SSPL. These three units were taken over by the government after they were made sick by the private owners. Proper utilization of their capacity could not be made due to lack of will on the part of the government, mismanagement at the administrative level and high level corruption.

With the pharmaceutical industry taking a leap towards biotechnology development world-wide, only the public sector drug companies, with the backing of the Central Government, could have faced the challenge effectively from the MNCs in the new situation.

Mergers and Acquisitions

International and national level mergers, acquisitions and takeovers have now become a common phenomenon in the pharmaceutical industry. Internationally American Home Product merged with Cyanamid, SKB with Sterling, Rhone Poulenc took over Fashions, BSF with Boots, Glaxo with Burroughs Welcome, Ciba Geigy with Sandoz, Warner Hindustan with Parke Davis, Hoechst with Rhone Poulenc etc. are some of the examples of big take overs. By mergers and acquisitions these companies became even larger with more financial power at their disposal over their competitors.

In coming days, with the help of international financial companies the MNCs will capture and take control of Indian companies to control the Indian market.

To match the situation created by international mergers and takeovers, Indian companies are adopting the same path. For example Wockhardt took over Merind and Tata Pharma, Ranbaxy took over Croslands, Nicholas Piramal took over Roche, Boehringer, Sumitra Pharma. The inevitable results are job loss of workers. Because of overlapping of jobs large numbers of workers are declared surplus. After merger Glaxo-Welcome and Ciba-Sandoz announced a reduction of 15 thousand and 10 thousand of their work force respectively world-wide. Upjohn and Pharmacia decided to close 24 of their 57 plants in different countries after their merger.

Some countries are adopting the 'buy and grow' method. They are taking over some popular brands and increasing their business. SKB took over Crocin from Duphar, Ranbaxy took over 7 leading brands from Gufic, Dr. Reddy's Lab purchased 6 products of Dolphin and two each from Pfimex and SOL Pharma. Sun pharma purchased all leading brands of NATCO, after selling the popular brands the companies are becoming sick and closing their shutters throwing the workers on the street.

The governments permission to the MNCs to come to India with 100% equity have threatened the existing companies with the same origin and their workers.

Through the process of mergers, acquisitions and takeovers MNCs will gradually perpetuate their grip on the Indian industry by the creation of a limited number of mega companies having monopoly control and domination world wide. In the absence of competition people will have to pay any price as it happens in the sellers market.

Conclusion

The present government at the centre is bringing a bill in the winter session of Parliament to change the Indian Patent Act 1970. The change in the Act is not in the interest of the people of the country. Now patents have become an object of business instead of development. Considering the wide gap of industrial and technological development between developed and developing countries monopoly rights through the patent system should not be allowed to the rich nations. Today 85% of the patents are being controlled by the TNCs of the rich nations. 'Globalization is hurting poor people, not just the poor countries. In this process poor countries and poor people will become increasingly marginalized', says the 1997 world development report of UNDP.

The main aim is to impose the conditionality of WTO and to change the Indian Patent Act as MNCs need more markets and are eyeing Asia which is the largest continent of the world where 60% of the world population lives but contributes only 20% of the world pharmaceuticals business. With a high rate of population growth it is expected that the need of drugs will tremendously increase in the third world countries including India in the next millennium. India contributes 16.1% of the world population, but it produces only 1.2% of world drug production . Hence the MNCs are trying to have more control over the pharmaceutical markets of the developing nations.

Developed countries are backing their own big companies to capture markets in other countries even at the cost of the interest of the people there. The United States has successfully battled for the inclusion of strict intellectual property rules in international trade agreements such as NAFTA and GATT. Often the U.S. position has literally been drafted by PhRMA. These trade agreements disregard public health considerations and have forced dramatic changes in the intellectual property rules the world over. Still PhRMA is not satisfied. And when PhRMA is not happy the office of U.S. Trade Representative (USTR) is not happy, says the editorial comment of *Multinational Monitor*.

Table 5.4 Some top Pharma company mergers in the world.

Company	Merger	Year of merger	Value of merged company
Dow Chemicals	Marion Labs	1986	$ 6.21 bn.
Bristol Myers	Squibb Corp	1989	12.09 bn.
Beecham group	Smith, Kline & French	1989	7.9 bn.
American Home Products	American Cynamide	1994	9.7 bn.
Hoffman La Roche	Syntex Lab.	1994	5.3 bn.
Eli Lyly	PCS Health System	1994	4 bn.
Sandoz	Gerber	1994	3.7 bn.
Smith Kline Beecham	Sterling	1994	2.9 bn.
Glaxo	Burroughs Wellcome	1995	14.2 bn.
Hoechst	MMD Roussel	1995	7.2 bn.
Pharmacia	Upjohn	1995	7 bn.
Rhone-Poulenc Rorers	Fison	1995	2.7 bn.
BASF	Boots	1995	1.3 bn.
Ciba Geigy	Sandoz	1996	30.1 bn.
Hoffman la Roche	Comage Ltd.	1997	1 bn.
Hoechst A.G.	Rhone Poulenc	1998	
Astra	Zeneca	1998	67 bn.

Table 5.5 Percentage of drug production and world population in some countries.

Country	% of world drug production	% of world population
USA	28.2%	4.7%
Germany	7.7%	1.5%
France	7.1%	1.1%
U.K.	3.4%	1.1%
Brazil	1.7%	2.8%
India	1.2%	16.1%

5.4 Indian Pharmaceutical Industry Trends 2010

Indian domestic pharmaceutical market has seen growth at a CAGR of about 12% in the last 5 years. About 67 million Indians are expected to reach the age of 67 years by 2011. People of this age group spends around 3 to 4 times more on drugs than people in younger age groups. This indicates substantial growth of Indian pharmaceutical industry. Patented drug are expected to have a 10% market share of pharmaceutical industry in 2010. Incomes of people in rural India are on a rise and the distribution network of drugs is also very strong. These factors are contributing to a high growth of India's rural pharmaceutical market. The positive approach towards product patent product has encouraged the Indian pharmaceutical companies to invest more in Research and Development. Indian pharmaceutical market is expected to have compound annual growth rate of 9.5 per cent by 2011.

Indian Pharmaceutical Industry - Future Perspectives

Future trends of Indian pharmaceutical industry seems to be in positive tone. Consumer spending on healthcare services and products has increased in India due to the increasing affordability, shifting disease patterns and modest healthcare reforms. Healthcare budget of an average Indian household is expected to grow from 7% in 2005 to 13% in 2025. The future trends of Indian pharmaceutical industry can be listed as under.

- By 2015, India will probably open a US$ 8 billion market for multi national pharmaceutical companies selling expensive drugs as predicted by the FICCI-Ernst & Young India study.
- The domestic India Pharma market is likely to reach US$ 20 billion by 2015.
- A whopping amount of US$ 6.31 billion will be invested in the Indian pharmaceutical industry as per the estimates of the Ministry of Commerce, Government of India.
- Indian pharmaceutical off-shoring industry is predicted to be a US$ 2.5 billion opportunity by 2012 all because of low cost of R&D.
- Patented drugs are predicted to capture up to a 10% share of the total Indian pharmaceutical industry by 2015 with a market size of US$2 billion.
- The branded generics market will continue to dominate the Indian pharmaceutical industry. Sixty one drugs worth US $ 80 billion will go off patent at the US Patent and Trademark Office between 2011 and 2013. Indian pharmaceutical industry is all set to gain from the patent expiry of some blockbuster drugs by producing their generic equivalents. However, the influence of physicians will remain high that will ensure fair competition on the basis of product quality and scientific detailing.
- By 2015, the specialty and super-specialty therapies will account for 45% of the Pharma market. The growing lifestyle disorders, particularly metabolic disorders

like diabetes and obesity as well as coronary heart disease and hypertension, cardiovascular, neuropsychiatry and oncology drugs will gain considerable significance.

- Although there will be a shift towards specialty therapies, mass therapies will remain important in the Indian pharmaceutical industry. This will be, primarily due to the gap between the prevalence of common diseases and their treatment rates. Diseases like anemia, diarrhea, gastro-intestinal & respiratory problems, acute pain, infections etc. is suffered by a large number of population. The growing income levels will also increase spending on basic healthcare and the consumption of mass therapy drugs for acute ailments.

The Indian pharmaceuticals industry has grown reasonably during the past decade and has the potential to transform itself over the next decade too. The domestic Pharma market of India will play a crucial role in fighting the growing diseases. However, the full potential of Indian pharmaceuticals can only be achieved through sustained, progressive and collaborative efforts by the government and the pharmaceutical industry as a whole.

Export and Import of Drugs and Pharmaceuticals

The Indian pharmaceutical industry, now a $17 billion(over Rs 68,000 crore) Industry, has shown tremendous progress in terms of infrastructure development, technology base creation and a wide range of products. It has established its presence and determination to flourish in the changing environment. The industry now produces bulk drugs belonging to all major therapeutic groups requiring complicated manufacturing technologies. Formulations in various dosage forms are being produced in GMP compliant facilities. Strong scientific and technical manpower and pioneering work done in process development have made these possible. The country now ranks 4th worldwide accounting for 8% of world's production by volume and 1.5% by value. It ranks 17th in terms of export value of bulk actives and dosage forms. Indian exports are destined to more than 200 countries around the globe including highly regulated markets of US, Europe, Japan and Australia.

The country is also showing excellent performance on the Pharma export front. The figures of exports under this category during the current decade have been:

(Figures in Rs. Crores)

2001-02	2002-03	2003-04	2004-05	2005-06	2006-07
9751	12826	15213	17857	22116	24942

Technological Strengths

The following attributes constitute the basis of the technological strengths of the Indian Pharmaceutical Industry: --

Self-reliance displayed by the production of 70% of bulk drugs and almost the entire requirement of formulations within the country

- Low cost of production
- Low R&D costs
- Innovative Scientific manpower
- Excellent and world-class national laboratories specialising in process development and development of cost effective technologies.
- Increasing balance of trade in Pharma sector
- An efficient and cost effective source for procuring generic drugs especially the drugs going off patent in the next few years.
- An excellent centre for clinical trials in view of the diversity in population.

Restricted Items for Import

Import of most of the bulk drugs, intermediates and formulations under the rules is free except for a quite a few narcotic drugs & psychotropic substances, that were restricted as per Exim Policy 2002-2007 at the instance of the Department of Revenue. On account of structural similarities and non availability of specific codes for many narcotic drugs & psychotropic substances, a large number of organic chemicals including vital bulk drugs & intermediates required by the Pharma industry were also put under restricted category by virtue of their coverage under 9 residual categories of "Others". Keeping in view the difficulties of a large number of genuine actual users of these substances, at the instance of this Department import restrictions on the narcotic drugs & psychotropic substances including those under "others" were lifted. At the same time a new regime for import of narcotic drugs & psychotropic substances has been brought in by DIRECTOR GENERAL OF FOREIGN TRADE. Import of all Drugs & Pharmaceuticals is subject to registration and other requirements as administered by Drug controller General of India under the provisions of Drugs & Cosmetics Act.

Small Scale Units in Drugs and Pharmaceuticals

As per the guidelines issued by the Ministry of Micro, Small & Medium Enterprises, the investment limit for units to qualify as a small-scale unit is Rs.5 crore. After latest amendments in the list of items reserved for SSI units in March 2007 only following four items having relevance to the drugs & pharmaceutical industry are left as reserved for exclusive manufacture by the small-scale units:

1. Niacinamide
2. Pyrazolones
3. Lanolin anhydrous
4. Potassium Citrate- industrial grade

Pharmaceutical Advisory Forum

Through Drug Policies announced from time to time, Government of India has been trying to ensure abundant availability of good quality essential pharmaceuticals of mass consumption at reasonable prices. At the same time strengthening the indigenous capability for cost effective quality production of medicines has been an important objective. To help realize this and in order to provide a Forum for a meaningful dialogue amongst all the stakeholders on various issues concerning the drug policy, it was decided to constitute a Pharmaceutical Advisory Forum in the Department of Chemicals & Petrochemicals

The Pharmaceutical Advisory Forum was constituted in July 2004 having following composition:

1. Hon'ble Minister for Chemicals & Fertilizers (Chairman)
2. Hon'ble Minister of State for Chemicals and Fertilizers (Member)
3. Health Ministers of All States/UTs (Members)
4. Secretary, Dep't. of Chemicals & Petrochemicals Government of India. (Member)
5. Secretary, Dep't. of Health Government of India. (Member)
6. Chairman, NPPA (Member)
7. Drugs Controller General of India (Member)
8. Joint Secretary (Pharmaceuticals), Department of Chemicals & Petrochemicals (Member Secretary)
9. Member Secretary, NPPA (Member)
10. Director (Pharmaceuticals), Department of Chemicals & Petrochemicals (Convener)
11. Drugs Controller of all States/UTs (Member)
12. Joint Secretary (Drugs), Dept. of Health, GOI (Member)
13. Two representatives of Consumer to be nominated by Dept. of Chemicals & Petrochemicals from each States/UTs. (Member)
14. One representative of Chemist Associations from each States/UTs. (Member)
15. One representative each of Drug Industry Association viz., IDMA, BDMA, OPPI, IPA and AISSPMA. (Member)

So far, three meetings of the Pharmaceutical Advisory Forum have been held at Vigyan Bhavan, New Delhi on 11.02.2006, 23.09.2006 and 15.5.2007 respectively. Important suggestions emanating from the deliberations of these meetings have already received serious consideration and steps are being taken to act upon them.

Pharmaceutical Export Promotion Council

Pharmaceutical Export Promotion Council (Pharmexcil) having its Headquarters at Hyderabad and Regional offices at Mumbai and Delhi, was set up by the Ministry of Commerce and Industry, Government of India vide Notification No 64 dated the 12th May, 2004. Under Para 3.12.1 of Export and Import Policy 2002-2007, Pharmexcil is the only Designated Agency for issue of Registration and Membership Certificates for Pharmaceutical Exports dealing in products/services like: -

Bulk Drugs (APIs), Drug Intermediates, Drug Formulations, Biotechnology, Biological Products, Herbal Products (Ayurveda, Siddha & Unani), Medicinal Plants, Homeopathy, Nutraceuticals and Physiochemical, Diagnostics, Contact Research; contract Manufacturing , Clinical Research, Surgical, Collaborative Research and Technologies/ Consultancy.

Objectives The objectives of the Council (Pharmexcil) are to extend all assistance to the pharmaceutical industry in India to explore their opportunities. Towards achieving this aim, the Council is taking delegations to various countries, organizing Business meets etc. encouraging export activities by arranging fund support under MAI programmes of the Government.

Services This Council is a Government sponsored single window contact to the world of Pharmaceuticals from India and an only authorized agency for issue of Registration cum Membership Certificate (RCMC) for pharmaceutical exports under Foreign Trade Policy of Government of India. Apart from this, the Council is also providing following

(a) Trade Enquiries received from foreign Embassies /Buyers

(b) Market Development assistance as provided by Ministry of Commerce for business tours to foreign countries.

(c) Arrange one to one Buyer/Seller Meets in India/Abroad.

(d) Arrange Exhibitions in India and Abroad for market promotion.

(e) Assist in Regulatory matters with domestic and Foreign Government agencies.

(f) Provide financial assistance for Product Registration charges, Research and Development, Product showcasing etc. as per rules.

(g) Arrange Conferences/Seminars in domestic and foreign countries - for market and technical up-gradation of information

Working Groups/ Joint Working Groups / Sub-Groups

India-EU Joint Working Group

Under India-EU Sub-Commission on Trade, India-EU Joint Working Group (JWG) on Pharmaceuticals and Biotechnology was set up under the Co-Chairmanship of Joint Secretary (Pharma) since 2006. D.G. Enterprises is the counterpart from the EU side. The first meeting of the said JWG was held on 18th July 2006 at Brussels where in the Terms of Reference for the JWG was finalized. Its 2nd meeting was held on 30th and 31st May 2007 at New Delhi.

Indo Tunisia Joint Working Group

A Joint Working Group on Drugs & Pharmaceuticals under the Aegis of the Indo-Tunisian Joint Commission has been constituted since 2004. Three meetings have since been held. The Tunisian Government has given permission to 5 Indian Companies for registering their products in Tunisia.

Sub Group on Pharmaceuticals under the aegis of Indo-Russian Working Group on Trade and Economic Cooperation (IRWGTEC)

Under the Indo-Russian Working Group on Trade and Economic Cooperation (IRWGTEC) a sub group on pharmaceuticals is functioning under this Department and provides inputs to IRWGTEC.

Under the said JWG the issues discussed were various areas of cooperation like promotion of Trade and exports of pharmaceuticals to these countries, Joint Venture Cooperation in manufacture as well as R&D, regulatory cooperation, HRD and Training taking part in Exhibitions and Trade Fairs.

Working Group on Drugs and Pharmaceuticals

The report includes a number of measures aimed at accelerating the growth of Indian Drugs and Pharmaceuticals Industry in the globalize scenario and at the same time benefit the common man in line with the Common Minimum Programme of the Union Government. Some of the important measures for the welfare of common man and ensuring growth of the domestic Drugs and Pharmaceuticals Industry as envisaged in the Report include: -

(i) Creation of 5 new NIPER like institutions to generate requisite HR in this field.

(ii) Interest subsidy to Pharma Industry for Schedule M compliance.

(iii) Setting up 10 Pharma Parks to provide global environment to the Pharma industry.

(iv) Creation of District Drug Banks for BPL families.

(v) Provision for Price and availability of Cancer medicines Fund.

(vi) Measures for Pharma PSUs welfare including revival of sick PSUs.

(vii) Strengthening and up gradation of infrastructure at NPPA and NIPER and Pharmexcil.

Pharmaceutical Export Promotion Cell

An Export Promotion Cell in the Pharmaceutical Division has been functioning with the objective of boosting pharmaceutical exports and to act as a nodal center for all queries/issues regarding pharmaceutical exports.

An Export Promotion Cell in the Pharmaceutical Division has been functioning with the objective of boosting pharmaceutical exports and to act as a nodal center for all queries/issues regarding pharmaceutical exports.

In order to give adequate attention to day-to-day problems faced by the exporters, there were interactions with various Ministries/Departments and our Missions abroad. The Cell collects statistical data on export and import of pharmaceuticals in the country and provides commercially useful information for developing and increasing drugs and pharmaceutical exports. It is acting as nodal center for all queries and issues regarding Pharma exports. The Cell also undertakes promotional activities for acceleration of pharmaceutical exports and considers suggestions for modifications in EXIM POLICY from the industry. The Cell has also been entrusted with the organization of seminars and workshops on standards, quality control requirements of important countries so as to prepare the domestic companies for exporting their products. Database on the status of pharmaceutical industry in many countries is available in the cell for the benefit of Indian exporters.

The Department has been associated with Department of Commerce in the promotion of exports and various events by way of GCC Africa and Latin America meets at Hyderabad and CIS meeting in Mumbai were organized. In these events there were interaction between Indian exporters and foreign buyers and regulatory officials.

Pharma exports touched a level of over Rs. 24942 crores during 2006-07. Exports constitute a substantial part of the total production of Pharmaceuticals in India. Another note worthy feature of export is more of dosage form export to advanced markets like

Europe, US, CIS Africa etc. The trend of exports is as follows: -

YEAR	EXPORT (Rs. in Crores)
1998-1999	6256.06
1999-2000	7230.16
2000-2001	8757.47
2001-2002	9751.20
2002-2003	12826.10
2003-2004	15213.24
2004-2005	17857.80
2005-2006	22578.98
2006-2007	24942.00

Licensing and FDI Policy

Industrial Licensing for all bulk drugs cleared by Drug Controller General (India), all their intermediates and formulations has been abolished, subject to stipulations laid down from time to time in the Industrial Policy. 100% FDI is also permissible for the manufacture of Drugs and Pharmaceuticals.

Indian Pharmaceutical Industry Strong Medium Term Visibility in Regulated Market Generics and Domestic Growth

- Global generic opportunities over the medium term are supported by large patent expiries and growing generic penetration backed by government initiatives in the regulated markets.
- The domestic formulations business continues to report strong growth aided by increasing expenditure on healthcare; changing disease profile on account of lifestyle related diseases and growing penetration in tier II&III markets.
- For most large Indian pharmaceutical companies, the domestic formulations business has been a core earnings contributor even as other segments face challenges either from increased competition or weak economic scenario globally.
- Globally generics players continue to face competitive environment with increasingly crowded space for filing ANDAs (abbreviated new drug application) challenges as well as aggressive defense by innovators including patent extensions and market authorization. Certain Indian generic majors are pursuing differentiated model with target on niche and "difficult-to-manufacture" molecules. Cost control, however, remains the key to success in the generic business.

- Increasing generic penetration in relatively untapped developed markets such as Japan however offers strong long-term potential as generic companies scout for investment opportunities to establish a foothold in these markets.
- Focus on establishing presence in the branded segment (domestic/semi-regulated markets) through in-organic investments or in-licensing route continues.
- Contract Research & Manufacturing (CRAMS) segment is affected by weak economic environment forcing companies to rationalize inventory levels. Slowdown in investments in new molecule research also affected business for contract research providers. There are, however, early signs of recovery.
- Patent expiries and increasing focus by Governments to reduce healthcare costs continue to put pressure on big pharmaceutical companies to pursue cost reduction including through outsourcing of non-core activities - supporting long-term prospects for CRAMS business. Upfront investments on infrastructure and establishing a diversified clientele, however, remain as challenges facing this segment.
- On the export front, companies are facing increasing working capital engagement in certain semi-regulated markets.
- Exports to the regulated markets would remain a strong growth driver for Indian companies.
- However, in spite of the sheer size of the opportunities, there are significant challenges in this business such as margin pressure; legal issues; parallel launch of authorized generics; access to distribution channels, increasing compliance costs and Government mandated changes in business environment in several countries.
- R&D investments in product development (for generic fillings) and Novel Drug Delivery System (NDDS) research continue to increase. However, investments in New Chemical Entities (NCEs) have generally been curtailed by several players on the back of lackluster response in the initial phase and funding challenges.
- Overall, investments in capital expenditure and acquisitions are likely to remain buoyant in the medium term. Balance sheets of major pharmaceutical companies remain strong providing some room for debt rising.

Growth prospects for domestic branded formulations remain favorable

The Indian pharmaceutical industry continues to witness 12-14% growth year-on-year driven by increasing expenditure of healthcare; changing disease profile; rising disposable income levels and growing penetration of health insurance besides regulatory reforms. New product introductions contribute to around 6-8% of the total growth, with the rest being contributed by a combination of volume and price increase. Amongst therapeutic areas, chronic segments such as anti-diabetics, CVS, CNS and oncology have been growing at fairly strong rates owing to changing lifestyle patterns and have been the key drivers of growth. The key acute infective, which were affected in the past owing to pricing pressure (as a result of drug pricing control), resulting in lower growth for the industry have also in the recent period reported stable growth. Expanding reach in under-penetrated markets has also supported the growth of companies with a large field force presence. It is estimated that only 35% population has access to modern medicines in the aforementioned under penetrated tier II/III markets.

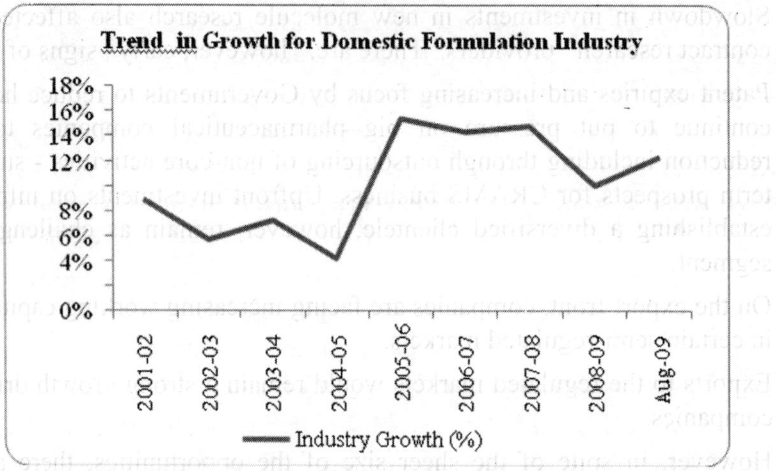

Source: Industry Research; ICRA Estimates

The industry structure remains highly fragmented, with top ten pharmaceutical companies accounting for only ~35% of total pharmaceutical sales. However, the leading players continue to retain their market share owing to their strong distribution reach, strong field force and new product launches. While the domestic branded formulations business continues to offer high gross margin, many of the innovator companies are now aggressively targeting this segment, which is likely to increase the competitive pressures. Also, potential changes in price control mechanism remain an area of uncertainty for the industry. If the scope of price control is expanded, there could be significant adverse impact on the profitability of domestic branded business.

Profitability indicators remain stable for formulation entities

The profitability indicators of leading formulations companies have remained fairly stable over the past six quarters except for marginal fluctuation during October-March 2009. As evidenced below, slight contraction in margins during the aforementioned period was largely on account of spike in input material prices and foreign currency fluctuations during the same period. In spite competition, profitability in the domestic branded business remains healthy supported by new product launches; investments on branding; increasing presence in chronic segments and above all an efficient operating cost structure.

Chart2a and 2b: Trend in operating and net margins for formulation companies

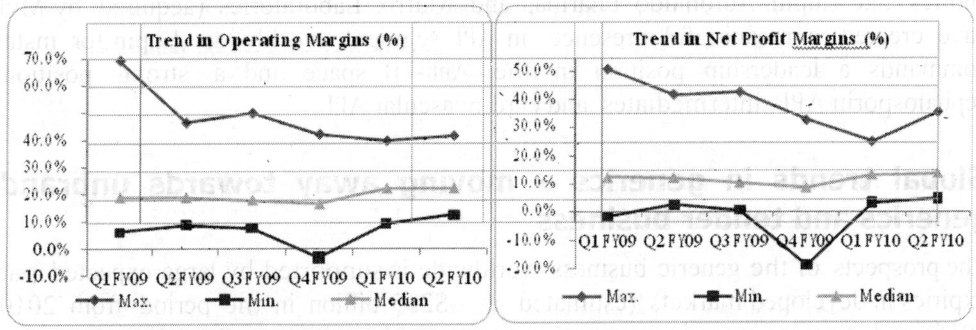

Source: Prowess, ICRA Estimates; ICRA Sample

Bulk Drug players faced margin contraction during the last fiscal

The sample of Active Pharmaceutical Ingredients (APIs)/Bulk Drugs companies also reported a similar trend with fluctuation in OPBDIT margins during H2 FY09. In terms of return indicators, bulk drug manufacturers typically generate lower return on capital employed as compared to formulation companies owing to higher capital investments. With bulk drug business being completely driven by scale of operations, most Indian companies barring a few large ones are relatively small companies, which results in high product concentration and pricing related vulnerabilities.

Chart3a and 3b: Trend in operating and net margins for API companies

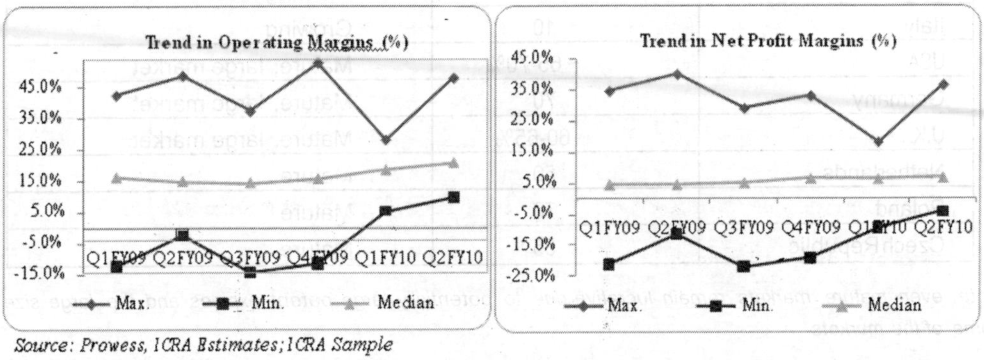

Source: Prowess, ICRA Estimates; ICRA Sample

Many small companies in the API segment have been struggling for survival and offer room for consolidation within the industry. The bulk drug companies also remain dependent on Chinese companies for certain key intermediates and there have been instances of disruption in supplies leading to significant adverse impact on their profitability. The Indian generic companies, traditionally a key client segment for API manufacturers, have also backward integrated into bulk drugs (especially for critical APIs for products targeting the developed markets) to have better control on cost and quality, thereby limiting business for pure API players. Amongst Indian companies, entities like Lupin, Aurobindo Pharma, and Matrix Laboratories (acquired by Mylan) have created a meaningful presence in API segment worldwide. Lupin for instance commands a leadership position in the Anti-TB space and a strong position in cephalosporin API/ intermediates and cardiovascular API.

Global trends in generics – moving away towards unbranded generics and tender business

The prospects of the generic business worldwide is supported by large expected patent expiries in developed markets (estimated at ~$235 billion in the period from 2010 to 2015) and growing generic penetration supported by initiatives from Governments and Insurance Companies to control healthcare costs. While the United States remains the largest generic market in the world with a fairly high (~65-70%) generic penetration, the growth potential in some of the smaller developed markets remains higher due to rapid growth in penetration expected over the medium term.

Table 5.6 Some developed markets, their current generic penetration and growth potential.

Country	Estimated generic	Comments on penetration
Japan	19	Growing, large market
France	20	Growing, large market
Spain	18	Growing
Italy	10	Growing
USA	~65-70%	Mature, large market
Germany	70	Mature, large market
U.K.	60-65%	Mature, large market
Netherlands	50	Mature
Poland	70	Mature
Czech Republic	55	Mature

Note: even mature markets remain lucrative due to potentially large patent expiries and the large size of some of the markets

A key concern in the developed markets is the rapid increase in healthcare costs, which is aggravated by an ageing population. Some of these markets are shifting away from branded generics to unbranded generics or tender market; in the process, the pricing power of generics companies is getting rapidly eroded. Government legislation and insurance companies are increasingly incentivizing pharmacists/ medical practitioners and patients with lower copayments to prescribe/ substitute branded medicine with cheaper generic alternatives. In addition, the rising bargaining power of large distributors, retailers and insurance companies are potential dampener to pricing power of generic companies. The generic companies also face challenges from adoption of aggressive product life cycle management strategies such as patent extensions, switching to OTC category, product substitution and launch of authorized generics, which can significantly erode attractiveness of the Para I[1] exclusivities. All these have significantly increased the costs and capped potential upsides from patent challenges for generic companies. In the last two years, there has been greater emphasis on patent settlements by Indian generics, which significantly reduces launch uncertainties and litigation costs and hence is a positive. These however are likely to come under greater regulatory scrutiny in the future.

Cost-effectiveness and superior quality remains the key drivers for success in the generics business. However first to file (FTF) opportunities and Para IV related exclusivities continue to provide significant profit upsides in developed markets because of limited competition during these periods. In the absence of a healthy pipeline of FTF/ exclusive products, these one-off upsides could lead to significant volatilities in performances. Most of the large Indian companies in the past have displayed large swings in their performance in developed markets depending on the availability of such one-off upsides in a particular year. This volatility could be corrected only through a strong pipeline of products to ensure steady flows of one- offs over the years. Also, patent settlements help reduce uncertainties in costs and timing of inflows from product launches.

Service levels and product pipelines remain extremely critical in developed markets, especially as these markets are dominated by large distributors/ retailers that enjoy tremendous bargaining power. Clearly while low cost is a necessary condition, it does not provide sufficient enough differentiation in the business. Strong management focus on legal and R&D skills is necessary to ensure emphasis on product development of FTF/ exclusive products, which remains a key success factor. A portfolio that includes products beyond commodity generics is necessary to maintain healthy profitability, as competitive pressures drive down prices by up to 99%+ post patent expiry in many products. A strong product pipeline can go a long way in sustaining interest of large distributors/ retailers and capturing of market share. A fewer products with reasonable market share is a more profitable strategy than having large number of products with

---

[1]The US market offers 180-day exclusivity to successful patent challenges through Para IV fillings, which can potentially offer a large profitable entry in this market

insignificant market share. Further, generic companies need to develop strong relationships with the channels to ensure an adequate market share. Also in recent periods regulatory compliance for developed markets has been a cause of concern for a number of companies. While most Indian manufacturers have been able to resolve 483s/ regulatory concerns flagged by international regulatory agencies, our discussion with industry indicates that there is likely to be some increase in compliance cost over the near term to meet the quality norms in these markets.

The global generics companies like Teva, Mylan etc, are scaling up rapidly, while Indian companies continue to be relatively small in comparison. The global generics business has been undergoing steady consolidation. In the US generic market, the top four players now account for ~61% market share as compared to around ~35% share 10 years back. Large generic companies like Teva, Sandoz, and Mylan have widely diversified products and a much bigger pipeline as compared to Indian companies. The largest Indian generic players are currently around $1.5 billion in revenues – this is against $5-11 billion. range for the three largest players globally. The sheer scale of these entities and the resultant advantages may necessitate some consolidation in the Indian generics business over the longer term.

Japanese market offers new growth avenue for Indian generic players

Amongst the key markets outside the United States and Europe, the Japanese market offers potential to drive significant growth in the medium term. With healthcare reforms aimed to reduce healthcare budgets and generic friendly policies being adopted by the Japanese Government, the pharmaceutical market is gradually opening up to generics. The current generic penetration in Japan, estimated at 6-7%, is amongst the lowest in the world. As a result, despite being the second largest pharmaceutical market in the world, the Japanese marketranks only as the sixth largest generic market. The Japanese Government has set a target of reaching a generic penetration of 30% by 2012, implying strong growth potential in the market.

The Japanese pharmaceutical market is characterised by a complex regulatory framework, thereby creating a high entry barrier. Thus, partnerships with local generic companies and/or acquisitions of local companies are emerging as the likely route to gain presence. Indian generic players have also made inroads in the Japanese market. The generic pricing in the market however remains favourable as compared to markets in Europe and the United States. Lupin, Ranbaxy and Cadila Healthcare are amongst the front runners. While Lupin gained access in the Japanese market through the acquisition of Kyowa Pharmaceuticals in 2007. Ranbaxy is exploring opportunities of marketing its generic products through Daiichi's distribution network post its acquisition by the latter.

Table 5.7 Indiangeneric companies in the Japanese pharmaceutical market

Lupin	Acquired Kyowa Pharmaceutical (generic company) in Japan in FY 08; actively pursuing integration with Indian operations in terms of product launches and material sourcing
Ranbaxy	Aims to leverage its wide-product basket with Daiichi Sankyo distribution network
CadilaHealthcare	Acquired Nippon Universal in 2007. Plans to increase presence through generic launches
Dr. Reddy's Lab.	Plans to establish presence in the Japanese market; Inorganic investment could be a possible route
Torrent Pharmaceutical	Established subsidiary

Aggressive brand defense by innovators remains a challenge

Generic business by its nature grows at the expense of branded products on patent expiry, bringing in potential conflict of interest between the two. While generic companies continue to seek ways to accelerate entry into the market through development of non-infringing processes/ patent challenges, innovator companies seek to extend their product life through effective patent defense. In recent times, the pressure on innovator companies has increased due to large impending patent expiries and shrinking new product pipelines. Aggressive product lifecycle management by innovators includes filing new patents; changing product benefit claims and labeling; switching to OTC products and launching of authorized generics. All these have effectively either delayed the entry of generics in the market or reduced benefits from patent challenges, thus restricting potential upsides for generic companies. With rising complexity of brand defense, evaluating likely response by innovator companies to patent challenges remains a critical input in pipeline planning for generic companies.

Strategic alliances by innovator companies

As mentioned earlier, potentially large patent expiries over the next five years and weak pipeline quality have increased the pressure on innovator companies to explore other avenues including generic business. While the global pharmaceutical business is expected to register moderate single digit growths, the growth in generic business is likely to be in double digits, reflecting the attractive potential of the business. Some of the global innovator companies already have their generic arms which are aggressively pursuing the business in all markets. In recent periods, a number of innovator companies have explored alliances and M&A in the generic space. Some examples include the acquisition of Ranbaxy by Daiichi; Zentiva by Sanofi; Glaxo's tie-up with Aspen. In recent periods some of the innovator companies have entered into alliances with Indian generic companies. These alliances are designed to exploit the low-cost manufacturing skills of Indian players with the reach of innovator companies in the branded generic space across world markets.

Table 5.8 Collaborations by Indian Companies

Companies	Partner	Comment
Aurobindo Pharma	Pfizer	100 plus oral dosages across NA, Europe, LA and
		Asia across CVS, CNS and anti-infective
Dr. Reddy's	GlaxoSmith	To market its portfolio of products across
		markets outside India, including co-arrangements
Strides Arcolab	Pfizer	Generic oncology products, primarily
		the US market
Claris Life	Pfizer	Sterile injectibles covering anti-infective, and other critical care products

M&A activities by Indian companies

Acquisitions have played a vital role for Indian companies in establishing their presence in international markets. Most acquisitions have either been in the generic or CRAMS space. Only a handful of acquisitions have been in the $200 million plus range, with a majority being small-sized acquisitions in value terms. Investments in generic space have been aimed at gaining presence in newer markets and acquiring marketing and distribution front-end. In the CRAMS space, access to new clients and technologies has been key rationale for acquisitions. The initial phase of investments has been in regulated markets (European Union and North America). However, the focus is now shifting to semi-regulated markets in Africa, Latin America, and South-East Asia. These markets offer potential for profitable growth with relatively easier regulatory pathways. Except for certain transactions, most acquisitions have in relatively small sized.

The performance of the investments by Indian companies overseas has so far been a mixed bag. Unanticipated change in market dynamics, inability to move sourcing to low-cost locations and contract cancellation have been some of the factors affecting performance. Certain companies have also faced challenges in securing new contracts, particularly in the CRAMS space. Unanticipated changes in market dynamics like those in Germany (market moved rapidly from branded generics to tender market) have also eroded value for some acquisitions. Indian companies are also looking at in-licensing opportunities to enter into the branded segment in regulated markets through patent acquisitions.

Biogenerics space offers strong long-term potential; Indian companies stepping up investments

In addition to strong potential offered by patent expiries, generic companies are also eyeing the dissimilar space as a key long-term growth potential avenue. As per industry estimates, nearly 41 molecules worth US$ 57 billion in sales in the biopharmaceutical space are expected to go off patent over the next six years.

Generic majors as well Indian generic companies have stepped up investments in this space and expect to tap the emerging opportunity. While the segment does offer strong potential, uncertainties related to clear regulatory pathway for bioequivalence studies act as a restraint. Moreover, the biologics space is also characterized by technology barriers in terms of complex product development & production process besides being highly capital intensive segment. Strategic alliances between generic and biotech companies are likely to strengthen in the future. Generic major – Teva has collaborated with Lonza to capitalize on biologics development & manufacturing expertise and infrastructure Amongst Indian companies, Dr. Reddy's, Biocon and Lupin are amongst the front runners in this space and are currently in the i nvesting in product development.

Chart 4: Worldwide sales (in US$ billion) of biologics by patent expiration

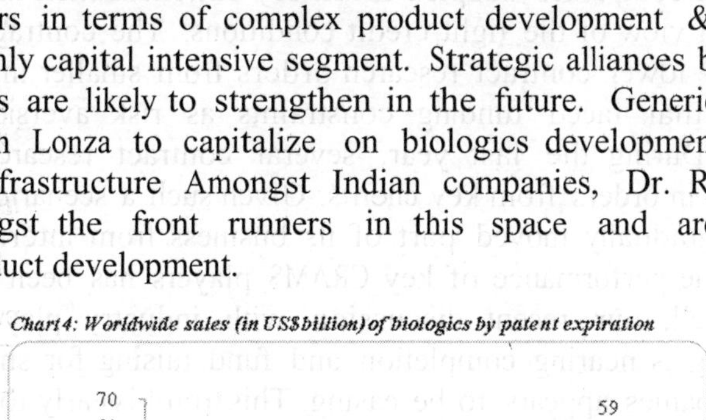

Source: Teva's analyst presentation

Significant up-front investments and client relationships is the key in CRAMS

With innovator companies focusing on cost rationalization, outsourcing opportunities across the value chain–from low volume drug discovery activities to higher volume commercial scale manufacturing- have emerged over the past few years. Within the CRAMS segment, Indian companies such as Piramal Healthcare, Jubilant Organosys, Dishman Pharmaceuticals, and Divi's Labs have invested significantly in establishing expertise and infrastructure across contract research and manufacturing space. While contract research largely involves providing drug discovery and development services, contract manufacturing includes outsourcing manufacturing of intermediates and APIs as per the specific requirements of innovator/generic companies. Establishing relations with several innovator companies is a necessary precursor in scaling up this business, which also entails significant investments in manufacturing and R&D capabilities. Innovator companies typically look for strong R&D capabilities and human resources as the key criteria while selecting contract research companies, while the ability to ensure low-cost manufacturing is seen as their key strength.

CRAMS affected by inventory rationalization measures and tight fund raising environment

The CRAMS space witnessed subdued performance during the last 12-18 months as global pharmaceutical companies adopted inventory rationalization as one of the cost reduction initiative in view of the tight credit conditions. The contract research space was also affected by lower contract research orders from smaller innovator R&D and biotech companies that faced funding constraints as risk aversion to fund new projects increased. During the last year, several contract research players faced significant slowdown in orders from key clients. Given such a scenario, players such as Piramal Healthcare gradually moved part of its business from international assets to Indian facilities. While performance of key CRAMS players has been lackluster in the current fiscal as well, our recent discussion with industry players suggest that inventory de-stocking is nearing completion and fund raising for small and medium-sized innovator companies appears to be easing. This trend is early to assess, but could lend some stability to the business environment.

Players focusing on collaborations in the drug discovery space

Besides providing pure vanilla contract research services, leading Indian contract research led companies have also been targeting collaborative approach in the drug discovery space with leading innovators companies, demonstrating their importance within the overall drug discovery and development value chain. Companies such as Biocon and Jubilant Organosys have been that front run of such transactions.

Outlook

In 2008-09, while most sectors have faced some challenges emerging from global economic slowdown, the pharmaceutical industry world-wide and generic business in particular has been relatively recession proof except for certain specific segments. Some large players in India witnessed significant financial stress during 2008-09 – most of it was related to impact of forex fluctuations on derivatives exposure and foreign currency liabilities. The other areas involving some stress included large acquisitions – some of the large overseas acquisitions by Indian companies failed to deliver in expected lines due to reasons ranging from unexpected changes in the business environment to contract cancellations (in CRAMS business). In third-party API business there have been sharp fluctuations in performance, contributed by a large fluctuation in raw material costs. Also, many of these API units remain vulnerable due to relatively high product and/or client concentration.

Table 5.9 Key collaborations for leading companies

Company	Association	Comments
Jubilant	Eli Lilly	Targeting multiple therapeutic areas; functional
		all discovery functions with joint venture for drug
	Forest Labs	Collaboration in the area of metabolic disorder
	Astra Zeneca	To deliver steady streams of discovery
		research funding spanning over five years
Biocon	Bristol Myers	Research partnership
	Mylan	Collaboration to develop and manufacture generic
	Amylin	Collaboration to develop and manufacture
		therapeutic for potential treatment of diabetes
Zydus Cadila	Eli Lilly	Collaboration for drug discovery and
		cardiovascular space
	KaraBio	Collaboration for drug discovery and development
		inflammatory disorders

Exports to the regulated markets would remain a strong growth driver for Indian companies. However, there are multiple challenges such as margin pressure; legal issues; parallel launch of authorized generics; access to distribution channels, increasing compliance costs and Government mandated changes in business environment in several countries. Margin pressures continue in the regulated generics markets because of a host of factors, such as increasing competition from India and other low-cost manufacturing locations; more aggressive brand defense by innovator companies (through authorized generics, for instance); increasing bargaining power of large distributors in these markets and pressure from Government and insurance companies to cut costs. Further, the attractiveness of the US market has suffered some setback, especially for the large generics targeting exclusivity. The reasons include, among others, legal challenges by patent holders, which delays and increase the cost of launch; and authorized generics taking away a large market share and profit from the generic patent challenger during exclusivity periods. These factors have sharply impacted the exclusivity-related profits that generic players seek from the US market. The attractiveness of relatively fragmented European market and new markets like Japan however has increased as generic penetration continues to rise rapidly in these markets.

While the supply-side environment for the generics business in major export markets appears to have turned adverse, the same is partly mitigated by the favorable outlook for the demand side. An ageing population and increase in healthcare costs continue to put pressure on all major Pharma markets like the United States, Europe and Japan, thereby encouraging higher penetration of generics through a mix of legislation and incentives to doctors and pharmacies.

For formulations companies, the domestic branded generics business has traditionally been the cash cow, providing steady cash flows that serve as a buffer against the uncertainties of international ventures. The growth prospects continue to remain strong on back of increasing healthcare awareness, rising penetration in semi-urban and rural markets and changing disease profile. Most MNC Pharma majors have also stepped up their focus on Indian market exploring opportunities of expanding their product portfolio. Uncertainty related to potential changes in the scope of price control, however, remains a negative. Regulatory price controls are however an integral part of the Pharma business world-wide. The risks of adverse developments in the domestic market also highlight the importance of geographical diversification as a risk mitigating measure in the Pharma industry.

On the CRAMS front, Indian players are focusing on providing services across the value chain spanning from development stage to commercial scale production. Relatively lower exposure to small biotech companies has been a risk mitigant during the downturn for these entities. With several drugs going off-patent and big Pharma increasing exposure to cost efficient sourcing locations, opportunities remain favorable for CRAMS players to provide developmental services and subsequently graduate to commercial scale production.

ICRA currently has 46 entities with long-term ratings (excluding 'SO' ratings) in the pharmaceutical sector. About 17% of these entities are rated in the 'AA' category. Most of these entities have a fairly strong and profitable domestic branded formulations business, which has been a stable source of cash flows over the years. Around 22% of the entities are rated in the non-investment graded. Most of these entities are relatively small entities, often in API business and suffer from high product and or client concentration.

Financials of formulation companies

Table 5.9 *Median of formulation companies – annual audited numbers*

In Million	2009	2008	2007	2006
Revenue	15,427	13,016	12,273	9,752
Gross profit	6,032	4,827	4,668	3,846
OPBDIT	3,048	2,497	2,545	1,594
Net profit	780	1,766	1,699	1,024
Net cash accrual	818	1,436	1,600	820
OPM (%)	19.9%	19.0%	18.7%	16.9%
NPM (%)	9.8%	12.0%	12.7%	10.3%
RoCE (%)	21.7%	21.9%	20.6%	15.5%
TD/ OPBDIT	1.6	1.8	1.7	2.6
TD/ TNW	0.8	0.6	0.6	0.6
FFO/TD	0.4	0.2	0.3	0.2
Debtors	76	86	81	76
Inventory	112	128	114	129
NWC/OI (%)	30.1%	36.2%	29.5%	33.2%

Note: Year ending 2009 include audited year ending Mar-09 and Dec-08 and so on

List of ICRA (industrial credit rating agency) Rated Entities

Table 5.10 List of ICRA Rated Formulation Companies

S. No.	Company Name	Long-Term Rating	Short-Term Rating
1	Amneal Pharmaceuticals Limited	LBB	
2	Biological E Limited	LBB+	A4+
3	Bliss GVS Pharma Limited	LBBB	A3+
4	Cadila Pharmaceuticals Limited	LBBB+ (stable)	A2+
5	Dr. Reddy's Laboratories Limited	LAA+	A1+
6	Fresenius Kabi Oncology Limited	LBBB+	A2+
7	Ind Swift Limited	LBBB	A3+
8	Indoco Remedies Limited	LA+ (stable)	A1+
9	Intas Pharmaceuticals Limited	LAA	A1+

Contd

S. No.	Company Name	Long-Term Rating	Short-Term Rating
10	Khandelwal Laboratories Private Limited	LBBB- (stable)	A3
11	Lupin Limited	LAA+	A1+
12	Merck Limited	LAA	A1+
13	Natco Pharma Limited.	LA+	A1
14	Piramal Healthcare Limited	LAA	A1+
15	Ranbaxy Laboratories Limited		A1+
16	Tablets (India) Limited	LBBB-	A3
17	Torrent Pharmaceuticals Limited	LAA	A1+
18	Troikaa Pharmaceuticals Limited	LBBB-	A3
19	Twilight Litaka Pharma Limited	LBBB	A2
20	Unichem Laboratories Limited		A1+

Table 5.11 List of ICRA Rated Bulk Drug Companies

S. No.	Company Name	Long Term- Rating	Short Term- Rating
1	Aarti Drugs Limited	LBBB+ (stable)	A2
2	Anu's Laboratories Limited	LBBB	A3+
3	Apex Drugs & Intermediates Limited	LBBB-	A3
4	Arch Pharmalabs Limited		A1
5	Biocon Limited	LAA+	A1+
6	Dhanuka Laboratories Limited	LBB+	A4+
7	Elam Pharma Private Limited	LB+	A4
8	Enaltec Labs Private Limited	LBB-	A4
9	Hikal Limited	LB+	A4
10	Ind Swift Laboratories Limited	LBBB+	A2+
11	Megafine Pharma (P) Limited	LBBB- (stable)	A3
12	Novodigm Limited	LA-	A1
13	Sara Exports	LBB+	A4+
14	Shasun Chemicals & Drugs Limited	LBBB- (negative)	A3
15	Shodhana Laboratories	LBBB	A2
16	Sri Krishna Pharmaceuticals Limited	LBBB-	A3
17	SR Drugs &Intermediates Pvt. Limited	LBBB-	A3
18	Surya Pharmaceutical Limited	LBBB-	A3
19	Unimark Remedies Limited	LBBB+	A2
20	Vamsi Labs Limited	LB-	A4

Table 5.12 List of Other Pharmaceutical Companies rated by ICRA

S. No.	Company Name	Long-Term Rating	Short-Term Rating
1	Akums Drugs & Pharma Limited	LBBB+	A2+
2	Aurigene Discovery Technologies Limited	LAA+ (SO)	A1+ (SO)
3	Biocon Biopharma Private Limited	LAA (SO)	
4	Clinigene International Limited	LAA(SO)	A1+(SO)
5	Enem Nostrum Remedies Private Limited	LB+	A4
6	Medreich Limited	LBBB	A2
7	Merck Specialities Private Limited		A1+
8	Next Wave India	LBB+	A4+
9	RFCL Limited	LA-	A1
10	Rusan Pharma Limited	LBBB-	A3
11	Syngene International Limited	LAA-	A1
12	Sai Advantium Pharma Limited	LBBB-	
13	TIL Exports Private Limited	LBBB-	A3

Note- Other Pharmaceutical Companies mainly include contract research and manufacturing companies

Key Acquisitions by Indian Companies

Table 5.13 Key acquisition concluded/announced by major pharmaceutical companies during the last two year

Company	Acquisition	Details	Rationale/Key Benefits
Dr. Reddy's Labora tories	Dow Pharma's	**Region** – Europe (two sites in the UK) **Area** – CRAMS **Investment** – US$ 32.1 million	Complements DRL's existing custom pharmaceutical business through access to relevant customers, process technology, associated products and R&D team; Contributed Rs. 1,021 million to DRL's turnover in FY09.
	BASF's ormulation manufacturin g unit in the US	**Region** – USA **Area** – CRAMS **Investment-** US$ 40,466	Access to contract manufacturing of generic prescription and OTC products in the US market through customer contracts, related ANDAs and NDAs and a manufacturing facility.

Contd...

	Jet Generici SRL	**Region** – Europe (Italy) **Area** – Generics **Investment** – Euro 2.34 million	Establish presence in the Italian generic market; provides access to product portfolio, a pipeline of registration applications and a marketing set-up.
Piramal Health care	Minrad International Inc. & RxElite	**Region** – USA **Area** – Generic Inhalation Anesthetics **Investment** – US$ 52 million (including US$ 12 million for working capital)	Strengthen presence in the global inhalation anesthetics segment through access to process-based intellectual property for two main products i.e. sevoflurane and desflurane. RxElite's acquisition allows access to sales & distribution network for Minrad in the US.
Lupin Limited	Kyowa Pharmaceuticals	**Region** – Japan **Area** – Generics **Investment** – US$ 63 million*	Establish a strong foothold in a relatively complex & highly regulated Japanese market; Kyowa is positioned as the tenth largest generic company in Japan.
	Harmason Pharma	**Region** – Germany **Area** – Generics **Investment** – Rs. 311 million	Access to German market through an approved product pipeline and an established field force
	Pharma Dynamics	**Region** – South Africa **Area** – Generics **Investment** – Rs. 901 million**	Access to South African generic market through an established distribution and marketing set-up
Ranbaxy	Zenotech Laboratories	**Region** – India **Investment** – Rs. 1,385	Strengthen presence in the areas of biosimilars and oncology (injectibles)
	Vectra		
Jubilant Organsys	Draxis Pharmaceuticals	**Region** – North America **Area** – CRAMS **Investment** – US$ 253 million	Strengthens Jubilant's CRAMS business in North America with capabilities to manufacture sterile and non-sterile products and provides access to the niche radiopharmaceuticals market.

Table 5.14 Key acquisition concluded/announced by major pharmaceutical companies during the last two year

Company	Acquisition	Details	Rationale/Key Benefits
Jubilant Organsys	Hollister Stier Laboratories LLC	**Region** – North America **Area** – CRAMS **Investment** – US$ 140.7 million	Strengthens Jubilant' CRAMS business with addition of contract manufacturing of sterile injectibles
Zydus Cadila	Etna Biotech	**Region** – Italy **Area** – Vaccines **Investment**	Access to a highly evolved research platform for developing new vaccines and technology
	Quimica e Farmaceutica Nikkho do Brasil Ltda. (Nikkho)	**Region** – Brazil **Area** – Generics **Investment** – US$ 26 million	Entry into the Brazilian branded generics market through established therapeutic products and sales network
	Simayla Pharmaceuticals	**Region** – South Africa **Area** – Generics **Investment**	Entry into the South African generics market through the well established product portfolio and marketing setup of the acquired company
	Laboratorios Combix	**Region** – Spain **Area** – Generics **Investment**	Strengthens the company's presence in Europe through an entry into the Spanish generics market
Wockhardt	Negma Laboratories	**Region** – France **Area** – Generics **Investment** – US$ 265 million	Access to a portfolio of patents and help establish the company as the biggest Indian pharmaceutical player in Europe with an entry into the French generics market
	Morton Grove	**Region** – USA **Area** – Generics **Investment** – US$ 38 million	Strengthens the company's position in the US market through an established portfolio of 31 products
Dishman Pharma	Vitamins & fine chemicals businesses of Solvay Pharmaceuticals, BV	**Region** – Netherlands **Area** – Vitamins **Investment**	Provides an opportunity to the company to bring fine chemical expertise to India

Contd...

Sun Pharma	TaroPharmaceutical Industries Ltd.	**Region** – North America **Area** – Generics **Investment** – US$ 454 million	Strengthens the company's position in North America by leveraging on Taro's strong product portfolio and manufacturing facilities
	Chattem Chemicals, Inc.	**Region** – USA **Area** – API **Investment** Undisclosed	Strengthens the company's presence in the controlled (narcotic) substance API business
Glenmark	Seven Formulation brands of Actavis and Biovena	**Region** – Poland **Area** – Generics **Investment**	Strengthens company's presence in the European generics market through entry into Poland
	Medicamenta	**Region** – Europe **Area** – Generics **Investment**	Provides entry into two of the fastest growing European markets viz. Czech Republic and Slovakia through the established sales & marketing setup and EU GMP approved manufacturing facility
Aurobindo Pharma	TAD Italy	**Region** – Italy **Area** – Generics **Investment**	Entry into the highly regulated Italian generic market through more than 70 ready-to-market products

Questions

1. Explain the progress of Pharma Industry in the last 3 decades in India?
2. Explain the future trends and prospects of Pharma Industry in India?
3. Discuss the role of Pharma Industry in Indian economic progress and nation building?
4. Explain export and import potential of pharmaceuticals in India?
5. Explain the basic drug research progress in the country?
6. Add a note on the following (a) strengths and weakness of Indian Pharma. Industry.
7. Explain the role of public sector units in Pharma.sector in India?
8. Write short notes on the following:
   (a) global Pharma industry challenges. (b) Hindustan antibiotics Ltd.
9. Explain the market share of different therapeutic categories in India?
10. Write short notes on the following (a) structure of Pharma industry in India
    (b) export and import trade.

Chapter - 6

Insurance

6.1 Insurance

Insurance is a form of *risk management* primarily used to *hedge* against the *risk* of a contingent, *uncertain* loss. Insurance is defined as the equitable transfer of the risk of a loss, from one entity to another, in exchange for payment. An **insurer** is a company selling the insurance; an **insured** or **policyholder** is the person or entity buying the insurance policy. The **insurance rate** is a factor used to determine the amount to be charged for a certain amount of insurance coverage, called the **premium**. *Risk management*, the practice of *appraising* and controlling risk, has evolved as a discrete field of study and practice.

- The transaction involves the insured assuming a guaranteed and known relatively small loss in the form of payment to the insurer in exchange for the insurer's promise to compensate (*indemnify*) the insured in the case of a large, possibly devastating loss. The insured receives a *contract* called the *insurance policy* which details the conditions and circumstances under which the insured will be compensated

Insurance involves *pooling* funds from many insured entities (known as exposures) in order to pay for relatively uncommon but severely devastating losses which can occur to these entities. The insured entities are therefore protected from risk for a fee, with the fee being dependent upon the frequency and severity of the event occurring. In order to be insurable, the risk insured against must meet certain characteristics in order to be an *insurable risk*. Insurance is a commercial enterprise and a major part of the financial services industry, but individual entities can also *self-insure* through saving money for possible future losses.

Insurability

Risk which can be insured by private companies typically share seven common characteristics.

1. ***Large number of similar exposure units:*** Since insurance operates through pooling resources, the majority of insurance policies are provided for individual members of large classes, allowing insurers to benefit from the *law of large numbers* in which predicted losses are similar to the actual losses.
2. ***Definite Loss:*** The loss takes place at a known time, in a known place, and from a known cause. The classic example is death of an insured person on a life insurance policy. Fire, automobile accidents, and worker injuries may all easily meet this criterion. Other types of losses may only be definite in theory. Occupational disease, for instance, may involve prolonged exposure to injurious conditions where no specific time, place or cause is identifiable. Ideally, the time, place and cause of a loss should be clear enough that a reasonable person, with sufficient information, could objectively verify all three elements.
3. ***Accidental Loss:*** The event that constitutes the trigger of a claim should be fortuitous, or at least outside the control of the beneficiary of the insurance. The loss should be 'pure,' in the sense that it results from an event for which there is only the opportunity for cost. Events that contain speculative elements, such as ordinary business risks, are generally not considered insurable.
4. ***Large Loss:*** The size of the loss must be meaningful from the perspective of the insured. Insurance premiums need to cover both the expected cost of losses, plus the cost of issuing and administering the policy, adjusting losses, and supplying the capital needed to reasonably assure that the insurer will be able to pay claims. For small losses these latter costs may be several times the size of the expected cost of losses. There is little point in paying such costs unless the protection offered has real value to a buyer.
5. ***Affordable Premium:*** If the likelihood of an insured event is so high, or the cost of the event so large, that the resulting premium is large relative to the amount of protection offered, it is not likely that anyone will buy insurance, even if on offer. Further, as the accounting profession formally recognizes in financial accounting standards, the premium cannot be so large that there is not a reasonable chance of a significant loss to the insurer. If there is no such chance of loss, the transaction may have the form of insurance, but not the substance.
6. ***Calculable Loss:*** There are two elements that must be at least estimable, if not formally calculable: the probability of loss, and the attendant cost. Probability of loss is generally an empirical exercise, while cost has more to do with the

ability of a reasonable person in possession of a copy of the insurance policy and a proof of loss associated with a claim presented under that policy to make a reasonably definite and objective evaluation of the amount of the loss recoverable as a result of the claim.

7. ***Limited risk of catastrophically large losses***: Insurable losses are ideally *independent* and non-*catastrophic*, meaning that the one losses do not happen all at once and individual losses are not severe enough to bankrupt the insurer; insurers may prefer to limit their exposure to a loss from a single event to some small portion of their capital base, on the order of 5 *percent*. Capital constrains insurers' ability to sell *earthquake insurance* as well as wind insurance in hurricane zones. In the U.S., *flood risk* is insured by the federal government. In commercial fire insurance it is possible to find single properties whose total exposed value is well in excess of any individual insurer's capital constraint. Such properties are generally shared among several insurers, or are insured by a single insurer who syndicates the risk into the *reinsurance* market.]

When a company insures an individual entity, there are basic legal requirements. Several commonly cited legal principles of insurance include:

Indemnity: The insurance company indemnifies, or compensates the insured in the case of certain losses only up to the insured's interest

Insurable interest: The insured typically must directly suffer from the loss. Insurable interest must exist whether property insurance or insurance on a person is involved. The concept requires that the insured have a "stake" in the loss or damage to the life or property insured. What that "stake" is will be determined by the kind of insurance involved and the nature of the property ownership or relationship between the persons.

Utmost good faith: The insured and the insurer are bound by a *good faith* bond of honesty and fairness

Contribution*:* Insurers which have similar obligations to the insured contribute in the indemnification, according to some method

Subrogation: The insurance company acquires legal rights to pursue recoveries on behalf of the insured; for example, the insurer may sue those liable for insured's loss

Causa Proxima or Proximate Cause: The cause of loss (the "peril") must be covered under the insuring agreement of the policy, and dominant cause must not be *excluded*

Indemnification

To "indemnify" means to make whole again, or to be put in the position that one was in, to the extent possible, prior to the happening of a specified event or peril. Accordingly, life insurance is generally not considered to be indemnity insurance, but rather "contingent" insurance (i.e., a claim arises on the occurrence of a specified event). There are generally two types of insurance contracts that seek to indemnify an insured:

1. an "indemnity" policy and
2. a "pay on behalf" or "on behalf of" policy.

The difference is significant on paper, but rarely material in practice.

An "indemnity" policy will never pay claims until the insured has paid out of pocket to some third party; for example, a visitor to the home slips on a floor that you left wet and sues you for rs.10,000 and wins. Under an "indemnity" policy the homeowner would have to come up with the rs.10,000 to pay for the visitor's fall and then would be "indemnified" by the insurance carrier for the out of pocket costs (the rs.10,000).

Under the same situation, a "pay on behalf" policy, the insurance carrier would pay the claim and the insured (the homeowner) would not be out of pocket for anything. Most modern liability insurance is written on the basis of "pay on behalf" language.

An entity seeking to transfer risk (an individual, corporation, or association of any type, etc.) becomes the 'insured' party once risk is assumed by an 'insurer', the insuring party, by means of a *contract,* called an insurance 'policy'. Generally, an insurance contract includes, at a minimum, the following elements: the parties (the insurer, the insured, the beneficiaries), the premium, the period of coverage, the particular loss event covered, the amount of coverage (i.e., the amount to be paid to the insured or beneficiary in the event of a loss), and exclusions (events not covered). An insured is thus said to be "*indemnified*" against the loss covered in the policy.

When insured parties experience a loss for a specified peril, the coverage entitles the policyholder to make a 'claim' against the insurer for the covered amount of loss as specified by the policy. The fee paid by the insured to the insurer for assuming the risk is called the 'premium'. Insurance premiums from many insured are used to fund accounts reserved for later payment of claims—in theory for a relatively few claimants—and for *overhead* costs. So long as an insurer maintains adequate funds set aside for anticipated losses (i.e., reserves), the remaining margin is an insurer's *profit*.

Effects

Insurance can have various effects on society through the way that it changes who bears the cost of losses and damage. It can increase fraud. On the other hand, it can help societies and individuals prepare for catastrophes and mitigate the effects of catastrophes on both households and societies.

Insurance can influence the probability of losses through *moral hazard, insurance fraud,* and preventive steps by the insurance company. Insurance scholars have typically used *morale hazard* to refer to the increased loss due to unintentional carelessness and moral hazard to refer to increased risk due to intentional carelessness or indifference.[6] Insurers attempt to address carelessness through inspections, policy provisions requiring certain types of maintenance, and possible discounts for loss mitigation efforts. While in theory insurers could encourage investment in loss reduction, some commentators have argued that in practice insurers had historically not aggressively pursued loss control measures - particularly to prevent disaster losses such as hurricanes - because of concerns over rate reductions and legal battles. However, beginning around 1996 insurers began to take a more active role in loss mitigation through *building codes*.

Insurers' business model

Underwriting and investing

The business model can be reduced to a simple equation: Profit = *earned premium* + investment income - incurred loss - underwriting expenses

Insurers make money in two ways:

1. Through *underwriting*, the process by which insurers select the risks to insure and decide how much in premiums to charge for accepting those risks;
2. By investing the premiums they collect from insured parties.

The most complicated aspect of the insurance business is the *underwriting* of policies. Using a wide assortment of data, insurers predict the likelihood that a claim will be made against their policies and price products accordingly. To this end, insurers use *actuarial science* to quantify the risks they are willing to assume and the premium they will charge to assume them. Data is analyzed to fairly accurately project the rate of future claims based on a given risk. Actuarial science uses *statistics* and *probability* to analyze the risks associated with the range of perils covered, and these scientific principles are used to determine an insurer's overall exposure. Upon termination of a given policy, the amount of premium collected and the investment gains thereon minus the amount paid out in claims is the insurer's *underwriting profit* on that policy. Of course, from the insurer's perspective, some policies are "winners" (i.e., the insurer pays out less in claims and expenses than it receives in premiums and investment income) and some are "losers" (i.e., the insurer pays out more in claims and expenses than it receives in premiums and investment income); insurance companies essentially use actuarial science to attempt to underwrite enough "winning" policies to pay out on the "losers" while still maintaining profitability.

An insurer's underwriting performance is measured in its *combined ratio* which is the *ratio of losses* and expenses to earned premiums. A combined ratio of less than 100 percent indicates underwriting profitability, while anything over 100 indicates an underwriting loss. A company with a combined ratio over 100% may nevertheless remain profitable due to investment earnings.

Insurance companies earn *investment* profits on “float”. “Float” or available reserve is the amount of money, at hand at any given moment, that an insurer has collected in insurance premiums but has not paid out in claims. Insurers start investing insurance premiums as soon as they are collected and continue to earn interest or other income on them until claims are paid out.

Naturally, the "float" method is difficult to carry out in an economically depressed period. *Bear markets* do cause insurers to shift away from investments and to toughen up their underwriting standards. So a poor economy generally means high insurance premiums. This tendency to swing between profitable and unprofitable periods over time is commonly known as the "underwriting" or *insurance cycle*.

Property and casualty insurers currently make the most money from their auto insurance line of business. Generally better statistics are available on auto losses and underwriting on this line of business has benefited greatly from advances in computing.

Claims

Claims and loss handling is the materialized utility of insurance; it is the actual "product" paid for. Claims may be filed by insured directly with the insurer or through brokers or agents. The insurer may require that the claim be filed on its own proprietary forms, or may accept claims on a standard industry form.

Insurance company claims departments employ a large number of *claims adjusters* supported by a staff of *records management* and *data entry clerks*. Incoming claims are classified based on severity and are assigned to adjusters whose settlement authority varies with their knowledge and experience. The adjuster undertakes an investigation of each claim, usually in close cooperation with the insured, determines if coverage is available under the terms of the insurance contract, and if so, the reasonable monetary value of the claim, and authorizes payment.

The policy holder may hire their own *public adjuster* to negotiate the settlement with the insurance company on their behalf. For policies that are complicated, where claims may be complex, the insured may take out a separate insurance policy add on, called loss recovery insurance, which covers the cost of a public adjuster in the case of a claim.

Adjusting liability insurance claims is particularly difficult because there is a third party involved, the plaintiff, who is under no contractual obligation to cooperate with the insurer and may in fact regard the insurer as a *deep pocket*. The adjuster must obtain legal counsel for the insured (either inside "house" counsel or outside "panel" counsel), monitor litigation that may take years to complete, and appear in person or over the telephone with settlement authority at a mandatory settlement conference when requested by the judge.

If a claims adjuster suspects underinsurance, the *condition of average* may come into play to limit the insurance company's exposure.

In managing the claims handling function, insurers seek to balance the elements of customer satisfaction, administrative handling expenses, and claims overpayment leakages. As part of this balancing act, *fraudulent insurance practices* are a major business risk that must be managed and overcome. Disputes between insurers and insured over the validity of claims or claims handling practices occasionally escalate into litigation; see *insurance bad faith*.

History of Insurance

In some sense we can say that insurance appears simultaneously with the appearance of human society. We know of two types of economies in human societies: money economies (with markets, money, financial instruments and so on) and non-money or natural economies (without money, markets, financial instruments and so on). The second type is a more ancient form than the first. In such an economy and community, we can see insurance in the form of people helping each other. For example, if a house burns down, the members of the community help build a new one. Should the same thing happen to one's neighbor, the other neighbors must help? Otherwise, neighbors will not receive help in the future. This type of insurance has survived to the present day in some countries where modern money economy with its financial instruments is not widespread.

Turning to insurance in the modern sense (i.e., insurance in a modern money economy, in which insurance is part of the financial sphere), early methods of transferring or distributing risk were practiced by *Chinese* and *Babylonian* traders as long ago as the *3rd* and *2nd millennia* BC, respectively. Chinese merchants traveling treacherous river rapids would redistribute their wares across many vessels to limit the loss due to any single vessel's capsizing. The Babylonians developed a system which was recorded in the famous *Code of Hammurabi*, c. 1750 BC, and practiced by early *Mediterranean* sailing *merchants*. If a merchant received a loan to fund his shipment, he would pay the lender an additional sum in exchange for the lender's guarantee to cancel the loan should the shipment be stolen or lost at sea.

Achaemenian monarchs of Ancient Persia were the first to insure their people and made it official by registering the insuring process in governmental notary offices. The insurance tradition was performed each year in Norouz (beginning of the Iranian New Year); the heads of different ethnic groups as well as others willing to take part, presented gifts to the monarch. The most important gift was presented during a special ceremony. When a gift was worth more than 10,000 Derrik (Achaemenian gold coin) the issue was registered in a special office. This was advantageous to those who presented such special gifts. For others, the presents were fairly assessed by the confidants of the court. Then the assessment was registered in special offices.

The purpose of registering was that whenever the person who presented the gift registered by the court was in trouble, the monarch and the court would help him. Jahez, a historian and writer, writes in one of his books on *ancient Iran*: "[W]whenever the owner of the present is in trouble or wants to construct a building, set up a feast, have his children married, etc. the one in charge of this in the court would check the registration. If the registered amount exceeded 10,000 Derrik, he or she would receive an amount of twice as much."

A thousand years later, the inhabitants of *Rhodes* invented the concept of the '*general average*'. Merchants whose goods were being shipped together would pay a proportionally divided premium which would be used to reimburse any merchant whose goods were jettisoned during storm or sink age.

The *Greeks* and *Romans* introduced the origins of health and life insurance c. 600 AD when they organized guilds called "benevolent societies" which cared for the *families* and paid *funeral* expenses of members upon *death*. *Guilds* in the *middle Ages* served a similar purpose. The *Talmud* deals with several aspects of insuring *goods*. Before insurance was established in the late 17th century, "friendly societies" existed in England, in which people donated amounts of money to a general sum that could be used for emergencies.

Separate insurance contracts (i.e., insurance policies not bundled with loans or other kinds of contracts) were invented in *Genoa* in the 14th century, as were insurance pools backed by pledges of landed estates. These new insurance contracts allowed insurance to be separated from investment, a separation of roles that first proved useful in marine insurance. Insurance became far more sophisticated in post-*Renaissance Europe*, and specialized varieties developed.

Some forms of insurance had developed in London by the early decades of the seventeenth century. For example, the will of the English colonist *Robert Hayman* mentions two "policies of insurance" taken out with the diocesan Chancellor of London, Arthur Duck. Of the value of £100 each, one relates to the safe arrival of Hayman's ship in Guyana and the other is in regard to "one hundred pounds assured by the said Doctor Arthur Ducke on my life". Hayman's will was signed and sealed on 17 November 1628 but not proved until 1633.[13] Toward the end of the seventeenth century, London's growing importance as a centre for trade increased demand for marine insurance. In the late 1680s, *Edward Lloyd* opened a coffee house that became a popular haunt of ship owners, merchants, and ships' captains, and thereby a reliable source of the latest shipping news. It became the meeting place for parties wishing to insure cargoes and ships, and those willing to underwrite such ventures. Today, *Lloyd's of London* remains the leading market (note that it is not an insurance company) for marine and other specialist types of insurance, but it works rather differently than the more familiar kinds of insurance.

Insurance as we know it today can be traced to the *Great Fire of London*, which in 1666 devoured more than 13,000 houses. The devastating effects of the fire converted the development of insurance "from a matter of convenience into one of urgency, a change of opinion reflected in Sir Christopher Wren's inclusion of a site for 'the Insurance Office' in his new plan for London in 1667."[14] A number of attempted fire insurance schemes came to nothing, but in 1681 *Nicholas Barbon*, and eleven associates, established

England's first fire insurance company, the 'Insurance Office for Houses', at the back of the Royal Exchange. Initially, 5,000 homes were insured by Barbon's Insurance Office.[15]

The first insurance company in the *United States* underwrote fire insurance and was formed in Charles Town (modern-day *Charleston*), *South Carolina*, in 1732. *Benjamin Franklin* helped to popularize and make standard the practice of insurance, particularly against *fire* in the form of *perpetual insurance*. In 1752, he founded the *Philadelphia Contributionship for the Insurance of Houses from Loss by Fire*. Franklin's company was the first to make contributions toward fire prevention. Not only did his company warn against certain *fire hazards*, it refused to insure certain buildings where the risk of fire was too great, such as all wooden houses. In the United States, *regulation* of the insurance industry is highly *Balkanized*, with primary responsibility assumed by individual *state* insurance departments. Whereas insurance markets have become centralized nationally and internationally, state insurance commissioners operate individually, though at times in concert through a *national insurance commissioners' organization*. In recent years, some have called for a dual state and federal regulatory system (commonly referred to as the *Optional federal charter* (OFC)) for insurance similar to that which oversees state banks and national banks.

Types of Insurance

Any risk that can be quantified can potentially be insured. Specific kinds of risk that may give rise to claims are known as "perils". An insurance policy will set out in detail which perils are covered by the policy and which is not. Below are (non-exhaustive) lists of the many different types of insurance that exist. A single policy may cover risks in one or more of the categories set out below. For example, auto insurance would typically cover both property risk (covering the risk of theft or damage to the car) and liability risk (covering legal claims from causing an accident). A *homeowner*'s insurance policy in the U.S. typically includes property insurance covering damage to the home and the owner's belongings, liability insurance covering certain legal claims against the owner, and even a small amount of coverage for medical expenses of guests who are injured on the owner's property.

Business insurance can be any kind of insurance that protects businesses against risks. Some principal subtypes of business insurance are (a) the various kinds of *professional liability insurance*, also called *professional indemnity insurance*, which are discussed below under that name; and (b) the business owner's policy (BOP), which bundles into one policy many of the kinds of coverage that a business owner needs, in a way analogous to how homeowners insurance bundles the coverage that a homeowner needs.

Auto insurance

Auto insurance protects you against financial loss if you have an accident. It is a contract between the insured and the insurance company. You agree to pay the premium and the insurance company agrees to pay losses as defined in the policy. Auto insurance provides property, liability and medical coverage:

1. Property coverage pays for damage to or theft of the car.
2. Liability coverage pays for the legal responsibility to others for bodily injury or property damage.
3. Medical coverage pays for the cost of treating injuries, rehabilitation and sometimes lost wages and funeral expenses.

An auto insurance policy comprises six kinds of coverage. Most countries require you to buy some, but not all, of this coverage. If you're financing a car, the lender may also have requirements. Most auto policies are for six months to a year.

Home Insurance

Home insurance provides compensation for damage or destruction of a home from disasters. In some geographical areas, the standard insurances exclude certain types of disasters, such as flood and earthquakes that require additional coverage. Maintenance-related problems are the homeowners' responsibility. The policy may include inventory, or this can be bought as a separate policy, especially for people who rent housing. In some countries, insurers offer a package which may include liability and legal responsibility for injuries and property damage caused by members of the household, including pets.

Health

Health insurance policies or other publicly-funded health programs will cover the cost of medical treatments. Dental insurance, like medical insurance, is coverage for individuals to protect them against dental costs. In the U.S. and Canada, dental insurance is often part of an employer's benefits package, along with health insurance.

Accident, Sickness and Unemployment Insurance

- *Disability insurance* policies provide financial support in the event the policyholder is unable to work because of disabling illness or injury. It provides monthly support to help pay such obligations as *mortgage loans* and *credit cards*. Short-term and long-term disability policies are available to individuals, but considering the expense, long-term policies are generally obtained only by those with at least six-figure incomes, such as doctors, lawyers, etc. Short-term disability insurance covers a person for a period generally up to six months, paying a stipend each month to cover medical bills and other necessities.

- *Long-term disability insurance* covers an individual's expenses for the long term, up until such time as they are considered permanently disabled and thereafter. Insurance companies will often try to find other ways to employ the person and reintegrate them back into the work force in preference to and before declaring them unable to work at all and therefore totally disabled. Insurance companies, for obvious reasons, frequently go to great lengths, including undercover surveillance via video cam and repeated independent medical evaluations by company doctors, in hopes of avoiding the necessity of paying permanent disability stipends to a claimant.
- If you are in the market to purchase long-term disability insurance, try to find out whether the prospective insurer has ONLY their own doctors handle ALL claims (including the questionable ones), or whether they hire out to firms who perform medical file reviews and Independent Medical Examinations, and whose doctors have nothing to gain or lose regardless of the opinion they derive from looking at your records or performing an exam. Your claim, should it eventuate to be disability of a permanent nature, is often more likely to be approved if "questionable" claims (those that don't involve loss of all four limbs) are hired out to independent firms for file reviews and/or IMEs as opposed to always being handled by in-house doctors working solely for the insurance company. Independent companies, such as University Disability Consortium, for instance, perform medical file reviews and IMEs for insurance companies, plaintiff and defense attorneys, among others, and because they have no stake or say-so regarding the final determination of a claimant's disability status, provide totally unbiased reports and IMEs and are, as a result, more likely to facilitate a desirable outcome for the person seeking permanent disability status than are reports and exams performed by doctors who work for the insurance company and have a great deal to gain or lose (e.g., bonuses, their jobs) when disability claims are upheld. So, caveat emptor: beware the practices of your prospective provider regarding claims of total disability prior to handing over those exorbitant fees they demand per LTD (long-term disability) policy.
- *Disability overhead insurance* allows business owners to cover the overhead expenses of their business while they are unable to work.
- *Total permanent disability insurance* provides benefits when a person is permanently disabled and can no longer work in their profession, often taken as an adjunct to life insurance.
- *Workers' compensation* insurance replaces all or part of a worker's *wages* lost and accompanying medical expenses incurred because of a job-related injury.

Casualty

Casualty insurance insures against accidents, not necessarily tied to any specific property.

- *Crime insurance* is a form of casualty insurance that covers the policyholder against losses arising from the criminal acts of third parties. For example, a company can obtain crime insurance to cover losses arising from *theft* or *embezzlement*.
- *Political risk insurance* is a form of casualty insurance that can be taken out by businesses with operations in *countries* in which there is a risk that *revolution* or other *political* conditions will result in a insurance.

Life Insurance

Life insurance provides a monetary benefit to a decedent's family or other designated beneficiary, and may specifically provide for income to an insured person's family, *burial, funeral* and other final expenses. Life insurance policies often allow the option of having the proceeds paid to the beneficiary either in a lump sum cash payment or an annuity.

Annuities provide a stream of payments and are generally classified as insurance because they are issued by insurance companies and regulated as insurance and require the same kinds of actuarial and investment management expertise that life insurance requires. Annuities and *pensions* that pay a benefit for life are sometimes regarded as insurance against the possibility that a *retiree* will outlive his or her financial resources. In that sense, they are the complement of life insurance and, from an underwriting perspective, are the mirror image of life insurance.

Certain life insurance contracts accumulate *cash* values, which may be taken by the insured if the policy is surrendered or which may be borrowed against. Some policies, such as annuities and *endowment policies*, are financial instruments to accumulate or *liquidate wealth* when it is needed.

In many countries, such as the U.S. and the UK, the *tax law* provides that the interest on this cash value is not taxable under certain circumstances. This leads to widespread use of life insurance as a tax-efficient method of *saving* as well as protection in the event of early death.

Property

Property insurance provides protection against risks to property, such as fire, *theft* or *weather* damage. This includes specialized forms of insurance such as *fire insurance*, *flood insurance*, *earthquake insurance*, *home insurance*, inland marine insurance or *boiler insurance*.

- Automobile insurance, known in the *UK* as *motor insurance*, is probably the most common form of insurance and may cover both legal *liability* claims against the *driver* and loss of or damage to the insured's *vehicle* itself. Throughout the *United States* an auto insurance policy is required to legally operate a motor vehicle on public roads. In some jurisdictions, bodily injury compensation for automobile accident victims has been changed to a *no-fault* system, which reduces or eliminates the ability to sue for compensation but provides automatic eligibility for benefits. Credit card companies insure against *damage* on rented cars.
    - Driving School Insurance provides cover for any authorized driver whilst undergoing tuition; cover also unlike other motor policies provides cover for instructor liability where both the pupil and driving instructor are equally liable in the event of a claim.
- *Aviation insurance* insures against hull, spares, deductibles, hull wear and liability risks.
- *Boiler insurance* (also known as boiler and machinery insurance or equipment breakdown insurance) insures against accidental physical damage to equipment or machinery.
- *Builder's risk insurance* insures against the risk of physical loss or damage to property during construction. Builder's risk insurance is typically written on an "all risk" basis covering damage due to any cause (including the negligence of the insured) not otherwise expressly excluded. Builder's risk insurance is coverage that protects a person's or organization's insurable interest in materials, fixtures and/or equipment being used in the construction or renovation of a building or structure should those items sustain physical loss or damage from a covered cause.
- *Crop insurance* "Farmers use crop insurance to reduce or manage various risks associated with growing crops. Such risks include crop loss or damage caused by weather, hail, drought, frost damage, insects, or disease, for instance."
- *Earthquake insurance* is a form of property insurance that pays the policyholder in the event of an *earthquake* that causes damage to the property. Most ordinary homeowners insurance policies do not cover earthquake damage. Most earthquake insurance policies feature a high *deductible*. Rates depend on location and the probability of an earthquake, as well as the *construction of the home*.
- A *fidelity bond* is a form of casualty insurance that covers policyholders for losses that they incur as a result of fraudulent acts by specified individuals. It usually insures a business for losses caused by the dishonest acts of its employees.
- *Flood insurance* protects against property loss due to flooding. Many insurers in the U.S. do not provide flood insurance in some portions of the country. In

response to this, the federal government created the *National Flood Insurance Program* which serves as the insurer of last resort.

- *Home insurance*, also commonly called hazard insurance or homeowners insurance (often abbreviated in the real estate industry as HOI), is the type of property insurance that covers private homes.
- Landlord insurance covers residential and commercial properties which are rented to others. Most homeowner's insurance covers only owner-occupied homes.
- *Marine insurance* and marine cargo insurance cover the loss or damage of ships at sea or on inland waterways, and of cargo in transit, regardless of the method of transit. When the owner of the cargo and the carrier are separate corporations, marine cargo insurance typically compensates the owner of cargo for losses sustained from fire, shipwreck, etc., but excludes losses that can be recovered from the carrier or the carrier's insurance. Many marine insurance underwriters will include "time element" coverage in such policies, which extends the indemnity to cover loss of profit and other business expenses attributable to the delay caused by a covered loss.
- *Surety bond* insurance is a three party insurance guaranteeing the performance of the principal.
- *Terrorism insurance* provides protection against any loss or damage caused by terrorist activities.
- Volcano insurance is an insurance that covers volcano damage in Hawaii.
- Windstorm insurance is an insurance covering the damage that can be caused by hurricanes and tropical cyclones.

Liability

Liability insurance is a very broad superset that covers legal claims against the insured. Many types of insurance include an aspect of liability coverage. For example, a homeowner's insurance policy will normally include liability coverage which protects the insured in the event of a claim brought by someone who slips and falls on the property; automobile insurance also includes an aspect of liability insurance that indemnifies against the harm that a crashing car can cause to others' lives, health, or property. The protection offered by a liability insurance policy is twofold: a legal defense in the event of a lawsuit commenced against the policyholder and indemnification (payment on behalf of the insured) with respect to a settlement or court verdict. Liability policies typically cover only the negligence of the insured, and will not apply to results of willful or intentional acts by the insured.

- Public *liability insurance* covers a business against claims should its operations injure a member of the public or damage their property in some way.

- *Directors and officers liability insurance* protects an organization (usually a corporation) from costs associated with litigation resulting from mistakes made by directors and officers for which they are liable. In the industry, it is usually called "D&O" for short.
- Environmental liability insurance protects the insured from bodily injury, property damage and cleanup costs as a result of the dispersal, release or escape of pollutants.
- Errors and omissions insurance: See "Professional liability insurance" under "Liability insurance".
- *Prize indemnity insurance* protects the insured from giving away a large prize at a specific event. Examples would include offering prizes to contestants who can make a half-court shot at a basketball game, or a hole-in-one at a golf tournament.
- *Professional liability insurance*, also called *professional indemnity insurance*, protects insured professionals such as architectural corporation and medical practice against potential negligence claims made by their patients/clients. Professional liability insurance may take on different names depending on the profession. For example, professional liability insurance in reference to the medical profession may be called *malpractice insurance.* Notaries public may take out *errors and omissions insurance (E&O).* Other potential E&O policyholders include, for example, real estate brokers, Insurance agents, home inspectors, appraisers, and website developers.

Credit

Credit insurance repays some or all of a *loan* when certain things happen to the borrower such as *unemployment*, *disability*, or *death.*

- *Mortgage insurance* insures the lender against default by the borrower. Mortgage insurance is a form of credit insurance, although the name *credit insurance* more often is used to refer to policies that cover other kinds of debt.
- Many credit cards offer payment protection plans which are a form of credit insurance.

Other types

- *All-risk insurance* is an **insurance** that covers a wide-range of incidents and perils, except those noted in the policy. All-risk insurance is different from peril-specific insurance that cover losses from only those perils listed in the policy.[21] In car insurance, all-risk policy includes also the damages caused by the own driver.

- *Business interruption insurance* covers the loss of income, and the expenses occurred, after a covered peril interrupts normal business operations.
- *Collateral protection insurance* or CPI, insures property (primarily vehicles) held as collateral for loans made by lending institutions.
- *Defense Base Act* Workers' compensation or DBA Insurance provides coverage for civilian workers hired by the government to perform contracts outside the U.S. and Canada. DBA is required for all U.S. citizens, U.S. residents, U.S. Green Card holders, and all employees or subcontractors hired on overseas government contracts. Depending on the country, Foreign Nationals must also be covered under DBA. This coverage typically includes expenses related to medical treatment and loss of wages, as well as disability and death benefits.
- *Expatriate insurance* provides individuals and organizations operating outside of their home country with protection for automobiles, property, health, liability and business pursuits.
- Financial loss insurance or Business Interruption Insurance protects individuals and companies against various financial risks. For example, a *business* might purchase coverage to protect it from loss of *sales* if a fire in a *factory* prevented it from carrying out its business for a time. Insurance might also cover the failure of a *creditor* to pay *money* it owes to the insured. This type of insurance is frequently referred to as "business interruption insurance." *Fidelity bonds* and *surety bonds* are included in this category, although these products provide a benefit to a third party (the "obligee") in the event the insured party (usually referred to as the "obligor") fails to perform its obligations under a contract with the obligee.
- *Kidnap and ransom insurance*
- *Legal Expenses Insurance* covers policyholders against the potential costs of legal action against an institution or an individual.
- Locked funds insurance is a little-known hybrid insurance policy jointly issued by governments and banks. It is used to protect public funds from tamper by unauthorized parties. In special cases, a government may authorize its use in protecting semi-private funds which are liable to tamper. The terms of this type of insurance are usually very strict. Therefore it is used only in extreme cases where maximum security of funds is required.
- Media Insurance is designed to cover professionals that engage in film, video and TV production.
- Nuclear incident insurance covers damages resulting from an *incident involving radioactive materials* and is generally arranged at the national level. See the *Nuclear exclusion clause* and for the United States the Price-Anderson Nuclear Industries Indemnity Act)

- *Pet insurance* insures pets against accidents and illnesses - some companies cover routine/wellness care and burial, as well.
- Pollution Insurance which consists of first-party coverage for contamination of insured property either by external or on-site sources. Coverage for liability to third parties arising from contamination of air, water, or land due to the sudden and accidental release of hazardous materials from the insured site. The policy usually covers the costs of cleanup and may include coverage for releases from underground storage tanks. Intentional acts are specifically excluded.
- Purchase insurance is aimed at providing protection on the products people purchase. Purchase insurance can cover individual purchase protection, warranties, guarantees, care plans and even mobile *phone insurance*. Such insurance is normally very limited in the scope of problems that are covered by the policy.
- Title insurance provides a guarantee that title to *real property* is vested in the purchaser and/or *mortgagee*, free and clear of *liens* or encumbrances. It is usually issued in conjunction with a search of the public records performed at the time of a *real estate* transaction.
- *Travel insurance* is an insurance cover taken by those who travel abroad, which covers certain losses such as medical expenses, loss of personal belongings, travel delay, personal liabilities, etc.

Insurance financing vehicles

- Fraternal insurance is provided on a cooperative basis by *fraternal benefit societies* or other social organizations.
- *No-fault insurance* is a type of insurance policy (typically automobile insurance) where insured are indemnified by their own insurer regardless of fault in the incident.
- Protected Self-Insurance is an alternative risk financing mechanism in which an organization retains the mathematically calculated cost of risk within the organization and transfers the catastrophic risk with specific and aggregate limits to an insurer so the maximum total cost of the program is known. A properly designed and underwritten Protected Self-Insurance Program reduces and stabilizes the cost of insurance and provides valuable risk management information.
- *Retrospectively Rated Insurance* is a method of establishing a premium on large commercial accounts. The final premium is based on the insured's actual loss experience during the policy term, sometimes subject to a minimum and maximum premium, with the final premium determined by a formula. Under this

plan, the current year's premium is based partially (or wholly) on the current year's losses, although the premium adjustments may take months or years beyond the current year's expiration date. The rating formula is guaranteed in the insurance contract. Formula: retrospective premium = converted loss + basic premium × tax multiplier. Numerous variations of this formula have been developed and are in use.

- Formal *self insurance* is the deliberate decision to pay for otherwise insurable losses out of one's own money. This can be done on a formal basis by establishing a separate fund into which funds are deposited on a periodic basis, or by simply forgoing the purchase of available insurance and paying out-of-pocket. Self insurance is usually used to pay for high-frequency, low-severity losses. Such losses, if covered by conventional insurance, mean having to pay a premium that includes loadings for the company's general expenses, cost of putting the policy on the books, acquisition expenses, premium taxes, and contingencies. While this is true for all insurance, for small, frequent losses the transaction costs may exceed the benefit of volatility reduction that insurance otherwise affords.
- *Reinsurance* is a type of insurance purchased by insurance companies or self-insured employers to protect against unexpected losses. *Financial reinsurance* is a form of reinsurance that is primarily used for capital management rather than to transfer insurance risk.
- *Social insurance* can be many things to many people in many countries. But a summary of its essence is that it is a collection of insurance coverage (including components of life insurance, disability income insurance, unemployment insurance, health insurance, and others), plus retirement savings, that requires participation by all citizens. By forcing everyone in society to be a policyholder and pay premiums, it ensures that everyone can become a claimant when or if he/she needs to. Along the way this inevitably becomes related to other concepts such as the justice system and the *welfare state*. This is a large, complicated topic that engenders tremendous debate, which can be further studied in the following articles (and others):
    - *National Insurance*
    - *Social safety net*
    - *Social security*
- Social welfare provision
- Stop-loss insurance provides protection against catastrophic or unpredictable losses. It is purchased by organizations who do not want to assume 100% of the liability for losses arising from the plans. Under a stop-loss policy, the insurance company becomes liable for losses that exceed certain limits called deductibles.

Closed community self-insurance

Some communities prefer to create virtual insurance amongst themselves by other means than contractual risk transfer, which assigns explicit numerical values to risk. A number of *religious* groups, including the *Amish* and some *Muslim* groups, depend on support provided by their *communities* when *disasters* strike. The risk presented by any given person is assumed collectively by the community who all bear the cost of rebuilding lost property and supporting people whose needs are suddenly greater after a loss of some kind. In supportive communities where others can be trusted to follow community leaders, this tacit form of insurance can work. In this manner the community can even out the extreme differences in insurability that exist among its members. Some further justification is also provided by invoking the *moral hazard* of explicit insurance contracts.

Insurance companies

Insurance companies may be classified into two groups:

- *Life* insurance companies, which sell life insurance, annuities and pensions products such as life insurance corporation of India etc.
- *Non-life*, *General*, or *Property/Casualty* insurance companies, which sell other types of insurance like reliance general insurance limited etc.

General insurance companies can be further divided into these sub categories.

- Standard Lines
- Excess Lines

In most countries, life and non-life insurers are subject to different regulatory regimes and different *tax* and *accounting* rules. The main reason for the distinction between the two types of company is that life, annuity, and pension business is very long-term in nature — coverage for life assurance or a pension can cover risks over many *decades*. By contrast, non-life insurance cover usually covers a shorter period, such as one year.

In the United States, standard line insurance companies are "mainstream" insurers. These are the companies that typically insure autos, homes or businesses. They use pattern or "cookie-cutter" policies without variation from one person to the next. They usually have lower premiums than excess lines and can sell directly to individuals. They are regulated by state laws that can restrict the amount they can charge for insurance policies.

Excess line insurance companies (also known as Excess and Surplus) typically insure risks not covered by the standard lines market. They are broadly referred as being all insurance placed with non-admitted insurers. Non-admitted insurers are not licensed in the states where the risks are located. These companies have more flexibility and can react faster than standard insurance companies because they are not required to file rates and forms as the "admitted" carriers do. However, they still have substantial regulatory requirements placed upon them. State laws generally require insurance placed with surplus line agents and brokers not to be available through standard licensed insurers.

Insurance companies are generally classified as either mutual or *stock* companies. Mutual companies are owned by the policyholders, while stockholders (who may or may not own policies) own stock insurance companies. *Demutualization* of mutual insurers to form stock companies, as well as the formation of a hybrid known as a mutual holding company, became common in some countries, such as the United States, in the late 20th century.

Other possible forms for an insurance company include reciprocals, in which policyholders 'reciprocate' in sharing risks, and Lloyd's organizations.

Insurance companies are rated by various agencies such as *A. M. Best*. The ratings include the company's financial strength, which measures its ability to pay claims. It also rates financial instruments issued by the insurance company, such as bonds, notes, and securitization products.

Reinsurance companies are insurance companies that sell policies to other insurance companies, allowing them to reduce their risks and protect themselves from very large losses. The reinsurance market is dominated by a few very large companies, with huge reserves. A rein surer may also be a direct writer of insurance risks as well.

Captive insurance companies may be defined as limited-purpose insurance companies established with the specific objective of financing risks emanating from their parent group or groups. This definition can sometimes be extended to include some of the risks of the parent company's customers. In short, it is an in-house self-insurance vehicle. Captives may take the form of a "pure" entity (which is a 100% subsidiary of the self-insured parent company); of a "mutual" captive (which insures the collective risks of members of an industry); and of an "association" captive (which self-insures individual risks of the members of a professional, commercial or industrial association). Captives represent commercial, economic and tax advantages to their sponsors because of the reductions in costs they help create and for the ease of insurance risk management and the flexibility for cash flows they generate. Additionally, they may provide coverage of risks which is neither available nor offered in the traditional insurance market at reasonable prices.

The types of risk that a captive can underwrite for their parents include property damage, public and product liability, professional indemnity, employee benefits, employers' liability, motor and medical aid expenses. The captive's exposure to such risks may be limited by the use of reinsurance.

Captives are becoming an increasingly important component of the risk management and risk financing strategy of their parent. This can be understood against the following background:

- heavy and increasing premium costs in almost every line of coverage;
- difficulties in insuring certain types of fortuitous risk;
- differential coverage standards in various parts of the world;
- rating structures which reflect market trends rather than individual loss experience;
- Insufficient credit for deductibles and/or loss control efforts.

There are also companies known as 'insurance consultants'. Like a mortgage broker, these companies are paid a fee by the customer to shop around for the best insurance policy amongst many companies. Similar to an insurance consultant, an 'insurance broker' also shops around for the best insurance policy amongst many companies. However, with insurance brokers, the fee is usually paid in the form of commission from the insurer that is selected rather than directly from the client.

Neither insurance consultants nor insurance brokers are insurance companies and no risks are transferred to them in insurance transactions. Third party administrators are companies that perform underwriting and sometimes claim handling services for insurance companies. These companies often have special expertise that the insurance companies do not have.

The financial stability and strength of an insurance company should be a major consideration when buying an insurance contract. An insurance premium paid currently provides coverage for losses that might arise many years in the future. For that reason, the viability of the insurance carrier is very important. In recent years, a number of insurance companies have become insolvent, leaving their policyholders with no coverage (or coverage only from a government-backed insurance pool or other arrangement with less attractive payouts for losses). A number of independent rating agencies provide information and rate the financial viability of insurance companies

Questions

1. Explain the concept of health insurance?
2. Discuss in detail about marine insurance?
3. What is general insurance? Discuss the various general insurance policies available to the customer?
4. Explain the insurance scenario in India?
5. Explain in detail the principles of insurance with suitable examples?

Chapter - 7

Governance in Pharmacy

7.0 Pharmacy Council of India (PCI)

Profile, Functions and Duties

- The Pharmacy education and profession in India upto graduate level is regulated by the PCI, a statutory body governed by the provisions of the Pharmacy Act, 1948 passed by the Parliament.
- The Pharmacy Act 1948 was enacted on 4.3.48 with the following preamble- "An Act to regulate the profession of pharmacy. Whereas it is expedient to make better provision for the regulation of the profession and practice of pharmacy and for that purpose to constitute Pharmacy Councils".
- The PCI was constituted on 9.8.49 under section 3 of the Pharmacy Act.

Objectives

- Regulation of the Pharmacy Education in the Country for the purpose of registration as a pharmacist under the Pharmacy Act.
- Regulation of Profession and Practice of Pharmacy.

Functions and Duties

- To prescribe minimum standard of education required for qualifying as a pharmacist. (Ref.: section 10 of the Pharmacy Act)
- Framing of Education Regulations prescribing the conditions to be fulfilled by the institutions seeking approval of the PCI for imparting education in pharmacy.
- To ensure uniform implementation of the educational standards through out the country.

- Inspection of Pharmacy Institutions seeking approval under the Pharmacy Act to verify availability of the prescribed norms.
- To approve the course of study and examination for pharmacists i.e. approval of the academic training institutions providing pharmacy courses.
- To withdraw approval, if the approved course of study or an approved examination does not continue to be in conformity with the educational standards prescribed by the PCI.
- To approve qualifications granted outside the territories to which the Pharmacy Act extends i.e. the approval of foreign qualification.
- To maintain Central Register of Pharmacists.

The Education Regulations

- The Education Regulations are framed under section 10 of the Act and prescribe:-
    - Qualification for pharmacists.
    - Minimum qualification for admissions to Diploma Course in Pharmacy, Duration of the course, No. of hours to be covered for theory and practical, mode of examinations, eligibility for appearing in the examinations, minimum pass marks for passing examination etc.
    - Period and other conditions for practical training etc..
    - Detailed syllabus of Diploma in Pharmacy.
    - Conditions to be fulfilled by the institutions for approval of course of study under section 12 of the Act. (Ref.: Appendix B). These conditions include details of infrastructural facilities which an institution seeking approval of the course of study has to create i.e. accommodation area, qualification, experience and No. of teaching staff, staff-student ratio, non teaching staff, equipments, museum, library etc.
    - Conditions to be fulfilled by the examining authority conducting examinations of the students.
    - Conditions to be fulfilled by the institutions to be recognised for giving practical training.
    - Practical training contract form for pharmacists.
    - Presently, the "Education Regulations 1991 For The Diploma Course In Pharmacy" (E.R.91) are in vogue.

Qualification for Registration as A Pharmacist

- The minimum qualification for registration as a pharmacist is a pass in "Diploma course in Pharmacy" (D.Pharm) from an institution approved u/s 12 of the Act.

D.Pharm is a two years course after 10+2 (science academic stream) followed by 500 hours of practical training spread over a period of 3 months.

- "Degree course in Pharmacy" (B.Pharm) from an institution approved by the PCI u/s 12 of the Act. B.Pharm is a 4 years course after 10+2 (science academic stream).

Regulation of Pharmacy Education under the Pharmacy Act

- By prescribing minimum qualification for registration as a pharmacist.
- By prescribing norms to be fulfilled by the pharmacy institutions seeking approval for the purpose of registration as a pharmacist.
- Uniform implementation of prescribed norms all over the country.
- Verification of the prescribed norms by inspecting pharmacy institutions.
- Granting approval or otherwise (withdrawal of approval/rejection of application) depending on the merits of the case.

Regulation of Pharmacy Profession under the Pharmacy Act

- Registration as a pharmacist is done by the State Pharmacy Council constituted under section 19 of the Pharmacy Act.
- Minimum Statutory requirements for registration as a pharmacist under the Pharmacy Act. (Ref. section 32(2) of the Pharmacy Act) –

  (a) Applicant should have attained the age of 18 years & pay the prescribed fee.

  (b) Applicant should reside or carry on the business or profession of Pharmacy, in the State.

  (c) Applicant should have passed an approved examination.

  Or

  Should possess a qualification approved under section 14 of the Pharmacy Act.

  Or

  is a registered pharmacist in another state.

- An approved examination is "Diploma in Pharmacy" or "Degree in Pharmacy" from an institution approved under section 12 of the Pharmacy Act.
- An approved examination is "Diploma in Pharmacy" or "Degree in Pharmacy" from an institution approved under section 12 of the Pharmacy Act.

- Section 42 of the Pharmacy Act states that no person other than a Registered Pharmacist shall compound, prepare, mix, or dispense any medicine on the prescription of a medical practitioner and whosoever contravenes it shall be punishable with imprisonment for a term which may extend to six months, or with fine not exceeding one thousand rupees or with both.
- Section 26A of the Pharmacy Act empowers the State Pharmacy Council, with the previous sanction of the State Govt. to appoint inspectors, who may –
  (a) inspect any premises where drugs are compounded or dispensed;
  (b) enquire whether a person who is engaged in compounding or dispensing of drugs is a registered pharmacist;
  (c) investigate any complaint made in writing in respect of any contravention of this Act;
  (d) institute prosecution under the order of the Executive Committee of the State Council;
  (e) exercise such other powers as may be necessary for carrying out the purposes of Chapters III, IV and V of this Act or any rules made thereunder.

The Procedure followed in Decision Making Process;

- PCI grants approval to a pharmacy institution for the conduct of "Course of Study" and "Examination" for the purpose of registration as a pharmacist.
- Whenever any prospective institution applies, procedure for seeking approval is intimated
- On receipt of duly filled in application and complete documents, an inspection is arranged to verify the availability of prescribed norms.
- Inspection Report on receipt is forwarded to institution for rectification of the shortcomings, if any, within a stipulated time period.
- Inspection Report alongwith the compliance report if received from institution is placed before the Executive Committee of the Council for consideration.
- The recommendations of the Executive Committee are placed before the Central Council for approval.
- The decision of the Central Council is conveyed to the institution and all concerned like Examining Authority, State Pharmacy Council etc.

- Decision regarding approval and withdrawal is also notified in the Gazette of India.

The norms set by the PCI for the Discharge of its Functions;

- The Education Regulations are prescribed and amended from time to time by the PCI with due approval of the Ministry of Health and Family Welfare, Govt. of India.
- Presently, Education Regulations, 1991 are in vogue which can be obtained from the office of the PCI- in person, by paying Rs. 40/-.
- By post, by submitting a Demand Draft of Rs. 90/- in favour of Pharmacy Council of India, payable at New Delhi.

The rules, regulations, instructions, Manuals and Records, held by PCI;

- Pharmacy Act, 1948.
- Education Regulations, 1991.
- Regulations of the Pharmacy Council of India.
- Standing Orders of the Pharmacy Council of India.
- Pharmacist Oath.
- Procedure for seeking approval of the PCI under the Pharmacy Act.

The Particulars of any arrangement that exists for consultation with or representation by the Members of the Public in Relation to the Formulation of its policy or implementation thereof;

- The public can always represent to PCI and the suggestions received from members of Public are taken into account while formulating policy or its implementation.

COUNCIL, COMMITTEES OF PCI AND AS TO WHETHER MEETINGS OF COUNCIL, COMMITTEES ARE OPEN TO THE PUBLIC, OR THE MINUTES OF SUCH MEETING ARE ACCESSIBLE FOR PUBLIC;

- Detail of Council/Committees of the PCI.

  Central Council –

It consists of representatives of –

(a) Teachers u/s 3(a)

(b) Central Govt. u/s 3(b)

(c) Medical Council of India u/s 3(c)

(d) Director-General, Health Services, ex-officio u/s 3(d)

(e) Drugs Controller, India, ex-officio u/s 3(dd)

(f) Director of the Central Drugs Laboratory, ex-officio u/s 3(e)

(g) University Grants Commission & All India Council for Technical Education u/s 3(f)

(h) State Pharmacy Council u/s 3(g)

(i) State Govt. u/s 3 (h)

- Committees of PCI
- Executive Committee.
- Law Committee.
- Education Regulations Committee.
- Professional Pharmacy and Public Relation Committee.
- Finance Committee.
- Four representatives of the Press and other visitors, not exceeding four at a time may be admitted, at the discretion of the President, to the meetings on production of permits from the Secretary. The Press representatives shall be required to obtain the previous approval of the Secretary for the publication of their report of the proceedings. The President at any time may hold the meetings in camera in which case all visitors including Press representatives will be required to withdraw.
- As per regulation 34 of Regulation of PCI, the minutes of the Central Council are "Confidential".

7.1 Pharmaceutical Export Promotion Council (Set up by Ministry of Commerce and Industry, Govt. of India) (Pharmexcil)

The Industry: Indian Pharmaceutical Industry has made phenomenal progress over the years and made its impact in the global market. Indian Pharmaceutical industry has been recognized as reliable source for drugs and drug intermediates, pharmaceutical formulations. Tremendous opportunities are available for Indian Pharma industry in post 2005 era to manufacture and export many products getting off-patented. Its immense strength in manufacturing quality medicines at affordable prices made the Indian Pharma industry to compete both in regulated and non-regulated markets. This industry is playing a vital role in the Indian economy with Rs.14500 crores export turnover in the year 2003-04 with a growth rate of 12%.

Apart from its strengths in manufacturing and exporting allopathic medicines, India is known for its own systems of medicines with about 7000 units manufacturing various Indian system of medicines viz., Ayurveda, Unani, Siddha, Homeopathy etc. Though strong in cultivation/manufacture of Indian system of medicines, India's share in the global herbal market, estimated at US$ 63 billion, is less than 0.2%, which shows that there is a tremendous scope for export market.

Fast growing Biotech industry estimated at about US$ 2 billion market, is a another part of Indian Pharma industry in India, which has great potential in the international market and which needs focused attention to improve its performance in the international market.

- US$ 5 billion industry
- Produces 70% APIs, almost the entire requirement of formulations within the country
- Ranks 4th in the world, accounting 8% of world production by volume and 2% by value
- Very strong in Indian medicine systems of Ayurvedic, Homoepathy, Unani, Siddha and Herbals medicines
- Fast growing Biotech industry with US$ 2 billion market
- Low cost of production
- Low R&D costs
- Abundant scientific and technical manpower
- Strong intellectual capital
- Excellent world-calls national laboratories, specialized in development processes and cost effective technologies
- An efficient and cost effective source for procuring generic drugs, especially the drugs going off patent in the next few years
- An excellent center for clinical trials
- USFDA/WHO complying manufacturing facilities
- 15% of Indian Pharmaceutical scientists are in USA, hence good network

The Council

The dynamic growth of Indian Pharma Industry, a knowledge based industry, and the recommendations of four major Pharma associations made the Ministry of Commerce & Industry to realize the need for separate export promotion council. Accordingly, Pharmaceuticals Export Promotion Council (PHARMEXCIL) has been set up on

12.5.2004. With its notification No.61 dt. 16.3.2005, Director General of Foreign Trade made Pharmexcil the sole agency to issue RCMCs to all Pharma exporters.

The activities of the Council are administered by Committee of Administration consisting of representatives from major Pharma industries in India like J B Chemicals & Pharmaceuticals Limited, Suven Life Sciences Limited, Dr. Reddy's Laboratories, Aurobindo Pharma, Luipin, Ranbaxy, Novarties, Avantis, Ipca, Shasun, Sun Pharma, Zydus Cadila, Glowchem, Calyx etc., apart from Govt. officials from Central govt. and Govt. of Andhra Pradesh. Administrative support to the Council is extended by very rich experienced personnel from various fields like Govt. of India and Pharma industry.

The Role of Council

Issue of RCMC Organizing Trade delegations/Buyer-Seller Meetings at abroad Organizing Reverse Buyer-Seller Meetings in India Assisting members to get their MDA/MAI claims refunded from Govt. of India Issue of Certificate of Origin Organizing periodical Seminars/Interactive meetings on exports related issues Make suggestions to Govt. of India on policy issues relating to Pharma exports.

Make representations to Govt. of India and other agencies in India and abroad to get amicable solutions for the common problems of the industry.

Categories under Pharmexcil

Various pharmaceutical items like Bulk Drugs and its intermediates, Formulations, herbal, ayurvedic, unani and homeopathic medicines, biotech and biological products, diagnostics, surgicals, neutraceuticals, and pharma industry related services, collaborative research, contract manufacturing, clinical trials and consultancy etc come under the purview of Pharmexcil of Commerce & Industry to promote exports of Pharmaceutical products from India. Council Ministry assist the members in the following areas:

yer-Seller Meetings at abroad

Organizing Reverse Buyer-Seller Meetings in India

Assisting members to get their MDA/MAI claims refunded from Govt. of India Interactive meetings on exports related issues ved from abroad on policy issues relating to Pharma exports India and other agencies in India and abroad for the common problems of the industry

7.2 Pharmaceutical Associations in India

Indian Pharmaceutical Association

Indian Pharmaceutical Association (IPA) is the premier professional association of pharmacists in India, with a member base of over 10,000, spread across the length &

breadth of the nation. IPA operates in India through 17 state branches & more than 33 local branches. The members represent various facets of pharmaceutical profession viz. Industry, regulatory, community pharmacy, hospital pharmacy & education. IPA is also actively associated in managing several academic programmes. IPA is affiliated with international pharma associations like FIP, FAPA, CPA, AAPS, AAiPS, IPSF & WHO, for carrying out various collaborative professional activities which include organizing training programmes for professionals from industry, academics, regulatory & practice, making representations to the authorities on matters of professional interest & working towards constantly upgrading the standards of professional services offered by the pharmacists

Mission

The Indian Pharmaceutical Association (IPA) is the national professional body of pharmacists engaged in various facets of the profession of pharmacy. The IPA is committed to promote the highest professional and ethical standards of pharmacy, focus the image of pharmacists as competent healthcare professionals, sensitize the community, government and others on vital professional issues and support pharmaceutical education and sciences in all aspects.

Objectives

- To promote the sciences and arts of Pharmacy in all aspects.
- To impart suitable education and training to the members preparing for the profession of pharmacy or to those already engaged in the profession.
- To undertake, carry on or promote scientific and technical research, experiments and tests of all kinds in pharmaceutical and allied sciences.
- To edit and publish, journals, books, magazines, documents and other publications for promoting the causes of the profession of Pharmacy.
- To hold seminars, symposia, conferences and exhibitions for promoting the causes of profession of Pharmacy.

Member Benefit

Enroll as IPA members and enjoy exclusive member benefits.

- Be a part of the most elite group of the Pharma professionals in India and gain from their experience and expertise.
- Have access to the latest in national and international news in a crisp, defined format, along with focused profiles of products & niche therapeutic segments, in our monthly newsletter ***"Pharma Professional"*** brought out by Cygnus.

- Take advantage of the many training programmes, seminars, symposia, conferences and workshops organized by IPA, at a concessional rate and update yourself on the latest in technology, trade and regulations governing the various facets of Pharma industry.
- Network with the bigwigs of the Pharma world at the IPA seminars and conferences and further your career.
- Avail of complimentary copies of our monthly newsmagazine - ***Pharma Times*** for your entire membership term.
- Get subsidized subscriptions for our research based scientific publication – ***Indian Journal of Pharmaceutical Sciences (IJPS).***

Organisation of Pharmaceutical Producers of India (OPPI)

- Organisation of Pharmaceutical Producers of India (OPPI) established in 1965, is a premier association of research based international and large pharmaceutical companies in India and is also a scientific and professional body. It caters to the needs of Research based Pharmaceutical Industry thereby creating and sustaining an environment conducive to innovation and growth, simultaneously, facilitating industry and stakeholders partnership through various advisory and consultative processes to achieve the Healthcare objectives of the Nation.
- OPPI Members Follow:
    - Good Manufacturing Practices (GMP)
    - International Code of Pharmaceutical Marketing Practices
    - OPPI's position on Intellectual Property Rights (IPR)

  OPPI functions mainly on the following areas:
    - Continuous dialogue with the stakeholders
    - Actively engage in knowledge creation & knowledge sharing with value addition
    - Engage in 'Corporate Academia' Interaction
- OPPI identifies itself with the country's national healthcare objectives and encourages its members to make substantial contributions to social concerns and actively promotes Corporate Social Responsibility (CSR).
- OPPI is an active member of International Federation of Pharmaceutical Manufacturers Associations (IFPMA), Geneva.

Vision of OPPI

To be an Active Partner with Government, Non-Governmental Organisations (NGOs) and other healthcare providers in improving the health and quality of life of our people through reduced morbidity and mortality by discovering, developing and making available safe, cost-effective and quality medicines. In particular, to play an important role in improving the access to medicines of people in rural areas and those living at or below the poverty line.

To build on India's existing strengths in manufacturing and Distribution and substantially enhance the beginnings made in R&D in order to become one of the leading players in the global pharmaceuticals market.

To develop a realization that the degree of success that the Industry attains in these areas will be a direct function of the emphasis given to the development of a sound system of Intellectual Property Rights, Biological Sciences Research (particularly genomics and proteomics), Clinical Research & Development and Innovative Process Chemistry.

To make India a global sourcing base of high quality pharmaceuticals to international consumers.

To be one of the major creators of intellectual capital and wealth for the economy.

Bulk Drug Manufacturers Association

History

Bulk Drug Industry is the backbone of the self-reliant Pharmaceutical industry in India, playing a significant role in improving the health standards of the people.

Consists of Large, Medium and many small-scale units providing direct employment to about 2,00,000 and indirect employment to another 2,00,000 people.

The capital investment in the industry is about Rs.30000 Million. Today 90% of the domestic bulk drugs requirement is met by the Indian industry, itself. The Bulk Drug industry contributed about Rs 51,000 Million of exports, which is growing by over 15%-20% every year.

The growth and achievement of the Indian Drug Industry during the last five decades has been phenomenal and has been rated as one of the highest among the developing countries.

From a mere processing industry to begin with, India's bulk drug and pharmaceutical industry today has grown into a highly sophisticated one, meeting the International standards of Production, Technology and Quality Control.

The progress of the Drug industry has not only rendered the country self-sufficient in National Health Care, but also played a role in reversing the trend of Indian foreign trade profile from a predominantly importing country to a highly visible exporter to global marketing.

The Association

The Bulk Drug Manufacturers Association (India) was formed in 1991 with Hyderabad as its Head Quarters. This is an all India body representing most of the Bulk Drug Manufacturers of India.

The Association works for the consolidation of gains of the industry and serves as a coordinator and catalyst between the government and the industry for the growth of the industry.

Role of BDMA

Sends representations to the Concerned Ministries and Officials on various problems being faced by member industries, from time to time.

Sends information to its member industries on day to day matters through our newsletter and circulars where by the industry's immediate attention is invited for sharing their suggestions / views on the subject.

Conducts Regional, National Seminars periodically in different places on current technical topics.

Objectives

To provide a platform for encouraging discussion among the member industries on various subjects concerning the Bulk Drug Industry with a focus on formulating the industries' views on various matters such as national, technical, economic and commercial policies that concern the growth of the Bulk Drug industry in the country.

To create and encourage mutual help and cooperation among the members

To assist, cooperate and represent the collective opinion of the association members in formulation and execution of legislative measures by state or Central government authorities/regulators that affect, directly or indirectly, the industry, trade or commerce of the Bulk Drug sector.

To diffuse among its members information on all matters effecting the bulk drug industry and to print, publish, issue, circulate such papers, periodicals, books, circulars as may seem conducive to any of the objectives of the Association.

To encourage the discovery and investigate and make known the nature and merits of inventions, which may seem capable of being used by those engaged in Bulk Drug Industry.

To formulate methods for developing indigenous as well as export market for Bulk Drugs manufactured in India.

To establish or maintain laboratory for testing the quality standards of Bulk Drugs and other allied products and to establish or maintain Research & Development Centre for development of new drugs/improvement in existing drugs / processes etc., or any Hi-tech Research & Training Center, in the interest of the members of bulk drug industry and the country in general.

To under take arbitration and settlement of all commercial disputes arising between members with mutual consent of parties

To do all such lawful things as are incidental or conductive to in consonance with the attainment of the objects of the association.

7.3 Indian Drug Manufacturers Association (IDMA)

Indian Drug Manufacturers' Association (IDMA) was formed in 1961 to help Indian manufacturers and to protect the interest of the Indian consumer.

Membership of over 700 wholly-Indian large, medium and small companies.

Turnover of Indian pharma industry has grown exponentially from Rs.10 crore (about US$ 2 million) in 1948 to about Rs. 1,00,000 crore (US $ 21 billion) today, a growth rate of over 15%.

Members' Indian Market share – about 75% in formulations and about 85% in bulk drugs.

Exports of about Rs. 50,000 crore (over US $ 10 billion) last year growing at 22% average.

Members' Export Record – about 65% of India's total drugs & pharma exports.

More than 150 factories are approved by US FDA, UK-MCA, Australia and South Africa Authorities and many more are holding WHO-GMP certificates.

India is ranked 3rd largest country in terms of production volume and 13th in terms of value with 8% of World's Production but only 1.5% of value.

The Indian Pharmaceutical Industry employs over 4.2 million personnel, both in manufacturing and ancillary sectors.

The growth which the Indian Pharmaceutical Industry has achieved is mainly due to the Indian Patent Act, 1970.

IDMA has been in the forefront actively supporting Ministry of Health & Family Welfare in compiling and bringing out the Indian Pharmacopoeia for many years and also continues its whole-hearted support to the Indian Pharmacopoeia Commission (IPC) in its activities.

IDMA has been successfully organizing Pharmaceutical Analysts Convention (PAC) for many years with the active participation of the Regulatory Authorities, both Central and States. The 13th IDMA-APA PAC 2010 is being organized on 14th and 15th October 2010 in Mumbai.

IDMA Publications

IDMA Bulletin - a weekly communication medium with members and other interested readers now in 41st year.

Indian Drugs - Monthly scientific and technical journal now in 47th year.

IDMA Annual Publication - a reference compendium which contains a wealth of information and data on the Indian Pharmaceutical Industry. Latest 48th edition released.

Indian Herbal Pharmacopoeia – containing exhaustive monographs on herbal plants with medicinal value.

IDMA-APA Forum - for professional Pharmaceutical Analysts.

IDMA-PEG Newsletter - for Pharmaceutical Engineers.

Technical Monographs - Guidelines on standards in manufacture.

IDMA has instituted various Annual Awards as below: QUALITY EXCELLENCE AWARDS for Bulk Drug and Formulation manufacturing units.

IDMA BEST PATENT AWARDS for Best patents granted in India and globally for greater emphasis on innovative Research.

IDMA RESEARCH AWARDS and the **Best Review Article Award** for the best Original Research papers and Review Article published in 'Indian Drugs'.

IDMA J B MODY AWARDS for the top-ranking B. Pharm students of Indian Universities .

IDMA-APA EMINENT ANALYST AWARD in recognition of life-time contribution and expertise in the field of Quality Assurance/Quality Control.

IDMA-APA OUTSTANDING AND YOUNG ANALYST AWARDS to encourage and promote young professional analysts.

Activities

Various issues of policy or operational nature relating to the structure and implementation of the Drugs Cosmetics Rules at Central or State level are taken up with the authorities through representations and follow-up meetings. Some of the important issues which have been taken up with the authorities in recent times are :

1. Extension of validity of WHO-GMP certificates to five years.
2. Six months grace period needed for implementation of overseas pharmacopoeia.
3. IDMA's representation on DTAB.
4. Decentralisation of work regarding registration for import of drugs.
5. Delay in testing of drugs.

6. Licence/inspection fees for SSI sector.
7. Reduction in 4 years period for treating a drug as 'new' drug.
8. Adoption of manufacturer's method of analysis in case of dispute.
9. Menace of spurious drugs, etc.

Besides submitting suggestions for improvement/modification in the EXIM Policy, the Association regularly takes up with the authorities various strategic issues relating to the constraints faced by the member companies in implementation of the EXIM Policy provisions. The difficulties faced by the member companies at the Customs on operational side are also presented to the authorities. Association's representatives on the Chief Commissioner of Custom's Open House meeting also take-up operational issues for their necessary redresal.

Publications

IDMA is not only an Industry Association, but also a scientific and professional body which co-ordinates the activities of member-companies in this vital field. IDMA publishes two periodicals - one, a monthly scientific and technical journal "Indian Drugs" and the other, a weekly communication medium "IDMA Bulletin", and various other prestigious publications such as the Annual Publication, Indian Herbal Phamacopoeia, etc.

IDMA Bulletin

Expanding as rapidly as the Indian Pharmaceutical Industry, the IDMA Bulletin is a premier publication which covers all the essential information so vital to the industry, every week (IDMA Bulletin is published on 7th, 14th, 21st and 30th of every month). This makes it the ideal news source for the Pharmaceutical Industry - manufacturers, government officials, trade, allied manufacturers, educational institutions - practically everyone interested in the pharmaceutical sector. Send us an email to ppr@idmaindia.com if you wish to subscribe to this excellent source of information you need to know.

As the official publication of Indian Drug Manufacturers' Association, IDMA Bulletin, now in its 40th year of publication reaches over 25,000 professionals in this industry both in India and abroad. IDMA Bulletin is read by the top decision makers, the men who make the industry grow from strength to strength. This makes it an ideal medium for advertisers too. Send us an email now to ppr@idmaindia.com if you are interested in communicating your corporate message or publicise your product effectively to the Pharmaceutical Industry.

IDMA Drugs

Indian Drugs is a well known Scientific and Research journal published by IDMA on 28th day of every month for the past 46 years. IDMA seeks to promote original research in India in Pharmaceutical Sciences and in all major fields that fall within its ambit, through this reputed publication. Original Research Papers, Review Articles, Short Notes in five broad disciplines - Pharmaceutics, Pharmacology, Pharmaceutical Analysis, Pharmaceutical chemistry and Pharmacognosy & Phytochemistry are published from all over India and from many countries abroad after scrutiny by the Editorial Advisory Board.

IDMA Publications

IDMA BULLETIN (Weekly)
(Published on 7th , 14th , 21st , and 30th)

INDIAN DRUGS (Monthly)
(Published on 28th of every month)

APA FORUM (Quarterly)
(Published on January, April, July, October)

TECHNICAL MONOGRAPHS

TECHNICAL MONOGRAPH NO.1
Stability Testing of Existing Drug Substances and Products

TECHNICAL MONOGRAPH NO.2
Primary & Secondary Chemical Reference Substances

TECHNICAL MONOGRAPH NO.3
Investigation of Out of Specification (OOS) Test Results

TECHNICAL MONOGRAPH NO.4
Pharmaceutical Preformulation Analytical Studies

IDMA LIST OF MEMBERS
(Members Directory)
48th ANNUAL PUBLICATION 2010
(Updated Copy)

7.4 Medical Detailing and Selling

Pharmaceutical marketing, sometimes called medico-marketing, is the business of advertising or otherwise promoting the sale of pharmaceuticals or drugs. Evidences show that marketing practices can negatively affect both patients and the health care profession. Many countries have measures in place to limit advertising by pharmaceutical companies.

Pharmaceutical company spending on marketing far exceeds that spent on research. In Canada, $1.7 billion was spent in 2004 to market drugs to physicians; in the United States, $21 billion was spent in 2002. In 2005 money spent on pharmaceutical marketing in the US was estimated at $29.9 billion with one estimate as high as $57 billion. When the US number are broken down 56% was free samples, 25% was detailing of physicians, 12.5% was direct to consumer advertising, 4% on hospital detailing, and 2% on journal ads

History

The marketing of medication has a long history. The sale of miracle cures, many with little real potency, has always been common. Marketing of legitimate non-prescription medications, such as pain relievers or allergy medicine, has also long been practiced, although, until recently, mass marketing of prescription medications has been rare. It was long believed that since doctors made the selection of drugs, mass marketing was a waste of resources; specific ads targeting the medical profession were thought to be cheaper and just as effective. This would involve ads in professional journals and visits by sales staff to doctor's offices and hospitals. An important part of these efforts was marketing to medical students.

To health care providers

Marketing to health care providers takes four main forms: gifting, detailing, drug samples, and sponsoring continuing medical education . In Britain, Canada, New Zealand, and the United States 80-90% of physicians see pharmaceutical representatives. Of statements made by pharmaceutical representatives 11% are false and of the false statements all are in favour of the representatives drugs. While very few physicians consider themselves susceptible to detailing, 84% of them believed that their colleagues are.

The Partners Healthcare, Massachusetts' largest hospital and physician network, has adopted new guidelines prohibiting physicians and researchers from accepting gifts from pharmaceutical manufacturers. This will include meals or individual drug samples, and drug samples left by companies will be distributed through a centralized system, while educational programs and fellowships will be required to be centrally reviewed and approved.

Free samples

Free samples have been shown to affect physician prescribing behaviour. Physicians with access to free samples are more likely to prescribe brand name medication over equivalent OTC medications.Other studies found that free samples decreased the likelihood that physicians would follow standard of care practices.

Continuing medical education

Hours spent by physicians in industry-supported CME is greater than that from either medical schools or professional societies.

Pharmaceutical Representatives

Currently, there are approximately 100,000 pharmaceutical sales representatives in India pursuing some 830,000 pharmaceutical prescribers. A pharmaceutical representative will often try to see a given physician every few weeks. Representatives often have a call list of about 200 physicians with 120 targets that should be visited in 1-2 week cycles.

Because of the large size of the pharmaceutical sales force, the organization, management, and measurement of effectiveness of the sales force are significant business challenges. Management tasks are usually broken down into the areas of physician targeting, sales force size and structure, sales force optimization, call planning, and sales forces effectiveness. A few pharmaceutical companies have realized that training sales representatives on high science alone is not enough, especially when most products are similar in quality. Thus, training sales representatives on relationship selling techniques in addition to medical science and product knowledge, can make a difference in sales force effectiveness. Specialist physicians are relying more and more on specialty sales reps for product information, because they are more knowledgeable than primary care reps.

INDIA has 90,000 pharmaceutical representatives or 1 for every 6.3 physicians. The number and persistence of pharmaceutical representatives has placed a burden on the time of physicians. "As the number of reps went up, the amount of time an average rep spent with doctors went down—so far down, that tactical scaling has spawned a strategic crisis. Physicians no longer spend much time with sales reps, nor do they see this as a serious problem."

Marketers must decide on the appropriate size of a sales force needed to sell a particular portfolio of drugs to the target market. Factors influencing this decision are the optimal reach (how many physicians to see) and frequency (how often to see them) for each individual physician, how many sales representatives to devote to office and group practice and how many to devote to hospital accounts. To aid this decision, customers are broken down into different classes according to their prescription behavior and of course, their business potential.

Marketers attempt to identify the set of physicians most likely to prescribe a given drug. Historically, this was done by measuring the number of total prescriptions (TRx) and new prescriptions (NRx) per week that each physician writes. This information is collected by commercial vendors. The physicians are then "deciled" into ten groups based on their writing patterns. Higher deciles are more aggressively targeted. Some pharmaceutical companies use additional information such as:

- profitability of a prescription (script),
- accessibility of the physician,
- tendency of the physician to use the pharmaceutical company's drugs,
- effect of managed care formularies on the ability of the physician to prescribe a drug,
- the adoption sequence of the physician (that is, how readily the physician adopts new drugs in place of older, established treatments), and
- the tendency of the physician to use a wide palette of drugs
- influence that physicians have on their colleagues.

Data for drugs prescribed in a hospital are not usually available at the physician level. Advanced analytic techniques are used to value physicians in a hospital setting.

Physicians are perhaps the most important component in sales. They write the prescriptions that determine which drugs will be used by people. Influencing the physician is the key to pharmaceutical sales. Historically, this was done by a large pharmaceutical sales force. A medium-sized pharmaceutical company might have a sales force of 1000 representatives. The largest companies have tens of thousands of representatives around the world. Sales representatives called upon physicians regularly, providing advertising and free drug samples. This is still the approach today; however, economic pressures on the industry are causing pharmaceutical companies to rethink the traditional sales process to physicians.

Peer Influence

- ***Key opinion leaders:*** Key opinion leaders (KOL), or "thought leaders", are respected individuals, such as prominent medical school faculty, who influence physicians through their professional status. Pharmaceutical companies generally engage key opinion leaders early in the drug development process to provide advocacy and key marketing feedback Some pharmaceutical companies identify key opinion leaders through direct inquiry of physicians (primary research).

  Alternatives to segmenting physicians purely on the basis of prescribing do exist, and marketers can call upon strategic partners who specialize in delineating which characteristics of true opinion leadership, a physician does or does not possess. Such analyses can help guide marketers in how to optimize KOL engagements as bona fide advisors to a brand, and can help shape clinical development and clinical data publication plans for instance, ultimately advancing patient care.

- ***Colleagues:*** Physicians acquire information through informal contacts with their colleagues, including social events, professional affiliations, common hospital affiliations, and common medical school affiliations. Some pharmaceutical companies identify influential colleagues through commercially available prescription writing and patient level data .Doctor dinner meetings are an effective way for physicians to acquire educational information from respected peers. These meetings are sponsored by some pharmaceutical companies.

Journal Articles

Recent legal cases and US congressional hearings have provided access to pharmaceutical industry documents revealing new marketing strategies for drugs· Activities once considered independent of promotional intent, including continuing medical education and medical research, are used, including paying to publish articles about promoted drugs for the medical literature, and alleged suppression of unfavorable study results[] so now days seminars are going on to educate the physician.

Private and Public Insurers

Public and private insurers affect the writing of prescriptions by physicians through formularies that restrict the number and types of drugs that the insurer will cover. Not only can the insurer affect drug sales by including or excluding a particular drug from a formulary, they can affect sales by tiering, or placing bureaucratic hurdles to prescribing certain drugs.

To Consumers

Only two countries as of 2008 allow direct to consumer advertising (DTCA): the United States and New Zealand. Since the late 1970s, DTCA of prescription drugs has become important in the United States. It takes two main form: the promotion or creation of a disease out of a non-pathologic physical condition or the promotion of a medication· Many people will inquire about, or even demand a medication they have seen advertised on television. In the United States, recent years have seen an increase in mass media advertisements for pharmaceuticals. Expenditures on direct-to-consumer advertising have more than quintupled in the seven years between 1997 and 2005 since the FDA changed the guidelines, from $700 million in 1997 to more than $4.2 billion in 2005, according to the United States GAO (Government Accountability Office, 2006)·

The mass marketing to consumers of pharmaceuticals is banned in over 30 industrialized nations, but not in the US and New Zealand, which is considering a ban. Some feel it is better to leave the decision wholly in the hands of medical professionals; others feel that consumer education and participation in health is useful, but consumers need independent, comparative information about drugs (not promotional information·.

For these reasons, most countries impose limits on pharmaceutical mass marketing that are not placed on the marketing of other products. In some areas it is required that ads for drugs include a list of possible side effects, so that consumers are informed of both facets of a medicine. Canada's limitations on pharmaceutical advertising ensure that commercials that mention the name of a product cannot in any way describe what it does. Commercials that mention a medical problem cannot also mention the name of the product for sale; at most, they can direct the viewer to a website or telephone number operated by the pharmaceutical company.

Economics

Pharmaceutical company spending on marketing far exceeds that spend on research. In 2004 in India $1.7 billion a year was spent marketing drugs to physicians and in the United States $21 billion were spent in 2002· In 2005 money spent on pharmaceutical marketing in the India was estimated at $29.9 billion with one estimate as high as $57 billion· When the number are broken down 56% was free samples, 25% was detailing of physicians, 12.5% was direct to consumer advertising, 4% on hospital detailing, and 2% on journal ads. Approximately $20 billion could be saved if generics were used instead of equivalent brand name products.

Regulation

In India marketing and distribution of pharmaceuticals is regulated by the Drug and Cosmetic act, 1940. In general, pharmaceutical companies adhere to FDA regulatory guidelines which call for all DTC advertising and information to be accurate, to provide substantial evidence for any claims that are made, to provide a balance between the risks and benefits of the promoted drug, and to maintain consistency with labeling approved by the FDA.

Evolution of marketing

The emergence of new media and technologies in recent years is quickly changing the pharmaceutical marketing landscape in India. Both physicians and consumers are increasing their reliance on the Internet as a source of health and medical information, prompting pharmaceutical marketers to look at digital channels for opportunities to reach their target audiences.

In 2008, eighty-four percent of physicians used the Internet and other technologies to access pharmaceutical, biotech or medical device information – a twenty percent increase from 2004. At the same time, sales reps are finding it more difficult to get time with doctor's for in-person details. Pharmaceutical companies are exploring online marketing as an alternative way to reach physicians. Emerging e-promotional activities include live video detailing, online events, electronic sampling, and physician customer service portals such as MDLinx and Physicians Interactive.

Direct-to-consumer marketers are also recognizing the need to shift to digital channels as audiences become more fragmented and the number of access points for news, entertainment and information multiplies. Standard television, radio and print direct-to-consumer (DTC) advertisements are less relevant than in the past, and companies are beginning to focus more on digital marketing efforts like product websites, online display advertising, search engine marketing, social media campaigns, and mobile advertising to reach the over 145 million U.S. adults online for health information

7.5 Pharmaceutical E-Detailing

Pharmaceutical companies are realizing they can reach doctors more effectively over the Internet, instead of sending pharmaceutical sales representatives to doctors offices to promote drugs.

The Internet is rapidly transforming Medical Detailing to E-Detailing!

Doctor Net has the largest, highest quality medical industry email address database in the world, a perfect tool for E-Detailing. Here are examples of how our clients use DoctorNet for E-Detailing:

- Deliver video to doctors using the Video Email Service
- Invite doctors to attend CME courses on the efficacy of new drugs
- Broadcast surveys to doctors to collect marketing and clinical information
- Invite doctors to preview a new E-Detailing web site
- Promote a web site that provides drug samples
- Point doctors to a web site that provides drug information
- Announce new drugs or new research results
- Offer seminars or promote medical conventions

Net E-Detailing services, you can reach thousands of doctors instantly.

Benefits of E-Medical Detailing

- ✔ Increase attendance at your medical meeting or convention exhibit booth.
- ✔ Contact medical companies for business to business relationships.
- ✔ Send email to your doctor customers through name to email match.
- ✔ Increase medical industry targeted traffic to your web site.

- Send press releases to doctors and the medical industry.
- Send email to doctors you haven't previously contacted.
- Increase effectiveness of sales reps and detail people.
- Tap the medical expertise of doctors with surveys.
- Acquire new leads for your products and services.
- Promote continuing education courses to doctors.
- Make special offers for products or services.
- Increase your advertising and marketing ROI.
- Announce and promote products or services.
- Perform medical industry market research.
- Offer hospitals services and products.
- Enroll doctors in clinical trials.
- Contact hospitals for placements.
- Contact medical administrators.
- Recruit doctors for jobs.
- Boost your bottom line.

7.6 Mobile Medical Detailing

Pharmaceutical companies operate in one of the most fiercely competitive industries, where the battle for market share is relentless, brutal and very costly But as these companies introduce one blockbuster drug after another, their primary means for getting physicians to actually prescribe them the sales force is reaching a point of diminishing returns as mushrooming armies of sales representatives compete over dwindling access to physicians sending the cost of sales through the roof. Each day, companies are finding it increasingly difficult to rise above the noise, build strong relationships with physicians and influence them to boost sales.

A new breed of powerful handheld computers combined with mobile application software tailored to the needs of pharmaceutical sales reps now offers a compelling solution for building stronger relationships with physicians and driving market share while improving productivity and lowering costs. Compact, convenient and easy to use, these mobile detailing solutions make better use of sales reps' time by offering them a more comprehensive view of the company-physician relationship, easier access to the information they need to be more knowledgeable and better prepared for their sales calls and other tools to help make them more productive.

Mobile detailing solutions can also boost sales force automation (SFA) system adoption and return on investment by more quickly and accurately capturing and updating critical call reporting information, enabling management to have greater visibility into what is actually happening out in the field. Imagine the wealth of useful information that would be gathered if sales reps could simply point and click to complete their post call reports in about a minute immediately after each visit instead of trying to keep track of the information and enter it via a laptop at the end of the day.

Between 1995 and 2000, the amount of time spent with sales reps by the average US physician decreased from 12 minutes to seven minutes per day. If ROI of sales force growth is to be improved, companies must identify new ways of meeting the needs of their target audiences and must tailor their detailing programs accordingly. Companies that fail to improve their productivity will experience further ROI decline if sales forces continue to grow at existing rates.

Building Stronger Physician Relationships

Despite direct-to-consumer advertising, e-detailing, direct mail campaigns and a host of other creative marketing activities that play critical roles, the success of a pharmaceutical company still rests primarily on the ability of its sales force to build relationships with physicians and to influence their choice of drugs. While in the past pharmaceutical companies could hope to gain market share by simply increasing the size of their sales force, this is no longer the case.

Physicians must contend with a growing number of factors competing for their time and trying to influence their decisions. Consider the following:

- The number of sales reps has doubled in the past five to eight years
- At the same time, the number of details has risen by only 15 percent.
- Each year, nearly 100 new ethical drugs are approved making staying up-to-date that much more complex for physicians.
- Better-informed patients are requesting drugs by name
- Boston Consulting Group estimates 66 percent of physicians have instituted some sort of barrier for sales reps, such as an appointment policy, restricted timing, limits on the number of reps seen, etc.

With high-prescribing physicians having more than 50 sales reps visiting on a regular basis, only a handful will establish meaningful dialogues with them. The challenge therefore, is enabling sales reps to build these relationships more quickly to create a sustainable competitive advantage once a relationship is established, it is extremely hard to displace.

Confronted with greater competition for a shrinking supply of physician availability, pharmaceutical companies are discovering they can rise above the noise and increase the chance of building physician relationships by using mobile detailing solutions to get more accurate, timely and pertinent information out to and back from their sales force. Powerful, able to be turned on and used instantly regardless of whether wireless coverage is available, and requiring minimal training, the new generation of mobile detailing solutions based on Windows ® powered Pocket PC, Palm OS ® and RIM ® BlackBerry handheld devices have the potential to do for information access what the cell phone has done for voice communications.

Mobile detailing solutions can fundamentally change how sales reps utilize their time. They can be more effective while with physicians, more productive during their non-selling time and better able to capture important detail information and physician feedback and transmit it back to headquarters. By delivering more information when and where it's needed, a well designed mobile detailing solution can deliver:

- Enhanced physician interactions It provides reps with a single, integrated view of each physician and all his or her relationships with the company.
- Increased sales force productivity, and
- Greater return on SFA investments.

It enables sales reps to provide real value to the physician during their precious few minutes together by making them better informed, better prepared and better able to meet the needs of the physician. Finally, by closing the loop with timely and accurate feedback from the field, the mobile application helps the company and all the sales reps better understand their customers and market more effectively.

Enhanced Physician Interactions

In pharmaceutical sales, success comes down to how well the sales rep performs during those two to four minutes with the physician. The ability to be effective in that brief time determines the value to the physician, the likelihood of building a relationship and ultimately the success of the company. A sales representative, who is poorly prepared, doesn't have the information the physician needs or otherwise fails to live up to the physician's expectations will not be an effective influencer. 84% of physicians surveyed felt the time they spend with sales reps would be more valuable if the rep had immediate access to important drug or clinical trial information on their handheld device.

How can pharmaceutical companies ensure their sales reps have higher quality interactions with physicians? For many, the answer is better access to information. To do their jobs well, sales reps need access to vast quantities of information: the latest marketing materials, competitor activities and rebuttals, medical findings, clinical data and news alerts, detail objectives, account history, e-detail visit information and interests for each physician or medical office, prescriber histories, sample management records and other timely information. How is this information being delivered today? How useful is it? What can be done to make it better? In many cases, a mobile detailing solution offers an innovative and highly effective means to deliver more up-to-date information to sales reps in a way that is both more convenient and easier to use.

Armed with all this information, the sales rep can walk into the office knowing everything the physician needs and working at maximum efficiency. Reps can provide more pertinent information, get their messages across more clearly and be more responsive to physicians questions. The relationship is strengthened because the physician perceives the sales rep as a more valuable resource who is not wasting his or her time which in turn drives trust and a willingness to spend more time with the rep on an ongoing basis.Pharma sales reps need access to multiple data sources to maximize every physician interaction.

Increased Sales Force Productivity

Easy access to information enables sales reps to make much more productive use of the bulk of their time which is spent waiting, traveling, preparing for calls or doing administrative tasks. A mobile application can greatly reduce paperwork and other follow-up burdens by capturing critical detail information more quickly and accurately. Sample management can be done electronically. Prepping and call reporting can be done during what before would have been non-productive dead time. Because all the information to prepare for the call is stored in the handheld application, the sales rep can have it fresh in his or her mind when entering the doctor's office by reviewing it while sitting in the waiting room. During the detail with the physician, the sales rep can drop off samples, capture the doctor's signature electronically, reiterate the key product messages and access some information the physician needs. Immediately after the call, the sales rep can complete all the call reporting in the handheld application. This significantly compresses the preparation and detail-reporting processes, potentially reducing them to 15 minutes or less, making the sales rep more effective and efficient and eliminating preparation and follow-up work normally required at the beginning and end of the day.

At the next available opportunity, the information the sales rep has captured is uploaded to the home office where it provides sales management and brand teams with better insight into field activity, physician behavior, patient impact, and competitive dynamics.

The mobile sales solution provides a framework for maximizing the sales rep's out-in-the-field performance while ensuring management receives consistent and accurate follow-up data essential for driving physician-centric marketing activities.

Greater Return on SFA Investment

According to META Group, 55 to 75 percent of SFA projects fail to meet their objectives. Gartner research concurs, citing that to 85 percent of projects to supply sales with technology fail to deliver measurable ROI benefits due in large part to a lack of alignment between business objectives and application The primary cause of this failure is low adoption of SFA by sales professionals, due to the fact that sales reps get value from the application. It ends up being a burden, rather than a tool to help them do their jobs better.

A sales automation application has to provide tangible value to the sales rep in order to drive consistent and quality usage and thereby create value for the overall organization. A well-designed mobile sales solution embraces the existing SFA system such as Siebel, SAP or another solution and combines it with other business-critical information and application functionality sales people really need to do their jobs most effectively. Sales reps will gravitate to solutions that make them more effective in front of physicians and more productive during their day. The organization will finally get data mining value from its existing SFA investments.

The benefits extend well beyond simply a better return on an SFA investment. There is perhaps no other industry where call reporting is more critical to success and where adherence to call reporting requirements is so burdensome. The pharmaceutical industry is highly information intensive, but much of that information n" physician preferences, competitive actions, adverse events data, patient perceptions, etc. Without adequate call reporting compliance, this information remains mostly inaccessible, at least in a form that can be used for data mining, robbing management of the ability to make better informed decisions. Widespread adoption and use of the SFA system for call reporting closes the loop by providing more accurate and more timely information the company and other sales reps can use to understand their customers better and set sales and marketing strategies. Pharmco executives cite untimely data as a top problem in data mining.

Establish and Leverage Relationships

Without a doubt, building strong physician relationships enables pharmaceutical companies to not only increase sales, but also create higher barriers for the competition. Those who build these relationships first can leverage their franchises for decades. The first companies to deploy mobile detailing solutions have the opportunity to benefit most from the first-mover advantage, securing eeper physician relationships and capturing more data they can use to develop better strategies to gain market share. Companies who wait too long to implement mobile detailing solutions risk losing the chance to capture valuable relationships as physicians recognize the greater value being offered by better informed and prepared sales reps from companies deploying mobile detailing solutions.

Questions

1. Explain the constitution and functions of pharmacy council of India?
2. Explain the role of pharmacy council of India in regulating the pharmacy education in the country?

3. Explain in detail the phenomena of medical detailing? Add a note on the significance of e-detailing?
4. Explain the important functions of organization of Pharma .producers of India?
5. Write short notes on (a) Indian drug manufacturer's association (b) pharmaceuticals export promotion council (PHARMEXCIL).
6. Explain the importance and role of bulk drug manufacturers association in Indian Pharma scenario?
7. Write a note on the following:
   (a) Composition of PCI (b) Mobile Pharma Detailing

Chapter - 8

Drug Store Principles and Management

What is a drug?

A drug can be given three possible operational definitions:

- a chemical substance that affects the processes of the body or mind;
- any chemical compound used on or administered to humans or animals as an aid in the diagnosis, treatment or prevention of disease, or other abnormal condition, for the relief of pain or suffering, or to control or improve any physiologic or pathologic state;
- a substance used recreationally for its effects on the central nervous system.

Since the advent of the essential drug concept, essential drugs have been defined by WHO as those that are indispensable and necessary to satisfy the health care needs of the majority of the population. They should therefore be available and accessible at all times, in the appropriate dosage forms and at prices affordable to all. This definition does not in any way diminish the usefulness of any drug that may not be on any given essential drug list. It is a conscious attempt to utilize available resources on the most important drugs of benefit to the majority of the population while recognizing the competition in the public sector.

What is management?

Management is the act or art of being responsible or in charge and conducting or supervising some- thing (e.g. a health centre pharmacy, business, public undertaking) with a degree of skill and address. It is the judicious use of means to accomplish an end (i.e. public health). Management can also refer to the collective body of those who are responsible for an entity (e.g. a health centre) or who exercise executive, administrative super visor y and regulator y control (e.g. board of governors, village health committee).

Why manage drugs?

Three reasons can be given to explain why drugs need to be managed properly. Firstly, drugs are part of the link between the patient and health ser vices. Consequently, their availability or absence will contribute to the positive or negative impact on health. Secondly, poor drug management, particularly in the public sector of developing countries, is a critical issue, but major improvements are possible that can save money and improve access. Finally, drugs are no longer the responsibility of health workers only. Political, economic, financial and traditional considerations have become so crucial in health care that it has become imperative to look at drugs and health care from these perspectives.

All of these factors contribute to appropriate financial expenditure, avoid wastage, increase access and ensure that drugs are properly used. As is inherent within the Bamako Initiative, proper drug management may also be a source of revenue, which can be used to cater for other health care needs and in particular for disadvantaged populations.

Management Cycle

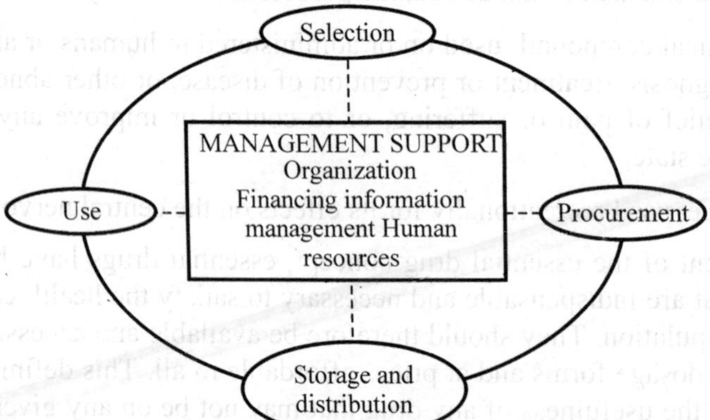

Policy and Legal Framework

The selection of drugs for use at health centers is usually determined at the national level by the Ministry of Health and is based on a number of factors. After determination of the quantities required, based on price, deliver y conditions and quality, the selected drugs go through a procurement process. After storage and distribution, the use of the drugs requires prescribing, packaging, dispensing and counseling. These tasks require qualified health workers or other relevant personnel with appropriate skills and attitudes. Management support tools are important for the acquisition of relevant skills in drug management.

Drug management cycle

Drug management functions are undertaken in four principal phases, which are interlinked and are reinforced by appropriate management support systems (i.e. tools). The following diagram (Diagram 1) illustrates the drug management cycle. From drug selection to drug use, passing through procurement, storage and distribution, a whole range of management capacities are required and necessitate using the appropriate tools within a given legal and policy framework.

Selection of drugs

Ministries of health normally determine the types of drugs and dosage forms that are selected for use in a country. Such selections ensure that available financial resources are used wisely provide a limited list of drugs and dosage forms that are appropriate to the health problems of a country or community. All levels of health care institutions are, thus, catered to:

- Primary,
- Secondary
- Tertiary.

Criteria for selection of drugs

Some criteria used in selecting drugs and their dosage forms, include the following: ntre Level

- Keeping costs of drugs and dosage forms affordable and cost-effective so as to optimize the use of financial resources;
- Having drugs available for the treatment of most prevalent diseases, ailments, sicknesses and so forth at the levels of care provided;
- Availability of safe, effective and good-quality drugs.

Basis for drug selection

Drugs are selected using the WHO Essential Drugs List as a model. Choice is based on: National health policy

- Free health care
- Subsidized health care
- Managed health care

National drug policy

- Free drug policy
- Subsidized cost of drugs or cost recover y
- Cost sharing

Patterns and prevalence of diseases

Quality and type of care provided

- Primary
- Secondary
- Tertiary

Available human resources

- Medical care (general and specialist care)
- Nursing care (nursing, midwifery, psychiatry)
- Pharmaceutical care (pharmacists, pharmacy technicians, clinical nurses)
- Financial resources.

International nonproprietary names (INNs), also known as generic names, are normally used in identifying selected drugs. However, the choice of drugs by generic names requires the existence of an effective Drug Regulator y Authority to ensure the availability of good-quality, safe, effective and affordable drugs.

Health centers usually have between ten and thirty drugs from the national essential drugs list. This small number of drugs makes procurement, storage and distribution easy. It also means that training prescribers and dispensers can be focused on a small number of drugs. This gives them experience with a smaller number of drugs and better recognition of adverse drug reactions. Patients' knowledge can be focused on the smaller number of drugs. This can improve adherence to instructions and reduce confusion.

Generic names

The drugs on the essential drugs list are referred to by their INN or generic names. The generic name is used in writing prescriptions as well as in purchasing drugs. The use of the generic name for these purposes has certain advantages:

- There is easy recognition of the type of drug, especially where many selected drugs exist in that class (e.g. all benzodiazepines have INNs ending

  with "-zepam");
- Drugs can be purchased from multiple sources, thus giving the advantage of buying at a competitive price;

- Product substitution is easy where bio-availability presents a clinical problem;
- The confusion associated with the use of brand names can be avoided.

Some people argue (without evidence) that generic drugs may be of poor quality. The quality of drugs and dosage forms available in a country is dependent on the regulator y measures implemented by the responsible authority. It is important to realize that quality control and naming of drugs are separate issues. Indeed, some manufacturers sell their brand-name products under a generic name at a lower price.

Examples of generic and brand names

Generic (INN)	Brand Names Acetyl
salicylic acid	Asprin®, Aspro®
Albendazole	Zentel® Ampicillin
Penbritin®	
Benzl benzoate	Ascabiol®
Benzylpenicillin	Megacillin®,
Specillin® Cimelidine	Tagamet®
Clotrimazole	Canesten® Cloxacillin
	Orbenin®
Cotrimoxazole (sulphametoxazole + trimethoprim)	Bactrim®, Septrim®
Dexamethasone	Dectancyl®, Dexone®
Diazepam	Valium®
Doxycycline	Doxigram®,
Monocline®	
Griseofulvin	Fulcine® Ibuprofen
	Brufen®
Promethazine	Phenergan®
Penytoin	Di-Hydan®, Dilantin®
Phenobarbital	Gardenal®
Propranolol	Inderal®Paracetamol
Panadol®Salbutamol	Ventolin® Sulfadoxine
+ pyrimethamine	Fansidar®

Drug Procurement

Procurement of drugs is based on selected drugs and dosage forms and available financial resources. Procedures adopted in procuring drugs include:

- Estimating quantity of each drug product required for a given period,
- Finding out the prices of the different drug dosage forms required,
- Allocating funds for each drug dosage form depending on:
- Priority nature of the drug and dosage form,
- Available finances.

Requisition for drug and dosage form is made after due consultation with prescribers.

Estimation of Drug Requirements

The estimate of the drug and dosage forms required for a given period is undertaken: To avoid shortages (out of stock) and ensure credible health care ser vice, to prevent excess stock and avoid waste (loss or mismanagement of financial resources).

Determining drug types and quantities required

Factors that influence choice and quantity of drugs include:

- Population which the health institution serves,
- Disease pattern,
- Seasonal variation in disease pattern,
- Monthly (rate of) drug consumption,
- Knowledge of quantity of each dosage form that is regularly consumed,
- Deliver y (lead) time,
- Time lag between placing orders and receiving the orders,
- Request indicator (re-order level):
- Quantity of drug product that serves as a signal for re-ordering.
- The maximum quantity of drugs held in stock is determined by:
- Distance from the central health ser vices area or regional medical store,
- Size of the health centre store,
- Number of clients (patients) visiting the health centre.

In this section, three factors—delivery (lead) time, monthly consumption and request indicator—are considered as the basis for calculating the appropriate quantity of a particular drug to be ordered.

Delivery (lead) time

It is important to establish how long it takes to have a drug delivered and receipted in the store so that the drug does not become out of stock. This period is called the delivery or lead time. Deliver y time may be days, weeks or even months. Deliver y time may be longer than two months because of the following reasons:

- Poor road conditions, particularly in the rainy season,
- Poor condition of deliver y vehicles,
- Increased work load at the issuing store,
- Non -availability of adequate resources at the central store,
- Consumption rate of drugs.

Monthly consumption

Monthly consumption may be collated with data obtained from:

- Bin (stock) cards,
- Daily use record, daily cash record,
- Drug register.

Normally, monthly consumption is obtained by:

- Calculating the average consumption over a period of time (e.g. six months)
- Or dividing the total consumption over the period by the number of months the drug dosage form was consumed.

Example 1: Monthly consumption

The first method of calculating monthly consumption is to add the quantity of drugs in stock at the beginning of a period (e.g., six months) to the quantity of drugs received during that same period and then subtract the quantity of drugs remaining at the end of the period.

April 2000, quantity of paracetamol 1,000 x 500-mg tablet containers in stock = 14

June 2000, quantity of paracetamol 1,000 x 500-mg tablet containers received = 8

September 2000, quantity of paracetamol 1,000 x 500-mg tablet containers, remaining stock = 6

Therefore, total quantity of paracetamol 1,000 x 500-mg tablet containers consumed over a six-month period = 14 + 8 – 6 = 16.

Average monthly consumption = 16/6

Average monthly consumption to the nearest container = 2 2/3

Example 2: Monthly consumption

A second method of calculating the average monthly consumption is to obtain data on consumption from the bin card on a monthly basis and then find an average over a period of time.

April 2000	2 x
1,000 tablets May 2000	4 x
1,000 tablets June 2000	2 x
1,000 tablets July 2000	2 x
1,000 tablets August 2000	3 x
1,000 tablets September 2000	3 x
1,000 tablets	
	16 x 1,000 tablets

Average monthly consumption is 16 x 1,000 tablets = 2 2/3 containers 6

Average monthly consumption of container to the nearest container = 3

Example 3: Monthly consumption

A third method of calculating average monthly consumption is to obtain data on actual consumption from the daily use record or daily use/cash record.

Data of monthly consumption of paracetamol 500-mg tablets over a six-month period.

April 2000	2,000 tablets
May 2000	3,100 tablets
June 2000	2,300 tablets
July 2000	2,100 tablets
August 2000	3,100 tablets
September 2000	3,200 table
Total six months	15,800 tab
Average monthly consumption of tablet is	15,800 = 2 [illegible] tablets 6

Each container has 1,000 tablets. Therefore the average monthly consumption of 1,000-tablet tin = 2633.3 = 2.6 tins 1000

Average monthly consumption of paracetamol 500-mg tablets to the nearest container = 3

Request indicator (re-order)

The request indicator (RI) is the level of drugs in stock; it indicates when fresh orders should be made. It is the quantity that is calculated to last between the period of placing the order and the deliver y of the new consignment.

The RI is marked with pencil in the space "RI" on the top right-hand corner of the stock card. It should be updated at least twice a year because consumption may vary due to seasonal changes or epidemics.

This will ensure that no shortage of stock occurs before the next consignment is expected. The stock should not be allowed to fall below this level before a new order is placed. Each stock card must have an RI that is updated from time to time as consumption varies.

The stock should never reach "zero level" before a request is made, as there will be a shortage of stock for some time. It is easy to calculate the RI once the monthly consumption is obtained.

If the deliver y time is three months and the monthly total consumption is 2633.3

RI is: 2633.3 tablets x 3 months = 7,900 tablets

Since the unit of issue is tins of 1,000 tablets, the above figure must be brought to the nearest tin, which is 7,900 = 7.90 = approximately 8 tins 1000

This means that when the stock of paracetamol is reduced to 8 tins, a new request must be made.

Quantity to be requested

The type and quantity of drug to be ordered will depend on the disease pattern of the area served by the health centre, the quantity for each dosage form previously consumed, when drugs were not out of stock, the period for which the new stock is to serve and the number of patients. In determining the quantity to be requested:

- Consider the lead or deliver y time.
- Consider the number of patients to be treated (using national treatment guidelines).

- Collaborate with the head of the health centre (prescriber) when making a new request. The prescriber is better placed to know for which item an extra quantity has to be requested because of epidemics or seasonal changes in disease pattern.
- Look through all the stock cards in a systematic manner and compare the RI with the current stock balances.
- Request only those items where the stock balance approaches the RI, equals the RI or is below the RI.

Examples

(a.) RI = 6 tins; Balance: 8 tins (number of patients = 100) (b.) RI = 6 tins; Balance: 6 tins (number of patients = 100) (c.) RI = 6 tins; Balance: 0 tins (number of patients = 100)

In the above three situations, consider the existing lead time of three months and add one month as RESERVE for unforeseen circumstances such as delay in deliver y, breakdown of deliver y vehicle, stock rupture at the central store, bad roads, unforeseen epidemic and so on.

Examples

(a) RI = -6 tins; current stock balance = 8 tins

In this case the RI is above by 2 tins.

Therefore, make the normal request less by 2 tins

Request quantity = 2 tins × 3 months + 1 month consumption (2 tins)

$= (2 \times 3) + 2 - 2$

$= 6$ tins

(b) RI = 6 tins; current stock balance = 6 tins Average monthly consumption is 6 tins/3 = 2 tins The quantity to be ordered is:

Average monthly consumption x Lead time + 1 month consumption for unforeseen events

= (2 tins × 3 months) + 2 tins

= 8 tins

(c) RI = 6 tins; current stock balance = 0 tins

In this case an extra quantity must be requested to cover the RI.

Request quantity = 2 tins x 3 months + 1 month consumption (2 tins) + RI (6 tins) quantity

$= (2 \times 3) + 2 + 6$

$= 14$ tins

In each case above, if previous data show that the number of patients would increase (e.g. malaria cases due to seasonal variations), then the quantities should be increased proportionally.

If the number of patients is expected to double, then the quantity should be multiplied by 2.

If the number of patients is expected to drop by half, then the quantity should be multiplied by 1/2.

Price of drugs

The prices of drugs are also determined at the national level. The factors to consider in determining price include:

- Purchase price,
- Shipping cost,
- Clearing and custom charges,
- Transportation charges,
- Markup to cover administrative and other costs.

In determining the price, a factor is also included to take care of inflation so that the revenue generated will not be eroded with time. This is important for the sustainability of the drug fund.

It is also important not to price drugs at the health centre below the national determined price. At the local level, the health committee may add another markup to cover local expenses.

Requisition, supply and receipt of drug request

Drugs that are ordered for use in the health centre must be approved for use in the centre. Drugs in the health centre should be relevant to the pattern of endemic diseases as well as the type of ser vices being provided in the health centre.

It is advisable to request drugs on a regular basis to prevent shortages. If drugs are not always available, patients may lose confidence in the health centre and will be discouraged from visiting it. It is important to make requests on a regular basis, as drugs will only be delivered when requested. The deliver y time should be taken into consideration in ensuring that drugs are not in short supply.

Requesting Regularly

Completing stores requisition/delivery (issue) form

It is advisable to make a request on a standard stores requisition/delivery (issue) form.

The stores requisition/delivery (issue) form should be produced in four copies. The original and two other copies of the form will be sent to the central store when completed. The fourth copy is kept in the dispensary to remind the health worker in charge of drugs or items requested.

Ensure that the following items are filled in correctly:

- Name of drug and dosage form;
- Unit of issue and quantity requested;
- The requisition number (it is preferable to begin with a new number each year, e.g. 1/00);
- The name of the dispensary and the date the requisition was made;
- The name and signature of the health worker making the requisition;
- Where the stores requisition/deliver y (issue) form is designed to contain all the items listed, fill in only the quantities of those items needed;
- Write down the approximate unit price of each requested item and the approximate total cost of each item;
- Name and signature of the health worker making the requisition;
- The head of the health centre and a representative of the health committee should endorse the stores requisition/delivery (issue) form.

Diagram 3

Model drug stores requisition / Delivery (Issue) Form

Request no______________________________ Institution:

Name of health worker: ____________________ Date:

Delivery note: _____________________________ Total number of packages: ____

Packed by (name): ____________________ Date _

Checked by (name): ____________________ Date ___

Handed over by (name): ____________________ Date

Received by (name): ____________________ Date

Item description	Unit of issue	Unit price	Quantity required	Total price	Quantity delivered	Total price	Signature	Remarks
1. Acetylsalicylic Acid 500 mg tab	1,000 tab							
2. Magnesium trisilicate	100 tab							
3. Chloroquine 100 mg b	1,000 tab							
4. ORS sachets	50 sachets							
5. Procaine	1 vial							

To be completed in four copies.

- Period for which supply is required, from ___to ____________

- The dispenser should comment on excess or short supply in the remarks column.

Name and signature of dispenser at health centre: ____________________

Name and signature of member of health committee: ____________________

Name and signature of head of heath centre: ____________________

Supply of drugs from medical stores Stores requisition/delivery (issue) form

A stores requisition/delivery (issue) form should accompany any supply made from the medical stores. Health centers normally receive their drug supplies from central, regional or health ser vices area medical stores. In very rare cases they may obtain drugs from other sources.

- Supplies are issued on the basis of request made to the medical store by the health centre on an approved stores requisition/deliver y (issue) form.
- The request should not be excessive and should preferably ask for quantities that can be used in between deliver y times.
- The quantity of drugs requested is made in the appropriate column of the form and is sent to the medical store from which drugs are supplied.
- The request is made on the basis of approved deliver y time, time frame or in emergency.
- The quantities of drugs delivered or issued from the medical stores should be entered in the appropriate column of the form.

The records of requisition and receipt of drugs from the medical store are kept in the health centre in an approved manner.

The delivery note from the central medical store should indicate what has been supplied as indicated in the stores requisition/deliver y (issue) form.

Receipt of drugs at Medical Store

- The consignment must come with two copies of the stores requisition/delivery (issue) form.
- Check that the quantity issued actually corresponds to the quantity indicated on the stores requisition/delivery (issue) form.
- Check off each drug after checking.
- Take note of the unit price of each drug and compare it to the previous unit price.
- Check that all original boxes, tins or bottles are unopened and are in good condition.
- Check the labels and ensure that there are no expired drugs being received.
- Any drugs already expired or soon to expire that cannot be consumed before expiration or drugs not in good condition should be returned for destruction or redistribution to other centers.
- Sign two copies of the stores requisition/deliver y (issue) forms if the above procedure has been completed.
- Return one copy of the signed stores requisition/delivery (issue) form to the medical stores, and place another copy in the "drug order" file.

- Place drugs with shorter expiration dates in front of the shelf so that they can be reached and used first.
- Remember to record the new stock on the respective stock (bin) cards.

Discrepancies when receiving drugs

Where there is a difference in the quantities of drugs issued and the quantities actually received, request the deliver y team to give an immediate explanation and make the necessary correction on the stores requisition/deliver y (issue) form. If there are broken bottles or leaking packages, hand these over to the deliver y team along with an internal drug return (IDR) form.

Discrepancies should always be recorded in the Remarks column on the stores requisition/delivery (issue) form.

Transfer voucher or internal drug return (IDR) form

The transfer voucher effects the movement of the following items to the medical store:

- Expiring drugs,
- Damaged or spoiled drugs,
- Drugs soon to expire,
- Excess stock resulting from wrong RI or low consumption.

The following rules should be kept in mind:

- It is important that drugs are not allowed to expire in the health centre because of changes in disease pattern or for any other reasons.
- Items that can be used elsewhere should be transferred immediately using an IDR form to the medical stores for subsequent redistribution (Diagram 4).
- Expired or spoiled items should be transferred immediately using the IDR form to the medical stores for destruction.
- Excess stock should normally be transferred at least 3 months before expiration to the medical store using the IDR form.

- An internal transfer directly from one dispensary to another without involving the central store is not permitted for accounting purposes.
- The IDR form should be filled in triplicate. The triplicate copy is retained in the health centre while the original and duplicate copies accompany the returned drugs.

Diagram 4
Example of Transfer Voucher or Internal Drug Return Form

Item description issue	Unit of issue	Expiry date	Quantity	Unit price	Amount	Remarks
Normal saline 500 ml	500 ml	9/04	10	800	8,000	*Leaking*

TOTAL 79,410

Delivered by: ____Received by:

For medical store use only

Voucher no. ___

2 copies returned to central store

This is the procedure for the transfer to the medical store of any of the following:

- Expired items,
- Damaged or spoiled items,
- Drugs soon to expire,
- Surplus quantities resulting from the wrong RI.

An internal transfer directly from one dispensary to another without including the central store should not be affected because this will create confusion in accounting. Diagram 5 illustrates an IDR flow.

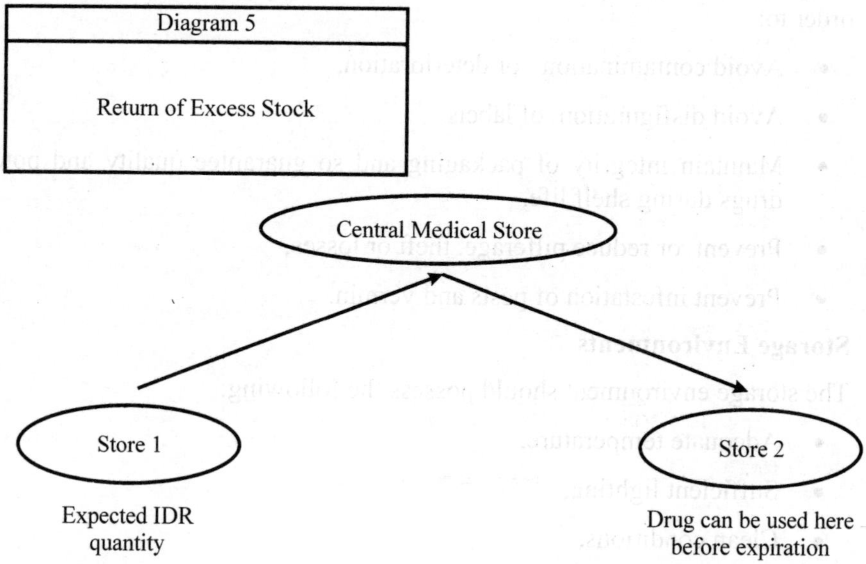

Some health centers have lying in-wards and outpatient clinics to which drugs are supplied. The health centre store will supply the drugs in accordance with the following:

- A request is made from the ward/clinic in an approved manner.
- Supplies are made on the basis of the request, and quantities of drugs supplied are recorded in an approved manner.
- Entries of quantities of drugs supplied are made on bin cards as well as the drug register maintained (in the store) for drugs received and supplied.

Normally, drugs are supplied from the health centre (dispensary) store to the dispensing area. Entries of such entries are also made on bin cards or the drug register maintained in the store bin an approved manner.

Drug donations

Donated drugs should be screened and separated into expired or poor-quality drugs, those approved for use at the health centre and those not approved. Those approved for use at the health centre should be retained and entered into the stock. The rest must be sent to the central store with an IDR form.

Drug storage

1. **Proper drug storage**

   Drugs are stored in a specially designed secure area or space of a building in order to:

   - Avoid contamination or deterioration,
   - Avoid disfiguration of labels,
   - Maintain integrity of packaging and so guarantee quality and potency of drugs during shelf life,
   - Prevent or reduce pilferage, theft or losses,
   - Prevent infestation of pests and vermin.

2. **Storage Environments**

   The storage environment should possess the following:

   - Adequate temperature,
   - Sufficient lighting,
   - Clean conditions,
   - Humidity control,
   - Cold storage facilities,
   - Adequate shelving to ensure integrity of the stored drugs.

3. **Arrangement of drugs on shelves**

   The following guidelines are for arranging drugs.

   - Shelves should be made of steel or treated wood.
   - Shelves should be strong and robust.
   - Drugs are arranged in alphabetical order of generic names.
   - Each dosage form of drug is arranged in separate and distinct areas.
   - Sufficient empty space should demarcate one drug or dosage form from another.

Most recently received drugs are placed behind old stock on the shelf except where new drugs have shorter expiration dates.

It is important to ensure the following rules in the dispensary and the store attached to the dispensary:

- Keep the environment clean.

- Always put lids properly on tins always and at the close of the day.
- Put drugs in a dry place protected from light and heat.
- Store liquids on a pallet on the floor or on the lowest shelf. The store must be cleaned daily and mopped at least once a week.

The storeroom

A well-arranged store enables easy identification of drugs and saves time when picking a drug from the shelves. The following procedure will facilitate managing the drugs in the store. Put drugs on the shelves in alphabetical order corresponding to the essential drug list. This helps remove drugs quickly and makes for easy inventor y control. The rule of FIRST IN FIRST OUT (FIFO) should be applied always. So, drugs that were received first should be used first, except where the new stock has shorter expiration dates than the old stock. In this regard, the principle of FIRST TO EXPIRE FIRST OUT (FEFO) should apply. To have access to drugs with shorter expiration dates first, put these in front of the shelves. Those with longer expiration dates should be placed behind those with shorter dates.

The Medical Store

Good arrangement facilitates dispensing work. Practice the following:

- Retain a daily drug use record in the dispensary.
- Provide a table for dispensing drugs.
- To facilitate work, do not overcrowd the dispensing table.
- Arrange documents in an orderly manner on the table, away from the dispensing area.
- Clean after each use tablet counters and place within easy reach on the table
- Avoid dispensing wrong drugs by arranging drugs on the table in alphabetical order so that the drug being dispensed is not confused with another.
- Always close drug containers from which drugs are not being dispensed to prevent spillage or dispensing the wrong drug.

Drug Distribution

At the health centre level, drug distribution concerns mainly dispensing drugs to patients. This requires an understanding of the patients (who may not speak or understand the language of the dispenser) and practical skills in dispensing and record-keeping.

Rational prescribing

Prescriptions should be written after a diagnosis or a health problem has been identified. The prescription will present the necessary drugs and measures sufficient to heal or improve the state of the patient. The prescription must then contain all the necessary information clearly written.

Known roman numerals usually written in prescriptions to represent dosage are: i, ii, iii, representing one, two and three.

Known roman numerals usually written in prescriptions to represent dosage are: i, ii, iii, representing one, two and three.

It is better to state dosage in terms of strength (e.g. 500 mg) than number of tablets. This is because some drug products are available in different strengths (e.g. diazepam 5 mg and 10 mg).

Avoid the use of decimal points when stating the strength of a drug—500 mg is preferred to .5 gm and 250 micrograms is preferred to .25 mg. This is because if the decimal point does not appear clearly, a wrong strength of drug may be dispensed as 25 mg instead of .25 mg. If a decimal point is not avoidable, then precede it with a 0 such as 0.25.

Too many abbreviations, illegible writing or ambiguous instructions can lead to errors in dispensing. It is therefore recommended that prescriptions should be unambiguous and written legibly.

Example: Rx

Paracetamol 500 mg tabs ii tds x 3 days

The prescription is clear as it states:

- The dosage form of the paracetamol—tablets,
- The strength of the paracetamol tablets—500 mg per tablet,
- The number of days for which the paracetamol tablets have been prescribed,
- The number of times the tablets should be taken each day,
- The number of paracetamol tablets to be taken each time.

Content of a Prescription

A prescription is a set of instructions written by a qualified prescriber to a dispenser for supply of drugs after counseling the patient on how to use the drug. It is very important that prescriptions are clearly written.

A prescription should have the following:

- Name of the patient and age (especially if a child),
- Date,

- Instructions about the prescribed drugs, including:
- Generic name and dosage form,
- Dose,
- Frequency of administration,
- Duration of treatment,
- Prescriber's signature and name.

Abbreviations commonly used in prescriptions

The following abbreviations are commonly used in prescriptions:

amp = ampoule
bid = twice daily
cap = capsule
g = gram
im = intramuscular
iv - intravenous **kg** = kilogram **mg** = milligram
mg/kg = milligram per kilogram
body weight (a way of calculating a dose to be prescribed)
ml = millilitre
mu = million (mega) unit
nocte = at bed time
od = once a day
prn = when necessar y
qid (qds) = four times daily
Rx = treatment
sc = subcutaneous
stat = at once
supp = suppositor y
tab = tablet
tbsp = tablespoonful (=10 ml)
tid/tds = thrice daily
tsp = teaspoonful (= 5 ml)
wt = weight

Duration of treatment is usually indicated by denominators: 7 = days, 12 = months and 52 = weeks. For example, 1/7 = one day, 2/12 = two months and 1/52 = one week.

Dispensing Drugs to Patients

Correct drug dispensing

Dispensed drugs should be appropriately labeled so that the patient can benefit optimally from the use of the drug. Expired drugs should not be dispensed. Correct dispensing ensures that:

- The right patient is served,
- A desired dosage form of the correct drug is given,
- The prescribed dosage and quantity are given,
- The right container that maintains the potency of the drugs is used,
- The container is appropriately labeled,
- Clear instructions are delivered verbally to the patient.

Dispensing procedure

- Ensure that the prescription has the name and signature of the prescriber and the stamp of the health centre.
- Ensure that the prescription is dated and has the name of the patient.
- If the prescription has not been written in a known (local) health centre, the prescriber of the centre should endorse it.
- Avoid dispensing without a prescription or from an unauthorized prescriber.
- Check the name of the prescribed drug against that of the container.
- Check the expiration date on the container.
- Calculate the total cost of the drug to be dispensed on the basis of the prescription where applicable.
- Inform the patient about the cost of the drug.
- Issue a receipt for all payments.
- Hand over the dispensed drug.

Dispensing prescriptions on part-payment

Where a patient does not have enough money to pay for all the drugs as prescribed, the dispenser is faced with a difficult situation. Consider the following scenario to resolve this situation:

(a) Cotrimoxazole 400/80 mg tab 2 bd x 5 days

(b) Chloroquine 150 mg tab 4 stat, then 2 tab bd x 2/7

- Either dispense all the 20 tablets of cotrimoxazole or the 10 tablets of chloroquine as prescribed and insist that the patient completes the dose dispensed.
- In case a patient is unable to pay for all the prescribed drugs, go to the prescriber and ask which of the two drugs should be dispensed first.
- Do not dispense a few tablets of cotrimoxazole and a few tablets of chloroquine as the patient will not come back to complete the prescription if he feels better.
- When the temporar y relief passes, the cotrimoxazole or chloroquine may not be effective again in that particular condition. condition.

Guiding principles in dispensing on cash basis

- Dispense drugs only on payment.
- Do not give free drugs to any person in the community, no matter what the person's social standing.
- Issue receipts for drugs sold.
- Display a price list of drugs for transparency and accountability, and to help patient's cross-check.

Packaging of drugs for patients

All drugs should be put in suitable and appropriately labeled containers to ensure correct use and maintain potency and quality during the period of use.

Tablets and capsules

- Do not use fingers to count tablets as this can lead to contamination of drugs

- Use a spoon to put tablets and capsules onto a counting tray.
- Count and put them in a labeled drug container or pack.
- Use a different labeled drug container or pack for each drug.
- Do not mix different drug items in one container.
- Close stock containers (e.g. tins, bottles) tightly after dispensing.
- Keep the spoon clean at all times.

Liquid preparations

- Provide appropriate bottles with caps for repackaging liquid preparations.
- Dispense liquid preparations in suitable containers.
- Do not use patients' own bottles
- Dispense each drug in a different bottle.

Labeling

- Label all containers in which drugs are dispensed.
- Use pictorial labels when a patient is not literate.
- Where envelopes are used, label them before drugs are packed.
- For liquid preparations, label the container(s) after putting in the liquid preparation.

The label on the container of dispensed drugs should contain the following in order to promote patient compliance:

- Drug name (use generic name),
- Strength (usually in mg),
- Quantity dispensed,
- Clear instructions for use in a familiar language,
- Cautionary label (e.g. "Keep out of reach of children"),
- Name of the patient,
- Name of the health facility,
- Date of dispensing.

Diagram 6

Example of Lables

LABEL A

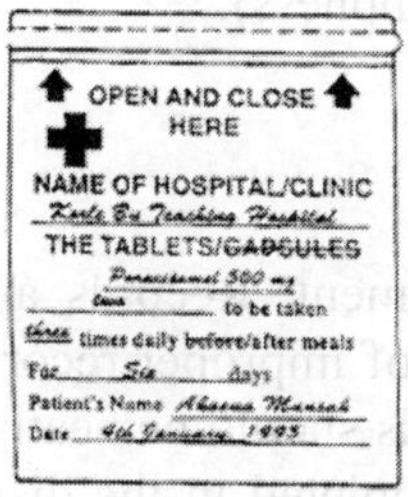

Label for **tablets** or capsules

LABEL B

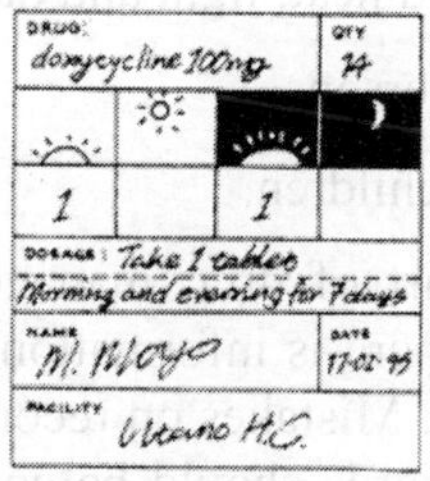

Pectoral label

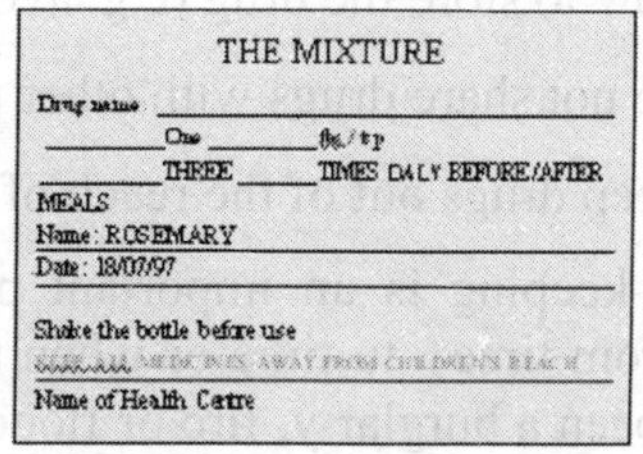

Lable for **Liquid preparations**

Use of Drugs Rational drug use

The rational use of drugs requires that the drug is prescribed for a particular patient after proper diagnosis of a health problem. Prescriptions should promote the rational use of drugs. Rational use of drugs requires that a particular patient with a specific health problem receives drugs according to the following:

- Appropriate dose,
- Appropriate dosage form,
- Appropriate route of administration,
- Appropriate frequency of administration,
- Appropriate duration of treatment,
- Appropriate information to the patient,
- Adequate follow up

Information to the patient

The health worker should be able to give the patient additional information to re-enforce the right instructions on the label. This should be in a language that is familiar to the patient. The information in the form of verbal instructions should including the following:

- How often to take the drug,
- When to take the drug (e.g. before or after the meals),

- How long the treatment is to last (e.g. why the entire course of an antibiotic treatment must be taken),
- How to take the drug (e.g. with water, chewing or swallowing),
- How to store the drug (e.g. avoid heat, light and dampness),
- Do not share drugs with other persons,
- Keep drugs out of the reach of children.

Record-keeping is an important part of drug management. Records are subject to auditing from time to time or when there is information of improper record-keeping or there has been a burglar y, fire or flood. Mistakes on records should be neatly crossed out and signed for but not obliterated. Records should be completed in the dispensary on a daily basis, and not later than a week after the event. This will enable easier compilation of drug consumption and cash receipts. The following stock management records should be completed in the order described in the following sections.

Consumption records to be kept at the store

Maintain a stock (bin) card for each dosage form of drug in the store where drugs are kept. Stock (bin) cards are important for good accountability of stock movements. The cards should be made of stiff cardboard and be placed near the drug products that they refer to on the shelves. If one dosage form is available in two different strengths, open separate stock cards for each strength. Stock, bin or tally cards are very useful tools in the management of stores. Follow these procedures:

- Maintain a stock (bin) card for each drug or dosage form of a drug in the store where drugs are kept.
- Enter quantity of seed stock in the "in" and "balance" columns with date, price and supplier.
- Enter quantity of any new stock in the "in" column with date, price, supplier and deliver y number.
- Enter balance of stock brought for ward in "balance" column with date.
- Entries of receipt and issue of drugs are made after the event.
- Always have a balance of stock entered in the "balance" column with date.
- Always issue out full containers of drugs from the sto[illegible] [illegible] enter [illegible] [illegible]ntity of drug issued in the "out" column.
- Physically check the actual balance of stock against cu[illegible] balance [illegible]k card from time to time to detect any discrepancy.
- Keep spoons and measuring cups within reach for dispensi[illegible]

Communicating with a patient in the dispensary

Keep separate stock (bin) cards for:

- Acetylsalicylic acid 300-mg tablets
- Acetylsalicylic acid 500-mg tablets.

Entries to be made in stock (bin) card

- When an item is received from the central store, enter the quantity received in the "IN" column on the stock card using a red pen.
- Add the number to the previous balance on the stock card to obtain the current balance.
- Enter the unit price.
- Enter the date and number of the deliver y note of the central store in the column "Ref. No."
- It is preferable to take a full container of a drug from the shelf in the store to the dispensing area when the stock in the dispensing area is finished or almost finished.

- Each time a full container of a drug is taken from the shelf to the dispensing area, an entry of the number of containers taken out is made in the stock (bin) card using a blue or black pen in the "OUT" column.
- Subtract the number of containers taken out from the previous balance in the stock card to obtain the current balance.

Diagram 8
Example of Stock (bin) card

Ako	Dispensary	Stock Card No. 1
ITEM: Paracetamol	Dosage 500 mg.	Unit of Issue
1,000 Tablets	RI89 x 1,000	

Date (1997)	Ref. No.	From/To	Quantity In	Quantity Out	Balance Price	Cost	Re marks	Sign ature
30/5		B/F				3		
5/6	51/97	From central store	7			10		
5/6		To central store				9		
					1		2,000	IDR
6/6		To dispensar y store To				8		Exp8/97
20/6		dispensar y store To			1	7	2,000	
4/7		dispensar y store To			1	6	2,000	
18/7		dispensar y store To			1	5	2,000	
4/8		dispensar y store To			1	4	2,000	
25/8		dispensar y store Stock			1	3	2,000	

Where RI represents the re-order level, the lowest stock level before an order is placed for the next stock.

8.1 Consumption Records at the Dispensary Level

There is a need to maintain a record on consumption of drugs at the dispensary through the use of a daily use record book.

- The daily use record book is used to make entries of all drugs dispensed on a daily basis.
- Maintain a daily use record in the daily use record book in the format shown in Diagram 9.
- Use a fresh page for making entries for each drug dosage form.

- Reserve a page or two for ever y month's consumption of drugs.
- Make entries from actual receipts issued.
- When a drug item is taken out of the dispensary store, an entry is made in the "OUT" column in the stock (bin) card in the store. An entry is also made in the "IN" column, with red pen, in the daily use record in the dispensing area as well as the date the entry was made.
- Add the quantity of drugs taken from the store to the dispensary to the previous balance in the daily use record to obtain current balance.
- Enter the dispensing date and the total quantity of dosage form dispensed daily in the "OUT" column.
- Subtract the quantity dispensed or used daily from the balance to obtain current balance.
- Enter any shortage in the "OUT" column and necessary remarks in the "REMARKS" column.

Discrepancies

Discrepancies should always be recorded in the "REMARKS" column (as in Diagram 9). Discrepancies may arise for one of the following reasons:

- Some of the tablets may have been crushed into powder or broken,
- A shortage may result from a mistake by the manufacturer,
- A shortage may occur in the containers when tablets issued are not recorded in the daily use record sheet,
- Arithmetic errors may result in shortages or excess stock.

Considering the case of acetylsalicylic acid tablets in Diagram 9, only proper record-keeping on a daily basis can give early warning of a possible shortage.

Example: The daily use record on 19/6 indicates that there is a balance of 42 tablets of acetylsalicylic acid. Actual balance is only 22 tablets. There is therefore a shortage of 20 tablets. If some powder or broken tablets are found in the container from which drugs were dispensed, the powder or broken tablets may account for the 20 tablets shortage in the daily use record book.

If there is nothing remaining in the container and entries were made of all drugs dispensed in the daily use record book, then it could be concluded that the shortage came from the manufacturer during packaging. Keep all available evidence and report to the medical store as soon as possible. The medical store may receive similar reports from other health centres and can then estimate the average shortage per container for that particular drug item and credit your account.

This irregularity may also be reported by the medical store to the suppliers for compensation, where possible. This exercise can only be accurately done with proper documentation in the daily use record book. This exercise will explain shortages declared at the end of the financial year when an audit is carried out.

Example of Daily Record

Acetylsalicylic acid tablets 3,000 mg

Date (1997)	From/To	Quantity		Balance (Tabs)	Remarks
		In	Out		
2/6				20	
3/6	B/F	1,000		1,020	
4/6	From dispensar y store		60	960	
5/6	To patients To patients To		48	912	
6/6	patients To patients To		84	828	
9/6	patients To patients To		60	768	
10/6	patients To patients To		84	684	
11/6	patients To patients To		84	600	
12/6	patients To patients		120	480	
13/6	Shortage		48	432	
16/6			150	282	
17/6	From store		84	198	
18/6	To patients		60	138	
19/6			96	42	
20/6			20	22	
23/6				1,022	
23/6				902	
24/6		120		150	
25/6	From store			180	20
26/6	To patients	1,000 "		160	Crumbled
27/6	Monthly consumption for	" " "		180	tablets
30/6	June 1997			1,232	
30/6		1,000		992	

Receipts for drugs dispensed

- When payments are made for the drugs dispensed, it is advisable that the fees for the dispensed drugs are collected and receipts issued before the drug is given to the patient.

- Every dispensary should have a receipt book in duplicate form.
- Every patient should be issued a receipt for drugs purchased (see Diagram 10 for example).
- Use carbon paper to produce a duplicate copy.
- Stamp the original receipt with "PAID" on receipt of cash payment for the dispensed drugs.
- Give the original receipt to the patient and retain the duplicate in the receipt booklet.

Example of Receipt

Receipt for drugs

Dispensary ______________________________ Name Date

Name of drug	Qty. sold	Unit Price	Amount
Chloroquine	10	3,000	30,000
Aspirin	10	2,000	20,000
Seller		Total	50,000

Daily use/cash record

The daily use/cash record has to be filled on a daily basis and in particular when payments are made for dispensed drugs. The following data could be transferred from the duplicate copies of the receipt book to the daily use/cash record sheet when the last patient (client) for the day has been served:

- Date,
- Name of patient,
- Receipt number,
- Quantity of each drug dispensed,
- Money collected from the patient.

Draw a line under the last entry for the day in your daily use/cash record sheet using a red pen. The quantity of drugs is expressed as number of tablets (for tablets) or volume in ml. (for liquids) dispensed. Add up the quantities of each drug dispensed and cash collected to give the details of daily transactions.

Daily/use Cash Record Bank

			Item									Daily cash received	Signature	
Date	Patient's name	Rec. No.												

Financial record book

The total daily cash from the column "CASH RECEIVED" of a daily use/cash record should be transferred to the financial record book (FRB) and the new balance calculated in the FRB as shown in table

Example of Financial Record Book

Date	Cash collected	Cash paid out	Balance	Remarks
8/7/00	B/F		210,000	
9/7/00	15,100		225,000	
10/7/00	5,060		230,160	
11/7/00	6,960		237,120	
12/7/00	9,860		46,980	
15/7/00	11,340	20,000*	58,320	*Paid to CMS
16/7/00	17,100		75,420	
17/7/00	6,705		82,125	
18/7/00	980		83,106	
19/7/00	7,565		90,670	
22/7/00	12,420		103,090	

***Cash in hand* = 103,090**

Audited on 23/7/00 by ________________________________ Chairman of ________________ health committee.

Dispensary Data Flow

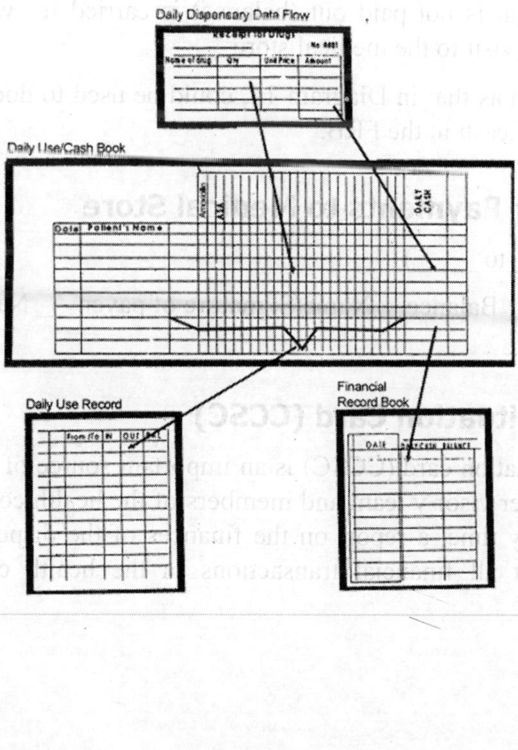

Custody of cash

Commercial banks usually do not have branches in most villages where health centres are located. It is, therefore, important to adopt convenient methods for securing all cash and always having money available for the replenishment of drugs.

The following procedures can be helpful in the handling of cash:

- Locally-made durable safe cash should be provided and buried in the floor in such a way that it cannot easily be located by other people. This safe should be used in such a way that once money has been deposited, it can only be taken out in the presence of a member of the health committee or super visor y team who has one of the keys.
- Purchase money orders with cash collected. Address such money orders to the medical store, if possible, and keep in the safe for making payment to the medical store during the next supply.
- Take money along for making payments for supplies whenever a trip is made to the medical store.
- The deliver y team could collect cash for supplies made to the health centre when delivering supplies.
- Only person from the central store team should collect money from the health centre!
- Any amount that is not paid out (balance) is carried for ward and used to pay during the next visit to the medical store.
- A receipt, such as that in Diagram 14, could be used to document the collection and payment of cash in the FRB.

Model Receipt for Payments to Medical Store

Turnover (From ______to _____) _____

Paid to central store __ Balance _ Name/Signature of payer __ Name/Signature of receiver ______ Date __

Current Capital Situation Card (CCSC)

The current capital situation card (CCSC) is an important source of financial information for the dispensary, super visor y team and members of the health committee. It should be possible to give, at any time, a report on the finances of the dispensary using the CCS card. This means that all financial transactions in the health centre dispensary are documented.

This document is used to follow up the value of stock and cash in the dispensary at any time. When a drug consignment is received, the cash value of stock at the dispensary increases. When an internal drug return is made, it reduces the dispensary's value of stock. At any time, the value of stock/cash should be equivalent to the figure on the CCSC.

The following transactions are recorded on the CCSC as shown in Diagram 15:

- When drugs are received, their total value is entered in the column "SUPPLY" and this is added to the previous balance.
- Cash paid to the medical store should be entered in the column "CASH PAID" and subtracted from the previous balance.
- All internal drug returns should also be expressed in cash and entered in the column "IDR" wit a red pen and subtracted from the previous balance. Note "IDR" under "REMARKS".
- Any price revision is entered in the column "SUPPLY" and added to or subtracted from the previous balance depending on whether the revision has resulted in an increase or decrease in the value of stock. Note "Price Revision" under "REMARKS".
- Whenever there is an inventor y-taking exercise, enter the value of stock taking in the column "BALANCE". The balance represents the amount of cash in hand and the drugs not dispensed (in stock) reflected as cash.

Name of Dispensary: *Gazawa*

Date	Supply	IDR	Cash	Balance Paid	Remarks
8/1/97	2,000,000			2,000,000	1st supply
8/97					
2/4/97				1,480,000	
2/4/97			520,000	2,084,00	
2/4/97	604,000			1,897,955	Supply
2/4/97				1,987,205	IDR(00142)
1/96	89,250	186,045			Pricerevision
28/6/97				1,387,205	
28/6/97				2,108,305	
28/6/97				2,108,305	
26/9/97	721,100		60,000	2,928,250	Supply
26/9/97				2,222,515	Stock Taking
	820,045				Supply

Monthly Return Form

The monthly return form is used at the end of each month to collect data for the medical store. This data will help the medical store to assess monthly consumption in the health centre and determine the future purchases at the health centre. This financial progress of the dispensary in relation to attendance at the health centre can also be assessed with the data. The information on the monthly return form (Diagram 16) is:

- Cash collected for the month (as in the FRB),
- Total number of patients that attended the health centre. Information provided by the head of the health centre,
- Quantities of each drug dispensed for the month (refer to daily use record or the daily use/cash record sheet.

Example of Dispensary Monthly Return Form

Dispensary: ____________________ Month and Year:

Monthly turnover (in local currency): ____________________

(Refer to FRB)

Health centre attendance for month: ____________________

Items sold during the month Quantity

Acetylsalicylic acid 500 mg tab ____________

Acetyl salicylic acid 250 mg tab ____________

Benzyl benzoate 25% lotion ____________

Chloroquine 100 mg tablet

Diethyl carbamazine 100 mg tablet ____________

Folic acid 5 mg tablet

Name of health worker: ____________

Signature of health worker: ____________

Date:

Inventory Form

The inventory form is used at the end of each financial year or at any time it becomes necessary to undertake an inventor y exercise in the dispensary. Both shortages and excesses can be found in the exercise. In either situation, a thorough investigation needs to be done (e.g. reviewing all additions and subtractions in the inventor y sheets). It is advisable to carry out an inventor y exercise at six-monthly intervals (or even quarterly) in order to identify any problems early enough rather than waiting for the end of the year. A representative of both the medical store and the health committee should participate in the inventory exercise. The following activities should be carried out during the inventory:

- Any cash in hand should be counted first and included in the inventor y figures.
- Any supply made before the inventory must be counted with the other items.
- Count all drugs in the store and dispensing area and record the numbers. Use a tablet counter to prevent contamination.
- Do not open full tins and packages to count the contents.
- Verify all full tins and packages to make sure that their contents are intact.
- Calculate the total value of stock by adding the values of all items.
- Compare this number with the current balance in the CCSC. The two should correspond if there has been efficient management of stock and cash during the period being audited.
- These figures will be used by an external auditor to prepare a balance sheet for the dispensary.
- The health worker should pay for any deficits established at the end of the audit.
- Profits declared in the audit report should be put back into the health system.

Example of Inventory Form

Place: Date

Item	Quantity	Unit Price	Total Cost
Acetylsalicylic acid 500 mg tablet			
Cotrimoxazole 400/800 mg tablet			
Benzyl benzoate 25% lotion B/100 ml	________		
Chloroquine 150 mg tablet			
Mebendazole 100 mg tablet			
Folic acid 5 mg tablet			
Total:	________		

30 ________

800 ________

500 ________

10 ________

10 ________

5 ________

Cash in hand: ________

Total capital: ______________________________

Amount on CCSC: ______________________________

Deficit/Surplus amount: ______________________________

Name/Signature of health worker: ______________________________

Name/Signature of head of centre: ______________________________

Name/Signature of health committee representative: ______________________________

Name/Signature of person taking over Dispensary, where applicable): _

Storage of Documents

For easy reference, documents should be numbered and put into different files. Various colors of files may be used for easy reference. The following documents should be put into different files:

- Daily use/cash record,
- Financial documents (e.g. IDR),
- Requisition/deliver y form,
- General correspondence,
- Miscellaneous.

Keep all used documents (e.g. receipt booklets, FRB, stock cards, CCSC) in safe custody for at least five years before they are thrown away.

Security measures in the dispensary

Necessary security measures in the dispensary must be implemented in order to avoid theft.

1. **Doors, windows, roofs and ceilings**

   Install an inner wooden door shutter and an outer metallic door shutter as shown in Diagram 18. All locks on the door should be functioning well. Ensure that all the doors are closed and locked at the end of each day. There should be one window in the dispensary to provide light for serving patients. The window should have strong burglar bars and a metallic shutter. The roof and ceiling of the building should be made of materials that will prevent any illegal entry into the dispensary.

2. **Safe and keys**

   A solid safe locally made to reduce cost should be installed in the dispensary for deposit of cash from daily sales. The safe should be buried in the floor in the dispensary in an area not accessible to other people. Keys should be kept by the individual responsible for the dispensary at all times. In the absence of the dispenser, the head of the health centre should make alternative arrangements for safe custody of the keys.

3. **Watchman**

An honest watchman should be employed to keep watch over the health centre and dispensary on a regular basis.

Handing over the dispensary

The dispenser may have to be away for one of the following reasons:

- Annual leave,
- Maternity leave,
- Sick leave.

The chairman of the health committee and the head of the health centre should make arrangements for temporary staff to serve in the dispensary during the absence of regular staff. Use the inventory form to establish the current stock with the person taking over. The out- going and incoming staff should sign the inventor y, and the health committee representative and head of the health centre should endorse it. Cash should be personally handed to the person taking over. Do not take any money away. Send a copy of the "handing over" note to the head of the health centre. Upon return from leave, the regular dispenser should follow the same procedure in taking over. In an emergency, the head of the health centre should arrange adequate coverage of the dispensary for the period of the emergency.

What to do in case of burglary

If there is any burglar y in the dispensary, follow this procedure:

- Do not go into the dispensary, and do not make any sale.
- Write and inform the head of the health centre and the chairman of the health committee.
- Follow up so that the head of the health centre reports immediately to the police.
- An inventor y of the dispensary similar to Diagram 17 should be done in the presence of the police or any other person designated by the head of the health centre.
- Compare the inventor y stock with the stock on the bin (stock) cards or daily use/cash record so as to assess the quantities of drugs stolen.

- A copy of the report of inventor y should be sent to the head of the health centre and to the medical store.
- The health committee should immediately reinstate the necessary security measures to prevent further burglary.
- Start sales only after the head of the health centre and the health committee so authorize.

Supervision/inspection

1. Role of supervision/inspection

Two teams should be involved in conducting inspection of the dispensary. The first is the team from the appropriate authority. A pharmacist should be a member of this team. The second team is represented by some members of the health committee.

Among other duties, the team should do the following:

- Ensure that drugs are properly arranged on shelves in the dispensary.
- Check that security measures are in place.
- Collect a few names with dates at random from receipt books, cross-check with the health centre consultation register and verify if those patients were actually consulted before coming to the dispensary.
- Recalculate at random the figures in the FRB to ensure that they are correct.
- In consultation with the health committee, make payments following laid down criteria.
- Decide with the health committee who will be responsible for deficits and surpluses.
- Make advance payment of salary to the health committee who will later pay the health worker on a monthly basis.
- Pay incentives where approved.
- Recommend to the health committee further work to be done in the dispensary.
- Give on-the-job training so that records are always kept up-to-date.
- Establish a report on-the-spot on observations and leave a copy in the health centre.
- Confirms the availability of all approved drugs on the list.

Role of Health Committee

The health committee should be mobilized to realize the following in proper functioning of the dispensary:

- Go through previous inspection reports made by the appropriate authority and note any action to be taken.
- Check the general cleanliness of the dispensary.
- Comparé monthly turnover at the dispensary in relation to the number of patients that were seen at the health centre.
- Confirm the availability of all approved drugs on the list in the dispensary.

The committee has to meet on a regular basis with the head of the health centre to plan activities for the health centre and dispensary and prepare strategies for the implementation of planned activities. The health committee should be mobilized to do the following:

- Oversee necessary security measures in the dispensary.
- Provide adequate furniture for the centre.
- Procure shelves for the drugs.
- Use an appropriate method to select a candidate to work in the dispensary.
- Follow up training of selected candidates at the medical store.
- Engage the trained candidate on contract.
- Inspect financial documents and detect any deficits early enough.
- Check that all administrative records in the dispensary are up-to-date.
- Ensure maintenance, cleanliness and proper-set up of the dispensary.
- Participate in handing over the dispensary in case of any absence.
- Sensitize the population on the advantages of the use of the dispensary.
- Assist in receiving drugs for the health centre, when necessary.
- Assist in all inventor y taking.
- Employ a watchman for the dispensary and health centre.

Active Ingredient — that portion of a drug dosage form that has therapeutic properties.

Basic Unit — the smallest unit in which a drug can be conveniently dispensed or administered.

Brand or Trade Name —this is a name given to a drug product by its manufacturer. Only the company that has the trade name for this product manufactures it or has it manufactured under license.

Branded Generic—Generic drug product marketed under brand name.

Central Store—A store within a health care deliver y system charged with the storage and distribution of drugs.

Community Health Worker—A trained health worker designated to work within the community and offering curative, preventive and promotive health services.

Current Capital Situation Card (CCSC) — A card showing the financial situation of a dispensary of any given time.

Delivery (Lead) Time — The time between which an order for new stock is placed and the time it is received.

Dispensary — An area suitably designed for the preparation and distribution of drugs to the patients.

Dispensary Store — A store for keeping stock of drugs within the dispensary area.

Dispense — To prepare and supply to a patient a course of therapy on the basis of a prescription.

Dispenser — A general term for anyone who dispenses drugs. It is specifically used to mean anyone who is not a graduate pharmacist but is trained to dispense medications, maintain stock records and assist in procurement activities.

Dispensing—The preparation and distribution of a course of therapy to a patient, with appropriate instructions, based on a prescription.

Dosage Form — The form of a finished drug product (e.g. tablets, capsule, elixir, suppository).

Drug Potency — The extent to which a drug product contains the specified amount of active ingredient.

Drug Product—A unique combination of drug(s), strength and dosage form (e.g., paracetamol 500 mg tab) in which a drug is administered.

Drug Product Strength — This is the quantity of active ingredient(s) of a drug(s) in a dosage form.

Drug Use — The process of diagnosing, prescribing, labeling, packaging and dispensing to ensure adherence of the patient to the given drug treatment.

Expiration Date — The expiration date indicates the date after which the manufacturer can no longer guarantee the stability, safety and potency of a drug.

FEFO — A system of stock movement based on First to Expire First Out.

FIFO — A system of stock movement based on First In First Out.

Generic Name — A generic name is the unique INN given to the active ingredient(s) of a drug and is recognized worldwide.

Generic Product — A generic product is a drug that is manufactured by an authorized manufacturer under nonproprietary or approved names. A generic product may be marketed under its generic name or brand name.

Health Centre — The lowest level of public health care establishment to which qualified health workers are deployed.

Health Committee — The committee selected from ordinary citizens in the community to over- see the proper running of health facilities within the community, including the managing of drug supplies.

Inventory — The sum of all items held in stock at any time.

International Nonproprietary Name (INN) — Internationally recognized name for a chemical entity.

Labeling — Placing written or symbolic instructions on the immediate container in which drugs are dispensed.

Prescriber —A qualified health worker authorized to write prescriptions.

Prescribing — The act of determining what medication the patient should have and the correct dosage and duration of treatment.

Prescription — A set of instructions written by a qualified or authorized prescriber to a dispenser for supply of drugs and provision of information to the patient.

Procurement —The process of acquiring supplies, including those obtained by purchase, donation and manufacture.

Rational Drug Use — The rational use of drugs implies the selection of an appropriate drug for the correct patient; given in the correct dose, dosage form, route, frequency and duration. The patient must also receive appropriate instructions on how to use the drugs.

RI — stands for request indicator, the lowest stock level of a drug product before an order is placed for new stock.

Revolving Drug Fund—A drug sales programme in which revenues from drug fees are used to replenish drug supplies.

Shelf Life — The length of time a drug may be stored without affecting its usability, safety, purity or potency.

Stock (Bin) Card — A card that records receipts, issues and balances of items held in a store. The bin card is kept in the store with the physical stock.

Unit of Issue of Drug from the Dispensary—At the dispensary, the unit of issue is a tablet, capsule, bottle or vial because only a few of those are dispensed to a patient.

Unit of Issue of Drug from the Store—The unit of issue for a request from the store is usually full of tins, packets or boxes of say 1,000 tablets or 100 vials, as the case may be.

User Fees — Charges paid by the user for a service.

8.2 Community Pharmacy Principles and Practices

Over the past four decades there has been a trend for pharmacy practice to move away from its original focus on medicine supply towards a more inclusive focus on patient care. The role of the pharmacist has evolved from that of a compounder and supplier of pharmaceutical products towards that of a provider of services and information and ultimately that of a provider of patient care. Increasingly, the pharmacist's task is to ensure that a patient's drug therapy is appropriately indicated, the most effective available, the safest possible, and convenient for the patient. By taking direct responsibility for individual patient's medicine related needs, pharmacists can make a unique contribution to the outcome of drug therapy and to their patients' quality of life. The new approach has been given the name pharmaceutical care. The most generally accepted definition of this new approach is:

"Pharmaceutical care is the responsible provision of drug therapy for the purpose of achieving definite outcomes that improve a patient's quality of life". (Hepler and Strand, 1990)[2]

In adopting this definition in 1998, the International Pharmaceutical Federation (FIP) added one significant amendment: "achieving definite outcomes that improve or maintain a patient's quality of life". The practice of pharmaceutical care is new, in contrast to what pharmacists have been doing for years. Because pharmacists often fail to assume responsibility for this care, they may not adequately document, monitor and review the care given. Accepting such responsibility is essential to the practice of pharmaceutical care.

In order to fulfill this obligation, the pharmacist needs to be able to assume many different functions. The concept of the seven-star pharmacist, introduced by WHO and taken up by FIP in 2000 in its policy statement on Good Pharmacy Education Practice, sees the pharmacist as a caregiver, communicator, decision - maker, teacher, life-long learner, leader and manager.

The knowledge base of pharmacy graduates is changing. As these graduates move into practice, so pharmacy practice itself will change, to reflect the new knowledge base. However, pharmacists already in practice were mainly educated on the basis of the old paradigm of pharmaceutical product focus. If the pharmacists are to contribute effecetively to the new patiencentred pharmaceutical practice, they must have the opportunity to acquire the new knowledge and skills required for their new role. To do this they must become life - long learners, one of the roles of the new pharmacist. There is an important and rewarding professional role for pharmacists beyond pharmaceutical product supply and management. The pharmaceutical product should be seen not as an end in itself – as often emphasized in pharmaceutical education and practice – but rather as a means to an end. Where medicines are used for the greatest possible benefit of each individual patient and of society as a whole, this will result in improvements in health as well as cost savings. New pharmacists should have the knowledge and skills needed to take up their new role and responsibilities and to function as collaborative members of the health care team the number of medicines on the market has increased dramatically over the last few decades, bringing some real innovations but also considerable challenges in controlling the quality and rational use of medicines.

In developing and industrialized countries alike, efforts to provide health care, including pharmaceutical care, are facing new challenges. These include the rising costs of health care, limited financial resources, a shortage of human resources in the health care sector, inefficient health systems, the huge burden of disease, and the changing social, techno - logical, economic and political environment which most countries face. While globalization has brought countries closer together in trade of products and services and in recognition of academic degrees and diplomas, for example, it has led to rapid changes in the health care environment and to new complexities due to increased travel and migration. Access to medicines of assured quality remains a major concern worldwide. One third of the world's population does not yet have regular access to essential medicines. For many people, the affordability of medicines is a major constraint. Those hardest hit are patients in developing and transitional economies, where 50% –90% of medicines purchased are paid for out- of-pocket. The burden falls most heavily on the poor, who are not adequately protected either by current policies or by health insurance. The logistical aspects of distribution – often see as the pharmacist's traditional role, especially in health institutions – represents another challenge. Moreover, in many developing countries 10% –20% of sampled medicines fail quality control tests.

A Statement on Ensuring the Quality and the Safety of Medicinal Products to Protect the Patient was jointly signed by FIP and the International Federation of Pharmaceutical Manufacturers Associations (IFPMA) in 2000. Its common goal is to protect the well - being of patients in all parts of the world by ensuring that all medicinal products are of good quality and proven safety and efficacy. Both the pharmaceutical industry and the pharmaceutical profession also recognized the need for a regulatory and marketing environment which encourages investment in new innovative medicines and allows their timely introduction and availability to patients worldwide another major challenge is ensuring that medicines are used rationally. This requires that patients receive medications appropriate to their clinical needs, in doses that meet their own individual requirements for an adequate period of time, and at the lowest cost to them and their community. However, rational use of medicines remains the exception rather than the rule. For those people who do receive medicines, more than half of all prescriptions are incorrect and more than half of the people involved fail to take them correctly. In addition, there is growing concern at the increase in the global spread of antimicrobial resistance, a major public health problem. A recent report by WHO4 revealed findings of up to 90% resistance to original first- line antibiotics such as ampicillin and cotrimoxazole for shigellosis, up to 70% resistance to penicillin for pneumonia and bacterial meningitis, up to 98% resistance to penicillin for gonorrhoea, and up to 70% resistance to both penicillins and cephalosporins for hospital-acquired staphylococcus aureus infections. In 2000, the FIP Council adopted a Statement of Policy on Control of Resistance to Antimicrobials5 which provides a list of recommendations for governments and health authorities on the appropriate measures needed to combat antimicrobial resistance. The statement also declares that pharmacists are ready to collaborate actively with physicians, regulatory authorities and other health professionals in efforts to combat antimicrobial resistance and to participate in public information campaigns on this. These challenges – both to access to medicines of assured quality and to their rational use – underscore the urgency of the need for global health sector reform. Against this backdrop of ongoing and profound changes in health care delivery systems, a paradigm shift in pharmacy practice is occurring. Public health interventions, pharmaceutical care, rational medicine use and effective medicines supply management are key components of an accessible, sustainable, affordable and equitable health care system which ensures the efficacy, safety and quality of medicines. It is clear that pharmacy has an important role to play in the health sector reform process. To do so, however, the role of the pharmacist needs to be redefined and reoriented. Pharmacists have the potential to improve therapeutic outcomes and patients' quality of life within available resources, and must position themselves at the forefront of the health care system. The movement towards pharmaceutical care is a critical factor in this process. While efforts to communicate the correct information to patients are as important as providing the medicine itself,6 pharmacists also have a vital contribution to make to patient care through managing drug therapy and concurrent non - prescription or alternative therapies. Over the past 40 years, the pharmacist's role has changed from that of compounder and dispenser to one of "drug therapy manager". This involves responsibilities to ensure that wherever medicines are provided and used, quality products are selected, procured, stored, distributed, dispensed and administered so that they contribute to the health of patients, and not to their harm. The scope of pharmacy practice now includes patient centered care with all the cognitive functions of counseling, providing drug information and monitoring drug therapy, as well as technical aspects of pharmaceutical services, including medicines supply management. It is in the additional role of managing drug therapy that pharmacists can now make a vital contribution to patient care.

What is health?

Pharmacy practice does not take place in a vacuum, but in the health care environment. It aims to improve health. Health is a broad concept which can embody a wide range of meanings from technical to moral and philosophical. It is perhaps the most important human resource. The most quoted definition of health was formulated in the Constitution of WHO in 1946. It is a positive definition which stresses well - being.

"Health is a state of complete physical, mental and social well-being, not merely the absence of disease or infirmity." (WHO, 1946)[7]

Over the years, WHO has taken forward the debate and has revised its definition of health. "Health is the extent to which an individual or group is able, on the one hand, to realize aspirations and satisfy needs; and, on the other hand, to change or cope with the environment. Health is therefore, seen as a resource for everyday life, not an object of living; it is a positive concept emphasizing social and personal resources, as well as physical capacities."

There is no single definition that unifies the perceptions about health. Our understanding of it depends on the many different contexts in which life is lived and health is perceived. Health is a human right and access to health care, including essential medicines, is a derived right. Health is essential for sustainable economic and social development. For example, in many parts of the world, the HIV/AIDS pandemic reduces economic achievements and national health outcomes. Health is thus a very precious resource.

The Pharmacy Profession

Medicinal therapy is the most frequently used form of treatment intervention in any health practice setting. Its use has grown dramatically as the population has aged, the prevalence of chronic disease has increased, new infectious diseases have emerged and the range of effective medications has broadened. In addition, more and more so - called "life -style medicines" – treatments for ailments like baldness, dry skin, wrinkles or erectile dysfunction – are being marketed. Increasingly medicines can be purchased in new settings, and are handled by non - pharmacists. Compounding has been largely replaced by the commercial manufacture of nearly all formulations. Medicines can be bought in supermarkets, in drug stores or at markets. They can also be obtained by mail order or over the Internet; they are sold by medical practitioners and dispensed by computerized dispensing machines. Under these circumstances it is pertinent to ask the following questions: Do we still need pharmacists? What is the value of pharmacy services? Professions exist to serve society. Hence the mission of the pharmacy profession must address the needs of society and individual patients. At one time, the acts of deciding on drug therapy and implementing it were relatively simple, safe and inexpensive. The physician prescribed and the pharmacist dispensed. However, there is substantial evidence to show that the traditional method of prescribing and dispensing medication is no longer appropriate to ensure safety, effectiveness and adherence to drug therapy. The consequences of medicine - related errors are costly in terms of hospitalizations, physician visits, laboratory tests and remedial therapy. In developed countries, 4%–10% of all hospital in- patients experiences an adverse drug reaction – mainly due to the use of multiple drug therapy, especially in the elderly and patients with chronic diseases. In the USA, for example, it is the 4th–6th leading cause of death and is estimated to cost up to US$130 billion a year. Elsewhere, in the UK it accounted for £466 million (over US$812 million) in 2004. In 1998, FIP published a Statement of Professional Standards on Medication Errors Associated with Prescribed Medication which aims to define the term "medication error" and to suggest a standard nomenclature to categorize such errors and their severity. The Statement also makes recommendations to members of the health care delivery system designed to improve safety in the manufacturing, ordering, labelling, dispensing, administration and use of medicines.

While appropriate drug therapy is safer and more cost- effective than other treatment alter- natives, there is no doubt that the personal and economic consequences of inappropriate drug therapy are enormous. It is important for society to be assured that spending on pharmaceuticals represents good value for money. In view of their extensive academic back- ground and their traditional role in preparing and providing medicines and informing patients about their use, pharmacists are well positioned to assume responsibility for the management of drug therapy. The accountability of health professionals for their actions is another major issue in health care provision. In the traditional relationship between the doctor as prescriber and the pharmacist as dispenser, the prescriber was accountable for the results of pharmacotherapy. That situation is changing in rapidly evolving health systems. The practice of pharmaceutical care assumes the pharmacist to be responsible for patients under their care, and society will not only accept that assumption but hold the profession to it. At the same time, other professions such as medical doctors, nurses and medical and pharmacy assistants also acquire competence and feel confident to function as drug therapy managers. In some countries they are moving aggressively to do so. Pharmacy students and practitioners must be educated to assume the responsibility for managing drug therapy, so that they can maintain and expand their position in the health care system and are compensated for their role in providing pharmaceutical care.

The accountability of health professionals for their actions is another major issue in health care provision. In the traditional relationship between the doctor as prescriber and the pharmacist as dispenser, the prescriber was accountable for the results of pharmacotherapy. That situation is changing in rapidly evolving health systems. The practice of pharmaceutical care assumes the pharmacist to be responsible for patients under their care, and society will not only accept that assumption but hold the profession to it.

At the same time, other professions such as medical doctors, nurses and medical and pharmacy assistants also acquire competence and feel confident to function as drug therapy managers. In some countries they are moving aggressively to do so. Pharmacy students and practitioners must be educated to assume the responsibility for managing drug therapy, so that they can maintain and expand their position in the health care system and are compensated for their role in providing pharmaceutical care.

Dispensing is, and must remain, a responsibility of the pharmacy profession. While fewer pharmacists may be actually engaged in dispensing medication, predominantly in rural areas, more pharmacists will be managing the dispensing process and assuming responsibility for its quality and outcomes. While change may generate potential threats, it can also open up immense opportunities. The pharmacy profession has a responsibility to identify new opportunities for pharmacy practice in a changing health sector context, to assess and to test them, and to demonstrate their ability to implement them successfully.

New Dimensions of Community Pharmacy Practice

Pharmaceutical Care

Pharmaceutical care is a ground-breaking concept in the practice of pharmacy which emerged in the mid-1970s. It stipulates that all practitioners should assume responsibility for the outcomes of drug therapy in their patients. It encompasses a variety of services and functions – some new to pharmacy, others traditional – which are determined and provided by the pharmacists serving individual patients. The concept of pharmaceutical care also includes emotional commitment to the welfare of patients as individuals who require and deserve pharmacists' compassion, concern and trust. However, pharmacists often fail to accept responsibility for this extent of care. As a result, they may not adequately document, monitor and review the care given. Accepting such responsibility is essential to the practice of pharmaceutical care.

Pharmaceutical care can be tendered to individuals and populations. "Population - based pharmaceutical care" uses demographic and epidemiological data to establish formularies or medicine lists, develop and monitor pharmacy policies, develop and manage pharmacy networks, prepare and analyze reports of drug utilization/costs, conduct drug utilization reviews and educate providers on medicine policies and procedures.

Without individual pharmaceutical care, however, no system can manage drug therapy and monitor medicine - related illness effectively. The population - based functions identified above need to occur either before or after patients are seen and provide valuable information, but cannot replace patient-specific services while patients are being seen. Medicine - related illnesses occur frequently even with medicines that are in a system's formulary or medicines list, since these medicines are often prescribed, administered or used inappropriately. Patients need pharmacists' services at the time they are receiving care. Successful pharmacotherapy is specific for each patient. It includes individual drug therapy decisions, reaching concordance (an agreement between the patient and the health care provider on the therapeutic outcome and how it may be achieved), and critical patient monitoring activities. For each individual patient's drug treatment, the pharmacist develops a care plan together with the patient. Patients can then contribute to successful outcomes by taking part of the responsibility for their own care and not relying solely on caregivers, in the former paternalistic style. A stepwise approach to patient care is described in detail in Chapter 2.

Pharmaceutical care does not exist in isolation from other health care services.[9] It must be provided in collaboration with patients, physicians, nurses and other health care providers. Pharmacists are responsible directly to patients for the cost, quality and results of pharmaceutical care. In 1998, a Statement of Professional Standards in Pharmaceutical Care was adopted by FIP. It provides guidance to pharmacists and national health care organizations as they begin to implement broad pharmaceutical services in their countries. FIP supports them concept of pharmaceutical care but recognizes the individual needs of different countries.

Evidence-based Pharmacy

In an increasingly complex health care environment, it has become difficult to compare the effectiveness of different treatments. Health care interventions can no longer be based on opinion or individual experience alone. Scientific evidence, built up from good quality research, is used as a guide, and adapted to each individual patient's circumstances.

Meeting Patient's Needs

In patient centered health care, the first challenges are to identify and meet the changing needs of patients. Pharmacists need to ensure that people can access medicines or pharmaceutical advice easily and, as far as possible, in a way and at a time and place of their own choosing. They can empower patients by engaging them in dialogue to communicate knowledge which enables them to manage their own health and treatment. Although patients are exposed to a wide range of information from package inserts, promotional materials, advertising in the media and through the Internet, this information is not always accurate or complete. The pharmacist can help informed patients to become accurately informed patients by offering unbiased relevant evidence-based information and by pointing to reliable sources. Counseling on disease prevention and lifestyle modification will pro-mote public health, while shared decision-making on how to take medicines through a concordant approach will optimize health outcomes, reduce the number of medicine-related adverse events, cut the amount of medicine which is wasted and improve adherence to medical treatment.

Chronic patient care – HIV/AIDS

Throughout history the world has never faced a health challenge like the HIV/AIDS pandemic. In order to respond adequately, health systems, especially in resource-limited set-tings, are undergoing a shift in health care provision from acute health care services to chronic patient care. With an estimated 40 million people living with HIV worldwide and 3 million people dying of AIDS in 2004 alone, the HIV/AIDS pandemic represents an extraordinary human, human rights and humanitarian crisis and a tragedy of immense social, economic and public health impact. In 2004, the world's nursing, medical and pharmacy leaders issued a resolution stating that all health professionals should commit the necessary funds and resources to rise to the challenge of HIV/AIDS. Health professionals, including pharmacists, should also act as strong advocates and social leaders.

The availability of financial resources for the provision of antiretroviral therapy (ART) in resource - limited settings is steadily increasing. The United Nations Declaration of Commitment on HIV/AIDS and the World Health Organization's announcement declaring HIV/AIDS to be a global public health emergency the urgent need for scaling up ART in resource -limited settings. In 2003, WHO made a commitment to treat 3 million people by the end of 2005. More recently, in July 2005 leaders of the G - 8 nations committed to the goal of scaling up access to HIV/AIDS treatment, care and prevention services with a view to moving towards universal access to ART by 2010.

Human resources are the most critical component of health systems and delivery. However, in many of the communities where ART is urgently needed, there is a significant shortage of skilled human resources to provide routine health care. People with many different skills (including management, administration, supply management, clinical care and community - based care) are needed for the safe and effective delivery of ART. Successful outcomes in delivering ART have relied on strategies to reduce dependence on highly skilled health professionals by sharing aspects of patient care and follow - up among different cadres of health care workers, the community and family members. To address the lack of highly skilled human resources, existing skills should be upgraded to cope with the demands of delivering ART and care services. Strategies will depend on health sector policies and the chosen service delivery approach.

One of the key health professionals that must be mobilized and involved is the pharmacist. Pre -service and ongoing training of pharmacists in providing HIV/AIDS prevention, care and treatment is essential. The content and delivery of training for pharmacists will depend on their allocated roles and responsibilities. Since pharmacists' knowledge, attitudes and behavior influence the way in which HIV care, treatment and prevention services are delivered and used, adherence to chronic HIV/AIDS care and treatment is one of the key areas where pharmacists need to be involved.

In 2003, the FIP Council adopted a Statement of Professional Standards on the Role of the Pharmacist in Encouraging Adherence to Long Term Treatments. There are many reasons for seeking to improve adherence to long-term therapies for chronic diseases such as HIV/ AIDS. The benefits include better health outcomes and improved quality of life and improved safety for the patient, as well as cost savings for all stakeholders. Pharmacists and other health professionals providing services involving treatment with medicines should make every effort to assist patients who wish to do so to improve adherence to their treatments.

In 1997, the role of pharmacists in efforts to combat HIV/AIDS was acknowledged in a joint Declaration by FIP and WHO. In 2004, FIP launched an International Network for Pharmacists on HIV/AIDS (www.fip.org/hivaids) which focuses on three main areas: training, documentation and exchange of experience. It includes training modules, policy documents, useful publications, links to relevant national and international organizations, an events calendar to which additional events can be added, and a mailing list to allow pharmacists to exchange points of view and experiences. This network will help to link up pharmacists throughout the world working in the field of HIV/AIDS and will help pharmacists to become leaders in the battle against the pandemic.

Self-medication

In 1996, a Statement of Principle, entitled Self- Care (including Self-Medication): The Professional Role of the Pharmacist, was adopted by the FIP Council. It sets out FIP's policies regarding the responsibilities of pharmacists concerning advice on self-medication. Areas covered by the statement include pharmacy premises, sales promotion, advice on the treatment of symptoms, specific requests for medicines (i.e., by name), referral notes and confidentiality. This Statement was followed in 1999 by a joint Declaration on Responsible Self-Medication which was signed by the FIP Council together with the World Self-Medication Industry (WSMI). This provides guidance to pharmacists, patients and the industry regarding the safe and effective use of non-prescription medicines.

The Pharmacist's Expanding Role

As the experts in medicines, pharmacists have always been known as an accessible and trusted source of advice and treatment. Today, their contribution to health care is developing in new ways to support patients in their use of medicines and as a part of clinical decision-making across the range of specialisms.

Pharmacies are open all day, are convenient for most people to get to and there is no need for an appointment to see the pharmacist. All this makes pharmacies the natural first port of call for help with common ailments.

Self- treatment of common ailments is becoming more popular as a growing range of safe, effective medicines becomes available from the pharmacy without the need for a doctor's prescription. Pharmacists have the expertise to advise both on the choice of medicines and their safe and effective use. The right choice of self- treatment can prevent some conditions from developing or help others clear up more quickly.

Quality Assurance of Pharmaceutical Care Services

A basic concept which should underlie all health care services and pharmacy practice is that of assuring the quality of patient care activities. Donabedian defined the three elements of quality assurance in health care as being structure, process and outcome. The processes used in the various settings of pharmacy practice all comply with the same principles, although they may differ in application. They will be described in detail in this handbook. Quality assurance processes of pharmaceutical care services serve to contribute towards better patient outcomes.

Definitions of the quality assurance of pharmaceutical care should encompass both technical standards and patients' expectations. While no single definition of health service quality applies in all situations, the following common definition is a helpful guide:

"*Quality assurance is that set of activities that are carried out to monitor and improve performance so that the health care provided is as effective and as safe as possible*".

Quality assurance can also be defined as "all activities that contribute to defining, designing, assessing, monitoring, and improving the quality of health care". These activities can be performed as part of the accreditation of pharmacies, supervision of pharmacy health workers, or other efforts to improve the performance and the quality of health services.

The Quality Assurance Project of the Center for Human Sciences in Bethesda, USA, lists four core principles which have emerged to guide quality assurance in health care:

1. Focus on the client/patient
2. Focus on systems and processes
3. Focus on measurement
4. Focus on teamwork

The implementation and practice of pharmaceutical care must be supported and improved by measuring, assessing and improving pharmacy practice activities, utilizing the conceptual framework of continuous quality improvement. A key lesson is that in many cases quality of pharmacy services can be improved by making changes to the health care system or pharmacy system without necessarily increasing resources. Improving the processes of pharmacy practice not only creates better outcomes but also reduces cost through eliminating waste, unnecessary work and repetition of work already done. Thus quality improvement must address both the resources (structures) and activities carried out (processes) to ensure or improve the quality of pharmaceutical care (outcomes).

Clinical Pharmacy

The term "clinical pharmacy" was coined to describe the work of pharmacists whose primary job is to interact with the health care team, interview and assess patients, make specific therapeutic recommendations, monitor patient responses to drug therapy and provide medicines information. Clinical pharmacists work primarily in hospitals and acute care settings and provide patient- oriented rather than product-oriented services. In some countries, the pharmacy profession has evolved to the point at which clinical pharmacy with patient-focused practice is no longer the exception but the rule for most pharmacists. Yet clinical pharmacy is still practiced exclusively in inpatient settings and hospitals, where access to patient data and the medical team is available.

The medical record, also known as the patient chart or file, is a legal document including hospital -specific admission information, initial patient history and physical examination, daily progress notes made by health care professionals who interact with the patient, consultations, nursing notes, laboratory results, diagnostic procedures, dietary recommendations, radiology and surgery reports. Most charts also include sections for medication orders and clinical pharmacy progress notes on pharmacokinetic dosing and other relevant therapeutic comments and recommendations.

Clinical pharmacy requires an expert knowledge of therapeutics, a good understanding of disease processes and knowledge of pharmaceutical products. In addition, clinical pharmacy requires strong communication skills with solid knowledge of the medical terminology, drug monitoring skills, provision of medicines information, therapeutic planning skills and the ability to assess and interpret physical and laboratory findings. Pharmacokinetic dosing and monitoring is a special skill and service provided by clinical pharmacists. Clinical pharmacists are often active members of the medical team and accompany ward rounds to contribute to bedside therapeutic discussions. The impact of clinical pharmacy services has been well documented in inpatient settings, and to a lesser extent in ambulatory and community settings. The value and acceptance of clinical pharmacy services were first documented in the 1970s and 1980s. In the USA, many schools of pharmacy have introduced curricula requiring all pharmacy students to study clinical pharmacy, leading to a professional Doctorate of Clinical Pharmacy.

Pharmacovigilence

Medicines safety is another important issue. Because of intense competition among pharmaceutical manufacturers, products may be registered and marketed in many countries simultaneously. As a result, adverse effects may not always be readily identified and so are not monitored systematically. Pharmacovigilence is a structured process for the monitoring and detection of adverse drug reactions (ADRs) in a given context.

Data derived from sources such as Medicines Information, Toxicology and Pharmacovigilence Centers have great relevance and educational value in the management of the safety of medicines. Medicine - related problems, once detected, need to be assessed, analyzed, followed up and communicated to regulatory authorities, health professionals and the public. Pharmacovigilence includes the dissemination of such information. In some cases, medicines may need to be recalled and withdrawn from a market, a process that entails concerted action by all those involved at any point in the medicines supply chain. Pharmacists have an important contribution to make to post-marketing surveillance and pharmacovigilence

The value of professional pharmacist services

Through its impact on individual patients' state of health, pharmaceutical care improves the quality and cost-effectiveness of health care systems. Improvements at the micro-level impinge on the overall situation at the macro-level, i.e., communities benefit when individuals within them enjoy better health. Ultimately the population at large will also benefit as system-wide improvements occur.

Pharmacists' services and involvement in patient centered care have been associated with improved health and economic outcomes, a reduction in medicine-related adverse events, improved quality of life, and reduced morbidity and mortality. These accomplishments have been achieved through gradual expansion of traditional role and, in some cases, through the emergence of collaborative drug therapy management programmes. Nonetheless, the potential for pharmacists to effect dramatic improvements in public health remains largely untapped.

A recent review investigated the effectiveness of professional pharmacist services in terms of consumer outcomes, and where possible, the economic benefits. Its key findings illustrate the value of a range of services, including continuity - of- care after hospital discharge and education to consumers and to health practitioners. Overall, this review demonstrates that there is considerable high quality evidence to support the value of professional pharmacy services in improving patient outcomes or medication use in the community setting. Elsewhere, an Australian study on the economic impact of increased clinical intervention rates in community pharmacy found that adequately trained and remunerated pharmacists generated savings (on health care, medicines and pharmacy practice costs) six times greater than those of a control group with no access to the same education or remuneration. It was estimated that adequately trained and remunerated pharmacists would save the health care system 15 million Australian dollars (approx. US$100 million). An adequate level of remuneration for pharmacists is key to ensuring that they move towards good pharmacy practice, and in particular towards pharmaceutical care. However, efforts to ensure that pharmacists are adequately recompensed will require effective documentation of what pharmacists actually do to improve outcomes as well as agreement by funders that what they do has economic value.

The Pharmacy Practice Activity Classification (PPAC)

As pharmacists increasingly focus their practices on the provision of pharmaceutical care and expect to be compensated for pharmaceutical care services, the need for a consistent and broadly accepted classification of pharmacy practice activities becomes evident. Although many systems exist to record pharmacists' activities, until now the profession has lacked a widely accepted way to describe or document these activities in a common language. The Pharmacy Practice Activity Classification (PPAC) initiated by the American Pharmacists Association (APhA) provides a common language that, if used consistently, will yield comparable data among studies. This in turn can contribute to building databases for statistically sound determinations about pharmacists' patient centered activities and whether they improve patient outcomes and the use of resources. Such systems are already used by other health professions (e.g., medicine, nursing). An important purpose of the PPAC is to provide a solid foundation to support systems for remuneration that can be used for billing.

The PPAC is focused primarily on activities of licensed, practicing pharmacists across the continuum of health care settings. The classification captures a range of activities from traditional dispensing to direct patient care services. It is recognized that pharmacists occupy other roles – in the pharmaceutical industry, administration, regulatory agencies, professional associations, public health, and academia – that are not directly related to patient care. The benefits of consensus on a uniform classification system include: advancing the recognition of pharmaceutical care as a key component of pharmacy practice, leading to an understanding of the value of and need for compensation for the delivery of pharmaceutical care services

The Pharmacy Practice Activity Classification

A. Ensuring appropriate therapy and outcomes

A.1 Ensuring appropriate pharmacotherapy

A.2 Ensuring patient's understanding/adherence to his or her treatment plan

A.3 Monitoring and reporting outcomes

B. Dispensing medications and devices

B.1 Processing the prescription or medicine order

B.2 Preparing the pharmaceutical product

B.3 Delivering the medication or device

C. Health promotion and disease prevention

C.1 Delivering clinical preventive services

C.2 Surveillance and reporting of public health issues

C.3 Promoting safe medication use in society

D. Health systems management

D.1 Managing the practice

D.2 Managing medications throughout the health system

D.3 Managing the use of medications within the health system

D.4 Participating in research activities

D.5 Engaging in interdisciplinary collaboration

- increasing interdisciplinary links and encouraging collaboration with other health care professionals, by defining common goals and patient interventions
- facilitating and standardizing research directed towards establishing the value of services in optimizing patient care
- supporting pharmacists to better manage their practices
- assisting in developing quality assurance systems and quality of care guidelines for practices
- facilitating documentation of pharmaceutical care activities in computer-based patient record systems.

The pharmacist as a member of the health care team

The health care team consists of the patient and all the health care professionals who have responsibility for patient care. This team needs to be well defined, and collaboration needs to be actively sought. Pharmacists have an important role to play in this team. They will need to adapt their knowledge, skills and attitudes to this new role, which integrates traditional pharmaceutical science with clinical aspects of patient care, clinical skills, management and communication skills, active collaboration with medical teams and solving of medicine-related problems. If they are to be recognized as full members of the health care team, pharmacists will need to adopt the essential attitudes required by health professionals working in this area: visibility, responsibility, accessibility in a practice aimed at the general population, commitment to confidentiality and patient orientation. Pharmacists will need to be competent and possess both vision and a voice to fully integrate themselves into the health care team.

The World Health Professions Alliance was established in 1999 to facilitate close collaboration between FIP, the World Medical Association (WMA), International Council of Nurses (ICN) and World Dental Federation (FDI) in support of governments, policy-makers and WHO in order to better deliver cost- effective quality health care worldwide (www.whpa.org). Through this alliance, over 20 million health care professionals can be reached worldwide, providing a valuable source of knowledge and experience.

Pharmacy Practice Settings

The role of the pharmacist takes different forms in various parts of the world. The pharmacist's involvement with pharmaceuticals can be in research and development, formulation, manufacturing, quality assurance, licensing, marketing, distribution, storage, supply, information management, dispensing, monitoring or education. Supply and information management activities have been termed "pharmaceutical services" and continue to form the foundation of pharmacy practice. Pharmacists practice in a wide variety of settings. These include community pharmacy (in retail and other health care settings), hospital pharmacy (in all types of hospital from small local hospitals to large teaching hospitals), the pharmaceutical industry and academia. In addition, pharmacists are involved in health service administration, in research, in inter- national health and in nongovernmental organizations (NGOs).

Levels of practice and decision-making

Pharmacy practice takes place at different levels. The ultimate aim of activities at all these levels is to benefit patients by improving and maintaining their health. Activities at individual patient level comprise all aspects of providing and managing a patient's drug therapy (i.e., pharmaceutical care, including clinical pharmacy services). At this level, decisions are made on issues of pharmaceutical care and triage (i.e., prioritization of care, patient follow-up and therapeutic outcome monitoring).

Some of the activities at the level of supply management in community and hospital pharmacy such as manufacture, compounding, procurement and distribution of medicines are seen as routine or "back office" activities and are not discussed in this handbook. However, these activities remain important, as the availability of medicines of assured quality at affordable prices is a prerequisite for any pharmaceutical care. For official recognition and reimbursement for interventions in the health care system, pharmacists usually need to comply with a wide range of rules relating to health care. Important aspects include terminology, standards, documentation, responsibility and accountability.

At the level of an institution, such as a hospital, clinic, managed care organization or pharmacy, tools used for medicines selection include formularies, standard treatment guide-lines and medicines utilization reviews. These tools are typically developed by Drug and Therapeutics Committees or by National Essential Medicines Committees. The development process is no longer confined to the developing group, but involves professionals at all levels and is increasingly based on clinical evidence rather than isolated expert opinions. These tools should be accepted by individual health care providers and should be implemented.

At the system level (e.g., at national, federal, state or district level), planning, management, legislation, regulation and policy are the enabling environment in which any health care system develops and operates. The system level also includes standards of practice and mandates for pharmacy that are managed at national, federal, regional, state or district level depending on the country. National medicines policies have become an integral part of many countries' national health policies. At the international level, there are moves to harmonize approaches worldwide – an approach that warrants greater attention in view of the global reach of the pharmaceutical industry and pharmacy practice. At community and population level, pharmaceutical practice comprises the activities which support the other levels (i.e., information, education and communication to promote public health, the provision of medicines information, research, dissemination of new information, education and training of staff, consumer groups, community-based organizations and health system researchers).

Health promotion, disease prevention and lifestyle modification are activities at community level that have a public health focus. Pharmacists can offer public health interventions more conveniently than other groups since they are easily accessible and recognized as experts in matters of health. Pharmacists are a trusted source of information and advice on health and medicines. However, they cannot operate in isolation and must accept joint responsibility with all health professionals to serve community and public health goals.

The seven-star pharmacist

To be effective health care team members, pharmacists need skills and attitudes enabling them to assume many different functions. The concept of the "seven-star pharmacist" was introduced by WHO and taken up by FIP in 2000 in its policy statement on Good Pharmacy Education Practice to cover these roles: caregiver, decision-maker, communicator, manager, life-long learner, teacher and leader. For the purposes of this handbook we have added the function of the pharmacist as a researcher.

The roles of the pharmacist are described below and include the following functions:

- ***Caregiver:*** Pharmacists provide caring services. They must view their practice as integrated and continuous with those of the health care system and other health professionals. Services must be of the highest quality.

- ***Decision*** - maker: The appropriate, efficacious, safe and cost- effective use of resources (e.g., personnel, medicines, chemicals, equipment, procedures, practices) should be the foundation of the pharmacist's work. At the local and national levels, pharmacists play a role in setting medicines policy. Achieving this goal requires the ability to evaluate, synthesize data and information and decide upon the most appropriate course of action.
- ***Communicator:*** The pharmacist is in an ideal position to provide a link between pre - scriber and patient, and to communicate information on health and medicines to the public. He or she must be knowledgeable and confident while interacting with other health professionals and the public. Communication involves verbal, non-verbal, listening and writing skills.

Manager: Pharmacists must be able to manage resources (human, physical and financial) and information effectively; they must also be comfortable being managed by others, whether by an employer or the manager/leader of a health care team. More and more, information and its related technology will provide challenges as pharmacists assume greater responsibility for sharing information about medicines and related products and ensuring their quality.

- Life - long- learner: It is impossible to acquire in pharmacy school all the knowledge and experience needed to pursue a life - long career as a pharmacist. The concepts, principles and commitment to life - long learning must begin while attending pharmacy school and must be supported throughout the pharmacist's career. Pharmacists should learn how to keep their knowledge and skills up to date.
- ***Teacher:*** The pharmacist has a responsibility to assist with the education and training of future generations of pharmacists and the public. Participating as a teacher not only imparts knowledge to others, it offers an opportunity for the practitioner to gain new knowledge and to fine -tune existing skills.
- ***Leader:*** In multidisciplinary (e.g., team) caring situations or in areas where other health care providers are in short supply or non - existent the pharmacist is obligated to assume a leadership position in the overall welfare of the patient and the community. Leadership involves compassion and empathy as well as vision and the ability to make decisions, communicate, and manage effectively. A pharmacist whose leadership role is to be recognized must have vision and the ability to lead. And the added function of:
- ***Researcher:*** The pharmacist must be able to use the evidence base (e.g., scientific, pharmacy practice, health system) effectively in order to advise on the

rational use of medicines in the health care team. By sharing and documenting experiences, the pharmacist can also contribute to the evidence base with the goal of optimizing patient care and outcomes. As a researcher, the pharmacist is able to increase the accessibility of unbiased health and medicines - related information to the public and other health care professionals.

Pharmacy practice: a commitment to implement change

Policy Changes

The first WHO Consultative Groups on the Role of the Pharmacist met in New Delhi in 1988 and in Tokyo in 1993. In 1994, the 47th World Health Assembly called for the development and implementation of national medicines policies aimed at improving access to and rational use of medicines. National medicines policies, which have been developed in over 100 WHO Member States, provide a framework for good pharmaceutical practice. The WHO Revised Drug Strategy relating to the role of the pharmacist was also addressed in the 1994 resolution of the World Health Assembly. This resolution recognizes the key role of pharmacists in public health, including the use of medicines. It emphasizes their responsibility to provide informed and objective advice on medicines and their use, to promote the concept of pharmaceutical care, and to participate actively in illness prevention and health promotion. The third and fourth WHO consultative groups on the role of the pharmacist met in Vancouver in 1997 and in The Hague in 1998.

Other documents on good pharmaceutical practice include the WHO document "Good Pharmacy Practice (GPP) in Community and Hospital Pharmacy Settings" and the FIP documents "Guidelines for Good Pharmacy Practice" of 1993, revised in 1997, and "Good Pharmacy Practice in Developing Countries: Recommendations for stepwise implementation." FIP has issued statements on professional standards for continuing professional development, good pharmacy education practice[38] and pharmaceutical care. Although many countries have already established their own good practice guidelines, the levels of knowledge about them, the ways in which they are used and monitored, and the ways in which practitioners learn how to apply them vary tremendously. This handbook is designed to help improve this situation.

A change in pharmacy education and a new learning approach

Pharmacists stand at the interface between research and development, manufacturer, prescriber, patient and the medicine itself. WHO has called for greater involvement of pharmacists in the general health care system and wider use of their broad academic background. In its statement of policy, FIP says that the changes in the pharmacist's role must be reflected in the basic and continuing education of pharmacists, with a greater focus on student learning. The new paradigm for pharmacy requires that pharmacists are far more than experts in pharmaceutical chemistry and pharmaceutics. They have to understand and apply the principles behind all the activities necessary to manage drug therapy. In 1999, the European Association of Faculties of Pharmacy (EAFP) proposed a shift during the pharmacy study Programme from laboratory-based sciences to practice and clinical sciences. The movement towards the patient care approach has occurred to varying degrees in some countries such as the UK and the USA. It encompasses care in its widest application, i.e., the opportunity for pharmacists to change and improve patient outcomes as integral, active members of the patient care team. However, pharmacy curricula have long been neglected at many learning institutions, which has helped perpetuate the undervalued status of pharmacists in the health care sector, particularly in developing countries. In traditional pharmacy curricula, the emphasis is often on the technical aspects of pharmacy, rather than on professional practice. The forces behind the changes in pharmaceutical education are many and varied, and increasing in both number and intensity. The major economic and political forces affecting the health care system in most countries are also having an impact on the practice of pharmacy. As a result, radical changes are needed in pharmaceutical education. The role and function of pharmacists and pharmaceutical staff need to be reappraised and the educational out- comes of the evolving pharmacy curriculum should be clearly defined. The use of outcomes statements will help to drive curriculum development. Educational outcomes can be used as a new organizing framework that integrates science, professional attributes, inter professional practice, and professionalism across new major headings of pharmaceutical care, systems management, and public health, as they are in the practice of pharmacy. Education outcomes should include the following:

- Pharmaceutical care with provision of both patient-centered care and population-centered care
- Systems management of resources (human, medical, informational and technological) and medication use systems
- Public health assuring effective and quality health and prevention services and developing public health policy.

The educational change will require not only extensive curriculum revision and restructuring, but also a major commitment to faculty development to prepare teachers to educate pharmacists in a different way. The type and depth of didactic and experiential material to be included will be different. The amount and allocation of educational resources will have to change. Schools and colleges of pharmacy should create, establish and evaluate practice models that could be used within evolving health care environments. Courses should take into consideration the needs of the target audience, learning outcomes, course content, teaching methods, learning resources, participant assessment, course evaluation, and quality assurance when being introduced into the curriculum. In recent years, there has been a shift in health sciences education towards a problem - based learning approach. Problem - based pharmacy curricula have been introduced at universities in a number of countries, including the UK, Australia, the Netherlands and South Africa. In some countries, outcome competencies (Unit Standards) have been defined against which practice may be compared. These standards are used to assess health professionals' knowledge and skills in pre - registration examinations or in continuing professional development (CPD). CPD, including research and reflection on the outcomes of actions, contributes to the maintenance of life - long competency to practice. In its statement on CPD, FIP establishes a framework within which pharmacists can meet this obligation. These are times of enormous change in health care and in the pharmacy profession. At no time in its recent history has the profession been faced with such challenges and opportunities. While the profession should articulate pharmaceutical care as the major contribution it has to offer to society, pharmaceutical education needs to develop the outcomes, competencies, content and process of the educational curriculum that is required to prepare students to render pharmaceutical care at the entry points in the health care system.

Summary

Although the number of pharmaceutical products on the market is increasing, access to essential medicines is still lacking in many parts of the world. Rising health care costs and changing social, technological, economic and political environments have made health care reforms necessary throughout the world. New approaches are needed at individual and at population level to provide safe and effective pharmacotherapy to patients in an ever more complex environment. Pharmacists are in an excellent position to meet the need for professionals to assure the safe and effective use of medicines. To do so, pharmacists must assume greater responsibility than they currently do for the management of drug therapies for the patients they serve. This responsibility goes well beyond the traditional dispensing activities that have long been the mainstay of pharmacy practice. While supervision of the routine medicines distribution process must remain the responsibility of pharmacists, their direct involvement in medicine distribution will decrease, since these routine activities will be handled by qualified pharmacy assistants. However, the number of supervisory activities will increase. Thus, pharmacists' responsibilities must be expanded to include monitoring therapeutic progress, consulting with prescribers, and collaborating with other health care practitioners on behalf of patients. The movement towards pharmaceutical care is a critical factor in this process.

The value of pharmacists' services in terms of clinical, economic and social outcomes has been documented. The Pharmacy Practice Activity Classification (PPAC) initiated by the American Pharmacists Association (APhA) provides a common language for a consistent classification of pharmacy practice activities that represents a new way to describe or document pharmacists' activities in a common language. Pharmacy is practiced across a range of both traditional and new settings and levels of decision - making. As members of the health care team, pharmacists need to be able to assume many different functions. The concept of the seven -star pharmacist was introduced by WHO and FIP to describe these roles. Pharmacists have the potential to improve therapeutic outcomes and patients' quality of life within available resources, and must position themselves appropriately within the health care system. Pharmaceutical education has a corresponding responsibility to produce graduates who are competent to deliver pharmaceutical care. Outcome competencies contribute to quality assurance by providing readily accessible standards against which practice may be measured.

8.3 Sales Promotion

Sales promotion is one of the four aspects of *promotional mix*. (The other three parts of the *promotional mix* are *advertising*, *personal selling*, and *publicity/public relations*.) Media and non-media marketing communication are employed for a pre-determined, limited time to increase consumer demand, stimulate market demand or improve product availability. Examples include:

- *contests*
- *point of purchase* displays
- *rebate* (*marketing*)
- free travel, such as free flights

Sales promotions can be directed at either the *customer*, sales staff, or *distribution* channel members (such as *retailers*). Sales promotions targeted at the consumer are called **consumer sales promotions**. Sales promotions targeted at retailers and wholesale are called **trade sales promotions**. Some sale promotions, particularly ones with unusual methods, are considered gimmick by many.

Consumer sales promotion techniques

- *Price deal:* A temporary reduction in the price, such as happy hour Loyal Reward Program: Consumers collect points, miles, or credits for purchases and redeem them for rewards. Two famous examples are Pepsi Stuff and Advantage. Cents-off deal: Offers a brand at a lower price. Price reduction may be a percentage marked on the package.

- *Price-pack deal:* The packaging offers a consumer a certain percentage more of the product for the same price (for example, 25 percent extra).

- Coupons: coupons have become a standard mechanism for sales promotions.

- Loss leader: the price of a popular product is temporarily reduced in order to stimulate other profitable sales Free-standing insert (FSI): A coupon booklet is inserted into the local newspaper for delivery. On-shelf couponing: Coupons are present at the shelf where the product is available. Checkout dispensers: On checkout the customer is given a coupon based on products purchased. On-line couponing: Coupons are available on line. Consumers print them out and take them to the store. Mobile couponing: Coupons are available on a mobile phone. Consumers show the offer on a mobile phone to a salesperson for redemption. Online interactive promotion game: Consumers play an interactive game associated with the promoted product. See an example of the Interactive Internet Ad for tomato ketchup.
- Rebates: Consumers are offered money back if the receipt and barcode are mailed to the producer.
- Contests/sweepstakes/games: The consumer is automatically entered into the event by purchasing the product.
- Point-of-sale displays:-
  - Aisle interrupter: A sign that juts into the aisle from the shelf.
  - Dangler: A sign that sways when a consumer walks by it.
  - Dump bin: A bin full of products dumped inside.
  - Glorifier: A small stage that elevates a product above other products.
  - Wobbler: A sign that jiggles.
  - Lipstick Board: A board on which messages are written in crayon.
  - Necker: A coupon placed on the 'neck' of a bottle.
  - YES unit: "your extra salesperson" is a pull-out fact sheet.
- Kids eat free specials: Offers a discount on the total dining bill by offering 1 free kids meal with each regular meal purchased.

Trade sales promotion techniques

- Trade allowances: short term incentive offered to induce a retailer to stock up on a product.
- Dealer loader: An incentive given to induce a retailer to purchase and display a product.
- Trade contest: A contest to reward retailers that sell the most product.
- Point-of-purchase displays: Extra sales tools given to retailers to boost sales.

- Training programs: dealer employees are trained in selling the product.
- Push money: also known as "spiffs". An extra commission paid to retail employees to push products.

Trade discounts (also called functional discounts): These are payments to distribution channel members for performing some function.

8.4 Attributes of a Good Salesman!

Good Salesmanship isn't about never loosing a sale. It's about learning from every lost sale and never letting history repeat itself in that arena! Everyone can't be a good salesman. It requires a great deal of competence or excellence. Following are a few qualities that a master salesman must develop.

Deliver more than you promise: For instance, if your customer is promised a good quality product on a particular date but the product reaches him before time and the quality too is better than expected, you have acquired a loyal customer for life! This is how a super-salesman works! He pursues the practice of rendering service that is greater in quantity and finer in quality than he is expected to deliver, thereby bringing profit not just for himself.

Make mistakes, but learn to profit from them: For a good salesman, no effort is ever lost. A good salesman not only never repeats his sales blunders, but learns from them. A good observation is a plus point. Learning from others mistakes helps prevent business gaffes too! Also, any mistake made is thoroughly analyzed to look for a solution. Good is sure to come out of it! A Good salesman understands that a coordination of different minds for the attainment of a single purpose is sure to produce positive results.

Have an aim: Another attribute of a good salesman or quality he must develop is his working towards the attainment of a particular goal or quota, within delineated time. A good salesman never goes with an intention of selling all he can. There has to be a specific objective to be attained.

A good sales man before making his sales pitch always tries to put himself in the customer's shoes. This provides a much better understanding of the customers� needs and how those requirements can be amply fulfilled.

The most important attribute of a salesman is his passion and his keenness to complete a sale. This infectious enthusiasm is immediately picked up by the prospective clients, which makes it easier to build a relationship of mutual trust. Good Salesmanship is a combination of the elements of persuasion, creativity, education and the ideal of mutual benefits. A quality salesman must have a good knowledge of products (special features and uses), knowledge about customers (nature, types, habits and buying motives).

The technique of selling and terms and conditions of the sale-delivery, prices, packing, credit facilities available etc.

Also, he must have ample familiarity with sales promotion activities such as distribution of samples, coupons, premiums, exhibitions and clearance sales.

At the same time the objectives must remain to properly introduce new products, win new customers, and to improve public image of the company.

Besides, personal and moral qualities of honesty, integrity, loyalty are a must! A successful salesman should be co-operative, courteous, well mannered, and outgoing. He should be intelligent with a presence of mind, imagination, confidence, observation, sharp memory, foresightedness and above all the power to take quick decisions. A pleasing personality only adds to the selling process. A good appearance, good tastes, good habits and impressive voice are sure to make a lasting impression. Finally, a good salesman is one who proves beneficial to both the sellers and the buyers. While ensuring that the need of the customer is suitably met, a good salesman ascertains a profit!

Questions

1. Explain the process of sales promotion in detail?
2. Discuss the ideal qualities of salesmanship?
3. Discuss the various issues involved in community pharmacy and the role played by community pharmacist?
4. Explain the guidelines for the administration of medication?
5. Explain the various accounting procedures followed in a drug store?
6. Explain the procedure followed for the procurement of drugs for a drug store?
7. Explain the following (a) Location of a drug store (b) Medication errors in dispensing.

Glossary

Acapulco gold - A very potent strain of marijuana from Acapulco, Mexico.

Accidental death benefit - In a life insurance policy, benefit in addition to the death benefit paid to the beneficiary, should death occur due to an accident. There can be certain exclusions as well as time and age limits.

Accounting period - Any period of time designated for which financial statements are prepared. Refer to FISCAL PERIOD.

Accounting procedures - All procedures that discover, identify, record, classify, maintain, and summarize financial information to either produce financial reports or to provide internal control.

Acid – LSD

Acid head - user of LSD, "Acid Freak"

Actual cash value - Cost of replacing damaged or destroyed property with comparable new property, minus depreciation and obsolescence. For example, a 10-year-old sofa will not be replaced at current full value because of a decade of depreciation.

Actuarial basis - A basis used in computing the amount of contributions to be made periodically to a fund or account so that the total contributions plus the compounded earnings thereon will equal the required payments to be made out of the fund or account. A Pension Trust Fund for a public employee retirement system is an example of a fund concerned with actuarial basis data.

Actuary - A specialist in the mathematics of insurance who calculates rates, reserves, dividends and other statistics. (Americanism: In most other countries the individual is known as "mathematician.")

Actus - Mescaline or Peyote

ADA - An acronym for the Americans with Disabilities Act of 1990.

Adaptation - Goods or service adapted in either product, distribution or advertising form to take account of unique conditions in any one country(ies).

Administering agency - An agency designated by the Office of Financial Management to provide general oversight of financial accounting activity. An administering agency is also responsible for the cash management of the funds it administers.

Advertising - Any form of marketing communication in the paid media.

Agency - Every state agency, office, board, commission, department, state institution, or state institution of higher education, which includes all state universities, regional universities. The Evergreen State College, and community and technical colleges.

Agency code - The four character numeric code assigned by the Office of Financial Management to designate the distinct operational units of state government. Agency codes are used for the identification of state agencies. Agencies are to use only the code assigned to their agency unless specified elsewhere in this manual. Refer to AGENCY.

Agency funds - Agency funds are used to account for the assets held by the state as an agent for individuals, private organizations, and other governments. Agency funds are purely custodial in nature. Refer to FIDUCIARY FUNDS.

Agent - A channel institution which represents one or more suppliers for a fee.

Agent -individual who sells and services insurance policies in either of two classifications:

1. Independent agent represents at least two insurance companies and (at least in theory) services clients by searching the market for the most advantageous price for the most coverage. The agent's commission is a percentage of each premium paid and includes a fee for servicing the insured's policy.
2. Direct or career agent represents only one company and sells only its policies. This agent is paid on a commission basis in much the same manner as the independent agent.

Aggressive exporter - An organisation which develops clear marketing strategies for what it intends to do in a foreign markets.

Airhead - Under the influence of marijuana

Alcohol - Booze, juice, sauce

Alley juice - Very cheap wine, "Grapes"

Allocation - A part of a lump-sum appropriation that is designated for expenditure by specific governmental units and/or for specific purposes, activities, or objects. Refer to EXPENDITURE AUTHORITY.

Allotment - An agency's plan of estimated expenditures, revenues, cash disbursements, and cash receipts for each month of the biennium.

Allowance for uncollectibles - A contra-asset valuation account used to indicate the portion of accounts receivable that is estimated to be uncollectible.

Amortization - The gradual reduction or liquidation of an amount over a period of time according to a specified schedule (such as, the retirement of a debt by serial payments to the creditor or in a sinking fund) either by a direct credit, or debit; or through the use of a valuation account.

Amphetamines - Speed, crystal, crank, meth, black beauties, bennies, uppers, dexies, 357 magnums

Ancillary costs - Costs that are directly attributable to asset acquisition, such as freight and transportation costs, site preparation costs, and professional fees, that are necessary to place a capital asset into its intended state of operation. Ancillary costs are capitalized as part of the cost of a capital asset. For an investment, ancillary costs include legal fees and commissions and are included as part of the cost of the investment.

Angel dust - Phencyclidine or PCP

Annuitization - Process by which you convert part or all of the money in a qualified retirement plan or nonqualified annuity contract into a stream of regular income payments, either for your lifetime or the lifetimes of you and your joint annuitant. Once you choose to annuitize, the payment schedule and the amount is generally fixed and can't be altered.

Annuity - A series of equal money payments made or received at equal intervals over a designated period of time.

Annuity - An agreement by an insurer to make periodic payments that continue during the survival of the annuitant(s) or for a specified period.

Anthropology - The discovery of beliefs, motives and values through the study of a society's overt and covert behaviour.

Appraisal – 1. The act of appraising. 2. The estimated value resulting from such action. Refer to APPRAISE.

Appraise - To make an estimate of value of an asset, for example an investment or capital asset, particularly of the value of property.

Appropriation - A legislative authorization for an agency to make expenditures for specific purposes from designated resources available or estimated to be available during a specified time period.

Approved for reinsurance - Indicates the company is approved (or authorized) to write reinsurance on risks in this state. A license to write reinsurance might not be required in these states.

Area organization - A form of international organisational structure used by highly marketing oriented organisations with stable products.

Art collection - An individual work of art or group of items of original artwork such as paintings, sculptures, craftwork or other materials commonly identified as a work of art. Art collections that are considered inexhaustible and meet certain criteria are not required to be capitalized. Agencies meeting the criteria for not capitalizing a collection have the option of capitalizing art collections as non-depreciable capital assets. Art collections that are exhaustible (such as those whose useful lives are diminished by display or educational/research applications) are to be capitalized and depreciated.

Artillery - Equipment for shooting drugs

Assets - A probable future economic benefit obtained or controlled by a particular entity as a result of past transactions or events. These economic resources can be tangible or intangible.

Assets - Assets refer to "all the available properties of every kind or possession of an insurance company that might be used to pay its debts." There are three classifications of assets: invested assets, all other assets, and total admitted assets. Invested assets refer to things such as bonds, stocks, cash and income-producing real estate. All other assets refer to nonincome producing possessions such as the building the company occupies, office furniture, and debts owed, usually in the form of deferred and unpaid premiums. Total admitted assets refer to everything a company owns. All other plus invested assets equals total admitted assets. By law, some states don't permit insurance companies to claim certain goods and possessions, such as deferred and unpaid premiums, in the all other assets category, declaring them "nonadmissable."

Attitudes and values - A predisposition towards a person or object based on cultural mores and values which is a precursor of behaviour.

Audit - A systematic collection of the sufficient, competent evidential matter needed to attest to the fairness of management's assertions in the financial statements or to evaluate whether management has efficiently and effectively carried out its responsibilities. The auditor obtains this evidential matter through inspection, observation, inquiries, and confirmations with third parties. Refer to COMPLIANCE AUDIT, CORRECTIVE ACTION PLAN, FINANCIAL AUDIT, PERFORMANCE AUDIT, AND SINGLE AUDIT.

Automated Clearing House (ACH) - A nationwide payment and collection system that provides for electronic distribution and settlement of funds. Although the term Electronic Fund Transfer (EFT) is technically more inclusive than the term ACH, the term EFT is often used synonymously with ACH..

Automated Teller Machine (ATM) - Computer controlled terminals located at a bank branch or other location, which enable a customer to perform basic banking activities (such as, withdrawals, deposits, or transferring funds) as they would through a bank teller.

Back-up - Permitting blood to back up into a syringe to ensure the needle is in a vein

Bad trip - Unpleasant LSD experience

Bag - Packet of drugs, usually a standard amount for sale

Bag man - Person who transports money

Balance of payments - A measure of all economic transactions between one country and all other countries.

Balance sheet - A financial statement that discloses the assets, liabilities, and equities of an entity at a specified date in conformity with generally accepted accounting principles (GAAP).

Balance sheet - An accounting term referring to a listing of a company's assets, liabilities and surplus as of a specific date.

Balloon - Small amount of contained narcotics

Bang - To inject narcotics

Barbs - Barbiturates; "downers, "reds"

Barter - The direct exchange of goods and services between two parties, often without cash considerations.

Base - Crack Cocaine

Basis of accounting - This refers to the methodology and timing of when revenues and expenditures or expenses are recognized in the accounts and reported in the financial statements. Refer to ACCRUAL BASIS, MODIFIED ACCRUAL BASIS and CASH BASIS.

Basis trading - The difference to new york futures, either on or off.

Bean - Capsules for drugs

Beat - To cheat someone

Benefit period - In health insurance, the number of days for which benefits are paid to the named insured and his or her dependents. For example, the number of days that benefits are calculated for a calendar year consist of the days beginning on Jan. 1 and ending on Dec. 31 of each year.

Bennies - Benzedrine; "peaches"

Benzos - Tranquillisers

Betterment - An addition made to, or change made in, a capital asset, other than maintenance, that is anticipated to prolong its expected useful life or to increase its capacity, efficiency, or quality of output.

Biennium - A 24-month fiscal period. In Washington, the biennium extends from July 1 of odd numbered years to June 30 of odd numbered years.

Big c - Cocaine

Big chief - Mescaline

Big man - supplier of drugs

Bill of lading - The receipt given by the shipping company to the shipper for goods accepted for carriage by sea. (as opposed to an airway bill of lading for goods carried by air).

Bills of exchange - An unconditional order in writing, addressed by one person (drawer) to another (drawee), signed by the person giving it (drawer), requiring the person to whom it is addressed (drawee) to pay on demand, at a fixed or determinable future date, a sum certain in money to, or to the order of, a specific person (payee) or to bearer.

Bindle - A small packet of drug powder

Black beauties - Amphetamines

Black hollies - Amphetamines

Black russian - Hashish

Black-out - Amnesia for events occurring while heavily intoxicated with alcohol, other sedative/hypnotic drugs

Blasted - High on drugs

Blazé - Marijuana

Block grant - A federal grant that consolidates, for a broad purpose, funding previously awarded for a wide range of activities.

Blotter – LSD

Blow - smoke Marijuana; sniff Cocaine

Blue devils – Amobarbital

Blues – Valium

Blunts - A cigar slit open and filled with marijuana

Bombed out - Very much intoxicated by narcotics

Bombita - Mixture of Cocaine and Heroin

Bond - A debt instrument issued through a formal legal procedure and secured either by the pledge of specific properties or revenues or by the general credit of the state.

Bong - a cylindrical water pipe for smoking narcotics, especially Marijuana

Book value - The net amount at which an asset or asset group appears on the books of account, as distinguished from its market or intrinsic value. In the case of assets subject to reduction by valuation allowances, book value refers to cost or stated value less the appropriate allowance.

Books of original entry - Books of original entry are a record in which the various transactions are initially and formally recorded and serve as the direct source of postings to ledgers (e.g. payroll register).

Booze - Alcohol (beer, wine, liquor)

Bread - Money

Brick - A kilogram (2.2 pounds) of tightly compacted Marijuana or Hashish

Bring down - Come off a drug

Broker - A channel institution which puts a specific buyer(s) and seller(s) in contact with one another in one or more commodity(ies) or service(s) with a view to achieving a sale or benefit.

Broker - Go-between for a drug deal

Broker - Insurance salesperson that searches the marketplace in the interest of clients, not insurance companies.

Broker-agent - Independent insurance salesperson who represents particular insurers but also might function as a broker by searching the entire insurance market to place an applicant's coverage to maximize protection and minimize cost. This person is licensed as an agent and a broker.

Brown - Heroin

B's - Heroin

Budget - A plan of financial operation embodying an estimate of proposed expenditures for a given period of time and the proposed means of financing them.

Budget - An amount of money set aside to cover the total cost of a communication campaign or other marketing activity.

Budgetary accounts - Accounts used to enter the adopted budget into the general ledger as part of the management control technique of formal budgetary integration.

Budgetary control - The control or management of a governmental unit in accordance with an approved budget for the purpose of keeping expenditures within the limitations of available appropriations and available revenues.

Buds – Marijuana

Bummer - Bad experience with drugs

Bundle - Multiple bags of a drug

Burn - Cheated bv a pusher

Burnout - Heavy user of drugs

Busted - Arrested on a drug-related charge

Buttons - Peyote or mushrooms

Buy - Purchase drugs

Buzzed - Mildly intoxicated

C - Cocaine

C.I.F - A contract of sale "cost, insurance freight" of the documents of title, not the goods, whereby the buyer is under an obligation to pay against the shipping documents irrespective of the arrival of the goods.

Candy - Barbiturates or Cocaine

Candyman - Drug supplier

Capital - Equity of shareholders of a stock insurance company. The company's capital and surplus are measured by the difference between its assets minus its liabilities. This value protects the interests of the company's policyowners in the event it develops financial problems; the policyowners' benefits are thus protected by the insurance company's capital. Shareholders' interest is second to that of policyowners.

Capital assets - Assets that meet the state's capitalization policy such as land, improvements to land, easements, buildings, leasehold improvements, vehicles, machinery, equipment, works of art and historical treasures, infrastructure, and all other tangible or intangible assets that are used in state operations and that have initial useful lives extending beyond one year. Capital assets do not include depletable resources such as minerals or timber.

Capital budget - The portion of a budget, or a separate budget, devoted to proposed additions to capital assets and the means of financing those additions.

Caps - Drug capsule

Captive agent - Representative of a single insurer or fleet of insurers who is obliged to submit business only to that company, or at the very minimum, give that company first refusal rights on a sale. In exchange, that insurer usually provides its captive agents with an allowance for office expenses as well as an extensive list of employee benefits such as pensions, life insurance, health insurance, and credit unions.

Cartwheels - Amphetamines

Case management - A system of coordinating medical services to treat a patient, improve care and reduce cost. A case manager coordinates health care delivery for patients.

Cash basis - A basis for accounting whereby revenues are recorded only when received and expenses are recorded only when paid without regard to the period in which they were earned or incurred.

Cash disbursements - Cash disbursements are any moneys (e.g., checks, cash, warrants, credit or debit card amounts, and EFTs (Electronic Fund Transfers) paid by the state during a period regardless of when the related obligations are incurred.

Cash discount - An allowance received or given if payment is completed within a stated period of time. Refer to TRADE DISCOUNT.

Cash equivalent - Short-term, highly liquid investments that are both 1. readily convertible to known amounts of cash and 2. so near their maturity that they present insignificant risk of changes in value because of changes in interest rates. Generally only investments with original maturities of three months or less meet this definition.

Cash receipts - Cash receipts are any moneys (e.g., checks, cash, warrants, credit or debit card amounts, or EFTs) received by the state during a period regardless of when the moneys are earned.

Cash/investments with escrow agent - An asset account reflecting deposits with escrow agents.

Casualty - Liability or loss resulting from an accident.

Casualty insurance - That type of insurance that is primarily concerned with losses caused by injuries to persons and legal liability imposed upon the insured for such injury or for damage to property of others. It also includes such diverse forms as plate glass, insurance against crime, such as robbery, burglary and forgery, boiler and machinery insurance and Aviation insurance. Many casualty companies also write surety business.

Charged up - Under the influence of drugs

Charlie - Cocaine

Chasing the dragon - A particular way of inhaling Heroin

Check - A written order on a bank to pay on demand a specified sum of money to a named person, out of money on deposit to the credit of the maker. A check differs from a warrant in that the latter is not necessarily payable on demand and may not be negotiable. It also differs from a voucher in that the latter is not an order to pay. Refer to WARRANT.

Check register - The document used to record pertinent details relating to expenditure/expense vouchers and coding for each check issued.

Cheer - LSD

Cheese - A starter form of Heroin containing Tylenol PM and up to 8 percent heroin

Child care facility - Space used by a child care provider to provide child care services for state government employees.

Child care provider - An entity that is, or commits to becoming, licensed to operate a Washington State day care facility, an entity that regularly provides care for children for periods of less than twenty-four hours.

China white - A very pure white Heroin

Chipping - Occasional use of drugs

Chippy - Person who uses drugs infrequently

Christina - Crystal Meth

Chronic - Marijuana

Claim - A demand made by the insured, or the insured's beneficiary, for payment of the benefits as provided by the policy.

Clean - Drug free; not having drugs in one's possession

Clearance pattern - The proportion of the total amount disbursed that is debited against the state's bank account each day after the disbursements.

Clearing account - An account used to accumulate total charges or credits so that they can be distributed later among the accounts to which they are allocable or so that the net differences can be transferred to the proper account.

Client - For travel regulation purposes, a person or entity that is entitled to receive agency services.

Client services - Services provided directly to agency clients including, but not limited to, medical and dental services, employment and training programs, residential care, and subsidized housing. Clients are considered to be those individuals who the agency has statutory responsibility to serve, protect, or oversee.

Cluster analysis - A technique for grouping similarities or differences between a set of objects or persons.

Coasting - Being high on drugs

Cocaine - Crack, coke, booth, blow, railers, snow, ringer, divits, toot, cola, rocks, blast, white dust, ivory flakes, nose candy, mobbeles

Coinsurance - In property insurance, requires the policyholder to carry insurance equal to a specified percentage of the value of property to receive full payment on a loss. For health insurance, it is a percentage of each claim above the deductible paid by the policyholder. For a 20% health insurance coinsurance clause, the policyholder pays for the deductible plus 20% of his covered losses. After paying 80% of losses up to a specified ceiling, the insurer starts paying 100% of losses.

Coke - Cocaine

Coke broke - Financially incapacitated from supporting Cocaine habit

Cold turkey - Sudden withdrawal from drugs

Collision insurance - Covers physical damage to the insured's automobile (other than that covered under comprehensive insurance) resulting from contact with another inanimate object.

Colombo - Marijuana grown in Columbia

Come down - The ending of a drug experience

Commission - Fee paid to an agent or insurance salesperson as a percentage of the policy premium. The percentage varies widely depending on coverage, the insurer and the marketing methods.

Commute - Travel between the official residence and other domicile of a state officer or employee and their official station or other place of work. Refer to OFFICIAL RESIDENCE and OFFICIAL STATION.

Comparative analysis - Comparing the same set of statistics within a category of one country with another for the purpose of estimating potential demand.

Compensatory time - Time worked by certain state employees that, if not used for paid time off, results in compensation to be cashed out in accordance with regulations or agency policy.

Competition - A product, organisation or individual, in either the same or another category which can be directly substituted one for the other in fulfilling the same needs or wants. .

Compliance audit - An examination leading to the expression of an opinion on the audited governmental unit's compliance with the various finance-related legal and contractual provisions. Refer to AUDIT.

Comprehensive Annual Financial Report (CAFR) - The official annual financial report of the state encompassing all funds and component units of the state. It includes an introductory section, management's discussion and analysis (MD&A), basic financial statements, required supplementary information other than MD&A, combining and individual fund statements, schedules, and a statistical section.

Comprehensive insurance - Auto insurance coverage providing protection in the event of physical damage (other than collision) or theft of the insured car. For example, fire damage or a cracked windshield would be covered under the comprehensive section.

Connect - To purchase drugs

Connection - Supplier of drugs

Consumable inventories - Supplies consumed in the course of an agency's operations; or incidental items held for resale.

Consumption method - The method under which inventories are recorded as an expenditure/expense when used. Refer to PURCHASES METHOD.

Control account - An account in the general ledger in which the aggregate of all debit and credit postings to a number of related accounts (called the subsidiary accounts) are recorded. For example, the Accounts Receivable account is a control account supported by the aggregate of the individual customer subsidiary accounts. Refer to GENERAL LEDGER and SUBSIDIARY ACCOUNTS.

Cooker - Usually a spoon or bottle cap used to heat drugs for injection

Cop - To obtain drugs

Copayment - A predetermined, flat fee an individual pays for health-care services, in addition to what insurance covers. For example, some HMOs require a $10 copayment for each office visit, regardless of the type or level of services provided during the visit. Copayments are not usually specified by percentages.

Corrective action plan - An agency response to audit findings that documents how deficiencies are to be corrected, how improvements are to be made, or demonstrates that audit findings are invalid or do not warrant any subsequent action. Refer to AUDIT.

Cost accounting - That method of accounting which provides for accumulating and recording of all the elements of cost incurred to accomplish a purpose, to carry on an activity or operation, or to complete a unit of work or a specific job.

Cost records - All ledgers, supporting records, schedules, reports, invoices, vouchers, and other records and documents reflecting the cost of projects, jobs, production centers, processes, operations, products, or services, or the cost of any of the component parts thereof.

Countertrade - An agreement by the customer to buy goods on condition that the seller buys some of the customer's own products in return.

Coverage - The scope of protection provided under an insurance policy. In property insurance, coverage lists perils insured against, properties covered, locations covered, individuals insured, and the limits of indemnification. In life insurance, living and death benefits are listed.

Coverage area - The geographic region covered by travel insurance.

Crack - Cocaine prepared for smoking

Credit card - A card entitling the holder to buy services or goods on credit.

Crystals - Methamphetamine

Culture - The sum total of learned behaviourial characteristics or traits which are manifest and shared by members of a particular society.

Currency swaps - A method to gain access to foreign capital at favourable rates comprising contracts to exchange cash flow relating to the debt obligations of the two counterparts to the agreement.

Current assets - Resources that are available, or can readily be made available, to meet the cost of operations or to pay current liabilities.

Current liabilities - Those obligations which are payable within one year from current assets or current resources.

Cut - to adulterate drugs

Cut out - To leave from someplace

Cut-off date - A selected date whereby transactions generally are stopped to provide for closing of the books of accounts for a given period, or for audit purposes.

Dagga - South African word for Marijuana

Darks - Heroin

Dealer - Someone who sells illegal drugs

Death benefit - The limit of insurance or the amount of benefit that will be paid in the event of the death of a covered person.

Debit card - A card that draws funds directly from a deposit account.

Debt - An obligation resulting from the borrowing of money or from the purchase of goods and services. Debts of the state include bonds, accounts payable, and other liabilities. Refer to BONDS PAYABLE, ACCOUNTS PAYABLE, LIABILITIES, LONG-TERM OBLIGATIONS and GENERAL LONG-TERM OBLIGATIONS.

Debt service funds - Debt service funds are used to account for the accumulation of resources for, and the payment of, general long-term obligation principal and interest. Refer to GOVERNMENTAL FUNDS.

Decentralised plans - A planning system taking into account differences in product/market conditions.

Deck - A packet of drugs

Deductible - Amount of loss that the insured pays before the insurance kicks in.

Deferred charges - An asset account reflecting costs which are not chargeable to the accounting period in which paid but are recorded as assets until amortized. An example is discount on bonds issued. Deferred charges differ from prepaid expenses in that deferred charges usually extend over a long period of time (more than five years) and are not a regularly recurring cost of operation. Refer to PREPAID EXPENSES.

Deficit - 1. The excess of the liabilities and reserves of a fund over its assets. 2. The excess of expenditures over revenues during an accounting period or, in the case of proprietary funds, the excess of expenses over revenues during an accounting period.

Demand pattern analysis - The analysis of in-country industrial sector growth patterns.

Deposit - Money or securities held in a bank or other financial institution. In the context of required note disclosures, deposits include cash and near cash items placed on account with a financial institution or fiscal agent. Some deposits (e.g., checking accounts) are subject to withdrawal upon demand without notice or penalty (demand deposits) and others (e.g., certificates of deposit) can only be withdrawn without penalty upon completion of a fixed period (time deposits).

Depreciation - The portion of the cost of a capital asset representing the expiration in the useful life of the capital asset attributable to wear and tear, deterioration, action of the physical elements, inadequacy, and obsolescence which is charged off during a particular period. In accounting for depreciation, the cost of a capital asset, less any salvage value, is prorated over the estimated useful life of such an asset. Refer to COMPOSITE METHOD and STRAIGHT-LINE METHOD.

Devaluation - The reduction in the value of one currency vis a vis other countries.

Dexies - Dexadrine, or"dex"

Diffusion theory - A classification for the adoption of innovation(s) through social phenomenon, characterised by a normal distribution.

Direct costs - Costs that include direct materials and labor. Refer to DIRECT EXPENSES.

Direct expenses - Expenses which are charged directly as a part of the cost of a product or service, or of a department or operating unit, as distinguished from overhead and other indirect costs which must be prorated among several products or services, departments, or operating units.

Disbursement - Payment by cash, warrant, check, journal voucher, EFT, or any other technological payment method approved by OFM.

Disease management - A system of coordinated health-care interventions and communications for patients with certain illnesses.

Disputed item - An item in question or lacking agreement by parties involved, such as an item appearing on a purchase card custodian statement that the card custodian disagrees with.

Distribution channel - An institution through which goods or services are marketed giving time and place utilities to users.

Dividend - The return of part of the policy's premium for a policy issued on a participating basis by either a mutual or stock insurer. A portion of the surplus paid to the stockholders of a corporation.

Division or cost center code - A code assigned by an agency to further identify its organizational structure.

Dollies - Methadone

Dolphins - Ecstasy

Donated assets - Assets acquired by gift, donation, or payment of a nominal sum, which is not reflective of the assets' true market value.

Donated inventories - Food or other items held for future distribution.

Double entry bookkeeping - A system of record keeping which requires two entries to the records (a debit and a credit) for every accounting event.

Downers - Tranquillisers

Dried out - Having gone through a withdrawal programme for drugs or alcohol

Drop - LSD

Drop - To take a drugs orally; a place where money or drugs are left

Druggie - A narcotic user or addict

Drunk pills - Valium

Dumping - The selling of goods or services in a buying country at less than the production unit price in the selling country, or the difference between normal domestic price and the price at which the product leaves the exporting country.

Dust - Narcotics in powder for

Duty - The actual custom duty based on an imported good either on an ad valorem, or specification amount per unit or combination of these two.

Dynamite - High quality, potent drugs

Earned premium - The amount of the premium that as been paid for in advance that has been "earned" by virtue of the fact that time has passed without claim. A three-year policy that has been paid in advance and is one year old would have only partly earned the premium.

Easy score - Obtaining drugs without difficulty

Economic feasibility - An application is economically feasible when, over a reasonable period of time, the application's cumulative benefits outweigh or are equivalent to the application's cumulative costs.

Economic feasibility study (EFS) - A cost/benefit analysis of a state agency's proposed electronic payment and/or disbursement project that should demonstrate the economic feasibility (net benefit) of the proposed project. Refer to Section 40.40.

Economical - Direct financial, work-related costs that occur at the least cost to the state and which the state is responsible to pay.

Effective interest rate - The rate of earning on a bond investment based on the actual price paid for the bond, the coupon rate, the maturity date and the length of time between interest dates, in contrast with the nominal interest rate.

Eggs - Tranquillisers

Eighth - One-eighth of a pound of drugs

Electronic Benefit Transfer (EBT) - The electronic transfer of government benefit funds to individuals through the use of automated card technology, automated teller machines (ATM) and point of sale (POS) terminals.

Electronic check - An electronic version or representation of a paper check. The account holder writes an e-check using a computer or other type of electronic device and transmits the e-check to the payee electronically. Like paper checks, e-checks are signed by the payer and endorsed by the payee. Rather than handwritten or machine-stamped signatures, however, e-checks are affixed with digital signatures. The payee deposits the e-check, receives credit, and the payee's bank clears the e-check to the paying bank. The paying bank validates the e-check and then charges the check writer's account for the check.

Electronic commerce/e-commerce - The commercial transaction of services in an electronic format.

Electronic Data Interchange (EDI) - A computer-to-computer exchange of information that is both computer-readable and computer-processable.

Electronic Data Processing (EDP) - Data processing by means of high-speed electronic equipment.

Electronic Fund Transfer (EFT) - Any transfer of funds, other than a transaction originated by check, draft, or similar paper instrument, which is initiated through an electronic terminal, telephone instrument, or computer or magnetic tape to authorize a financial institution to debit or credit an account.

Elephant - PCP

Elimination period - The time which must pass after filing a claim before policyholder can collect insurance benefits. Also known as "waiting period."

Emergency - A set of unforeseen circumstances beyond the control of an agency that either: (a) presents a real, immediate threat to the proper performance of essential functions; or (b) may result in material loss or damage to property, bodily injury, or loss of life if immediate action is not taken.

Employers liability insurance - Coverage against common law liability of an employer for accidents to employees, as distinguished from liability imposed by a workers' compensation law.

Encumbrance - A claim on property, such as a mortgage, a lien for work and materials, or a right of dower. The interest of the property owner is reduced by the amount of the encumbrance.

Encumbrance - A reservation of an expenditure authority for an obligation in the form of purchase orders or contracts. An encumbrance represents a commitment. It is not an expenditure.

Endowment - Refer to PERMANENT FUNDS.

Entitlement - A service or grant that, under federal law, must be provided to all eligible applicants.

Entity - The basic unit upon which accounting and/or financial reporting activities are focused.

Entry - The record of a financial transaction in the appropriate books of account.

Equipment - Tangible property other than land, buildings, improvements other than buildings, or infrastructure, which is used in operations and with a useful life of more than one year. Examples are furnishings, equipment, and software. Equipment may be attached to a structure for purposes of securing the item, but unless it is permanently attached to, or an integral part of, the building or structure, it is to be classified as equipment and not buildings.

E's - Ecstasy

Ethnocentrism - A home country orientation but with export of surplus production.

Exchange rate - The ratio of exchange of one currency to another.

Exclusions - Items or conditions that are not covered by the general insurance contract.

Expenditures - Decreases in net current financial resources. Expenditures include disbursements and accruals of the current period. Expenditures do not include encumbrances.

Expenses - Decreases in net total assets. Expenses represent the cost of operations incurred during the current period regardless of the timing of the related disbursements.

Experience - Trip on LSD

Export credit guarantee fund - A facility, provided by government treasury, to guarantee the development costs of exports or legal claims arising there from.

Export processing zone - A zone, designated within the country, enjoying tax privileges or other status, where goods and services can be brought into, reprocessed and re-exported.

Exporting - The marketing of surplus goods produced in one country into another country.

Expropriation - The annexation or seizure of national assets as an extreme form of political action.

Face value - As applied to securities, this term designates the amount of an insurer's liability stated in the security document.

Factory - Place where illicit drugs are prepared for sale.

Fidelity bond - A written promise to indemnify against losses from theft, embezzlement, defalcation, and misappropriation of public moneys by government officers and employees. Refer to SURETY BOND.

Fiduciary funds - Fiduciary funds are used to account for assets held by the state in a trustee capacity, or as an agent for others and that cannot be used to support the state's own programs. There are four types of fiduciary funds: private-purpose, pension (and other employee benefit), and investment trust funds, and agency funds. Refer to PRIVATE-PURPOSE TRUST FUNDS, PENSION (AND OTHER EMPLOYEE BENEFIT) TRUST FUNDS, INVESTMENT TRUST FUNDS, and AGENCY FUNDS.

Financial audit - An audit made by an independent external auditor for the purpose of issuing an audit opinion on the fair presentation of the financial statements of the state in conformity with GAAP. Refer to AUDIT.

First-in, first-out (FIFO) - An inventory valuation method, which allocates cost on the assumption that goods are consumed or sold in the order that they were acquired.

Fiscal period - Any period at the end of which a governmental unit determines its financial position and the results of its operations. Refer to ACCOUNTING PERIOD.

Fiscal year - In Washington State, a 12-month period extending from July 1 of one calendar year to June 30 of the next calendar year.

Fix - An injection of drugs

Fixed assets - Refer to CAPITAL ASSETS.

Fixtures - Attachments to buildings, which are not intended to be removed, and which cannot be removed without damage to the buildings. Those fixtures with useful lives presumed to be as long as that of the building itself are considered a part of the building; all others are classified as equipment.

Flake - Cocaine

Flash - LSD

Flea powder - Poor quality drugs

Flying - Under the influence of drugs

Football – Amphetarnine

Foreign exchange - Facilities' business across national boundaries, usually expressed in foreign currency bought or sold on the foreign exchange market.

Forward rates - A mechanism whereby the risk of changes in exchange rates can be covered by obtaining a new rate quote for a future exchange of currencies.

Freak out - A bad trip; an unexpected reaction to a drug

Front - To put money out before receiving the merchandise

Function - A group of related activities aimed at accomplishing a major service or regulatory program for which a government is responsible.

Fund balance - In governmental funds, this is the difference between fund assets and fund liabilities. Governmental fund balances should be segregated into reserved and unreserved amounts. Refer to RESERVED FUND BALANCE and UNRESERVED FUND BALANCE.

Fund capital asset - Capital assets recorded in proprietary and trust funds and used in the production of the goods or services provided or sold. Depreciation on fund capital assets is charged as an expense of the fund.

Fund equity - The difference between a fund's assets and liabilities. In governmental funds, it is referred to as fund balance. In proprietary funds, it is referred to as net assets. Refer to FUND BALANCE and NET ASSETS.

Fund financial statements - Financial statements presented for the state's governmental, proprietary and fiduciary funds. They display information about major funds individually and nonmajor funds in the aggregate for governmental and enterprise funds. Fiduciary statements include financial statements for fiduciary funds. Each of the three fund categories is reported using the measurement focus and basis of accounting required for that category. Refer to GOVERNMENTAL FUNDS, PROPRIETARY FUNDS, and FIDUCIARY FUNDS.

Funding technique - Procedures to minimize the time between the transfer of funds from the federal government and the payment of funds for program purposes by the state.

Future - A legally binding contract to deliver/take delivery on a specified date of a given quality and quantity of a commodity at an agreed price.

Fuzz - The police

Ganja - The Jamaican word for Marijuana

Gear - Heroin

General account - All premiums are paid into an insurer's general account. Thus, buyers are subject to credit-risk exposure to the insurance company, which is low but not zero.

General Agreement on Tariffs and Trade (GATT) - An institutional framework producing a set of rules and principles with the intention of liberalising trade between member countries.

General capital assets - Used in operations of governmental funds that are not assets of any fund, but of the government as a whole. Most often, general capital assets are acquired through the expenditure of the financial resources of governmental funds. General capital assets include all capital assets not accounted for in proprietary funds. The state accounts for general capital assets in the General Capital Assets Subsidiary Account and reports them in the governmental activities column in the government-wide financial statement of net assets.

General fund - The general fund is used to account for the financial activities of the general government not required to be accounted for in another account. Refer to GOVERNMENTAL FUNDS.

General journal - The journal in which all entries not recorded in special journals are recorded.

General ledger - A ledger containing the accounts in which are recorded, in detail or in summary, all transactions of the state. Refer to CONTROL ACCOUNT and SUBSIDIARY ACCOUNTS.

General liability insurance -Insurance designed to protect business owners and operators from a wide variety of liability exposures. Exposures could include liability arising from accidents resulting from the insured's premises or operations, products sold by the insured, operations completed by the insured, and contractual liability.

General long-term obligations subsidiary account - A record keeping mechanism that provides a basis for accountability and control over the state's long-term obligations other than those accounted for in proprietary and fiduciary funds.

General obligation bonds - Statewide bond issues that are secured by an unconditional pledge of the full faith, credit and taxing power of the state.

General revenues - Revenues that are not matched to specific program expenses are required to be reported as general revenues.

Generally Accepted Accounting Principles (GAAP) - These are the uniform minimum standards for financial accounting and reporting. They govern the form and content of the financial statements of an entity. GAAP encompass the conventions, rules, and procedures necessary to define accepted accounting practice at a particular time. They include not only broad guidelines of general application, but also detailed practices and procedures. The primary authoritative body on the application of GAAP to state and local governments is the Governmental Accounting Standards Board.

Generally Accepted Auditing Standards (GAAS) - These are the standards established by the AICPA for the conduct and reporting of financial audits. There are 10 basic GAAS, classed into three broad categories: general standards, standards of fieldwork and standards of reporting. The GAAS set forth the objectives of the audit and establish measures that can be applied to judge the quality of its performance.

Generally Accepted Government Auditing Standards (GAGAS) - These standards are for the conduct and reporting of both financial and performance audits in the public sector. The basic GAGAS standards are classed into three broad categories: general standards, fieldwork standards, and reporting standards.

Geocentrism - A world orientation with world market strategies.

Ghost billing account - A cardless billing program offered by many charge card and credit card companies that is designed to primarily accommodate airline ticket purchases.

Glass - Crystal Meth

Global environment - All semi or uncontrollable factors which a marketer has to account for in carrying out global operations.

Global evaluation - A four stage organisational development process evolving from first stage; domestic focus to a fourth stage; global marketing strategy of extension, adaptation and creation of market opportunities.

Global marketing - Marketing on a worldwide scale reconciling or taking commercial advantage of global operational differences, similarities and opportunities in order to meet global objectives.

Global products - Products designed to meet global market segments.

Gluey - A glue sniffer

Goofballs - Barbiturates

Governmental accounting - The composite activity of analyzing, recording, summarizing, reporting, and interpreting the financial transactions of a governmental entity.

Governmental funds - Governmental funds are used to account for most typical governmental functions focusing on the acquisition, use, and balances of a state's expendable financial resources and the related current liabilities. The accounting for governmental funds has a budget orientation using the current financial resources measurement focus and the modified accrual basis of accounting. There are five types of governmental funds: General, Special Revenue, Debt Service, Capital Projects, and Permanent Funds. Refer to GENERAL FUND, SPECIAL REVENUE FUNDS, DEBT SERVICE FUNDS, CAPITAL PROJECTS FUNDS, and PERMANENT FUNDS.

Government-wide financial statements - Financial statements that incorporate all of the state's governmental and business-type activities, as well as its nonfiduciary component units. There are two basic government-wide financial statements: the Statement of Net Assets and the Statement of Activities. Both basic government-wide financial statements are presented using the economic resources measurement focus and the accrual basis of accounting. Refer to BUSINESS-TYPE ACTIVITIES and GOVERNMENTAL ACTIVITIES.

Grace period - The length of time (usually 31 days) after a premium is due and unpaid during which the policy, including all riders, remains in force. If a premium is paid during the grace period, the premium is considered to have been paid on time. In Universal Life policies, it typically provides for coverage to remain in force for 60 days following the date cash value becomes insufficient to support the payment of monthly insurance costs.

Gram - A metric measure of weight

Grants - Awards of financial assistance, including cooperative agreements, in the form of money, or property in lieu of money, to an eligible grantee. The term does not include technical assistance which provides services instead of money, or other forms of assistance such as revenue sharing, loans, loan guarantees, interest subsidies, insurance or direct appropriations. Also, the term does not include assistance, such as fellowship or other lump sum awards, which the grantee is not required to account for. Refer to CAPITAL GRANTS and OPERATING GRANTS.

Grass - Marijuana

Green - Marijuana

Gross domestic product (GDP) - The value of all goods and services produced by a country's domestic economy in one year.

Gross leverage - The sum of net leverage and ceded reinsurance leverage. This ratio measures a company's gross exposure to pricing errors in its current book of business, to errors of estimating its liabilities, and exposure to its reinsurers.

Gross national product (GNP) - The market value of all goods and services outputted by residents of a country in one year including income from aboard.

Gun - equipment for injecting drugs

H - Heroin

Happy dust - Cocaine

Hash - Marijuana

Hawk - LSD

Hay - Marijuana

Hazard - A circumstance that increases the likelihood or probable severity of a loss. For example, the storing of explosives in a home basement is a hazard that increases the probability of an explosion.

Hazardous activity - Bungee jumping, scuba diving, horse riding and other activities not generally covered by standard insurance policies. For insurers that do provide cover for such activities, it is unlikely they will cover liability and personal accident, which should be provided by the company hosting the activity.

Health Maintenance Organization (HMO) - Prepaid group health insurance plan that entitles members to services of participating physicians, hospitals and clinics. Emphasis is on preventative medicine, and members must use contracted health-care providers.

Health Reimbursement Arrangement - Owners of high-deductible health plans who are not qualified for a health savings account can use an HRA.

Health savings account - Plan that allows you to contribute pre-tax money to be used for qualified medical expenses. HSAs, which are portable, must be linked to a high-deductible health insurance policy.

Heaven - Cocaine

Heavenly blue - Morning glory seeds; a hallucinogen

Heavy burner - A person who smokes a lot of dope, a burnout

Hedging - A mechanism to avoid the risk of a decline in the future market of a commodity, usually by entering into futures markets.

Herb - Marijuana

Heroin - china white, fix, horse, smack, whack, mother pearl, H. junk

Hierarchy of needs - The ordering of a person's needs into hierarchy of relative potency such that as lower order needs are fulfilled higher, unfulfilled order needs emerge, which require fulfillment. "

High - To be intoxicated on drugs

Hip-hop - Refers to a culture that includes rap music, art, dance, fashion, attitude

Hit- A single dose of drugs

Hog - PCP

Holding - In possession of drugs

Home grown - Locally grown Marijuana; local weed; ditch weed

Hooked - Addicted

Hopped up - Under the influence of drugs

Horse - Heroin

Household goods - All household goods, personal effects and property used in a dwelling, and normal equipment and supplies used to maintain the dwelling.

Hurricane deductible - Amount you must pay out-of-pocket before hurricane insurance will kick in. Many insurers in hurricane-prone states are selling homeowners insurance policies with percentage deductibles for storm damage, instead of the traditional dollar deductibles used for claims such as fire and theft. Percentage deductibles vary from one percent of a home's insured value to 15 percent, depending on many factors that differ by state and insurer.

Hype - Narcotic addict

Ice - Crystal Meth

Ice cream habit - Occasional drug use

Ideology - An individual's organisation or country's political belief.

Imprest account - An account into which a fixed amount of money is placed for the purpose of making change or minor disbursements. As disbursements are made, a voucher is completed to record the date, amount, nature, and purpose of the disbursement. At periodic intervals, or when the money is completely expended, a report with substantiating vouchers is prepared and the account is replenished for the exact amount of the disbursements, and appropriate general ledger accounts are charged. The total of cash and the substantiating vouchers should always equal the total fixed amount of money set aside in the imprest account. Refer to CHANGE ACCOUNTS and PETTY CASH.

Incidental expenses - Fees and tips given to porters, baggage carriers, hotel and restuarant staff, flight attendants, and others for personal services performed. This is not a miscellaneous expense. An allowance for incidental expenses is included within the daily subsistence rates for the area of travel.

Income elasticity measurements - A description of the relationship between the demand for goods and changes in income.

Income per capita - The market value of all goods and services outputted by a country divided by the total number of residents of that country.

Income statement - Refer to OPERATING STATEMENT; STATEMENT OF REVENUES, EXPENDITURES AND CHANGES IN FUND BALANCE; and STATEMENT OF REVENUES, EXPENSES, AND CHANGES IN FUND NET ASSETS OR FUND EQUITY.

Income taxes - Incurred income taxes (including income taxes on capital gains) reported in each annual statement for that year.

Indemnity - Restoration to the victim of a loss by payment, repair or replacement.

Independent audit - An audit performed by an independent auditor. Refer to FINANCIAL AUDIT, PERFORMANCE AUDIT, and INTERNAL AUDIT.

Inexhaustible capital assets - Refer to NON-DEPRECIABLE CAPITAL ASSETS.

Inflation - A condition where demand outstrips supply or costs escalate, affecting an upward change in prices.

Inflation protection - An optional property coverage endorsement offered by some insurers that increases the policy's limits of insurance during the policy term to keep pace with inflation.

Information system - A system for gathering, analysing and reporting data aimed at reducing uncertainty in business decision making.

Information technology related equipment - Includes capitalized and non-capitalized assets such as equipment, software and products used in processing information, office automation and telecommunications.

Infrastructure assets - Long lived capital assets that normally are stationary in nature and normally can be preserved for a significantly greater number of years than most capital assets. Examples of infrastructure assets include roads, sidewalks, bridges, tunnels, drainage systems, water and sewer systems, dams, and lighting systems. With the exception of the state highway system and emergency airfields operated by the Department of Transportation, which use the modified approach to depreciation, infrastructure assets are to be depreciated.

Insurable interest - Interest in property such that loss or destruction of the property could cause a financial loss.

Interactive plans - A planning system whereby headquarters sets a policy and framework and subsidiaries interpret these under local conditions.

Interest payable - A liability account reflecting the amount of interest owed by the state. In governmental funds, interest is to be recognized as an expenditure in the accounting period in which it becomes due and payable and the liability is to be recorded as interest payable at that time. In proprietary and trust funds, interest payable is recorded as it accrues, regardless of when payment is actually due.

Interest receivable - An asset account reflecting the amount of interest due to the state.

Interest-crediting methods - There are at least 35 interest-crediting methods that insurers use. They usually involve some combination of point-to-point, annual reset, yield spread, averaging, or high water mark.

Interfund accounts - Accounts in which activity between funds are reflected. Refer to INTERFUND ACTIVITY.

Interfund services provided and used - Sales and purchases of goods and services between funds for a price approximating their external exchange value. Refer to INTERFUND ACTIVITY.

Interfund transfers - Nonreciprocal transfers made without a requirement for repayment. Refer to EQUITY TRANSFERS, OPERATING TRANSFERS, and INTERFUND ACTIVITY.

Intergovernmental revenues - Revenues from other governments in the form of grants, entitlements, shared revenues, or payments in lieu of taxes.

Interim financial statement - A financial statement prepared before the end of the current fiscal period and covering only financial transactions during the period to date.

Internal audit - An appraisal activity conducted by auditors working for and within an organization of the diverse operations and controls within the organization to determine whether prescribed policies and procedures are followed, established standards are met, resources are used efficiently and economically, and the organization's objectives are being achieved.

Internal control - A management process for keeping an entity (agency, board, commission, department, division, institution, or program) on course in achieving its organizational objectives. A management control system, including comprehensive internal controls, should provide reasonable assurance that entity objectives are being met.

International monetary fund - A fund, with world wide country membership, (united nations) which lends money to countries on a short term basis to assist them balance of payments problems.

International product life cycle - A model which suggest that products go through a cycle whereby high income, mass consumption countries go through a cycle of exporting, loss of exports to final importers of products.

International products - Goods or services seen as having extended potential into other markets.

Inventory control point - A specific location, area, building, inventory type, etc., as defined in writing by the agency inventory officer where consumable inventories are aggregated for distribution, valuation, and/or reporting threshold purposes.

Investment in capital assets, net of related debt - One of the three components of net assets reported in government-wide and proprietary fund financial statements. It is comprised of capital assets, including restricted capital assets, net of accumulated depreciation and reduced by the outstanding balances of any bonds, mortgages, notes, or other borrowings that are attributable to the acquisition, construction, or improvement of capital assets of the state.

Investment income - The return received by insurers from their investment portfolios including interest, dividends and realized capital gains on stocks. It doesn't include the value of any stocks or bonds that the company currently owns.

Investment trust funds - Fiduciary funds used by the sponsor to report the external portion of investment pools. Refer to FIDUCIARY FUNDS.

Investments - Securities, real estate and other instruments held for the production of income or profit.

Invoice - A document submitted by a vendor, showing the character, quantity, price, terms, nature of delivery, and other particulars of goods delivered or of services rendered.

Issuance costs - Fees associated with the issuance of debt that may be withheld from the proceeds or paid separately including underwriter's fees and bond counsel fees. In governmental funds, issuance costs are reported as expenditures.

Jellies - Tranquillisers

Jive - Marijuana

Joint - A Marijuana cigarette

Joint ventures - An enterprise in which two or more investors share ownership and control over property rights and operations.

Joy popping - Occasional use of drugs

Judgment - An amount to be paid or collected by the state as the result of a court decision, including a condemnation award in payment for private property taken for public use.

Juice – Alcohol

Junk - Heroin, so named because it's never pure when sold on the street

Junkie - An opiate addict

Kickback - Relapse back into drug usage

Kiddie dope - Usually prescription drugs

Kif - North African word for Marijuana

Killer - Strong drug

Killer weed - Strong Marijuana, or marijuana sprinkled with PCP

L – LSD

Laddering - Purchasing bond investments that mature at different time intervals.

Last-In, First-Out (LIFO) - An inventory valuation method that allocates cost on the assumption that the last units acquired are the first units consumed or sold.

Laughing gas - Nitrous Oxide (inhalant)

Leapers - Amphetamines

Leasehold - The right to the use of real estate by virtue of a lease, usually for a specified term of years, for which consideration is paid.

Lease-purchase agreements - Contractual agreements which are termed "leases," but in substance they are purchase contracts.

Ledger - A group of accounts in which are recorded the financial transactions of the state. Refer to GENERAL LEDGER and SUBSIDIARY LEDGER.

Legal opinion - 1. The opinion of an official authorized to render it (e.g., attorney general). 2. In the case of governmental bonds, the opinion of a specialized bond attorney as to the legality of a bond issue.

Lemonade - poor-quality drugs

Letter of credit - A method of international payment whereby the buyer instructs his own country bank to open a credit with the seller's own country bank specifying the documents which the seller has to deliver to the bank for him/her to receive payment.

Lettuce - Money

Levy - A tax imposed by government, to meet a specific objective.

Liabilities - Probable future sacrifices of economic benefits, arising from present obligations of a particular entity to transfer assets or provide services to other entities in the future as a result of past transactions or events. The term does not include encumbrances.

Liability - Broadly, any legally enforceable obligation. The term is most commonly used in a pecuniary sense.

Liability insurance - Insurance that pays and renders service on behalf of an insured for loss arising out of his responsibility, due to negligence, to others imposed by law or assumed by contract.

Library resources - Exhaustible items used for reference or lending such as books, periodicals, and microfilm that have a useful life greater than one year. Library resources are capitalized, depreciated and controlled by a recognized cataloging system.

Licensed - Indicates the company is incorporated (or chartered) in another state but is a licensed (admitted) insurer for this state to write specific lines of business for which it qualifies.

Licensed for reinsurance only - Indicates the company is a licensed (admitted) insurer to write reinsurance on risks in this state.

Licensing - A method of foreign operation cooperation whereby an organisation in one country agrees to permit a firm in another country to use the manufacturing, processing, trademark, know-how or some other skill provided by the licensor.

Lid - One ounce or less of Marijuana

Lifetime reserve days - Sixty additional days Medicare pays for when you are hospitalized for more than 90 days in a benefit period. These days can only be used once during your lifetime. For each lifetime reserve day, Medicare pays all covered costs except for a daily coinsurance amount.

Lightening - LSD

Limited obligation bonds - These bonds, while backed by the full faith and credit of the state, are payable primarily from dedicated revenues of the state's motor vehicle fuel excise tax and other miscellaneous dedicated revenues.

Linctus - Methadone

Line - A dose of Cocaine arranged in a line on a smooth surface

Liquid acid - LSD

Liquidation - Payment of debt, cancellation of encumbrance, or conversion into cash.

Liquidity - Liquidity is the ability of an individual or business to quickly convert assets into cash without incurring a considerable loss. There are two kinds of liquidity: quick and current. Quick liquidity refers to funds--cash, short-term investments, and government bonds--and possessions which can immediately be converted into cash in the case of an emergency. Current liquidity refers to current liquidity plus possessions such as real estate which cannot be immediately liquidated, but eventually can be sold and converted into cash. Quick liquidity is a subset of current liquidity. This reflects the financial stability of a company and thus their rating.

Living benefits - This feature allows you, under certain circumstances, to receive the proceeds of your life insurance policy before you die. Such circumstances include terminal or catastrophic illness, the need for long-term care, or confinement to a nursing home. Also known as "accelerated death benefits."

Loans receivable - An asset account reflecting amounts that have been loaned to individuals or organizations external to the state, including notes taken as security for such loans. Loans to other governments should be recorded and reported separately.

Local products - Goods or services seen only suitable in one single market.

Location code - The identification code of the county in which the fixed asset is located.

Long-term obligations - Those obligations expected to mature at some future date and therefore not expected to be liquidated with currently existing resources or current assets. The long-term liabilities of specific enterprise, internal service, and trust funds are to be accounted for through those funds. All other unmatured general long-term liabilities are to be accounted for in the General Long-Term Obligations Subsidiary Account .

Loss control - All methods taken to reduce the frequency and/or severity of losses including exposure avoidance, loss prevention, loss reduction, segregation of exposure units and noninsurance transfer of risk. A combination of risk control techniques with risk financing techniques forms the nucleus of a risk management program. The use of appropriate insurance, avoidance of risk, loss control, risk retention, self insuring, and other techniques that minimize the risks of a business, individual, or organization.

Loss ratio - The ratio of incurred losses and loss-adjustment expenses to net premiums earned. This ratio measures the company's underlying profitability, or loss experience, on its total book of business.

Loss reserve - The estimated liability, as it would appear in an insurer's financial statement, for unpaid insurance claims or losses that have occurred as of a given evaluation date. Usually includes losses incurred but not reported (IBNR), losses due but not yet paid, and amounts not yet due. For individual claims, the loss reserve is the estimate of what will ultimately be paid out on that claim.

Low context culture - High reliance on explicit verbal or written communications or other explicit format.

Mainline - Inject a drug directly into a vein, to "shoot up"

Mainliner - A person who injects directly into the vein

Major fund - A governmental or enterprise account reported as a separate column in the basic fund financial statements. The General Fund is always a major fund. Otherwise, major funds are those accounts with revenues, expenditures/expenses, assets, or liabilities (excluding extraordinary items) that are at least 10 percent of corresponding totals for all governmental and enterprise accounts for the same item.

Man - Police

Manicure - Remove seeds from marijuana

Manufacturer - The name of either the manufacturer or the commonly accepted trade name.

Marching powder - Cocaine

Marijuana - Buds, bhang, dope, goof butt, grass, hash, hay, hemp, herb, jive, pot, rope, stinkweed, stuff, tea, weed, wacky tobaccky, whack,

Marijuana cigarette - Bone, doobie, joint, J, reefer, spiff

Market entry - The way in which an organisation enters foreign markets either by direct or indirect export or production in a foreign country.

Market holding price - The charging of a price at what the market can bear in order to hold market share.

Market positioning - The adoption of a specific market stance, either leader, challenger, follower, flanker or adopter, vis a vis competition.

Marketing - Planning, executing and controlling the conception, pricing, promotion and distribution of ideas, goods and services in order to build lasting, mutually profitable exchange relationships satisfying individual and organisational objectives.

Mary jane – Marijuana

Matchbox - Measurement for a small amount of Marijuana

Matrix organization - A complex form of organisational structure bringing together the competencies of geographic knowledge, product knowledge and know how, and functional competencies - financial, production and marketing - and a knowledge of the customer, industry and its needs.

Mazzies - Tranquillisers

Measurement focus - The accounting convention which determines: (1) which assets and which liabilities are included on the governmental unit's balance sheet; and (2) whether its operating statement presents "financial flow" information (revenue and expenditures) or "capital maintenance" information (revenues and expenses). Refer to CURRENT FINANCIAL RESOURCES MEASUREMENT FOCUS and ECONOMIC RESOURCES MEASUREMENT FOCUS.

Media - Any paid for communication channel including television, radio, posters etc.

Media scheduling - A timetable for the allocation of advertising messages in the media over a given time horizon.

Meet - Buyer and seller get together

Mercantilism - A nationalist doctrine of one nation prospering at the expense of another nation.

Merchandise - Drugs

Merchandise inventories - Merchandise held for resale to other agencies, other governmental units, or the public.

Mescaline - mess, crystal

Message - An informative communication about a product or service placed in a communication channel.

Meth - Methadone

Microdot - A tablet containing LSD

Mid period transfer - Occurs when an employee transfers to a new agency in the middle of a pay period other than the 1st working day after the end of pay cycle.

Miss emma - Morphine

Mitsubishi's – Ecstasy

Mixture - Methadone

Moggies - Tranquillisers

Money market investments - A short-term, highly liquid debt security, including commercial paper, banker's acceptances, and U.S. Treasury and agency obligations. (Asset-backed securities, derivatives, and structured notes are not included in this term.)

Monkey - drug dependency; a kilogram of a narcotic

Mortgage insurance policy - In life and health insurance, a policy covering a mortgagor with benefits intended to pay off the balance due on a mortgage upon the insured's death, or to meet the payments due on a mortgage in case of the insured's death or disability.

Mule - A carrier of drugs

Multinational products - Goods or services adapted to the perceived unique characteristics of national markets.

Multiple factor indices - A measure of potential demand indirectly using, as proxies, variables that either intuition or statistical analysis suggest can be closely correlated with the potential demand for the product under view.

Munchies - The hunger that follows after using Marijuana

Mushrooms - Magic mushrooms, shrooms, mushies

Mutual insurance companies - Companies with no capital stock, and owned by policyholders. The earnings of the company--over and above the payments of the losses, operating expenses and reserves--are the property of the policyholders. There are two types of mutual insurance companies. A nonassessable mutual charges a fixed premium and the policyholders cannot be assessed further. Legal reserves and surplus are maintained to provide payment of all claims. Assessable mutuals are companies that charge an initial fixed premium and, if that isn't sufficient, might assess policyholders to meet losses in excess of the premiums that have been charged.

Nailed - Arrested

Named perils - Perils specifically covered on insured property.

Narc - Narcotic agent

Nationalism - The assertion of indigenous culture by an individual, organisation or country.

Net assets - The difference between assets and liabilities. Refer to FUND EQUITY.

Net book value - Refer to BOOK VALUE.

Net income - A term used in accounting for proprietary funds to designate the excess of total revenues and operating transfers in over total expenses and operating transfers out for an accounting period.

Net income - The total after-tax earnings generated from operations and realized capital gains as reported in the company's NAIC annual statement on page 4, line 16.

Net investment income - This item represents investment income earned during the year less investment expenses and depreciation on real estate. Investment expenses are the expenses related to generating investment income and capital gains but exclude income taxes.

Net leverage - The sum of a company's net premium written to policyholder surplus and net liabilities to policyholder surplus. This ratio measures the combination of a company's net exposure to pricing errors in its current book of business and errors of estimation in its net liabilities after reinsurance, in relation to policyholder surplus.

Net premium - The amount of premium minus the agent's commission. Also, the premium necessary to cover only anticipated losses, before loading to cover other expenses.

Nominal interest rate - The contractual interest rate shown on the face and in the body of a bond and used to compute the amount of interest to be paid, in contrast to the effective interest rate.

Non-tariff barriers - Measures, public or private that cause intentionally traded goods or services to be allocated in such a way as to reduce potential real world income.

Non-appropriated funds - Moneys that can be expended without legislative appropriation. Only funds in accounts specifically established in state law as being exempt from appropriation fall into this category. Non-appropriated accounts can be either budgeted (and subject to OFM allotment approval) or non-budgeted.

Non-budgeted accounts - Accounts that are not subject to either the appropriation or allotment process.

Non-exchange transactions - A transaction in which a government either gives value (benefit) to another party without directly receiving equal value in exchange or receives value (benefit) from another party without directly giving equal value in exchange.

Nonoperating expenses - Expenses of a proprietary fund that are not directly related to the fund's principal operations.

Nonoperating Income (LOSS) - In a proprietary fund, the net difference between nonoperating revenues and nonoperating expenses. Refer to NONOPERATING REVENUES and NONOPERATING EXPENSES.

Nonoperating revenues - Proprietary fund revenues that are incidental to, or by-products of, the fund's principal operations.

Normal return night - That night of travel on which it was anticipated prior to the trip, that the traveler would return either to the official duty station or official residence after the completion of official state business.

Norml - National Organization for the Reform of Marijuana Laws; lobbies for lenient drug laws

Norries – Tranquillisers

Notes payable - A liability account reflecting amounts owed by the state from an unconditional written promise to pay a certain sum of money upon demand or at a fixed or determinable time.

Notes receivable - An asset account reflecting amounts owing to the state from an unconditional written promise to pay a certain sum of money on demand or at a fixed or determinable time.

Notes to the financial statements - The summary of significant accounting policies and other disclosures required for a fair presentation of the financial statements of the governmental unit in conformity with generally accepted accounting principles (GAAP) which are in addition to and not included on the face of the financial statements themselves. The notes to the financial statements are an integral part of the financial statements.

Nugget - Marijuana

O.D. - overdosed on drugs

Object of expenditure - As used in expenditure classification, this term applies to the character of the article purchased or the service obtained (rather than the purpose for which the article or service was purchased or obtained). Examples are salaries and employee benefits.

Occurrence - An event that results in an insured loss. In some lines of business, such as liability, an occurrence is distinguished from accident in that the loss doesn't have to be sudden and fortuitous and can result from continuous or repeated exposure which results in bodily injury or property damage neither expected not intended by the insured.

Official station - The city, town, or other location where the state official or employee's office is located, or the city, town, or location where the state official or employee's work is performed on a permanent basis. For the purposes of these travel regulations, Olympia, Tumwater and Lacey are considered to be the same official station. A state official or employee's official station is to be designated by the agency. It is to be determined by the needs of the agency and not assigned because it is the home or preferred living area of a state official or employee.

On - Under the influence of a drug

On a trip - Under the influence of drugs

On Ice - In jail

On the nod - Under the influence of narcotics or depressants

Operating budget - A plan of current expenditures and the proposed means of financing them. The operating budget is the primary means to ensuring that the financing, acquisition, spending, and service delivery activities of the state are controlled.

Operating expenses - Proprietary fund expenses that are directly related to the fund's principal operations.

Operating income - The excess of proprietary fund operating revenues over operating expenses.

Operating revenues - Proprietary fund revenues that are directly related to the fund's principal operations. They consist primarily of user charges for goods and services.

Operating statement - The financial statement disclosing the financial results of operations of a governmental unit during an accounting period in conformity with generally accepted accounting principles (GAAP).

Operating transfers - All interfund transfers other than equity transfers, e.g., legally authorized transfers from a fund receiving revenue to the fund through which the resources are to be expended. Refer to INTERFUND TRANSFERS.

Option - A bilateral contract giving its holder the right, but not the obligation to buy or sell a specified asset at a specific price, at or up to, a specific date.

Order number - The number of the purchasing document used for an acquisition of an asset.

Original budget - The first complete appropriated budget. The original budget may be adjusted by reserves, transfers, allocations, supplemental appropriations, and other legally authorized legislative and executive changes before the beginning of the fiscal year.

Original Issue Discount (OID) - The amount by which the par value of a security exceeds its public offering price at the time it was originally offered to an investor.

Original Issue Premium (OIP) - The amount by which the price paid for a security exceeds the security's par value.

Other income/expenses - This item represents miscellaneous sources of

Out of it - Under the influence of drugs

O.Z. - One ounce

Outside consultant - An independent contractor providing personal services.

Outstanding warrant record - A record used to record warrants issued by an agency which are not yet redeemed by the State Treasurer.

Overhead - Those elements of cost necessary in the production of a good or service which are not directly traceable to the product or service. Usually these costs relate to objects of expenditure that do not become an integral part of the finished product or service, such as rent, heat, lights, management, and supervision.

Paid-up additional insurance - An option that allows the policyholder to use policy dividends and/or additional premiums to buy additional insurance on the same plan as the basic policy and at a face amount determined by the insured's attained age.

Pakalolo - Hawaiian term for Marijuana

Panama gold, red - Potent Marijuana grown in Panama

Panic - Drugs not available

Paper mushrooms - LSD

Papers - rolling papers, used to make marijuana or tobacco cigarettes

Par value - In the case of bonds, the amount of principal that must be paid at maturity. Par value is referred to as the face value of the security.

Paraphernalia - Accessories used to take drugs

Participation rate - In equity-indexed annuities, a participation rate determines how much of the gain in the index will be credited to the annuity. For example, the insurance company may set the participation rate at 80%, which means the annuity would only be credited with 80% of the gain experienced by the index.

Passive exporter - An organisation which awaits orders or comes across them by choice.

PCP - (Phencyclidine) angel dust, kools sherms, high, wet daddies, dust, juice

Peace pills - PCP

Peanuts - Barbiturates

Pebbles - Crack Cocaine

Penetration price - The charging of a low price in order to gain volume sales conducted under conditions of little product uniqueness and elastic demand patterns.

Pension (and other employee benefit) trust funds - A fiduciary fund type used to report resources that are required to be held in trust for the members and beneficiaries of defined benefit pension plans, defined contribution plans, other post employment benefit plans, or other employee benefit plans. Refer to FIDUCIARY FUNDS.

Pepsi habit - occasional use of drugs

Percy - Cocaine

Performance audit - A systematic process of objectively obtaining and evaluating evidence regarding the performance of an organization, program, function, or activity. Evaluation is made in terms of its economy and efficiency of operations and effectiveness in achieving desired goals. The performance audit function provides an independent review of management's performance and the degree to which actual performance meets pre-stated goals. Refer to AUDIT.

Peril - The cause of a possible loss.

Periodic inventory - An inventory system whereby the agency performs a physical count of its inventory periodically, at least annually at fiscal year end.

Permanent funds - Permanent funds are used to report resources that are legally restricted to the extent that only earnings, and not principal, may be used for the purposes that benefit the state or it's citizens. Permanent funds include endowments where the funds or property donated to the state are required by contract, agreement or trust instrument to be maintained in tact. Refer to GOVERNMENTAL FUNDS.

Personal injury protection - Pays basic expenses for an insured and his or her family in states with no-fault auto insurance. No-fault laws generally require drivers to carry both liability insurance and personal injury protection coverage to pay for basic needs of the insured, such as medical expenses, in the event of an accident.

Personal lines - Insurance for individuals and families, such as private-passenger auto and homeowners insurance.

Personal service - Professional or technical expertise provided by a consultant to accomplish a specific study, project, task, or other work statement.

Petty cash - A sum of money set aside on an imprest basis. Cash held for making change or paying small obligations when the issuance of a formal voucher and warrant/check would be too expensive and time consuming. Petty cash includes both change and imprest accounts. Refer to IMPREST ACCOUNT.

Peyote - hallucinogenic cactus, buttons

Physical distribution - The act and functions of physically distributing goods and services including the elements of transport, warehousing and order processing.

Pickup - Purchase drugs

Piece - Usually one ounce of drugs

Pills - Ecstasy

Pinks - Second (Barbiturate)

Plant - A hiding place for drugs

Point of sale - An electronic payment system in a merchant location where consumers pay for retail goods and services, through the use of credit cards or debit cards that directly access and deduct funds from the customer's checking account.

Point-of-service plan - Health insurance policy that allows the employee to choose between in-network and out-of-network care each time medical treatment is needed.

Policy - The written contract effecting insurance, or the certificate thereof, by whatever name called, and including all clause, riders, endorsements, and papers attached thereto and made a part thereof.

Policyholder dividend ratio - The ratio of dividends to policyholders related to net premiums earned.

Polycentrism - A host country orientation on a subsidiary basis.

Poppers - Amyl Nitrate capsules (inhalant)

Posting - The process of transferring to a ledger account the data, either detailed or summarized, contained in a book or document of original entry.

Pot - Marijuana

Pot head - Marijuana user

Power hitter - A device (often plastic) used to deliver a blast of Marijuana smoke to the lungs

Pre-existing condition - A coverage limitation included in many health policies which states that certain physical or mental conditions, either previously diagnosed or which would normally be expected to require treatment prior to issue, will not be covered under the new policy for a specified period of time.

Premium - The price of insurance protection for a specified risk for a specified period of time.

Prepaid expenses - Payments made for those supplies and/or services (not inventory) acquired or purchased during an accounting period but not consumed or used at the end of the accounting period.

Price ceiling - The maximum price which can be charged bearing in mind competition and what the market can bear.

Price escalation - The difference between the domestic price and the target price in foreign markets due to the application of duties, dealer margins and/or other transaction costs.

Price floor - **The** minimum price which can be charged bounded by product cost.

Primary data - Unpublished data from individuals or organisations.

Product - A good or service offered by an organisation which affords a bundle of benefits both objective (physical) and subjective (image) to a user.

Product organization - A form of international organisational structure whereby executives in functional areas are given global responsibility.

Product strategy - A set of decisions regarding alternatives to the target market and the marketing mix given a set of market conditions.

Profit - A measure of the competence and ability of management to provide viable insurance products at competitive prices and maintain a financially strong company for both policyholders and stockholders.

Program - Any of the major activities of an agency expressed as a primary function or organizational unit. Agencies may not alter their program structure without the explicit approval of the legislature and the Office of Financial Management.

Promotion - The offer of an inducement to purchase, over and above the intrinsic value or price of a good service.

Proprietary funds - Proprietary funds are used to account for the state's ongoing organizations and activities that are similar to those often found in the private sector. These funds are considered self-supporting in that the services rendered by them are generally financed through user charges or on a cost reimbursement basis. Proprietary funds use the economic resources measurement focus and the accrual basis of accounting. There are two types of proprietary funds: enterprise funds and internal service funds. Refer to ENTERPRISE FUNDS and INTERNAL SERVICE FUNDS.

Prospective employee - Applicants for the position of director, deputy director, assistant director, state supervisor or equivalent or higher position, engineers or other personnel having both executive and professional status. In the case of institutions of higher education, prospective employees are limited to applicants being considered for academic positions above the rank of instructor, and professional or administrative employees in supervisory positions. In the case of community and technical colleges, such travel expenses may be paid for applicants being considered for full-time faculty positions or administrative employees in supervisory positions.

P's - Crystal Meth

Public funds - Moneys under the control of a treasurer or custodian belonging to, or held for the benefit of, the state or any of its political subdivisions, public corporations, municipal corporations, agencies, courts, boards, commissions, or committees, including moneys held as trustee, agent or bailee. RCW 39.58.010.

Purchase card - A credit card issued to a card custodian for the purpose of making authorized purchases on behalf of the agency.

Purchase card provider - An individual, company, firm, or combination thereof with which the state of Washington contracts for purchase card services.

Purchase card transaction log - A record kept by the card custodian that lists purchase card transactions in detail.

Purchase requisition - A form used by agencies to request the Office of State Procurement, Department of General Administration, to order materials, supplies, and equipment, or to request an amendment of a previous requisition. This form is used when an agency does not have general or specific authority to make the purchase or when the item does not fall within the statewide contracts.

Purchases method - The method under which inventories are recorded as expenditures when acquired. Refer to CONSUMPTION METHOD.

Purchasing card manager - An individual who serves as the administrator of the purchase card program within an agency and is responsible for providing training, advice, direction, consultation, and assistance to approving managers and card custodians.

Purchasing documents - Documents approved for use by agencies having local purchasing authority.

Purchasing power parity - The rate at which one unit of currency will purchase the same amount of goods and services as it bought in an equilibrium period, despite differential rates of inflation.

Quack - doctor

Qualified high-deductible health plan - A health plan with lower premiums that covers health-care expenses only after the insured has paid each year a large amount out of pocket or from another source. To qualify as a health plan coupled with a Health Savings Account, the Internal Revenue Code requires the deductible to be at least $1,000 for an individual and $2,000 for a family. High-deductible plans are also known as catastrophic plans.

Qualified travel provider - An internet travel provider, qualified travel agent, or other vendor under contract with the state to provide travel services to state employees.

Qualified versus non-qualified policies - Qualified plans are those employee benefit plans that meet Internal Revenue Service requirements as stated in IRS Code Section 401a. When a plan is approved, contributions made by the employer are tax deductible expenses.

Qualifying event - An occurrence that triggers an insured's protection.

Quick assets - Assets that are quickly convertible into cash.

Quick liquidity ratio - Quick assets divided by net liabilities plus ceded reinsurance balances payable. Quick assets are defined as the sum of cash, unaffiliated short-term investments, unaffiliated bonds maturing within one year, government bonds maturing within five years, and 80% of unaffiliated common stocks. These assets can be quickly converted into cash in the case of an emergency.

Quota - A specific imported amount imposed by one country on another, when once filled cannot be exceeded within a given time. When a quota is in force the price mechanism is not allowed to operate.

Rainbows - LSD

Rap - To talk with someone; or charged with a crime

Realized gain or loss - The difference between the net proceeds received and the cost, or amortized cost, or fair value of an investment when the investment is sold..

Receivables - Amounts due from private persons, businesses, agencies, funds, or governmental units that are expected to be collected in the form of moneys, goods, and/or services.

Receiving report - partial delivery (A18, A18-A) - A form used by agencies to document and authorize payment for partial deliveries of goods or services ordered by a single Purchase Order or Field Order.

Reconciliation - The process of correlating one set of records with another set of records and/or a physical inventory count that involves identifying, explaining. and correcting differences.

Recovery of expenditure - Those receipts which represent the recovery of current period expenditures and which are offset against the expenditure account.

Red devils - Seconal (Barbiturate)

Reefer - Marijuana

Refund - An amount paid back or credit allowed because of an over-collection or because of the return of merchandise.

Regiocentrism - A regional market orientation with world market strategies.

Register - A record for the consecutive entry of events, documents, or transactions, with proper notation of all the required information. The form is designed so that the entries are distributed, summarized, and aggregated for convenient posting to the accounts.

Regression analysis - The selection of an independent variable which accounts for the most variance in a dependent variable.

Regular workplace - The location where a state employee or state official normally performs his/her work (excludes meeting and conference rooms).

Reimbursement - 1. Repayments of amounts remitted on behalf of another party. 2. Interfund/Interagency transactions that constitute reimbursement to a fund/agency for expenditures/expenses initially made from it but that properly apply to another. These transactions are recorded as expenditures/expenses in the reimbursing fund/agency and as reductions of expenditures/expenses in the fund/agency reimbursed.

Reinsurance - In effect, insurance that an insurance company buys for its own protection. The risk of loss is spread so a disproportionately large loss under a single policy doesn't fall on one company. Reinsurance enables an insurance company to expand its capacity; stabilize its underwriting results; finance its expanding volume; secure catastrophe protection against shock losses; withdraw from a line of business or a geographical area within a specified time period.

Renewal - The automatic re-establishment of in-force status effected by the payment of another premium.

Replacement cost - The amount of cash or other consideration that would be required today to obtain the same asset or its equivalent.

Replacement cost - The dollar amount needed to replace damaged personal property or dwelling property without deducting for depreciation but limited by the maximum dollar amount shown on the declarations page of the policy.

Reserve - An amount representing actual or potential liabilities kept by an insurer to cover debts to policyholders. A reserve is usually treated as a liability.

Reserved fund balance - Those portions of fund balance that are not appropriated for expenditure or that are legally segregated for a specific future use. Refer to FUND BALANCE.

Restricted assets - Assets whose use is subject to constraints that are either (a) externally imposed by creditors (such as through debt covenants), grantors, contributors, or laws or regulations of other governments or (b) imposed by law through constitutional provisions or enabling legislation.

Restricted net assets - One of the three components of net assets reported in government-wide and proprietary fund financial statements. Net assets should be restricted when constraints are placed on net asset use either: 1. externally imposed by creditors, grantors, contributors, or laws or regulations of other governments, or 2. imposed by law through constitutional provisions or enabling legislation.

Retailer - A channel institution which acts as an intermediary between other channel institutions and the end user and who usually breaks bulk, charging a margin for its services.

Retainage payable - A liability reflecting amounts due on construction contracts not paid pending final inspection of the project or the lapse of a specified period, or both. The unpaid amount is usually a stated percentage of the contract price. Refer to CONTRACTS PAYABLE.

Revaluation - The increase in the value of one currency vis a vis other currencies.

Revenue - In governmental fund type accounts, revenues are increases in net current assets and are recognized in the accounting period in which they become measurable and available. In proprietary fund and trust fund type accounts, revenues are increases in net total assets and are recognized in the period in which they are earned and become measurable.

Revenue bonds - Bonds whose principal and interest are secured by specific sources of revenue and do not involve a pledge of the full faith and credit of the state. Revenue bonds are payable from identified sources of revenue which are generally derived from the assets acquired or constructed with bond proceeds. In addition to a pledge of revenues, such bonds sometimes contain a mortgage on the enterprise fund's property.

Revolving fund/account - 1. An internal service fund established to carry out a cycle of operations. The amounts expended from the fund are restored thereto from earnings from operations or by transfers from other funds, so that it is always intact. 2. An imprest account into which a fixed amount of money is placed for change-making purposes or minor disbursements. Refer to IMPREST ACCOUNT.

Riding the wave - Under the influence of drugs

Rig - The paraphernalia for injecting drugs

Ripped off- Robbed

Risk class - Risk class, in insurance underwriting, is a grouping of insureds with a similar level of risk. Typical underwriting classifications are preferred, standard and substandard, smoking and nonsmoking, male and female.

Risk management - Management of the pure risks to which a company might be subject. It involves analyzing all exposures to the possibility of loss and determining how to handle these exposures through practices such as avoiding the risk, retaining the risk, reducing the risk, or transferring the risk, usually by insurance.

Roach - The stub of a Marijuana cigarette

Roach clip - Any tweezers-like device used to hold a Marijuana cigarette stub that is too short to hold in the- fingers

Rocks - Crack Cocaine

Rolexes - Ecstasy

Roofies - Tranquillisers

Roll-up fund - A roll-up fund is a reporting entity. It is comprised of the various accounts that generally fall within the generic activity/nature of the roll-up fund's title.

Rugby balls - Tranquillisers

Rush - An intense surge of pleasure; Butyl Nitrate inhalant

Salvage value - An estimate of the amount that will be realized at the end of the useful life of a depreciable asset.

Sauce - Alcohol

Scat - Heroin

Schedules - Refer to SUPPORTING SCHEDULES.

School boy - Codeine

Scientific amortization method - Under the scientific amortization method, the total discount or premium is prorated to interim periods on the basis of a constant rate (as opposed to a constant dollar) to produce a level rate of yield.

Score - To locate and purchase a quantity of drugs

Script writer - A Doctor willing to write a prescription for faked symptoms

Search - The collection of relevant information by deliberate searching either formally or informally.

Secondary data - Published accessible data from a variety of sources.

Secondary market - The secondary market is populated by buyers willing to pay what they determine to be fair market value.

Securities - Bonds, notes, mortgages, or other forms of negotiable or nonnegotiable instruments.

Segment - A segment is an identifiable activity within an enterprise fund that has one or more bonds or other debt instruments outstanding with a revenue stream pledged in support of that debt and an external party that requires a separate accounting of revenues, expenses, gains, losses, assets and liabilities.

Self reference criterion - Perceptual distortion brought about by an individual's own cultural experience.

Sensi - Marijuana

Set up - to arrange to have a person arrested for drugs; combination of uppers and downers (Barbiturates and.Amphetamines)

Shared leave - The donated leave converted to hours by the receiving agency at the donee's rate of pay. This may be more or less than the literal hours donated depending on the relative salary rates of the respective employees.

Shoot up - To inject intravenously

Shooting gallery - Place where addicts inject drugs

Short-term liabilities - Short-term liabilities are legal obligations of the state that arise upon the receipt of goods or services. In governmental fund type accounts, they are payable from current financial resources. In proprietary fund type accounts, short-term liabilities are payable within one year.

Shotgun - A way of smoking Marijuana, by blowing smoke back through the joint into another's mouth

Single audit - A financial, internal control, and compliance audit of a nonfederal entity administering federal assistance awards including the financial statements of the entity.

Sinsemilla or sins - A potent type of Marijuana without seeds grown in Northern California

Skag - Heroin

Skimming price - The charging of a high price in order to gain maximum revenue conducted under conditions of product uniqueness and inelastic demand patterns.

Skin popping - To inject a drug under the skin

Skunk - Marijuana

Smack - Heroin

Small and attractive assets - Assets that do not meet the state's capitalization policy but that an agency considers particularly vulnerable to loss, thus subject to special property control.

Smart card - A card that has a pre-determined limit of cash, which is drawn down with every purchase. The smart card stores information on a microprocessor or memory chip rather than the magnetic stripe found on stored value and credit cards.

Smilies - LSD

Smoke - Marijuana

Snappers - Amyl Nitrate capsules (inhalant)

Snort - To inhale Cocaine through the nostrils

Snow - Cocaine

Snow bird - Dependent on Cocaine

Sole source - A consultant providing professional or technical expertise of such a unique nature that the consultant is clearly and justifiably the only practical source to provide the service. The justification is to be based on either the uniqueness of the service or sole availability at the location required.

Solid · Marijuana

Solvency - Having sufficient assets-capital, surplus, reserves-and being able to satisfy financial requirements--investments, annual reports, examinations--to be eligible to transact insurance business and meet liabilities.

Source document - Document used to initiate an individual accounting transaction.

Sourcing - A decision to have certain components in the value chain manufactured out of the country. Often called the "make of buy" decision.

Space cadet - Habitual user of Marijuana

Spaced - Unresponsive to surroundings

Spaced out - Under the influence of drugs

Special revenue funds - Special revenue funds are used to account for the proceeds of specific revenue sources (other than trusts for individuals, private organizations or other governments or for major capital projects) that are legally restricted to expenditure for specified purposes. Refer to GOVERNMENTAL FUNDS.

Speed - Amphetamines

Speed freak - Person who repeatedly takes Amphetamines, usually intravenously

Speedball - A mixture of Cocaine and Heroin; "Bombita"

Spike - Needle used to inject drugs

Spoons - Paraphernalia associated with Cocaine, often worn as jewelry

Standardisation - Same goods or services marketed in either product, distribution or advertising form, unchanged in any country.

Standardised plans - A uniform planning system applied globally, based on economics of scale and consumer uniformity.

Star dust - Cocaine

Stars - LSD

Stash - A place where drugs are hidden

State pilot - A state employee whose fifty percent or more of his or her working time is performing flight connected services and flying an aircraft that is clearly defined as a requirement of his or her job assignment.

Statement of activities - A government-wide financial statement that reports the net (expense) revenue of its individual functions. An objective of using the net (expense) revenue format is to report the relative financial burden of each of the reporting government's functions on its taxpayers.

Statute - A written law enacted by the Legislature and signed by the Governor.

Statutory reserve - A reserve, either specific or general, required by law.

Step on - To dilute drugs

Stick - A Marijuana cigarette STIMULANTS - pep pills

Stock insurance company - An incorporated insurer with capital contributed by stockholders, to whom earnings are distributed as dividends on their shares.

Stoned - Under the influence of drugs

Stones - Crack Cocaine

Straight - Not using drugs

Strategic business unit - A self contained grouping of organisations, products or technologies which serve an identified market and competes with identified competitors.

Strung out - Heavily addicted to drugs

Stuff- Drugs

Subrecipient - A non-federal entity that expends federal awards received from a pass-through entity to carry out a federal program, but does not include an individual that is a beneficiary of such a program. It also excludes vendors that receive federal funds in exchange for goods and/or services in the course of normal trade or commerce.

Subrogation - The right of an insurer who has taken over another's loss also to take over the other person's right to pursue remedies against a third party.

Subsidiary accounts - A group of related accounts supporting in detail the balance of a controlling account, usually kept in a subsidiary ledger. Refer to SUBSIDIARY LEDGER and CONTROL ACCOUNT.

Subsidiary ledger - A group of subsidiary accounts, the sum of the balances of which is equal to the balance of the related control account. Refer to GENERAL LEDGER and SUBSIDIARY ACCOUNTS.

Subsistence - Daily travel expenses covering meals, taxes, tips for meals and incidental expenses.

Sub-sub-object of expenditure code - Optional code assigned by an agency to further identify a particular expenditure item within a sub-object of expenditure.

Successive periods - In hospital income protection, when confinements in a hospital are due to the same or related causes and are separated by less than a contractually stipulated period of time, they are considered part of the same period of confinement.

Superman - LSD blotter with Superman imprint

Supplies - Assets consumed in the course of an agency's operations.

Surety bond - A written promise to pay damages or to indemnify against losses caused by the party or parties named in the document, through nonperformance or through embezzlement defalcation. Surety bonds also include fidelity bonds covering governmental officials and employees. Refer to FIDELITY BOND.

Surplus - The amount by which assets exceed liabilities.

Surveillance - The collection of relevant information which crosses an individual's scanning attention field.

Suspense account - An account that carries charges or credits temporarily pending the determination of the proper account or accounts to which they are to be posted. It does not appear in financial statements.

Tab - LSD

Tariff - An instrument of terms of access normally the imposition of a single or multiple excise rate on a imported good.

Taste - A small sample of drugs

Taxes - Compulsory charges levied by a government for the purpose of financing services performed for the common benefit.

Taxes receivable - An asset account reflecting the uncollected portion of taxes that have been levied.

Tea - Marijuana

Telecommuting - Involves the use of telephones and computers to enable an employee to work at a location other than their regular workplace. Telecommuting is a Commute Trip Reduction strategy that must be approved by an employee's agency.

Term bonds - Bonds whose entire principal matures on one date.

Term life insurance - Life insurance that provides protection for a specified period of time. Common policy periods are one year, five years, 10 years or until the insured reaches age 65 or 70. The policy doesn't build up any of the nonforfeiture values associated with whole life policies.

Termination benefits - Benefits given to employees when they leave state service either voluntarily (i.e. early retirement) or involuntarily (i.e. reduction in force). Examples of benefits include cash payments, enhancements to defined benefit pension or other postemployment benefit formulas, continued access to health insurance, severance pay, career counseling, and/or outplacement services.

Terms of access - The conditions imposed by one country which apply to the importation of goods from another country.

Thai sticks - Marijuana laced with Opium

The World Bank - Known also as the International Bank for Reconstruction and Development (IBRD). A bank, with world wide country membership, (United nations) which provides long term capital to and economic development.

Tina - Crystal Meth

To party - Refers to having a good time using alcohol and other drugs

Tobacco - Butt, chew, weed, cig,

Toke - Inhaling Marijuana or Hashish smoke

Tolley - Or toluene; a cheap, extremely harmful paint solvent (inhalant)

Toot - To sniff Cocaine

Tooter - Small, hollow tube (straw-like) to sniff Cocaine

Tort - A private wrong, independent of contract and committed against an individual, which gives rise to a legal liability and is adjudicated in a civil court. A tort can be either intentional or unintentional, and liability insurance is mainly purchased to cover unintentional torts.

Total loss - A loss of sufficient size that it can be said no value is left. The complete destruction of the property. The term also is used to mean a loss requiring the maximum amount a policy will pay.

Tracks - A row of needle marks on the skin

Trade discount - An allowance, usually varying in percentage with the volume of transactions, made without respect to the time when the account is paid. These discounts are commonly considered a reduction of the sales or purchase price and not earnings. The term is not to be confused with cash discount. Refer to CASH DISCOUNT.

Transfer pricing - The price at which goods or services are transferred between one country and another within the same organisation.

Transportation expenses - Those costs covering (a) travel by commercial carriers such as bus, train, ship, and airplane; (b) travel by privately owned motor vehicles, such as cars, motorcycles, vans, or trucks; (c) travel by rental motor vehicle; (d) or some combination of (a), (b), and/or (c).

Trap - A hiding place for drugs

Travel expenses - Those costs covering per diem expenses; transportation expenses; meals and/or coffee and light and miscellaneous refreshment business expenses regardless of travel status; and miscellaneous business expenses related to official state travel.

Travel status - The official status of a traveler when the traveler is away from both the official residence and the official station, exclusive of commuting between the traveler's official station and official residence, on state-related business.

Traveler - A person in travel status who is on official state business.

Treasury funds/accounts - Accounts which have cash on deposit in and under the control of the State Treasurer and are disbursed by means of a warrant. Treasury accounts are subject to appropriation unless specifically exempted.

Treasury trust funds/accounts - Accounts not required by law to be within the treasury and not subject to appropriation, but placed in the custody of the state treasurer due to certain circumstances.

Trial balance - A list of balances of the accounts in a ledger kept by double entry with the debit and credit balances shown in separate columns.

Trip - Under the influence of drugs

Tripper - LSD

Trips - LSD

Turf - A location where drugs are sold

Turkey - A substitute sold as a specific drug

Turned on - Introduced to drugs, or under the influence of drugs

Tweezes - A wild variety of psilocybin mushrooms (hallucinogen)

Unallotted - Appropriation authority not specifically scheduled for expenditure.

Unamortized discounts on bonds sold - Excess portion of the face value of bonds over the amount received from their sale that remains to be amortized over the life of the bonds.

Unanticipated receipts - Money received which has not been appropriated by the Legislature. The Governor has the authority to approve the allotment of such money within the guidelines of the intent in which they were received.

Uncle - Federal Agents

Underwriter - The individual trained in evaluating risks and determining rates and coverages for them. Also, an insurer.

Underwriter's discount - The fee an underwriter charges when purchasing bonds or certificates of participation (COPs) for resale to the public. The underwriter assumes the risk of ownership until the bonds are sold.

Underwriting - The process of selecting risks for insurance and classifying them according to their degrees of insurability so that the appropriate rates may be assigned. The process also includes rejection of those risks that do not qualify.

Underwriting guide - Details the underwriting practices of an insurance company and provides specific guidance as to how underwriters should analyze all of the various types of applicants they might encounter. Also called an underwriting manual, underwriting guidelines, or manual of underwriting policy.

Undesignated unreserved fund balance - Available expendable financial resources in a governmental fund that are neither legally restricted nor the object of tentative management plans.

Unearned premiums - That part of the premium applicable to the unexpired part of the policy period.

Unearned revenue - Refer to DEFERRED REVENUES.

Unexpended allotment - Portion of an allotment not yet expended.

Unexpended appropriation - Portion of an appropriation not yet expended.

Uninsured motorist coverage - Endorsement to a personal automobile policy that covers an insured collision with a driver who does not have liability insurance.

Universal life insurance - A combination flexible premium, adjustable life insurance policy.

Uppers - Stimulants, Amphetamines

Utilization - How much a covered group uses a particular health plan or program.

Valium - Ludes, drunk pills, v's blues

Vallies - Tranquillisers

Valuation - A calculation of the policy reserve in life insurance. Also, a mathematical analysis of the financial condition of a pension plan.

Variable life insurance - A form of life insurance whose face value fluctuates depending upon the value of the dollar, securities or other equity products supporting the policy at the time payment is due.

Variable universal life insurance - A combination of the features of variable life insurance and universal life insurance under the same contract. Benefits are variable based on the value of underlying equity investments, and premiums and benefits are adjustable at the option of the policyholder.

Vendor's remittance advice - A form used to accompany each warrant/check to notify the payee of what is being paid. The vendor's remittance advice is to reference the warrant/check number and the invoice number as appropriate.

Viator - The terminally ill person who sells his or her life insurance policy.

Voluntary reserve - An allocation of surplus not required by law. Insurers often accumulate such reserves to strengthen their financial structure.

Voucher - A written document that evidences the propriety of transactions and usually indicates the accounts in which they are to be recorded.

Voucher distribution form - A form used by agencies to substantiate and authorize payment when a Purchase Order or Field Order is not involved but where vendor invoices are employed.

Wacky tobaccky - Marijuana

Waiver of premium - A provision in some insurance contracts which enables an insurance company to waive the collection of premiums while keeping the policy in force if the policyholder becomes unable to work because of an accident or injury. The waiver of premium for disability remains in effect as long as the ensured is disabled.

Warrant - A payment instrument for each invoice voucher or other evidence of indebtedness validated by the State Treasurer for payment. Refer to CHECK.

Warrant register - A form used to record expenditure/expense vouchers and account classifications of each transaction in detail certified and issued by the State Treasurer. It is also used to summarize the information documented on the detailed warrant register.

Weed - Marijuana

Weighted average - An inventory valuation method which values ending inventory based on the average cost per unit for the period.

White - Cocaine

White lightening - LSD

Whole life insurance - Life insurance which might be kept in force for a person's whole life and which pays a benefit upon the person's death, whenever that might be.

Wholesaler - A channel institution which purchases and sells in bulk from either original suppliers and/or other channel intermediaries, charging a margin for its services

Window - LSD

Wire transfer - A type of electronic fund transfer that guarantees immediate available funds or same day settlement. The payments are conducted on the Federal Reserve System's federal wire (Fed Wire) network. Refer to ELECTRONIC FUND TRANSFER.

Wired - addicted to Amphetamines or Heroin

Works - equipment for injecting drugs

Xtc - Ecstasy

Yellow jackets - Nembutal, Barbiturate

Yen - A strong craving

Zero-coupon general obligation bonds - Bonds secured by an unconditional pledge of the full faith, credit and taxing power of the state. They are sold at a deep discount without coupons and appreciate to full value at maturity.

Zombie - Heavy user of drugs

Zonked - Extremely high on drugs